The Modern Library
of the World's Best Books

Selected Writings of
Edmund Burke

Selected Writings
of
Edmund Burke

Edited by *W. J. Bate*

Abbott Lawrence Lowell Professor of the
Humanities, Harvard University

The Modern Library, NEW YORK

Random House is the publisher of THE MODERN LIBRARY

Manufactured in the United States of America

Foreword

Any single-volume selection of Burke (any two- or three-volume selection) would seem thin. One of the best selections, eighty years ago, began by citing Hazlitt's remark that the only fair sample of Burke is "all that he wrote." This could be said of any major writer, of course. But it is particularly true of Burke. It is true not only because Burke wrote so much—and most of it of the highest quality. It is true because the kind of thing Burke wrote—especially what shows Burke at his best—is inevitably lengthy.

For Burke's real greatness comes in the patient study of detail, and his ability to retain the full sense of that detail as he moves through it with a vision gradually and genuinely earned. He is one of the most quotable of writers. Yet as Johnson said of Shakespeare, anyone who tried to recommend him by select quotations would succeed like the man in Hierocles who, when he offered his house for sale, carried a brick in his pocket as a specimen. There is another reason why excerpts are particularly unfair to Burke. It has to do with the long, moving drama of his life. For what he writes later is often a supplement to what he wrote earlier; and, though it is frequently forgotten, what he wrote earlier is a very necessary supplement to what, in very different (and in a sense rather tragic) circumstances, he wrote later.

The principal problem, for this small volume, was whether to give a very few of Burke's writings in their entirety, or else to offer a wider spread through mere excerpts from a large variety of his works. In either alternative something had to be sacrificed. The decision was a compromise: to offer as many complete texts of his major works as could be squeezed into the space, but then to supplement them, in a few cases, by necessary excerpts from others. By doing this we were able to give some works in their entirety, including at least two which, however praised, are not now easily available. (Works presented entire are: *Speech on American Taxation, On Conciliation with the Colonies, Letter to the Sheriffs of Bristol,* the concluding *Speech in General Reply* in the trial of Warren Hastings, *Thoughts on French Affairs,* and the *Letter to a Noble Lord.*) At the same time we were able to give substantial selections from five other works. Burke's youthful but brilliant *Sublime and Beautiful* was not included because it is readily available, difficult to represent in part, and a work that would perhaps appeal to a different audience from that interested in his major works. None of Burke's writings has been more frequently reprinted, during the last twenty years, than the *Reflections on the Revolution in France.* Because it is so conveniently available in inexpensive reprints, it seemed rather foolish to usurp this edition by another reprinting when the opportunity was available to present not only other aspects of Burke (such as the writings on America and India) but also other valuable works of his later period, such as the *Thoughts on French Affairs* and his noble valedictory, the *Letter to a Noble Lord.* Hence the *Reflections* are represented only in part. A more serious problem was Burke's great sixteen-year effort on behalf of India, which is once again becoming timely. For these works are less readily available. It was finally decided to give substantial selections from his classic *Speech on Fox's East India Bill,* and one complete speech from the impeachment of Warren Hastings. It is partly with a sense of these necessary omissions that the Introduction was written.

Table of Contents

V. THE FRENCH REVOLUTION

VI. LETTER TO A NOBLE LORD (1795)   485

EDMUND BURKE
Selected Works

Introduction

Because of the range of Burke's thinking, and because of his honesty toward the variety and complexity of human interests, it has always been possible to isolate a part of what he wrote, and then to use it in support of any reasonable cause. A liberal like the late Harold Laski could describe the theme of Burke's greater writing as "Reform in order to preserve." On the other hand, a conservative would be equally justified in describing it by the phrase, "Preserve in order to reform"—preserve what has proved to be a fertile soil for past development in order to have the means of continuing to develop.

It is not that Burke evades labels like "conservative" or "liberal" by simply taking a middle road. Instead, his career actively subsumes both and, by reminding us of their larger meanings, restores their value—as he restores the value of so much else. For his aim, more often than not, is to liberate what can conserve, and to conserve what liberates and protects. In this, as in so many other ways, what finally captures us is his example, valuable in its own right and also because of its rarity. It has been justly said that, like Shakespeare, he dazzles the strong and educated intellect far more than the feeble; that, in fact, he sways intelligent and cultivated readers as a demagogue would a mob. The extraordinary appeal of his example, continuing throughout the changes of almost two centuries, lies first, in what can only be called a generous capaciousness of mind, and secondly, in his unrivalled power to distil creative principles of thought and action from the concrete, practical facts of a situation.

3

[1]

Burke was born in Dublin, January 12, 1729, the son of
an Irish Protestant attorney and a Catholic mother. His
detestation of intolerance has rightly been said to have begun
with his family background. Though reared in the Church
of England, he was only too closely aware of the dis-
criminatory laws against the Catholics. Moreover, he was
educated at the school of a kindly, tolerant Quaker, Abraham
Shackleton, whose memory he revered, and with whose son,
Richard Shackleton, he formed a lifelong friendship.

Years later, as J. R. Green said, Burke's dress and manner
seemed Quaker-like, however much he differed from the
ordinary idea of a Quaker in his readiness to speak. Longinus,
whom Burke studied in college, mentions how we catch, as
if by infection, the traits of those we admire, and how by
means of this we acquire confidence in moving toward what
we ourselves hope to be. Already, in Burke's youth, we have
to do with a mind deeply stirred by the example of toleration
that he found in Shackleton, anticipating the protective
imagination that was later to champion multiplicity and
variety. Characteristically, forty years afterwards (1781),
when he met some Hindu Brahmins helplessly adrift in London, he was shocked to find them without a place where they
could eat as their customs dictated and could perform the
rites of their religion. He immediately took them to his home,
placing all that he had at their disposal for the rest of their
stay in England.

After attending Trinity College, Dublin (1743-48), Burke
was sent to London by his father to study law. The Irish
provincial was at once struck by the large variety of London.
But though he dutifully entered the Middle Temple (1750),
Burke, who was only twenty-one, experienced something of
a jolt. The study of law seemed to him a pinched and meager
diet. "Government," he said thirty years later, "is the exercise

of *all* of the great qualities of the human mind." And not long after he said this, Boswell heard him attack the legal education of the time for the "narrow and contracted notions" it encouraged. To the young Burke, literary occupations seemed freer and more attractive. The theater—a new experience for Burke—interested him, and he was eager to meet people connected with it. Back in Trinity College, where he had organized a small debating society, he had also begun a psychological study of aesthetics after reading the great classical treatise by Longinus, *On the Sublime*. Both activities were prophetic of his future. In fact, the coalescence of the two interests is a fairly passable key to the later Burke. And now, when he was in his middle and later twenties, Burke, somewhat on the rebound from his study of law, went back to the problem he had taken up at Trinity College, and completed the work that was later published as *A Philosophical Inquiry into the Origin of our Ideas of the Sublime and Beautiful* (1756). The psychological study of art really begins in the middle and later eighteenth century; and this essay was a pioneer. The later vogue of Burke's *Sublime and Beautiful* was enormous, especially in Germany. If, by 1800, it could seem a relatively crude performance, this was only because the book, to begin with, was a youthful effort of Burke's, and also because forty years of speculation had naturally been able to refine the subject further. In any brief account of Burke, what is significant about the book is, first, the originality and range it shows; and, second, Burke's practical interest in psychology—in the habitual responses of human nature.

While he was finishing the *Sublime and Beautiful*, Burke turned to two other projects that more closely anticipated his later career. The collected works of the late Lord Bolingbroke had appeared (1754). Already distrusting what he called "geometrical" reasoning about human nature and government—the quick, two-dimensional trust in system—

Burke wrote a jaunty but gifted parody of Bolingbroke called
A Vindication of Natural Society (1756). A little later
(1759) he became the editor of a new project for the publisher, Robert Dodsley, to be called the *Annual Register,*
consisting of a yearly review of the important events and
writings of the year. The *Annual Register* gave a stimulus—
and an outlet—to Burke's omnivorous curiosity. He had a
chance to deal with almost any subject. It also brought
needed money; for in 1757, he had married Jane Nugent,
the daughter of a physician, and they both looked forward
to having a family. Shortly afterwards, Burke became secretary to William Gerard Hamilton, known as "Single-Speech"
Hamilton because, in the golden age of English oratory, he
had given a maiden speech, carefully prepared, and, with a
few exceptions, did not speak again. Burke's talents proved
very useful to Hamilton; for Hamilton found that the only
subjects about which Burke did not know more than anyone
else were "gaming and music." The advantage to Burke was
less: Hamilton—a wealthy young man of Burke's own age—
could be petty as well as silent. One contemporary speaks of
him, perhaps too strongly, as an "envious reptile."

It was about this time (1764) that Burke became a member of the famous club—known simply as "The Club"—
which was to include such men as Samuel Johnson, Joshua
(later Sir Joshua) Reynolds, Oliver Goldsmith, Edward
Gibbon, Adam Smith, and the noted actor, David Garrick.
It was still a rather youthful group when he joined it.
Significantly, Burke, who was far from the celebrity he
was later to have, was already regarded by the members of
"The Club" with admiration. They could sense genius without demanding a passport beforehand. The constant tributes
of Johnson are always cited: "Burke's talk is the ebullition of
his mind"; "The first man everywhere"; "His stream of mind
is perpetual"; "Burke is the only man whose common conversation corresponds with the general fame which he has. . . .

Take up whatever topic you please, he is ready to meet you."

Burke's acquaintance with such men—he was still in his mid-thirties—was of the greatest value. The large generality of his thinking was exercised with them. They strengthened his bold, youthful decision not to huddle cautiously into specialism. And when he entered the House of Commons at the age of thirty-six (1765) he did so—figuratively speaking —under the auspices of these friends; and no group could be prouder than they of his early success. Parties in the modern sense were still in the process of forming. The political situation was highly fluid. Burke joined the so-called "Rockingham Whigs"—a group of liberal conservatives (or conservative liberals) that looked back to the "Glorious Revolution" of 1688 for its ancestry, and was led now by the Marquis of Rockingham. Burke, in fact, served as Rockingham's private secretary, and in time became the unofficial intellectual leader of the group, though he was to break from it later.

[2]

From here on, the greatest English statesman—at least the greatest English writer on statecraft—was to remain in the opposition. Only during the brief Rockingham Ministry (1782) did he hold any office—the not too important one of Paymaster-General. This one fact cannot be stressed too much. A man cannot remain in the opposition all his life without something happening to him.

Burke's important political writing begins with his pamphlet *Thoughts on the Cause of the Present Discontents* (1770). Comparatively stark in style when one thinks of his later writing, and rather heavily concerned, for the modern reader, with "dead politics," it remains a classic justification of the value of parties. But the great issue with which the early Burke is identified was, of course, the growing dispute between England and the American colonies. With its rapidly expanding empire, England was suddenly confronted with a problem unique in its history. Colonies which had been for a hundred and fifty years mere outposts for trade, speculation, or an escape for discontented individuals, were now quickly increasing in population, commerce, and ingenuity. Problems completely unforeseen a century before—even fifty years before—were multiplying. Interests at home, and the struggle of George III to reassert the power of the crown, clashed headlong with the demands of this novel situation; and the time-honored British issues of taxation and representation inevitably became subjects of contention. Burke's American speeches are perhaps less read now than they were during the nineteenth century. At least this is true in America. One reason may be the subconscious feeling of many Americans that, by stressing Burke's other writings, they are being less parochial. Yet, as John Morley long ago said, nothing else Burke wrote—even the generous, patient, eloquent labor on behalf of India, or the long, often clairvoyant, often querulous debate with the French Revolution—puts so cleanly and dramatically the essential philosophy of Burke as the American writings, especially the great speech *On Conciliation with the Colonies* (1775).

In his *Speech on American Taxation* (1774), Burke tried to brush aside the talk of abstract rights that he felt simply clogged the issue while inflaming passions. Repeatedly throughout his career he was to point out how easily human nature can rationalize and bend the notion of abstract rights to serve any purpose. The doctrine of "natural rights" can be used equally in support of such an uprising as the French Revolution, or of England's taxation of colonies in order to pay for the protection of them. "Natural rights" can serve as an argument against slavery; they can be invoked in support of keeping property (including slaves) for which one has paid; they can be used as a justification for taking land from a nation with more territory and less population; and they provide an admirable moral excuse for oppressing others who stand in the way of one's own interpretation of what they mean. Hence, in the *Speech on American Taxation*, trying to cut across "metaphysical distinctions" ("I hate the very sound of them"), he comes back to policies that have traditionally permitted growth:

> Again, and again, revert to your old principles—seek peace and ensure it—leave America, if she has taxable matter in her, to tax herself. I am not going into the distinctions of rights, nor attempting to mark their boundaries. I do not enter into these metaphysical distinctions. . . . Be content to bind America by laws of trade; you have always done it. Let this be your reason for binding their trade. Do not burden them by taxes; you were not used to do so from the beginning. Let this be your reason for not taxing. These are the arguments of states and kingdoms. Leave the rest to the schools; for there only may they be discussed with safety.

[**3**]

The speech *On Conciliation* enlarges on this enlightened practicality. The wrangle over rights and sovereignty is irrelevant and even trifling: a concrete, pressing situation exists which has to be faced and solved. The problem now is, first of all, to secure peace between the mother-country and the colonies. There is the sheer fact that "Peace implies reconciliation," and this, in turn, implies that concession will have to be made on one side or another. "In this state of things, I make no difficulty in affirming that the proposal ought to originate from us." This again is a matter of sensible expediency. For the colonies, being militarily weaker, would feel concession to be a display of fear, while there is no such embarrassment to the larger power.

Burke next reminds the Commons that the important point is the nature of America. For "we must govern America according to that nature . . . and not according to our own

imaginations, not according to abstract ideas of right, by
no means according to mere general theories of government,
the resort to which appears to me, in our present situation,
no better than arrant trifling."

1   He first stresses the number of people in the colonies—
already a third that of England. This, which should be "in
the front of our deliberation," proves that "no partial, narrow, contracted, pinched, occasional system" will work; that
"some degree of caution is required"; that "you ought not
. . . to trifle with so large a mass . . . you could at no time
do so without guilt; and be assured you will not be able to
do it long with impunity." Secondly, Burke mentions the
2   flourishing commerce of the colonies, as well as their agri-
cultural and material wealth. Here he pauses to give the
Commons as vivid a sense as he himself has of the life and
interests of those engaged in commerce, and, in the great
description of the whaling-fleets, sweeps geographically from
Hudson's Bay to Cape Horn, as he stresses the value of the
"wise and salutary neglect" of the British government in
allowing this initiative to flourish.

3   Then, moving into the subject of the "temper and character" of the colonists, he points out: (1) The inheritance of
British Law, reminding the Commons that the great contests
in England itself "were from the earliest times chiefly upon
the question of taxing." (2) The existence of the provincial
legislative assemblies, which have encouraged a habit of
independence. (3) The extreme dissenting religious spirit.
Practical   The Protestantism common in the northern colonies, for example, is "a refinement on the principle of resistance; it is
the dissidence of dissent, and the Protestantism of the Protestant religion." Moreover, colonists from other countries
have, in one way or another, tended to be dissenters from
the established religion of their nations. (4) The haughty
concept of personal freedom in the southern colonies, partly
because the very existence of slavery leads those who are

free to be especially "proud and jealous of their freedom."
(5) The number of men drawn to law as a profession,
encouraging a stubbornly argumentative habit of mind. (6)
The remoteness of the colonies: months pass between an
order and the execution of it ("Nothing worse happens to
you than does to all nations who have extensive empire . . .
the circulation of power must be less vigorous at the extremities. . . . The Turk cannot govern Egypt, and Arabia,
and Kurdistan, as he governs Thrace. . . . Despotism itself
is obliged to truck and huckster. The Sultan gets such
obedience as he can. *He governs with a loose rein that he
may govern at all*").

From this vivid and ample diagnosis, Burke then turns 4
(as he is always turning) to the pressing problem of what
to do, waiving debate whether these characteristics of the
colonists are desirable to the British or to anyone else: "the
question is not whether their spirit deserves praise or blame
—*what, in the name of God, shall we do with it? You have
before you the object,* such as it is—with all its glories, with
all its imperfections on its head. You see the magnitude, the
importance, the temper, the habits, the disorders." In this
large context he considers the possible choices of action: (1)
To prevent the colonists from further expansion by stopping
the crown grants of land (they would simply move in and
"occupy without grants"). (2) To prosecute their independent spirit as "criminal" or treasonable ("The thing seems a
great deal too big for my ideas of jurisprudence"; and, in
such a "narrow and pedantic" attempt to apply routine ideas
of a criminal trial to a great public contest, what is "the
method of drawing up an indictment against a whole people?" It is obviously not going to work). (3) The third
proposal is "to admit the people of our colonies into an
interest in the Constitution." The entire question of abstract
rights he puts aside; it reminds him of Milton's description
of the "great Serbonian bog . . . where armies whole have
solution

sunk." Urging again that the real question "is not whether
you have a *right* to render your people miserable, but
whether it is not in your interest to make them happy,"
Burke turns to precedents in the British past, concentrating
on Wales as an example; and then, with the confidence that
"Magnanimity in politics is not seldom the truest wisdom;
and a great empire and little minds go ill together," moves
his memorable resolutions.

Two years after the speech *On Conciliation*, Burke, who
was now representing the town of Bristol, was anxious lest
the legislation to suppress American liberties should also
affect England (parties, as he said, are only too quick "to
forget their *own* future safety in their desire of sacrificing
their enemies"). Accordingly, he wrote the famous *Letter to
the Sheriffs of the City of Bristol on the Affairs of America*
(1777), which is still one of the classic pronouncements
on political prudence and the imaginative use of fact—including the recognition of the fact that *"nothing in progression can rest on its original plan. We may as well think of
rocking a grown man in the cradle of an infant."*

[4]

The personal life of Burke, especially after he entered
Parliament, has often seemed elusive. This is partly because
his open character and the warm universality of his thought
have aroused far more sympathy than we ordinarily give to
other men, and we are more eager for details than we should
otherwise be. Also, the private papers of Burke, because of a
variety of accidents, have become available only recently.
Even so, close personal acquaintances thought him reticent
and at times rather mysterious. The brilliant studies of
Thomas Copeland have done much to explain this apparent
reticence. When Richard Shackleton—the son of Burke's old
Quaker schoolmaster—innocently agreed to a request to give

information about the background of his eminent friend, and wrote a valuable intimate account, Burke surprisingly turned on him, with harshness and unconcealed distress, mentioning the ease with which political enemies could "pursue me into the closest recesses of my life," and "hunt even to my cradle in hope of finding some blot against me." And Mr. Copeland has shown Burke's growing reserve in the presence of Boswell after it became plain that Boswell was taking copious notes on the conversation of his friends.

After his retirement from Parliament, when he was taunted by the young Duke of Bedford for accepting a pension, there was the bitter reply: "I was not, like his grace of Bedford, swaddled and rocked and dandled into a legislator. . . . At every step of my progress in life . . . and *at every turnpike I met, I was obliged to show my passport,* and again and again to prove my sole title to the honor of being useful to my country." Politics were far rougher in the eighteenth century than they have been since; accusations of the most vicious sort were more publicized. Whenever he pled for justice, Burke could easily be maligned. When the Indian crisis came to a head, and he led the impeachment of Warren Hastings, it was said that £20,000 (a sum almost equivalent to a million dollars now) was spent to attack Burke. In 1780, in the anti-Catholic riots, a mob tried to force Burke—one of the main opponents of the riots—to kiss the Bible and swear he was not a Catholic. Moreover, he was probably more caricatured, as Mr. Copeland points out, than any man of his day—often shown in the robes of a Jesuit, occasionally whipping himself; and there are plenty of hints about his lack of money. Christened "O'Bourke" after one of his early, moving speeches in the House of Commons, he had always thought of himself, in comparison with the great Whig noblemen (the "oaks" of England), as like those summer vines that, as they creep on the ground, may "belly into melons that are exquisite for size and flavour," yet are still "but annual plants that perish with our season, and leave no traces behind us."

Complications in his own <u>family life</u> added to his embarrassment as he moved into prominence. Burke's brother, Richard, and a man vaguely referred to as a "cousin," William Burke, had also come to London to make their fortune. Avid speculators in stocks, without the scruples of their great relative, they still had a claim on his loyalty. Before he knew it, Burke, even as a young man, and with his way yet to make, had agreed to share a common purse with them. As Sir Gilbert Elliott said later of Burke and his relatives: he "has now got such a train after him as would sink anybody but himself." He was always to have relatives attached to him, and served somewhat as the leader of the clan in London. It never occurred to him to turn his back on them. The one serious charge against Burke's integrity has come as a by-product of this. For his estate in Beaconsfield (1768), he borrowed part of the money from William Burke. A loan, it turns out, was made to William from Lord Verney, presumably in order for William to lend it again to Edmund; and when trouble later arose, Burke denied any debt of his own to Verney. His conduct on this occasion, of which a good deal has been made, can only be explained by his <u>extraordinary personal carelessness about domestic details</u> —a carelessness that could at times amount to stark oblivion. It is only fair to remember that such traits were by no means uncommon in public men at the time. Even the younger Pitt (the only man who could open a national budget without notes, as Macaulay said) was proudly indifferent to his domestic expenses, and left immense debts of which he had little conscious knowledge. The point, however, is not to excuse Burke, but only to suggest that the rather messy personal circumstances in which he found himself, while trying to fulfill his almost clannish family obligations, made him more sensitive to criticism. Moreover, these personal loyalties were retained somewhat absent-mindedly, while at the same time he devoted himself intensely, as if in a separate life, to the public ideas he espoused; and it was this separate life, this devoted professional commitment, that was always at the forefront of his attention. Hence the stories of the bizarre household of the Burkes at Beaconsfield. He farmed the land successfully, making constant experiments and improvements; but the house, cobwebbed and littered with papers, dispensed hospitality generously to all comers amidst confusion, brilliance, and domestic waste, with Burke himself utterly absorbed either in his work or in the interchange of ideas.

Caricature and misinterpretation followed him to the end. Even his voluntary retirement from Parliament, in his old age, was heralded as a defeat. And when, shortly afterward, his only son Richard Burke died at thirty-seven (the son, on whom Burke set so many hopes, was expected to become secretary to the Lord Lieutenant of Ireland), the calumny did not stop. It was said that Burke had become mad, and wandered about Beaconsfield kissing the cows and horses. Actually, he had been strolling quietly one day in the fields. And when a favorite horse of his dead son Richard came near, he had stopped to caress it, and then, suddenly, understandably, wept.

Boswell records a conversation in which Burke, ordinarily so equable, states: "I believe in any body of men in England I should have been in the Minority; I have always been in the Minority." Burke said this back in 1778, only three years after the great speech *On Conciliation with the Colonies*. It was to be some years yet before a more nearly complete admission of this to himself (it was never altogether complete) was to have its effect. But as the admission began to seem inevitable, it at least, with all its personal frustrations, freed him to turn to problems with more speculative liberty, and, as the years still passed, with a more splendid rhetoric.

[5]

During his first twenty-four years in Parliament, the conservative Burke found himself—except in one notable instance—constantly arguing for reform. His American speeches were quickly followed by efforts to lift the restraints that crippled Irish trade and manufacture. Pleading for a Britain in which "England and Ireland may flourish together" ("The world is large enough for us both. Let it be our care not to make ourselves too little for it"), Burke also supported measures that would ease the shockingly severe penal laws that were still inflicted on the Catholics. The mild Catholic Relief Act, passed by Parliament in 1778, aroused popular opposition, partly because the war with America had encouraged Catholic France and Spain to join against England. London mobs (the famous "Gordon Riots") incited by Lord George Gordon, plundered shops and houses, burned buildings (almost three hundred people were killed), and even invaded Parliament. Burke especially was an object of mob-hatred, though he walked the streets openly and deliberately. By supporting these reforms, he offended his constituency in Bristol. To the Bristol merchants, who were already chafing at his support of measures to ease the economic restraints of Ireland, Burke's hope to liberalize the anti-Catholic laws was the last straw. Knowing it was now useless to try to be re-elected from Bristol, he voluntarily withdrew after making an eloquent effort to explain his stand. Fortunately, he was able to be elected from Malton, in Yorkshire (1781).

At the same time that he was most involved in the Irish and Catholic questions, Burke was presenting his "Plan of Reform in . . . the Public Economy" (1780), containing a detailed analysis of the waste in administration of the Crown offices. Then, a few months later, he suddenly startled his supporters by turning against a new proposal, led by Fox and later championed by the younger Pitt, to reform the House of Commons by calling for more frequent elections and by adding new members on a more representative basis.

Burke's opposition seemed—and has always seemed—a dramatic change. But the most interesting thing about it is that it is not his *premises* that have changed, but something else. For repeatedly, Burke had surrounded every movement for reform that he had ever championed, with a context of thought only too richly aware of the need for caution: of the need to make sure that the change—if the change is to endure and be formative—must be "grafted" on the present growth of things. So, in the *Speech on Economical Reform,* urging that reform be early so that it can be temperate ("Early reformations are amicable arrangements with a friend in power; late reformations are terms imposed upon a conquered enemy"), Burke only a few months before had stressed that in long-delayed and therefore

> *hot* reformations, in what men more zealous than considerate call *making clear work,* the whole is generally so crude, so harsh, so indigested . . . that the very people who are most eager for it are among the first to grow disgusted at what they have done. Then some part of the abdicated grievance is recalled from its exile in order to become a corrective of the correction.

Again, in the reforming *Tract on the Popery Laws,* he had stressed that the repeal of old laws should involve the most cautious and comprehensive study because, like old houses, such laws often "lean on one another, and the operation is delicate." The point, in fact, is memorably put as far back as the *Thoughts on the Cause of the Present Discontents* (1770): "It is no inconsiderable part of wisdom, to know how much of an evil ought to be tolerated; lest, by attempting a degree of purity impracticable . . . instead of cutting off the subsisting ill practices, new corruptions might be produced for the concealment and security of the old." So now, on the issue of Parliamentary reform, Burke proceeds from the same context:

> There are many things in reformation which would be proper to be done if other things can be done along with them, but which, if they cannot be so accompanied, ought not to be done at all . . . Please God, I will walk with caution whenever I am not able clearly to see my way before me.

Burke's opposition to Parliamentary reform, therefore, involves no change in his general premises. The change is rather in the object to which they are applied. For here, for the first time, was a proposal that could in some way tamper (as he thought) with the actual roots of what had permitted all the growth that had been attained: the character of the House of Commons itself. As he states in the famous close of this speech (May 7, 1782) on Pitt's proposed changes:

> It is for fear of losing the inestimable treasure we have that I do not venture to game it out of my hands for the vain hope of improving it. I look with filial reverence on the constitution of my country, and never will cut it in pieces, and put it into the kettle of any magician, in order to boil it, with the puddle of their compounds, into youth and vigor. On the contrary, I will drive away such pretenders; I will nurse its venerable age, and with lenient arts extend a parent's breath.

This colorful close is a personal defense rather than an argument—a sort of apology for keeping the whole subject at a distance for at least a while. The speech is not one to which he devoted much effort. It is significantly bare even of rhetoric (except at the end) as well as analysis.

Too much can easily be made of Burke's stand on Parliamentary reform. In fact, too much has been made of it. Plainly, the whole matter was something of a nuisance, coming at the time it did. For many other considerations were now at the forefront of his mind. There is some reason to feel that he did not wish to see the boat rocked while the

waves were still high, or even rising, and that he meant what
he said when he asserted (the italics are his own) that he
reserved his right of dissenting "from any resolution whatsoever on the subject of an alteration in the representation and
election of the kingdom *at this time.*" Among the matters
occupying Burke's attention—he had been studying it in
especially careful detail throughout the year before he rose
to reply to Pitt's proposal for Parliamentary change—was
the subject of India.

[6]

"If I had asked for a reward," Burke wrote near the close
of his life, "which I have never done, it would be for the
sixteen years I laboured with the most assiduity and met with
the least success—I mean in the affairs of India." The East
India Company, chartered as far back as 1600, had gradually
become, as Burke said, "a state in the disguise of a merchant."
As its trading stations increased, it was allowed by the
Crown to protect them with armies, and even to commission
officers. With the disintegration of the Mogul Empire, from
which it obtained its privileges, the Company moved into the
vacuum. In this slow transformation of the East India Company into a vast state, with power over millions, there had
naturally been friction with Parliament. In time the Company
was forced to present its accounts to the Government; a
Supreme Court was set up in Bengal responsible to the
Crown; and in the hope of creating some order, the company
in 1773 appointed an able, energetic man, Warren Hastings,
as Governor-General. Finally, a committee was selected, with
Burke as its head, to study how British India could be
governed "with the greatest security and advantage to this
country, and by what means the happiness of the native inhabitants may be best promoted." The thickly detailed reports
that Burke wrote for this committee were followed by Fox's
East India Bill (1783), ultimately based on Burke's reports,

which asked nothing less than the transfer of the East India
Company's political powers to the Government. The appropriation of these powers inevitably conflicted with the ideal
of prescriptive rights that Burke had always championed. But
outweighing them were far more important rights.

Seeking—as he had done some years before with America
—to present the matter in such a way that "India might be
approximated to our understandings, and, if possible, our
feelings," Burke presents a vivid picture of the size of the
territories, and of the numbers of people involved, contrasting
them with the irresponsible government they were being given
by young men blithely unaware of the complexity of the
society they had come, in effect, to plunder:

> Animated with all the avarice of age and all the impetuosity
> of youth, they roll in one after another, wave after wave; and
> there is nothing before the eyes of the natives but an endless,
> hopeless prospect of new birds of prey and passage . . .
> Every rupee of profit made by an Englishman is lost forever
> to India. . . . England has erected no churches, no hospitals,
> no palaces, no schools; England has built no bridges, made no
> highroads, cut no navigations, dug no reservoirs. Every other
> conqueror of every other description has left some monument,
> either of state or beneficence, behind him. Were we to be
> driven out of India this day, nothing would remain to tell that
> it had been possessed, during the inglorious period of our
> dominion, by anything better than the orangoutang or the tiger.

The powerful generality of this speech, as always in Burke
at his greatest, reaches far beyond the immediate reform he
has in mind:

> All these circumstances are not, I confess, very favorable to
> the idea of our attempting to govern India at all. But there we
> are; there we are placed by the Sovereign Disposer; and we
> must do the best we can in our situation. *The situation of man
> is the preceptor of his duty*.

As soon as the bill was passed by the Commons, opposition

flared from every side, incited by every motive. (There were also some real flaws in the bill, and Fox had been hasty.) In the turmoil, George III, as Morley said, at last saw his chance. He brought pressure to bear on the House of Lords, which defeated the bill; and he immediately used the defeat as a reason to discharge the government, which was then assumed by the younger Pitt.

But Burke, it soon turned out, had only made a start. He continued the investigations that finally culminated in the famous impeachment of Warren Hastings as Governor-General. Early in 1786, he presented the articles of charge to the House of Commons; and in February, 1788, the Commons formally impeached Hastings before the House of Lords. The trial was one of the most spectacular events of the century. Most of the great orators of the day were involved—and the period is the golden era of English oratory. The galleries were crowded with the eminent men of the period. Four sittings were occupied by Burke's general introduction to the charges, and Hastings himself was visibly shaken. Then Charles James Fox opened the long charge concerning Cheyte Sing; and the theatrical Richard Brinsley Sheridan, in a self-consciously brilliant but shallow speech that lasted two days, took over the colorful charge concerning the ravishing of the property of the Princesses of Oude. Partly because of Macaulay's account of the trial, in his essay on Warren Hastings—probably the most colorful paragraphs in English historical writing—the opening parts of the trial, after a hundred and seventy-five years, are still one of the most vivid episodes in British history. After a few months, however, interest inevitably flagged: too many other matters were afoot, and the details were getting rather specialized and even boring. Burke doggedly clung to the charges. The trial dragged on, constantly interrupted or postponed; and Hastings was at last acquitted in 1794, six years later. Perhaps Burke sensed from the start that Hastings himself could not be convicted (however honestly Burke believed in Hastings' guilt), and was primarily concerned, as Bertram Newman said, to "secure the enactment, on a stage, visible to all England and Europe, of a palpable and spectacular warning that the imputation of grave public crimes against subject races should not pass without a solemn inquiry."

[7]

Burke's long study and plea on behalf of India show him (at least in two respects) at his very greatest. And this is completely aside from the obvious historical importance— aside from the fact that this spectacular, thorough airing of the whole matter was slowly, over generations, to leave its effect. It is also despite the two facts that Hastings himself, to begin with, was being made a scapegoat, and also that this huge mass of material is inevitably dated and is far too detailed to arouse much interest. No collected body of writing so highly praised has been so little read.

But the appeal is still hypnotic. For, first, simply as a sheer feat of mind, this *tour de force* of Burke is unrivalled in its own way, and compels unqualified admiration. He studied and digested every available work on the history, religions, geography, and economy of India. Moreover, "Bales of official correspondence, of pamphlets, folio volumes of reports," as Newman said, "so far from choking his assimilative powers, served to exercise his mind, to fire his imagination, and, most important, to widen his sympathies." Secondly, this assimilative power is constantly fed by a moral and imaginative vision that is richly meshed with fact and freighted with concreteness (not yet cut loose from this strong purchase, as some of the writings on the French Revolution were to be). Above all, there is the appeal of Burke's sense of process and time. In the trial of Warren Hastings, as Macaulay perceptively wrote, everything calculated to strike an imaginative and reflecting mind was present: interests that belonged to the near and distant were collected. "Every step in the proceedings carried the mind backward, through many troubled centuries, to the days when the foundations of our constitution were laid; or . . . over boundless seas and deserts," to a vast, distant land. In the hall of William Rufus, with its associations that reached back to Richard the Lionhearted, and in forms handed down since the Plantagenets, Burke, with his own vivid knowledge of England's long past, tried to present to this audience what he had learned of a remote subcontinent of so many millions. To the mediaeval and Far Eastern associations is also added the glance backward to the great orations of classical antiquity. Finally there is added (as in all of Burke's greater writing) a prophetic anticipation of the modern world's haunting sense of time.

For in one special, very important way, Burke is closer to the modern educated sensibility than any other writer between Shakespeare and Wordsworth. He is closer because of his constant sense of process, and the almost tender protectiveness of his imagination when it turns to the tragic past. If the phrase, "the tragic past," is used here, it is partly with the thought of Whitehead's distinction: that the essence of "tragedy" is not unhappiness, but rather the solemn, remorseless working out of events. The past is tragic partly because it is finished. There is the sheer fact that all that life is over, as our own will only too quickly be. What that vast diversity of life did, suffered, or hoped, can never be changed. As in Proust's great book, with its remarkable title (*À la Recherche du Temps perdu*), or Eliot's *Four Quartets,* the greater writing of the twentieth century—and perhaps of the nineteenth century—is saturated with the vivid sense of the way in which the past is forever locked in an unalterable pattern. Hence the tenderness to the past since the onset of the romantic era. It touches every aspect of our lives. Even Henry Ford, who could mutter that "History is bunk," devoted a good deal of worried and even sentimental effort to

salvaging the relics of a vanished America he himself had
helped to usher from the scene. The point is the modernity
of Burke in his sense of process and change: the fact that
there is always the sense of a large finished past which can
be rescued only by the interpretative imagination that medi-
tates on it, as music can come alive only when the printed
pattern of notes is scanned and repeated, for a little time, by
some later intelligence. And the past is tragic not only because it is irrevocable, without any second chance, so to
speak, but also because so much of it was blind (as we ourselves are now): blind because of the enormous waste, the
conflicts, frustrations, defeats; because of the freight it carries
of the diversity of each life, and of the ways in which the
cramped, primitive minds of all of us, poisoned by fear and
self-defense, torture each other in our bewildered stupidity.
The sense of all this stirs in Burke the desire to shelter this
huge accumulation of past life, and to give it, so to speak, at
least the shadow of a second chance, if only in the meditative
imagination that tries to learn from it. "Their imagination"
(he said later of the systematic theorists of the French
Revolution) "is not *fatigued* with the contemplation of
human suffering through the wild waste of centuries added
to centuries of misery and desolation. *Their humanity is at
their horizon,*—and, like the horizon, it always flies before
them."

But the earth, of course, belongs to the living. And this
almost obsessive desire to shelter, which extends to the
present and future as well as the past, especially focusses on
continuities in which the interplay of all three is sensed
dynamically. Those only, said Coleridge, have the true
"philosophical imagination" who can "interpret and understand the symbol that the wings of the air-sylph are forming
within the skin of the caterpillar." The vision of process that
increasingly absorbed Burke is that suggested by Yeats, a
century and a half later——

France

> And haughtier-headed Burke, that proved the State a tree,
> That this unconquerable labyrinth of the birds, century after
> century,
> Cast but dead leaves to mathematical equality.

Yeats catches the situation exactly. For in Burke's ideal of unity through slow, organic growth is the capacious sense of variety—of the "unconquerable labyrinth" of actual life ("dead leaves" being all that can be garnered by the "mathematical" or systematic hunt for simple, clean-cut shape). And the essence of the image lies in the fact that the tree, grown so slowly ("century after century"), offers shelter simply through the labyrinthine interlacing of its boughs. "Unconquerable" in its rooted strength, it provides an infinitely varied protection for the "birds"—the innumerable flickers of vivid life—that are ourselves.

[8]

Suddenly, when Burke was sixty, the French Revolution broke out, and with it began the final stage of Burke's own career. To the surprise of almost everyone, he threw himself against this violent change which was capturing the imagination of more people in Europe than anything else that had occurred for a century. Many well-meaning men in England felt that the changes in France were not only long overdue for France itself, but were even a suggestive model for other countries. The closing years of Burke's life are one protracted, interrupted, stubborn debate with this belief—with anything, in fact, that half-savored of this belief. For so long judicious, open-minded, saturated with fact, and idealizing the uses of fact, he could be forgiven if now, at last, he was a little obsessive, a little single-minded, and frequently repetitive. He had both a personal justification and also a very good reason. Shelved long since as a practicing states-man, except on committees, or as an orator, and repeatedly

disregarded (in his own mind) in almost everything he had
advocated, he was now less bound by the need of practical
decision. He was freer to speculate; and with one cause after
another removed from the realm of the possible, there was
naturally a human reluctance to quit this final cause, which
he continued henceforth to chew and worry. But the final
defense (if any defense is needed) is that he really came far
closer to sensing what the Revolution involved than anyone
else of his day or, in fact, of generations afterwards.

The first scene of this closing act in Burke's life begins with
the famous *Reflections on the Revolution in France* (1790),
which he continued to revise for almost a year before publishing. In the first part of the *Reflections,* he demolishes the
simple-minded connection that many people in England were
making between the French Revolution and the so-called
"Glorious Revolution" (1688) in England, when William III
and Mary were brought in to replace James II. In the English
Revolution of 1688, "the two principles of conservation and
correction" were working simultaneously. Prescriptive rights
were preserved, strengthened, and even broadened through
the reform. Burke then turns to what the French Assembly has
done, and the arbitrary "geometrical" blitheness with which,
in this new constitution, it imposes individual injustices in the
name of efficiency and equality, and, in its handling of older
institutions, slays the horse (so to speak) instead of using the
bridle. At the end he is ominously prophetic, especially when
he comes, directly and realistically, to the uses of power, and
to the future relations the Assembly must have with the Army.
Here, of course, Burke puts his finger on what was actually
to occur with the rise of Napoleon.

> In the weakness of one kind of authority, and in the fluctua-
> tion of all, the officers of an army will remain for some time
> mutinous and full of faction, *until some popular general, who*
> *understands the art of conciliating the soldiery, and who*
> *possesses the true spirit of command, shall draw the eyes of*

all men upon himself. Armies will obey him on his personal account. There is no other way of securing military obedience in this state of things. But the moment in which that event shall happen, *the person who really commands the army is your master;* the master (that is little) of your king, the master of your Assembly, the master of your whole republic.

The book is unquestionably one of the great books of the last two centuries. Fundamental distinctions, of the greatest value to the moralist and the student of human institutions, are scattered profusely. Moreover, Burke has on his side one undeniable fact of the greatest importance. The French Revolution did serve as both a prototype and a catalyst for forces that have grown with frightening strength and momentum in the modern world. The repercussions range from the local fact that France itself is even now a divided nation, a hundred and seventy-five years later, to the far larger one that the revolutionary philosophy (aggression through rationalization—through the use of abstraction, system, and the scrapping of precedent) has become endemic since World War I, resulting in the now familiar sprouting of militant *isms* (the militant use, that is, of theory and system as propaganda). Nazism, and the communism of Russia and later of China are, of course, the notable examples. Burke's later *Thoughts on French Affairs* (1791) puts the matter more crisply than he ever put it before or was to do again: the French Revolution bears "little resemblance or analogy to those which have been brought about in Europe upon principles merely political. *It is a revolution of doctrine and theoretic dogma.* It has a much greater resemblance to those changes which have been made upon religious grounds," the last one of which, on anything like a comparable scale, was the Protestant Reformation itself. To have perceived this is certainly a part—a very large part—of Burke's greatness.

But the insights in the *Reflections* do not burgeon organically from the context. Instead they flash out against a back-

drop that is often dark and suggestive but at other times only
fuzzy. The form of writing, in short, is rather new for Burke.
Now it can be justly replied that a change in form of writing
ought to be allowed a man. And perhaps the only fair criticism is that which Burke himself teaches at his finest, where
we see, in his own example, the constant development of
principle from and by means of complex fact. Viewed with
this demanding expectation, the *Reflections,* simply as a work
of art (or rather as a *single* work of thought, separated from
the rest of Burke) has a basic stagger in its walk. Taught by
him as much as anyone to prize organic structure, we can
only feel that *some* of the noble premises of the book (and
Burke asks us to accept them all as a unit) are simply not
applicable. Justly described by Russell Kirk as a book that
excels any other as a "foundation of conservative philosophy,"
it is still excelled by the collected writings of Burke as a
whole. This is high praise. But the reservation ought to be
kept in mind. As Hazlitt said, the only fair selection of Burke
is "all that he wrote." And in trying to relate this new, prophetic work (the starting-ground for all his later writing on
the French Revolution) to the context of his other writing, the
book itself must first be seen, with some sympathy, as the
writing of a man so long in the opposition. Though this in no
way detracts from the wisdom, the tone carries some of the
exasperation that was to become more frequent in his later
works.

Furthermore, in *Reflections on the Revolution in France,*
he was dealing with a nation rather different from those to
which he was accustomed and to which he had given such
tender and yet realistic study. In considering the American
colonies, he had shown an unrivalled ability to leap far afield
from the parochial scene; and he had spared no pains to
submerge himself in details. But he had been able to do this
because these colonies were still a part, and a heavy respon-

sibility, of growing Britain. So with India. In that devoted
labor, his conscience had been caught—was still being caught
—by the mesh of responsibility that England had created for
itself. Moreover, the huge sub-continent of India was not only
closely tied with England but also so different that a real
effort of imagination on Burke's part was challenged. India
combined the appeal of distance, of immense variety (variety
far greater than that of France), and the tug of British responsibility. But France, only across the channel, could be
taken more for granted, and could stimulate no such labor
in the older Burke. At least it could arouse no such steady,
imaginative effort in a statesman who was at last reversing
Goldsmith's complaint (that he gave up to party what was
meant for mankind),* and who was moving, inevitably, into
the more theoretical and poetic aspects of government.

Fundamentally, the *Reflections* and the works on the
French Revolution that follow can be seen for what they are
only if we realize that the personal intensity behind them is
inspired less by the complete facts of the Revolution in
France than by the dread lest the principles—and practices
—should touch the great, slow-growing tree of the British
Constitution. Anxiety, when personal enough, always nar-
rows our outlook. If only because he is now defensive—because he is at last exclusive rather than assimilative (and it
is assimilation that is Burke's great strength)—this noble,
capacious, at times petulant book can never be taken as the
principal key to Burke but only as one of the keys needed
to open the vault. Nothing said here in any way detracts from
either the general wisdom of the book or from its prophetic
interest, both of which are taken for granted. As Napoleon

---

* Who, born for the Universe, narrow'd his mind,
    And to party gave up, what was meant for mankind

  Who, too deep for his hearers, still went on refining,
    And thought of convincing, while they thought of dining.

said, "Had there been no Rousseau, there would have been
no Revolution. If there had been no Revolution, *I* would
have been impossible."

[9]

Burke, now near the end of his career, could not stay away
from the subject of the French Revolution, though a part of
him only too eagerly wished to have done with it. Plainly, by
the end of 1791, a great change in Europe was taking place.
And in a passage, cited seventy-five years later by Matthew
Arnold as "one of the finest things in literature," Burke
openly reminded himself—as well as others—that *if* a change
is about to take place, the important question is how to
deal with it. Constantly in his earlier writing he had put to
the forefront the undeniable existence of fact. And he did so
now, in the *Thoughts on French Affairs* (1791). Here, perhaps because he hoped that this would be the last pronounce-
ment he would ever make on the subject, Burke is deliberately
concise. He again stresses the uniqueness of the French
Revolution as a revolution "of doctrine and theoretic dogma,"
far transcending local or domestic problems. It is an ominous
cloud on the horizon. Quickly he surveys the nations of
Europe as they then were, from "nerveless" Spain to Germany. There is the clairvoyant remark that in time an even
more militant ideology will strike Germany: that there is
already slowly preparing in Germany "a revolution, in my
opinion, likely to be more decisive upon the general fate of
nations than that of France itself." Then, at the close of this
astonishing pamphlet, comes the question: *"What is to be
done?"* After stressing the almost infinite variables that have
to be kept in mind, he ends with the paragraph Arnold
praised as Burke's "return upon himself":

> The evil is stated, in my opinion, as it exists. The remedy
> must be where power, wisdom, and information, I hope, are
> more united with good intentions than they can be with me. I

have done with this subject, I believe, for ever. It has given
me many anxious moments for the last two years. If a great
change is to be made in human affairs, the minds of men will
be fitted to it; the general opinions and feelings will draw that
way. Every fear, every hope will forward it; *and then they who
persist in opposing this mighty current in human affairs, will
appear rather to resist the decrees of Providence itself, than
the mere designs of men. They will not be resolute and firm,
but perverse and obstinate.*

[10]

Twenty years before—or even ten—Burke could have followed his own precept, and put his own imagination directly
to the question he had once put to the Commons, in the
great speech *On Conciliation:* "The question is not whether
their spirit deserves praise or blame—*what, in the name of
God, shall we do with it? You have before you the object,
such as it is*—with all its glories, with all its imperfections on
its head. You see the magnitude, the temper, the habits, the
disorders." But as one cause after another had failed (as
Burke thought), and as the chance of office had receded until
it had been forgotten, his concern had now been sublimated
to a general conception of European order. And in a sense
the obsessive—at times prophetic—fear of all that the French
Revolution might mean was only his valedictory tribute to
the British Constitution: a tribute that his personal circumstances would never allow to become closer than a brilliantly
descriptive one. His quick temper, always an enemy of his
own ideals as well as his ambition, was becoming easier to
exasperate. From the beginning, extraordinary though brilliant lapses of taste (to use a Victorian euphemism) had
been common. He could fall at times into a Swiftian power
of obscene image that shocked even an eighteenth-century
House of Commons. Only the sturdy, admiring Johnson resisted the temptation to censure Burke for this. At most
Johnson would agree merely that Burke "has not in every

respect the highest elegance," and compare him to "a lion who lashes himself into fury with his own tail."

Moreover, external circumstances kept cruelly prodding Burke to continue his long debate with France, which was beginning to seem querulous and even comic to younger people. When Pitt solidified the Tory majority in 1790, the Whigs, in order to secure more strength, welcomed the support of reformists who were eulogizing the events in France. Startled, Burke wheeled about to attack their measures. Then came the dramatic break with Charles James Fox on the floor of the House of Commons (May 6, 1791) with its rather awful display of emotion. As a result, Burke was virtually read out of the party of which he had been so long the intellectual leader. The result was catastrophic for his own peace of mind. For it was Burke, of course, who was really responsible for the break rather than Fox. Put more justly, it was simply one of those terrible moments when thirty years of a man's life suddenly catch up with him, and then, unpredictably joining with accident, produce a tragic result. The Quebec Bill was up for discussion on April 21, 1791. Fox, a week before, had ended a speech by praising the French Constitution as nothing less than "the most stupendous and glorious edifice of liberty which has been erected . . . in any time or country." Burke, hardly believing he had heard such a thing, instinctively rose to answer; but he was shouted down by cries of "Question." Not until May 6 itself did he have a chance to answer. He was hopelessly heated by now. In making his reply, he was interrupted or called to order eight times as straying from the proper subject of discussion—that is, the Quebec Bill itself.

Younger members of the party had been feeling for some time that Burke talked too long; and his painstaking study of detail was becoming tedious—even more tedious to them, it would seem, than to his opponents. Then occurred an incident that would seem sentimental or even foolish had it involved another man. But in the case of Burke, it was rather terrible. Never given to self-pity (however self-righteously irritable at times), always just, he had become helplessly bewildered by the attacks from these comparative youths of his own party; and finally the inevitable association was made, in his own mind, with the classic victim of ingratitude in dramatic literature. Puzzled, hurt (at one point Fox walked out,* with twenty or thirty of his followers), Burke, stung into a sort of stammering, began to quote from *King Lear:*

> the little dogs, and all,
> Tray, Blanche, and Sweetheart. See, they bark at me!

The long scene, even in the third-person reporting of the *Parliamentary History* (XXIX. 363-428), is remarkable in the dramatic ebb and flow of feeling. This particular moment, it is true, is tactfully omitted—Burke's deplorable outburst, and the indignant response of the Commons at such a display. But the account immediately picks up the discussion that follows. Burke, regretting the lapse, tried to curb himself: he really tried for the moment to moderate his tone, to be reasonable. Then, still interrupted, he was at last reduced to the steps that personal pride can sometimes prod one to take. He was now not answering Fox but thirty years of life. Dropping the argument, he suddenly began, in ominous, measured tones (the third-person is almost *verbatim*):

> It was certainly indiscretion, at any period, but especially at his time of life, to provoke enemies, or give his friends occasion to desert him; yet if his firm and steady adherence to the British constitution placed him in such a dilemma, he would risk all, and. . . with his last words exclaim, "Fly from the French constitution." (Mr. Fox here whispered, that "there

---

* A grotesque touch, altogether in keeping with the *Lear*-like character of the episode, is that Fox was not stalking out in protest after all. Tired, and torn by the scene that he was afraid might arise, he simply went out for a moment's refreshment—actually just to get an orange—and his supporters, thinking (like Burke) that Fox was really leaving, sheep-like rose and followed.

was no loss of friends.") Mr. Burke said, yes, there *was* a loss
of friends—he knew the price of his conduct . . . their friendship was at an end.

Fox rose, astonished, reduced to weeping. He tried to answer
Burke. But Burke was now adamant, and five days later (May
11), speaking at last of his own years as "a very laborious
. . . though a very unimportant servant of the public," he
openly accepted, he said, the fact that a "sentence of banish-
ment had been pronounced" upon him:

> He stood, he said, a man publicly disgraced by his party
> . . . he had gone through his youth without encountering any
> public disgrace; and though he had then in his age been so
> unfortunate as to meet it, he did not solicit the right hon.
> gentleman's [Fox's] friendship, *nor that of any man, either on
> one side of the House or the other.*

The last step was taken. It had been long preparing. This
champion of party—this sober analyst of the uses of party—
was now without such a base. Moreover, this conscience and
capacious analyst of Empire was without active connection
with what he had dreamed of nourishing with "filial reverence." A few months after the fatal break with Fox, he wrote
the *Thoughts on French Affairs,* bending over backward not
to be "perverse and obstinate," and hoping to "have done with
this subject . . .   forever." But he still could not stop. He
wrote his moving *Appeal from the New to the Old Whigs*
(1792), in which he tried again to contrast the quiet English
Revolution of 1688 with the doctrinaire French Revolution.
Fanny Burney saw him in the summer of 1792. The conversation went well for a while ("How I wish," she wrote, "that
you could meet this wonderful man when he is easy, happy,
and with people he cordially likes"). But politics came up
in the conversation, and suddenly, she said, it gave "to his
face the expression of a man who is going to defend himself
from murderers." The *Appeal from the New to the Old*

Whigs was followed by the *Observations on the Conduct of the Ministry* (1793). Two years later he began the four *Letters on a Regicide Peace* (1795), though the last two were not published until after Burke's death in 1797. There are brilliant paragraphs in the *Regicide Peace* where Burke again argues that the philosophy of the leaders of the French Revolution exemplifies a new, fundamental disorder that will become increasingly militant: that it could in time "destroy all Europe." But despite the prophetic passages and the noble sense of European unity, the *Letters* have long been neglected except by the historian. As John Morley said long ago, they lack the saturation in fact and probabilities that makes Burke almost unique, though they could easily have established the reputation of a lesser man.

In 1794, the long, drawn-out trial of Warren Hastings came to an end. In the famous peroration to his speech on June 16, Burke—now about to retire—tried, at the close of his career in the House of Commons, to contrast the British Parliament with the hapless Parliament of Paris; he dwelt on its long history, and the responsibility it had to its past and to the future. But Hastings was acquitted the year after. To Burke's own mind, at least, this, like every other cause, had ended in failure.

[11]

Leaving Parliament, Burke retired to Beaconsfield. The grotesque cartoons in the newspapers had now become crueler. Always pictured as bespectacled (no cartoonist could seem to forget the glasses he wore, and his long sharp nose), he was lampooned as a Jesuit, though, except for the robes, he might seem even more a caricature of a Quaker schoolmaster. From the beginning, the ideal of Abraham Shackleton, his old Quaker teacher, had been formative and valuable. Unconsciously, perhaps, he was beginning to assimilate still more, at the end of his life, some of the external mannerisms

of both the man and the faith, however militant he had
now become about the "theoretic dogma" of the French
Revolution.

It was proposed to offer him a peerage, with the title of
Lord Beaconsfield. But his only son, Richard, suddenly died
in August, 1794, two months after Burke gave the famous
peroration to Parliament in the Hastings impeachment. To
the lonely, grief-stricken Burke, the peerage meant little.
With a continuity Burke would have valued, the title was
used years later. For when the great Victorian Prime Minister,
Benjamin Disraeli, whose life was a drama comparable to
that of Burke, was offered a peerage, he chose, as the highest
compliment he could ask, the title of Lord Beaconsfield. The
imaginative appeal in this continuity is that the full history
of Burke intimately involves the greater figures from the
middle nineteenth century to the present day. He has a large
part—in fact, no one has a larger part—in whatever Britain
has contributed to the government of societies. The two im-
perishable contributions of Britain to the modern world—to
the world that emerged from the Middle Ages, and is still our
world—are, of course, its government and also its unrivalled
literature. And in Burke, as in no one else, the two are
combined.

Arrangements for Burke's peerage naturally subsided after
the unexpected death of his son. But the younger Pitt, who
was now Prime Minister, at least secured a pension for his
great opponent. Burke, always negligent of his own affairs,
was poorly off; and the pension, which he was to receive only
for the three remaining years of his life, was suddenly attacked by an impetuous but aging youth, the Duke of Bedford, whose own family (the House of Russell) had received
enormous grants from the crown after the confiscation of the
monasteries by Henry VIII. Ironically, the Duke of Bedford,
who was what Samuel Johnson would call an "unideaed"
person, and who was hoping to establish himself as a man

with causes, had also been flirting with the Revolutionary party. The result was a final, even glorious discharge of lightning from a long-collecting cloud of feelings.

Never was a man so unfortunate in picking either a cause or an opponent as Bedford. For his attack provoked Burke's magnificent reply, *A Letter to a Noble Lord,* surely the most splendid valedictory that any statesman ever wrote. In this nearest approach that he ever made to autobiography, Burke mentions quickly his lifelong efforts to keep men like the Duke of Bedford himself "in that situation which alone makes him my superior"—his birth and his fortune. Then follows the most powerful use of antithesis in any writing of the entire century—finer than anything of the sort in Gibbon or probably even Johnson (Burke is indeed "the first man everywhere," said Johnson)—as he contrasts this modest pension with the staggering grants given to the House of Russell. The sustained climax is one of the great moments in English prose. Hazlitt considered the passage the "most splendid in Burke's writing"; and according to De Quincey, Burke himself, discussing the purely literary character of his work, cited these paragraphs as those over which he worked with most care:

> The crown has considered me after long service; the crown has paid the Duke of Bedford by advance. He has had a long credit for any service which he may perform hereafter. He is secure, and long *may* he be secure, in his advance, whether he performs any services or not. But let him take care how he endangers the safety of that constitution which secures his own utility or his own insignificance, or how he discourages those who take up even puny arms to defend an order of things which like the sun of heaven, shines alike on the useful and the worthless. His grants are ingrafted on the public law of Europe . . .

These grants, continues Burke, and all they symbolize, are secure against every change but one—that militantly preached by the envious, system-drunk leaders of the French Revolution, who, mechanically and revengefully, regard all previous rights as an automatic disqualification. "Such are *their* ideas, such *their* religion, and such *their* laws." But as to this country, he goes on, as he works to a final nobility of vision, so forgivably and even amusingly crossed by the Olympian sighs of exasperation at the end ("Amen! and so be it!")— "as long as the well-compacted structure" of this state—

> a fortress at once and a temple, shall stand inviolate on the British Sion—as long as the British monarchy, no more limited than fenced by the orders of the state, shall, like the proud Keep of Windsor, rising in the majesty of proportion, and girt with the double belt of its kindred and coeval towers . . . oversee and guard the subjected land—*so long the mounds and dikes of the low, fat Bedford level will have nothing to fear from all the pickaxes of all the levelers of France.* As long as . . . the king, and . . . the lords and commons of the realm . . . the constitutional frank-pledge of this nation; the firm guarantees of each other's being and each other's rights; the joint and several securities . . . for every kind and every quality of property and dignity—*as long as these endure, so long the Duke of Bedford is safe, and we are all safe together* —the high from the blights of envy and the spoliations of rapacity; the low from the iron hand of oppression and the insolent spurn of contempt. Amen! and so be it! and so it will be!

[12]

The last two years of Burke's life make rather sad reading. There are the scenes of Burke walking about Beaconsfield and weeping when he saw the horse that his dead son used to ride. There are more cheerful intervals, as when one of his friends found him playing with children and "rolling about with them," as the friend said, "on the carpet, and pouring out, in his gambols, the sublimest images mingled with the most wretched puns." The close of Burke's life especially contrasts with that hopeful day, so many years before, when the proudly happy members of the Club, especially Johnson and Reynolds (both dead by now), were eagerly awaiting the news of his first speech in Parliament. His roots had been with them from the beginning. Only a few years before he died, Burke had attended the last of the famous *Discourses* that Reynolds, as President of the Royal Academy, had given over a period of twenty-one years. Reynolds had grown increasingly liberal as he became older; and now, in his final *Discourse,* outlining a way of looking at art that creatively merges with that of the next century, he disowned much of his own painting, and humbly urged a far more dynamic use of tradition than he himself had shown. He ended with a memorable passage about Michelangelo, who himself had conserved the classical past while moving creatively toward the future. In a scene that could have taken place only in the later eighteenth century, Burke at once arose, during the applause to this magnificent farewell. And walking down the aisle toward his old friend, who had only two more years to live, he quoted the lines from *Paradise Lost* that could be applied to Burke himself:

> The Angel ended, and in Adam's ear
> So charming left his voice, that he awhile
> Thought him still speaking, still stood fix'd to hear.

When he retired from Parliament, Burke was obviously ill. It now seems likely that he had cancer of the stomach. Three years later, on July 9, 1797, he died. Fox generously proposed that he be buried in Westminster Abbey; but Burke had left a request that he be buried in the small churchyard at Beaconsfield.

I AMERICA AND THE BRITISH EMPIRE

Speech on American Taxation

During the last session of the last Parliament, on the 19th of April, 1774, Mr. Rose Fuller, member for Rye, made the following motion:—

"That an act made in the seventh year of the reign of his present Majesty, intituled, 'An act for granting certain duties in the British colonies and plantations in America; for allowing a drawback of the duties of customs upon the exportation from this kingdom of coffee and cocoa-nuts, of the produce of the said colonies or plantations; for discontinuing the drawbacks payable on china earthenware exported to America; and for more effectually preventing the clandestine running of goods in the said colonies and plantations,' might be read."

And the same being read accordingly, he moved,—

"That this House will, upon this day sevennight, resolve itself into a committee of the whole House, to take into consideration the duty of three-pence per pound weight upon tea, payable in all his Majesty's dominions in America, imposed by the said act; and also the appropriation of the said duty."

On this latter motion a warm and interesting debate arose, in which Mr. Burke spoke as follows.

[Inserted by the publisher, James Dodsley, when the Speech was first printed (1774); it may possibly have been written by Burke himself.]

Sir,—I agree with the honorable gentleman[1] who spoke last, that this subject is not new in this House. Very disagreeably

---

[1] Charles Wolfran Cornwall, Esq., lately appointed one of the Lords of the Treasury. [Burke]

to this House, very unfortunately to this nation, and to the peace and prosperity of this whole empire, no topic has been more familiar to us. For nine long years, session after session, we have been lashed round and round this miserable circle of occasional arguments and temporary expedients. I am sure our heads must turn and our stomachs nauseate with them. We have had them in every shape; we have looked at them in every point of view. Invention is exhausted; reason is fatigued; experience has given judgment; but obstinacy is not yet conquered.

The honorable gentleman has made one endeavor more to diversify the form of this disgusting argument. He has thrown out a speech composed almost entirely of challenges. Challenges are serious things; and as he is a man of prudence as well as resolution, I dare say he has very well weighed those challenges before he delivered them. I had long the happiness to sit at the same side of the House, and to agree with the honorable gentleman on all the American questions. My sentiments, I am sure, are well known to him; and I thought I had been perfectly acquainted with his. Though I find myself mistaken, he will still permit me to use the privilege of an old friendship; he will permit me to apply myself to the House under the sanction of his authority, and, on the various grounds he had measured out, to submit to you the poor opinions which I have formed upon a matter of importance enough to demand the fullest consideration I could bestow upon it.

He has stated to the House two grounds of deliberation: one narrow and simple, and merely confined to the question on your paper; the other more large and more complicated, —comprehending the whole series of the Parliamentary proceedings with regard to America, their causes, and their consequences. With regard to the latter ground, he states it as useless, and thinks it may be even dangerous, to enter into so extensive a field of inquiry. Yet, to my surprise, he had hardly laid down this restrictive proposition, to which his authority would have given so much weight, when directly, and with the same authority, he condemns it, and declares it absolutely necessary to enter into the most ample historical detail. His zeal has thrown him a little out of his usual accuracy. In this perplexity, what shall we do, Sir, who are willing to submit to the law he gives us? He has reprobated in one part of his speech the rule he had laid down for debate in the other, and, after narrowing the ground for all those who are to speak after him, he takes an excursion, himself, as unbounded as the subject and the extent of his great abilities.

Sir, when I cannot obey all his laws, I will do the best I can. I will endeavor to obey such of them as have the sanction of his example, and to stick to that rule which, though not consistent with the other, is the most rational. He was certainly in the right, when he took the matter largely. I cannot prevail on myself to agree with him in his censure of his own conduct. It is not, he will give me leave to say, either useless or dangerous. He asserts, that retrospect is not wise; and the proper, the only proper subject of inquiry, is "not how we got into this difficulty, but how we are to get out of it." In other words, we are, according to him, to consult our invention, and to reject our experience. The mode of deliberation he recommends is diametrically opposite to every rule of reason and every principle of good sense established amongst mankind. For that sense and that reason I have always understood absolutely to prescribe, whenever we are involved in difficulties from the measures we have pursued, that we should take a strict review of those measures, in order to correct our errors, if they should be corrigible,—or at least to avoid a dull uniformity in mischief, and the unpitied calamity of being repeatedly caught in the same snare.

Sir, I will freely follow the honorable gentleman in his historical discussion, without the least management for men or measures, further than as they shall seem to me to deserve it. But before I go into that large consideration, because I would omit nothing that can give the House satisfaction, I wish to tread the narrow ground to which alone the honorable gentleman, in one part of his speech, has so strictly confined us.

He desires to know, whether, if we were to repeal this tax, agreeably to the proposition of the honorable gentleman who made the motion, the Americans would not take post on this concession, in order to make a new attack on the next body of taxes; and whether they would not call for a repeal of the duty on wine as loudly as they do now for the repeal of the duty on tea. Sir, I can give no security on this subject. But I will do all that I can, and all that can be fairly demanded. To the *experience* which the honorable gentleman reprobates in one instant and reverts to in the next, to that experience, without the least wavering or hesitation on my part, I steadily appeal: and would to God there was no other arbiter to decide on the vote with which the House is to conclude this day.

When Parliament repealed the Stamp Act in the year 1766, I affirm, first, that the Americans did *not* in consequence of this measure call upon you to give up the former Parliamentary revenue which subsisted in that country, or even any one of the articles which compose it. I affirm also, that, when, departing from the maxims of that repeal, you revived the scheme of taxation, and thereby filled the minds of the colonists with new jealousy and all sorts of apprehensions, then it was that they quarrelled with the old taxes as well as the new: then it was, and not till then, that they questioned all the parts of your legislative power, and by the battery of such questions have shaken the solid structure of this empire to its deepest foundations.

Of those two propositions I shall, before I have done, give such convincing, such damning proof, that, however the contrary may be whispered in circles or bawled in newspapers, they never more will dare to raise their voices in this House. I speak with great confidence. I have reason for it. The ministers are with me. *They* at least are convinced that the repeal of the Stamp Act had not, and that no repeal can have, the consequences which the honorable gentleman who defends their measures is so much alarmed at. To their conduct I refer him for a conclusive answer to his objection. I carry my proof irresistibly into the very body of both Ministry and Parliament: not on any general reasoning growing out of collateral matter, but on the conduct of the honorable gentleman's ministerial friends on the new revenue itself.

The act of 1767, which grants this tea-duty, sets forth in its preamble, that it was expedient to raise a revenue in America for the support of the civil government there, as well as for purposes still more extensive. To this support the act assigns six branches of duties. About two years after this act passed, the ministry, I mean the present ministry, thought it expedient to repeal five of the duties, and to leave (for reasons best known to themselves) only the sixth standing. Suppose any person, at the time of that repeal, had thus addressed the minister: [2] "Condemning, as you do, the repeal of the Stamp Act, why do you venture to repeal the duties upon glass, paper, and painters' colors? Let your pretence for the repeal be what it will, are you not thoroughly convinced that your concessions will produce, not satisfaction, but insolence in the Americans, and that the giving up these taxes will necessitate the giving up of all the rest?" This objection was as palpable then as it is now; and it was as good for preserving the five duties as for retaining the sixth. Besides, the minister will recollect that the repeal of the Stamp Act

---

[2] Lord North, then Chancellor of the Exchequer.

had but just preceded his repeal; and the ill policy of that measure, (had it been so impolitic as it has been represented,) and the mischiefs it produced, were quite recent. Upon the principles, therefore, of the honorable gentleman, upon the principles of the minister himself, the minister has nothing at all to answer. He stands condemned by himself, and by all his associates old and new, as a destroyer, in the first trust of finance of the revenues,—and in the first rank of honor, as a betrayer of the dignity of his country.

Most men, especially great men, do not always know their well-wishers. I come to rescue that noble lord out of the hands of those he calls his friends, and even out of his own. I will do him the justice he is denied at home. He has not been this wicked or imprudent man. He knew that a repeal had no tendency to produce the mischiefs which give so much alarm to his honorable friend. His work was not bad in its principle, but imperfect in its execution; and the motion on your paper presses him only to complete a proper plan, which, by some unfortunate and unaccountable error, he had left unfinished.

I hope, Sir, the honorable gentleman who spoke last is thoroughly satisfied, and satisfied out of the proceedings of ministry on their own favorite act, that his fears from a repeal are groundless. If he is not, I leave him, and the noble lord who sits by him, to settle the matter as well as they can together; for, if the repeal of American taxes destroys all our government in America,—he is the man!—and he is the worst of all the repealers, because he is the last.

But I hear it rung continually in my ears, now and formerly,—"The preamble! what will become of the preamble, if you repeal this tax?"—I am sorry to be compelled so often to expose the calamities and disgraces of Parliament. The preamble of this law, standing as it now stands, has the lie direct given to it by the provisionary part of the act: if that can be called provisionary which makes no provision. I should be afraid to express myself in this manner, especially in the face of such a formidable array of ability as is now drawn up before me, composed of the ancient household troops of that side of the House and the new recruits from this, if the matter were not clear and indisputable. Nothing but truth could give me this firmness; but plain truth and clear evidence can be beat down by no ability. The clerk will be so good as to turn to the act, and to read this favorite preamble.

"Whereas it is *expedient* that a revenue should be raised in your Majesty's dominions in America, for making a more *certain* and *adequate* provision for defraying the charge of the *administration of justice and support of civil government* in such provinces where it shall be found necessary, and towards *further defraying* the expenses of *defending, protecting, and securing the said dominions.*"

You have heard this pompous performance. Now where is the revenue which is to do all these mighty things? Five sixths repealed,—abandoned,—sunk,—gone,—lost forever. Does the poor solitary tea-duty support the purposes of this preamble? Is not the supply there stated as effectually abandoned as if the tea-duty had perished in the general wreck? Here, Mr. Speaker, is a precious mockery:—a preamble without an act,—taxes granted in order to be repealed,—and the reasons of the grant still carefully kept up! This is raising a revenue in America! This is preserving dignity in England! If you repeal this tax, in compliance with the motion, I readily admit that you lose this fair preamble. Estimate your loss in it. The object of the act is gone already; and all you suffer is the purging the statute-book of the opprobrium of an empty, absurd, and false recital.

It has been said again and again, that the five taxes were repealed on commercial principles. It is so said in the paper

in my hand: [3] a paper which I constantly carry about; which
I have often used, and shall often use again. What is got by
this paltry pretence of commercial principles I know not;
for, if your government in America is destroyed by the *repeal
of taxes,* it is of no consequence upon what ideas the repeal
is grounded. Repeal this tax, too, upon commercial principles,
if you please. These principles will serve as well now as they
did formerly. But you know that either your objection to a
repeal from these supposed consequences has no validity, or
that this pretence never could remove it. This commercial
motive never was believed by any man, either in America,
which this letter is meant to soothe, or in England, which it
is meant to deceive. It was impossible it should: because
every man, in the least acquainted with the detail of commerce, must know that several of the articles on which the
tax was repealed were fitter objects of duties than almost any
other articles that could possibly be chosen,—without comparison more so than the tea that was left taxed, as infinitely
less liable to be eluded by contraband. The tax upon red and
white lead was of this nature. You have in this kingdom an
advantage in lead that amounts to a monopoly. When you
find yourself in this situation of advantage, you sometimes
venture to tax even your own export. You did so soon after
the last war, when, upon this principle, you ventured to impose a duty on coals. In all the articles of American contraband trade, who ever heard of the smuggling of red lead and
white lead? You might, therefore, well enough, without danger
of contraband, and without injury to commerce, (if this were
the whole consideration,) have taxed these commodities. The
same may be said of glass. Besides, some of the things taxed
were so trivial, that the loss of the objects themselves, and
their utter annihilation out of American commerce, would

---

[3] Lord Hillsborough's Circular Letter to the Governors of the Colonies, concerning the repeal of some of the duties laid in the Act of
1767. [Burke]

have been comparatively as nothing. But is the article of tea
such an object in the trade of England, as not to be felt, or
felt but slightly, like white lead, and red lead, and painters'
colors? Tea is an object of far other importance. Tea is perhaps the most important object, taking it with its necessary
connections, of any in the mighty circle of our commerce. If
commercial principles had been the true motives to the repeal,
or had they been at all attended to, tea would have been the
last article we should have left taxed for a subject of controversy.

Sir, it is not a pleasant consideration, but nothing in the
world can read so awful and so instructive a lesson as the
conduct of ministry in this business, upon the mischief of
not having large and liberal ideas in the management of great
affairs. Never have the servants of the state looked at the
whole of your complicated interests in one connected view.
They have taken things by bits and scraps, some at one time
and one pretence, and some at another, just as they pressed,
without any sort of regard to their relations or dependencies.
They never had any kind of system, right or wrong; but only
invented occasionally some miserable tale for the day, in
order meanly to sneak out of difficulties into which they
had proudly strutted. And they were put to all these shifts
and devices, full of meanness and full of mischief, in order
to pilfer piecemeal a repeal of an act which they had not the
generous courage, when they found and felt their error, honor-
ably and fairly to disclaim. By such management, by the
irresistible operation of feeble councils, so paltry a sum as
three-pence in the eyes of a financier, so insignificant an article
as tea in the eyes of a philosopher, have shaken the pillars of
a commercial empire that circled the whole globe.

Do you forget that in the very last year you stood on the
precipice of general bankruptcy? Your danger was indeed
great. You were distressed in the affairs of the East India
Company; and you well know what sort of things are involved

in the comprehensive energy of that significant appellation. I am not called upon to enlarge to you on that danger, which you thought proper yourselves to aggravate, and to display to the world with all the parade of indiscreet declamation. The monopoly of the most lucrative trades and the possession of imperial revenues had brought you to the verge of beggary and ruin. Such was your representation; such, in some measure, was your case. The vent of ten millions of pounds of this commodity, now locked up by the operation of an injudicious tax, and rotting in the warehouses of the Company, would have prevented all this distress, and all that series of desperate measures which you thought yourselves obliged to take in consequence of it. America would have furnished that vent, which no other part of the world can furnish but America, where tea is next to a necessary of life, and where the demand grows upon the supply. I hope our dear-bought East India Committees have done us at least so much good, as to let us know, that, without a more extensive sale of that article, our East India revenues and acquisitions can have no certain connection with this country. It is through the American trade of tea that your East India conquests are to be prevented from crushing you with their burden. They are ponderous indeed; and they must have that great country to lean upon, or they tumble upon your head. It is the same folly that has lost you at once the benefit of the West and of the East. This folly has thrown open folding-doors to contraband, and will be the means of giving the profits of the trade of your colonies to every nation but yourselves. Never did a people suffer so much for the empty words of a preamble. It must be given up. For on what principle does it stand? This famous revenue stands, at this hour, on all the debate, as a description of revenue not as yet known in all the comprehensive (but too comprehensive!) vocabulary of finance,—*a preambulary tax*. It is, indeed, a tax of sophistry, a tax of pedantry, a tax of disputation, a tax of war and rebellion, a tax for anything but benefit to the imposers or satisfaction to the subject.

Well! but whatever it is, gentlemen will force the colonists to take the teas. You will force them? Has seven years' struggle been yet able to force them? Oh, but it seems "we are in the right. The tax is trifling,—in effect it is rather an ex-oneration than an imposition; three fourths of the duty for-merly payable on teas exported to America is taken off,—the place of collection is only shifted; instead of the retention of a shilling from the drawback here, it is three-pence custom paid in America." All this, Sir, is very true. But this is the very folly and mischief of the act. Incredible as it may seem, you know that you have deliberately thrown away a large duty, which you held secure and quiet in your hands, for the vain hope of getting one three fourths less, through every hazard, through certain litigation, and possibly through war.

The manner of proceeding in the duties on paper and glass, imposed by the same act, was exactly in the same spirit. There are heavy excises on those articles, when used in Eng-land. On export, these excises are drawn back. But instead of withholding the drawback, which might have been done, with ease, without charge, without possibility of smuggling, and instead of applying the money (money already in your hands) according to your pleasure, you began your operations in finance by flinging away your revenue; you allowed the whole drawback on export, and then you charged the duty, (which you had before discharged,) payable in the colonies, where it was certain the collection would devour it to the bone,—if any revenue were ever suffered to be collected at all. One spirit pervades and animates the whole mass.

Could anything be a subject of more just alarm to America than to see you go out of the plain highroad of finance, and give up your most certain revenues and your clearest interest, merely for the sake of insulting your colonies? No man ever doubted that the commodity of tea could bear an imposition of three-pence. But no commodity will bear three-pence, or will bear a penny, when the general feelings of men are irritated, and two millions of people are resolved not to pay. The feelings of the colonies were formerly the feelings of Great Britain. Theirs were formerly the feelings of Mr. Hampden,[4] when called upon for the payment of twenty shillings. Would twenty shillings have ruined Mr. Hampden's fortune? No! but the payment of half twenty shillings, on the principle it was demanded, would have made him a slave. It is the weight of that preamble, of which you are so fond, and not the weight of the duty, that the Americans are unable and unwilling to bear.

It is, then, Sir, upon the *principle* of this measure, and nothing else, that we are at issue. It is a principle of political expediency. Your act of 1767 asserts that it is expedient to raise a revenue in America; your act of 1769, which takes away that revenue, contradicts the act of 1767, and, by something much stronger than words, asserts that it is not expedient. It is a reflection upon your wisdom to persist in a solemn Parliamentary declaration of the expediency of any object, for which, at the same time, you make no sort of provision. And pray, Sir, let not this circumstance escape you,—it is very material,—that the preamble of this act which we wish to repeal is not *declaratory of a right*, as some gentlemen seem to argue it: it is only a recital of the *expediency* of a certain exercise of a right supposed already to have been asserted; an exercise you are now contending for by ways and means which you confess, though they were obeyed, to be utterly insufficient for their purpose. You are therefore at this moment in the awkward situation of fighting for a phantom,—a quiddity,—a thing that wants, not only a

---

[4] John Hampden (1594-1643), who led the resistance to the imposition of "ship-money" on the ground that Charles I lacked the power to tax without the authority of Parliament.

substance, but even a name,—for a thing which is neither abstract right nor profitable enjoyment.

They tell you, Sir, that your dignity is tied to it. I know not how it happens, but this dignity of yours is a terrible incumbrance to you; for it has of late been ever at war with your interest, your equity, and every idea of your policy. Show the thing you contend for to be reason, show it to be common sense, show it to be the means of attaining some useful end, and then I am content to allow it what dignity you please. But what dignity is derived from the perseverance in absurdity is more than ever I could discern. The honorable gentleman has said well,—indeed, in most of his *general* observations I agree with him,—he says, that this subject does not stand as it did formerly. Oh, certainly not! Every hour you continue on this ill-chosen ground, your difficulties thicken on you; and therefore my conclusion is, remove from a bad position as quickly as you can. The disgrace, and the necessity of yielding, both of them, grow upon you every hour of your delay.

But will you repeal the act, says the honorable gentleman, at this instant, when America is in open resistance to your authority, and that you have just revived your system of taxation? He thinks he has driven us into a corner. But thus pent up, I am content to meet him; because I enter the lists supported by my old authority, his new friends, the ministers themselves. The honorable gentleman remembers that about five years ago as great disturbances as the present prevailed in America on account of the new taxes. The ministers represented these disturbances as treasonable; and this House thought proper, on that representation, to make a famous address for a revival and for a new application of a statute of Henry the Eighth.[5] We besought the king, in that well-

---

[5] Passed in the House of Commons, 8 February, 1769.

considered address, to inquire into treasons, and to bring the supposed traitors from America to Great Britain for trial. His Majesty was pleased graciously to promise a compliance with our request. All the attempts from this side of the House to resist these violences, and to bring about a repeal, were treated with the utmost scorn. An apprehension of the very consequences now stated by the honorable gentleman was then given as a reason for shutting the door against all hope of such an alteration. And so strong was the spirit for supporting the new taxes, that the session concluded with the following remarkable declaration. After stating the vigorous measures which had been pursued, the speech from the throne proceeds:—

"You have assured me of your *firm* support in the *prosecution* of them. Nothing, in my opinion, could be more likely to enable the well-disposed among my subjects in that part of the world effectually to discourage and defeat the designs of the factious and seditious than the hearty concurrence of every branch of the legislature in the resolution of *maintaining the execution of the laws in every* part of my dominions."

After this no man dreamt that a repeal under this ministry could possibly take place. The honorable gentleman knows as well as I, that the idea was utterly exploded by those who sway the House. This speech was made on the ninth day of May, 1769. Five days after this speech, that is, on the thirteenth of the same month, the public circular letter, a part of which I am going to read to you, was written by Lord Hillsborough, Secretary of State for the Colonies. After reciting the substance of the king's speech, he goes on thus:—

"I can take upon me to assure you, notwithstanding insinuations to the contrary from men with *factious and seditious views,* that his Majesty's *present administration have at no time entertained a design to propose to Parliament to lay any further taxes upon America, for the purpose of* RAISING A REVENUE; and that it is at present their intention to propose, the next session of Parliament, to take off the duties upon glass, paper, and colors, upon consideration of such duties *having been laid contrary to the true principles of commerce.*

"These have *always* been, and *still are,* the sentiments of *his Majesty's present servants,* and by which their conduct *in respect to America has been governed.* And *his Majesty* relies upon your prudence and fidelity for such an explanation of *his* measures as may tend to remove the prejudices which have been excited by the misrepresentations of those who are enemies to the peace and prosperity of Great Britain and her colonies, and to reëstablish that mutual *confidence and affection* upon which the glory and safety of the British empire depend."

Here, Sir, is a canonical book of ministerial scripture: the general epistle to the Americans. What does the gentleman say to it? Here a repeal is promised,—promised without condition,—and while your authority was actually resisted. I pass by the public promise of a peer relative to the repeal of taxes by this House. I pass by the use of the king's name in a matter of supply, that sacred and reserved right of the Commons. I conceal the ridiculous figure of Parliament hurling its thunders at the gigantic rebellion of America, and then, five days after, prostrate at the feet of those assemblies we affected to despise,—begging them, by the intervention of our ministerial sureties, to receive our submission, and heartily promising amendment. These might have been serious matters formerly; but we are grown wiser than our fathers. Passing, therefore, from the Constitutional consideration to the mere policy, does not this letter imply that the idea of taxing America for the purpose of revenue is an abominable project, when the ministry suppose none but *factious* men, and with seditious views, could charge them with it? does not this letter adopt and sanctify the American distinction of *taxing for a revenue?* does it not formally reject all future taxation on that principle? does it not state the ministerial rejection of such principle of taxation, not as the occasional, but the constant opinion of the king's servants? does it not say, (I care not how consistently,) but does it not say, that their conduct with regard to America has been *always* governed by this policy? It goes a great deal further. These excellent and trusty servants of the king, justly fearful lest they themselves should have lost all credit with the world, bring out the image of their gracious sovereign from the inmost and most sacred shrine, and they pawn him as a security for their promises:— *"His Majesty* relies on your prudence and fidelity for such an explanation of *his* measures." These sentiments of the minister and these measures of his Majesty can only relate to the principle and practice of taxing for a revenue; and accordingly Lord Botetourt, stating it as such, did, with great propriety, and in the exact spirit of his instructions, endeavor to remove the fears of the Virginian assembly lest the sentiments which it seems (unknown to the world) had *always* been those of the ministers, and by which *their* conduct *in respect to America had been governed,* should by some possible revolution, favorable to wicked American taxers, be hereafter counteracted. He addresses them in this manner:—

"It may possibly be objected, that, as his Majesty's present administration are *not immortal,* their successors may be inclined to attempt to undo what the present ministers shall have attempted to perform; and to that objection I can give but this answer: that it is my firm opinion, that the plan I have stated to you will certainly take place, and that it will never be departed from; and so determined am I forever to abide by it, that I will be content to be declared infamous, if I do not, to the last hour of my life, at all times, in all places, and upon all occasions, exert every power with which I either am or ever shall be legally invested, in order to obtain and *maintain* for the continent of America that *satisfaction* which I have been authorized to promise this day by the *confidential* servants of our gracious sovereign, who to my certain knowledge rates his honor so high *that he would rather part with his crown than preserve it by deceit."*

A glorious and true character! which (since we suffer his ministers with impunity to answer for his ideas of taxation) we ought to make it our business to enable his Majesty to preserve in all its lustre. Let him have character, since ours is no more! Let some part of government be kept in respect!

This epistle was not the letter of Lord Hillsborough solely, though he held the official pen. It was the letter of the noble lord upon the floor,[6] and of all the king's then ministers, who (with, I think, the exception of two only) are his ministers at this hour. The very first news that a British Parliament heard of what it was to do with the duties which it had given and granted to the king was by the publication of the votes of American assemblies. It was in America that your resolutions were pre-declared. It was from thence that we knew to a certainty how much exactly, and not a scruple more nor less, we were to repeal. We were unworthy to be let into the secret of our own conduct. The assemblies had *confidential* communications from his Majesty's *confidential* servants. We were nothing but instruments. Do you, after this, wonder that you have no weight and no respect in the colonies? After this are you surprised that Parliament is every day and everywhere losing (I feel it with sorrow, I utter it with reluctance) that reverential affection which so endearing a name of authority ought ever to carry with it? that you are obeyed solely, from respect to the bayonet? and that this House, the ground and pillar of freedom, is itself held up only by the treacherous underpinning and clumsy buttresses of arbitrary power?

If this dignity, which is to stand in the place of just policy and common sense, had been consulted, there was a time for preserving it, and for reconciling it with any concession. If

---

[6] Lord North.

in the session of 1768,[7] that session of idle terror and empty menaces, you had, as you were often pressed to do, repealed these taxes, then your strong operations would have come justified and enforced, in case your concessions had been returned by outrages. But, preposterously, you began with violence; and before terrors could have any effect, either good or bad, your ministers immediately begged pardon, and promised that repeal to the obstinate Americans which they had refused in an easy, good-natured, complying British Parliament. The assemblies, which had been publicly and avowedly dissolved for *their* contumacy, are called together to receive *your* submission. Your ministerial directors blustered like tragic tyrants here; and then went mumping with a sore leg in America, canting, and whining, and complaining of faction, which represented them as friends to a revenue from the colonies. I hope nobody in this House will hereafter have the impudence to defend American taxes in the name of ministry. The moment they do, with this letter of attorney in my hand, I will tell them, in the authorized terms, they are wretches "with factious and seditious views," "enemies to the peace and prosperity of the mother country and the colonies," and subverters "of the mutual affection and confidence on which the glory and safety of the British empire depend."

After this letter, the question is no more on propriety or dignity. They are gone already. The faith of your sovereign is pledged for the political principle. The general declaration in the letter goes to the whole of it. You must therefore either abandon the scheme of taxing, or you must send the ministers tarred and feathered to America, who dared to hold out the royal faith for a renunciation of all taxes for revenue. Them you must punish, or this faith you must preserve. The preservation of this faith is of more consequence than the duties on *red lead*, or *white lead*, or on broken *glass*, or *atlas-*

---

[7] In this session the address referred to above (cf. note 5), for reviving the statute of Henry VIII, was passed.

ordinary, or *demy-fine,* or *blue-royal,* or *bastard,* or *foolscap,*
which you have given up, or the three-pence on tea which
you retained. The letter went stamped with the public authority of this kingdom. The instructions for the colony
government go under no other sanction; and America cannot
believe, and will not obey you, if you do not preserve this
channel of communication sacred. You are now punishing the
colonies for acting on distinctions held out by that very ministry which is here shining in riches, in favor, and in power,
and urging the punishment of the very offence to which they
had themselves been the tempters.

Sir, if reasons respecting simply your own commerce,
which is your own convenience, were the sole grounds of the
repeal of the five duties, why does Lord Hillsborough, in dis-
claiming in the name of the king and ministry their ever
having had an intent to tax for revenue, mention it as the
means "of reëstablishing the confidence and affection of the
colonies?" Is it a way of soothing *others,* to assure them that
you will take good care of *yourself?* The medium, the only
medium, for regaining their affection and confidence is that
you will take off something oppressive to their minds. Sir, the
letter strongly enforces that idea: for though the repeal of the
taxes is promised on commercial principles, yet the means of
counteracting the "insinuations of men with factious and seditious views" is by a disclaimer of the intention of taxing
for revenue, as a constant, invariable sentiment and rule of
conduct in the government of America.

I remember that the noble lord on the floor, not in a former debate to be sure, (it would be disorderly to refer to it,
I suppose I read it somewhere,) but the noble lord was
pleased to say, that he did not conceive how it could enter
into the head of man to impose such taxes as those of 1767:
I mean those taxes which he voted for imposing, and voted
for repealing,—as being taxes, contrary to all the principles
of commerce, laid on *British manufactures.*

I dare say the noble lord is perfectly well read, because the duty of his particular office requires he should be so, in all our revenue laws, and in the policy which is to be collected out of them. Now, Sir, when he had read this act of American revenue, and a little recovered from his astonishment, I suppose he made one step retrograde (it is but one) and looked at the act which stands just before in the statute-book. The American revenue act is the forty-fifth chapter; the other to which I refer is the forty-fourth of the same session. These two acts are both to the same purpose: both revenue acts; both taxing out of the kingdom; and both taxing British manufactures exported. As the forty-fifth is an act for raising a revenue in America, the forty-fourth is an act for raising a revenue in the Isle of Man. The two acts perfectly agree in all respects, except one. In the act for taxing the Isle of Man the noble lord will find, not, as in the American act, four or five articles, but almost the *whole body* of British manufactures, taxed from two and a half to fifteen per cent, and some articles, such as that of spirits, a great deal higher. You did not think it uncommercial to tax the whole mass of your manufactures, and, let me add, your agriculture too; for, I now recollect, British corn is there also taxed up to ten per cent, and this too in the very head-quarters, the very citadel of smuggling, the Isle of Man. Now will the noble lord condescend to tell me why he repealed the taxes on your manufactures sent out to America, and not the taxes on the manufactures exported to the Isle of Man? The principle was exactly the same, the objects charged infinitely more extensive, the duties without comparison higher. Why? Why, notwithstanding all his childish pretexts, because the taxes were quietly submitted to in the Isle of Man, and because they raised a flame in America. Your reasons were political, not commercial. The repeal was made, as Lord Hillsborough's letter well expresses it, to regain "the confidence and affection of the colonies, on which the glory and safety of the British empire depend." A wise and just motive, surely, if ever there was such. But the mischief and dishonor is, that you have not done what you had given the colonies just cause to expect, when your ministers disclaimed the idea of taxes for a revenue. There is nothing simple, nothing manly, nothing ingenuous, open, decisive, or steady, in the proceeding, with regard either to the continuance or the repeal of the taxes. The whole has an air of littleness and fraud. The article of tea is slurred over in the circular letter, as it were by accident: nothing is said of a resolution either to keep that tax or to give it up. There is no fair dealing in any part of the transaction.

If you mean to follow your true motive and your public faith, give up your tax on tea for raising a revenue, the principle of which has, in effect, been disclaimed in your name, and which produces you no advantage,—no, not a penny. Or, if you choose to go on with a poor pretence instead of a solid reason, and will still adhere to your cant of commerce, you have ten thousand times more strong commercial reasons for giving up this duty on tea than for abandoning the five others that you have already renounced.

The American consumption of teas is annually, I believe, worth 300,000*l*. at the least farthing. If you urge the American violence as a justification of your perseverance in enforcing this tax, you know that you can never answer this plain question,—Why did you repeal the others given in the same act, whilst the very same violence subsisted?—But you did not find the violence cease upon that concession.—No! because the concession was far short of satisfying the principle which Lord Hillsborough had abjured, or even the pretence on which the repeal of the other taxes was announced; and because, by enabling the East India Company to open a shop for defeating the American resolution not to pay that specific tax, you manifestly showed a hankering after the principle of the act which you formerly had renounced. Whatever road you take leads to a compliance with this motion. It opens to you at the end of every visto. Your commerce, your policy, your promises, your reasons, your pretences, your consistency, your inconsistency,—all jointly oblige you to this repeal.

But still it sticks in our throats, if we go so far, the Americans will go farther.—We do not know that. We ought, from experience, rather to presume the contrary. Do we not know for certain, that the Americans are going on as fast as possible, whilst we refuse to gratify them? Can they do more, or can they do worse, if we yield this point? I think this concession will rather fix a turnpike to prevent their further progress. It is impossible to answer for bodies of men. But I am sure the natural effect of fidelity, clemency, kindness in governors is peace, goodwill, order, and esteem, on the part of the governed. I would certainly, at least, give these fair principles a fair trial; which, since the making of this act to this hour, they never have had.

Sir, the honorable gentleman having spoken what he thought necessary upon the narrow part of the subject, I have given him, I hope, a satisfactory answer. He next presses me, by a variety of direct challenges and oblique reflections, to say something on the historical part. I shall therefore, Sir, open myself fully on that important and delicate subject: not for the sake of telling you a long story, (which, I know, Mr. Speaker, you are not particularly fond of,) but for the sake of the weighty instruction that, I flatter myself, will necessarily result from it. It shall not be longer, if I can help it, than so serious a matter requires.

Permit me then, Sir, to lead your attention very far back, —back to the Act of Navigation, the cornerstone of the policy of this country with regard to its colonies. Sir, that policy was, from the beginning, purely commercial; and the commercial system was wholly restrictive. It was the system of a monopoly. No trade was let loose from that constraint, but merely to enable the colonists to dispose of what, in the course of your trade, you could not take,—or to enable them to dispose of such articles as we forced upon them, and for which, without some degree of liberty, they could not pay. Hence all your specific and detailed enumerations; hence the innumerable checks and counterchecks; hence that infinite variety of paper chains by which you bind together this complicated system of the colonies. This principle of commercial monopoly runs through no less than twenty-nine acts of Parliament, from the year 1660 to the unfortunate period of 1764.

In all those acts the system of commerce is established as that from whence alone you proposed to make the colonies contribute (I mean directly and by the operation of your superintending legislative power) to the strength of the empire. I venture to say, that, during that whole period, a Parliamentary revenue from thence was never once in contemplation. Accordingly, in all the number of laws passed with regard to the plantations, the words which distinguish revenue laws specifically as such were, I think, premeditately avoided. I do not say, Sir, that a form of words alters the nature of the law, or abridges the power of the lawgiver. It certainly does not. However, titles and formal preambles are not always idle words; and the lawyers frequently argue from them. I state these facts to show, not what was your right, but what has been your settled policy. Our revenue laws have usually a *title*, purporting their being *grants;* and the words *"give and grant"* usually precede the enacting parts. Although duties were imposed on America in acts of King Charles the Second, and in acts of King William, no one title of giving "an aid to his Majesty," or any other of the usual titles to revenue acts, was to be found in any of them till 1764; nor were the words "give and grant" in any preamble until the sixth of

George the Second.[8] However, the title of this act of George the Second, notwithstanding the words of donation, considers it merely as a regulation of trade: "An act for the better securing of the trade of his Majesty's sugar colonies in America." This act was made on a compromise of all, and at the express desire of a part, of the colonies themselves. It was therefore in some measure with their consent; and having a title directly purporting only a *commercial regulation,* and being in truth nothing more, the words were passed by, at a time when no jealousy was entertained, and things were little scrutinized. Even Governor Bernard, in his second printed letter, dated in 1763, gives it as his opinion, that "it was an act of *prohibition,* not of revenue." This is certainly true, that no act avowedly for the purpose of revenue, and with the ordinary title and recital taken together, is found in the statute-book until the year I have mentioned: that is, the year 1764. All before this period stood on commercial regulation and restraint. The scheme of a colony revenue by British authority appeared, therefore, to the Americans in the light of a great innovation. The words of Governor Bernard's ninth letter, written in November, 1765, state this idea very strongly. "It must," says he, "have been supposed *such an innovation as a Parliamentary taxation* would cause a great *alarm,* and meet with much *opposition* in most parts of America; it was *quite new* to the people, and had no *visible bounds* set to it." After stating the weakness of government there, he says, "Was this a time to introduce *so great a novelty* as a Parliamentary inland taxation in America?" Whatever the right might have been, this mode of using it was absolutely new in policy and practice.

Sir, they who are friends to the schemes of American revenue say, that the commercial restraint is full as hard a law for America to live under. I think so, too. I think it, if un-

---

[8] In the so-called Molasses Act of 1733.

compensated, to be a condition of as rigorous servitude as men can be subject to. But America bore it from the fundamental Act of Navigation until 1764. Why? Because men do bear the inevitable constitution of their original nature with all its infirmities. The Act of Navigation attended the colonies from their infancy, grew with their growth, and strengthened with their strength. They were confirmed in obedience to it even more by usage than by law. They scarcely had remembered a time when they were not subject to such restraint. Besides, they were indemnified for it by a pecuniary compensation. Their monopolist happened to be one of the riches' men in the world. By his immense capital (primarily employed, not for their benefit, but his own) they were enabled to proceed with their fisheries, their agriculture, their shipbuilding, (and their trade, too, within the limits,) in such a manner as got far the start of the slow, languid operations of unassisted Nature. This capital was a hot-bed to them. Nothing in the history of mankind is like their progress. For my part, I never cast an eye on their flourishing commerce, and their cultivated and commodious life, but they seem to me rather ancient nations grown to perfection through a long series of fortunate events, and a train of successful industry, accumulating wealth in many centuries, than the colonies of yesterday,—than a set of miserable outcasts a few years ago, not so much sent as thrown out on the bleak and barren shore of a desolate wilderness three thousand miles from all civilized intercourse.

All this was done by England whilst England pursued trade and forgot revenue. You not only acquired commerce, but you actually created the very subjects of trade in America; and by that creation you raised the trade of this kingdom at least fourfold. America had the compensation of your capital, which made her bear her servitude. She had another compensation, which you are now going to take away from her. She had, except the commercial restraint, every characteristic mark of a free people in all her internal concerns. She had the image of the British Constitution. She had the substance. She was taxed by her own representatives. She chose most of her own magistrates. She paid them all. She had in effect the sole disposal of her own internal government. This whole state of commercial servitude and civil liberty, taken together, is certainly not perfect freedom; but comparing it with the ordinary circumstances of human nature, it was an happy and a liberal condition.

I know, Sir, that great and not unsuccessful pains have been taken to inflame our minds by an outcry, in this House, and out of it, that in America the Act of Navigation neither is or never was obeyed. But if you take the colonies through, I affirm that its authority never was disputed,—that it was nowhere disputed for any length of time,—and, on the whole, that it was well observed. Wherever the act pressed hard, many individuals, indeed, evaded it. This is nothing. These scattered individuals never denied the law, and never obeyed it. Just as it happens, whenever the laws of trade, whenever the laws of revenue, press hard upon the people in England: in that case all your shores are full of contraband. Your right to give a monopoly to the East India Company, your right to lay immense duties on French brandy, are not disputed in England. You do not make this charge on any man. But you know that there is not a creek from Pentland Firth to the Isle of Wight in which they do not smuggle immense quantities of teas, East India goods, and brandies. I take it for granted that the authority of Governor Bernard in this point is indisputable. Speaking of these laws, as they regarded that part of America now in so unhappy a condition, he says, "I believe they are nowhere better supported than in this province: I do not pretend that it is entirely free from a breach of these laws, but that such a breach, if discovered, is justly punished." What more can you say of the obedience to any laws in any country? An obedience to these laws formed the acknowledgment, instituted by yourselves, for your superiority, and was the payment you originally imposed for your protection.

Whether you were right or wrong in establishing the colonies on the principles of commercial monopoly, rather than on that of revenue, is at this day a problem of mere speculation. You cannot have both by the same authority. To join together the restraints of an universal internal and external monopoly with an universal internal and external taxation is an unnatural union,—perfect, uncompensated slavery. You have long since decided for yourself and them; and you and they have prospered exceedingly under that decision.

This nation, Sir, never thought of departing from that choice until the period immediately on the close of the last war. Then a scheme of government, new in many things, seemed to have been adopted. I saw, or thought I saw, several symptoms of a great change, whilst I sat in your gallery, a good while before I had the honor of a seat in this House. At that period the necessity was established of keeping up no less than twenty new regiments, with twenty colonels capable of seats in this House. This scheme was adopted with very general applause from all sides, at the very time that, by your conquests in America, your danger from foreign attempts in that part of the world was much lessened, or indeed rather quite over. When this huge increase of military establishment was resolved on, a revenue was to be found to support so great a burden. Country gentlemen, the great patrons of economy, and the great resisters of a standing armed force, would not have entered with much alacrity into the vote for so large and so expensive an army, if they had been very sure that they were to continue to pay for it. But hopes of another kind were held out to them; and in particular, I well remember that Mr. Townshend, in a brilliant harangue on this subject, did dazzle them by playing before their eyes the image of a revenue to be raised in America.

Here began to dawn the first glimmerings of this new colony system. It appeared more distinctly afterwards, when it was devolved upon a person to whom, on other accounts, this country owes very great obligations. I do believe that he had a very serious desire to benefit the public. But with no small study of the detail, he did not seem to have his view, at least equally, carried to the total circuit of our affairs. He generally considered his objects in lights that were rather too detached. Whether the business of an American revenue was imposed upon him altogether,—whether it was entirely the result of his own speculation, or, what is more probable, that his own ideas rather coincided with the instructions he had received,—certain it is, that, with the best intentions in the world, he first brought this fatal scheme into form, and established it by Act of Parliament.

No man can believe, that, at this time of day, I mean to lean on the venerable memory of a great man, whose loss we deplore in common. Our little party differences have been long ago composed; and I have acted more with him, and certainly with more pleasure with him, than ever I acted against him. Undoubtedly Mr. Grenville was a first-rate figure in this country. With a masculine understanding, and a stout and resolute heart, he had an application undissipated and unwearied. He took public business, not as a duty which he was to fulfil, but as a pleasure he was to enjoy; and he seemed to have no delight out of this House, except in such things as some way related to the business that was to be done within it. If he was ambitious, I will say this for him, his ambition was of a noble and generous strain. It was to raise himself, not by the low, pimping politics of a court, but to win his way to power through the laborious gradations of public service, and to secure himself a well-earned rank in Parliament by a thorough knowledge of its constitution and a perfect practice in all its business.

Sir, if such a man fell into errors, it must be from defects not intrinsical; they must be rather sought in the particular habits of his life, which, though they do not alter the ground-work of character, yet tinge it with their own hue. He was bred in a profession. He was bred to the law, which is, in my opinion, one of the first and noblest of human sciences,—a science which does more to quicken and invigorate the under-standing than all the other kinds of learning put together; but it is not apt, except in persons very happily born, to open and to liberalize the mind exactly in the same proportion. Passing from that study, he did not go very largely into the world, but plunged into business,—I mean into the business of office, and the limited and fixed methods and forms established there. Much knowledge is to be had, undoubtedly, in that line; and there is no knowledge which is not valuable. But it may be truly said, that men too much conversant in office are rarely minds of remarkable enlargement. Their habits of office are apt to give them a turn to think the substance of business not to be much more important than the forms in which it is conducted. These forms are adapted to ordinary occasions; and therefore persons who are nurtured in office do admirably well as long as things go on in their common order; but when the high-roads are broken up, and the waters out, when a new and troubled scene is opened, and the file affords no prece-dent, then it is that a greater knowledge of mankind, and a far more extensive comprehension of things is requisite, than ever office gave, or than office can ever give. Mr. Grenville thought better of the wisdom and power of human legislation than in truth it deserves. He conceived, and many conceived along with him, that the flourishing trade of this country was greatly owing to law and institution, and not quite so much to liberty; for but too many are apt to believe regulation to be commerce, and taxes to be revenue. Among regulations, that which stood first in reputation was his idol: I mean the Act of Navigation. He has often professed it to be so. The policy of that act is, I readily admit, in many respects well understood.

But I do say, that, if the act be suffered to run the full length
of its principle, and is not changed and modified according
to the change of times and the fluctuation of circumstances,
it must do great mischief, and frequently even defeat its own
purpose.

After the war, and in the last years of it, the trade of
America had increased far beyond the speculations of the
most sanguine imaginations. It swelled out on every side. It
filled all its proper channels to the brim. It overflowed with
a rich redundance, and breaking its banks on the right and on
the left, it spread out upon some places where it was indeed
improper, upon others where it was only irregular. It is the
nature of all greatness not to be exact; and great trade will
always be attended with considerable abuses. The contraband
will always keep pace in some measure with the fair trade. It
should stand as a fundamental maxim, that no vulgar precaution ought to be employed in the cure of evils which are closely
connected with the cause of our prosperity. Perhaps this great
person turned his eyes somewhat less than was just towards
the incredible increase of the fair trade, and looked with
something of too exquisite a jealousy towards the contraband.
He certainly felt a singular degree of anxiety on the subject,
and even began to act from that passion earlier than is commonly imagined. For whilst he was First Lord of the Admiralty, though not strictly called upon in his official line, he
presented a very strong memorial to the Lords of the Treasury, (my Lord Bute was then at the head of the board,)
heavily complaining of the growth of the illicit commerce in
America. Some mischief happened even at that time from
this over-earnest zeal. Much greater happened afterwards,
when it operated with greater power in the highest department of the finances. The bonds of the Act of Navigation
were straitened so much that America was on the point of
having no trade, either contraband or legitimate. They found,
under the construction and execution then used, the act no

longer tying, but actually strangling them. All this coming
with new enumerations of commodities, with regulations which
in a manner put a stop to the mutual coasting intercourse of
the colonies, with the appointment of courts of admiralty under various improper circumstances, with a sudden extinction
of the paper currencies, with a compulsory provision for the
quartering of soldiers,—the people of America thought themselves proceeded against as delinquents, or, at best, as people
under suspicion of delinquency, and in such a manner as they
imagined their recent services in the war did not at all merit.
Any of these innumerable regulations, perhaps, would not
have alarmed alone; some might be thought reasonable; the
multitude struck them with terror.

But the grand manœuvre in that business of new regulating
the colonies was the fifteenth act of the fourth of George the
Third, which, besides containing several of the matters to
which I have just alluded, opened a new principle. And here
properly began the second period of the policy of this country
with regard to the colonies, by which the scheme of a regular
plantation Parliamentary revenue was adopted in theory and
settled in practice: a revenue not substituted in the place of,
but superadded to, a monopoly; which monopoly was enforced
at the same time with additional strictness, and the execution
put into military hands.

This act, Sir, had for the first time the title of "granting
duties in the colonies and plantations of America," and for
the first time it was asserted in the preamble "that it was *just*
and *necessary* that a revenue should be raised there"; then
came the technical words of "giving and granting." And thus
a complete American revenue act was made in all the forms,
and with a full avowal of the right, equity, policy, and even
necessity, of taxing the colonies, without any formal consent
of theirs. There are contained also in the preamble to that act
these very remarkable words,—the Commons, &c., "being desirous to make *some* provision in the *present* session of Parlia-

ment *towards* raising the said revenue." By these words it appeared to the colonies that this act was but a beginning of sorrows,—that every session was to produce something of the same kind,—that we were to go on, from day to day, in charging them with such taxes as we pleased, for such a military force as we should think proper. Had this plan been pursued, it was evident that the provincial assemblies, in which the Americans felt all their portion of importance, and beheld their sole image of freedom, were *ipso facto* annihilated. This ill prospect before them seemed to be boundless in extent and endless in duration. Sir, they were not mistaken. The ministry valued themselves when this act passed, and when they gave notice of the Stamp Act, that both of the duties came very short of their ideas of American taxation. Great was the applause of this measure here. In England we cried out for new taxes on America, whilst they cried out that they were nearly crushed with those which the war and their own grants had brought upon them.

Sir, it has been said in the debate, that, when the first American revenue act (the act in 1764, imposing the port-duties) passed, the Americans did not object to the principle. It is true they touched it but very tenderly. It was not a direct attack. They were, it is true, as yet novices,—as yet unaccustomed to direct attacks upon any of the rights of Parliament. The duties were port-duties, like those they had been accustomed to bear,—with this difference, that the title was not the same, the preamble not the same, and the spirit altogether unlike. But of what service is this observation to the cause of those that make it? It is a full refutation of the pretence for their present cruelty to America; for it shows, out of their own mouths, that our colonies were backward to enter into the present vexatious and ruinous controversy.

There is also another circulation abroad, (spread with a malignant intention, which I cannot attribute to those who say the same thing in this House,) that Mr. Grenville gave the colony agents an option for their assemblies to tax themselves, which they had refused. I find that much stress is laid on this, as a fact. However, it happens neither to be true nor possible. I will observe, first, that Mr. Grenville never thought fit to make this apology for himself in the innumerable debates that were had upon the subject. He might have proposed to the colony agents, that they should agree in some mode of taxation as the ground of an act of Parliament. But he never could have proposed that they should tax themselves on requisition, which is the assertion of the day. Indeed, Mr. Grenville well knew that the colony agents could have no general powers to consent to it; and they had no time to consult their assemblies for particular powers, before he passed his first revenue act. If you compare dates, you will find it impossible. Burdened as the agents knew the colonies were at that time, they could not give the least hope of such grants. His own favorite governor was of opinion that the Americans were not then taxable objects.

"Nor was the time less favorable to the *equity* of such a taxation. I don't mean to dispute the reasonableness of America contributing to the charges of Great Britain, *when she is able;* nor, I believe, would the Americans themselves have disputed it at a *proper time and season.* But it should be considered, that the American governments themselves have, in the prosecution of the late war, contracted very large debts, which it will take some years to pay off, and in the mean time occasion very *burdensome taxes for that purpose* only. For instance, this government, which is as much beforehand as any, raises every year 37,500*l.* sterling for sinking their debt, and must continue it for four years longer at least before it will be clear."

These are the words of Governor Bernard's letter to a member of the old ministry, and which he has since printed.

Mr. Grenville could not have made this proposition to the agents for another reason. He was of opinion, which he has declared in this House an hundred times, that the colonies could not legally grant any revenue to the crown, and that infinite mischiefs would be the consequence of such a power. When Mr. Grenville had passed the first revenue act, and in the same session had made this House come to a resolution for laying a stamp-duty on America, between that time and the passing the Stamp Act into a law he told a considerable and most respectable merchant, a member of this House, whom I am truly sorry I do not now see in his place, when he represented against this proceeding, that, if the stamp-duty was disliked, he was willing to exchange it for any other equally productive,—but that, if he objected to the Americans being taxed by Parliament, he might save himself the trouble of the discussion, as he was determined on the measure. This is the fact, and, if you please, I will mention a very unquestionable authority for it.

Thus, Sir, I have disposed of this falsehood. But falsehood has a perennial spring. It is said that no conjecture could be made of the dislike of the colonies to the principle. This is as untrue as the other. After the resolution of the House, and before the passing of the Stamp Act, the colonies of Massachusetts Bay and New York did send remonstrances objecting to this mode of Parliamentary taxation. What was the consequence? They were suppressed, they were put under the table, notwithstanding an order of Council to the contrary, by the ministry which composed the very Council that had made the order; and thus the House proceeded to its business of taxing without the least regular knowledge of the objections which were made to it. But to give that House its due, it was not over-desirous to receive information or to hear remonstrance. On the 15th of February, 1765, whilst the Stamp Act was under deliberation, they refused with scorn even so much as to receive four petitions presented from so respectable colonies as Connecticut, Rhode Island, Virginia, and Carolina, besides one from the traders of Jamaica. As to the colonies, they had no alternative left to them but to disobey, or to pay the taxes imposed by that Parliament, which was not suffered, or did not suffer itself, even to hear them remonstrate upon the subject.

This was the state of the colonies before his Majesty thought fit to change his ministers. It stands upon no authority of mine. It is proved by uncontrovertible records. The honorable gentleman has desired some of us to lay our hands upon our hearts and answer to his queries upon the historical part of this consideration, and by his manner (as well as my eyes could discern it) he seemed to address himself to me.

Sir, I will answer him as clearly as I am able, and with great openness: I have nothing to conceal. In the year sixty-five, being in a very private station, far enough from any line of business, and not having the honor of a seat in this House, it was my fortune, unknowing and unknown to the then ministry, by the intervention of a common friend, to become connected with a very noble person, and at the head of the Treasury Department. It was, indeed, in a situation of little rank and no consequence, suitable to the mediocrity of my talents and pretensions,—but a situation near enough to enable me to see, as well as others, what was going on; and I did see in that noble person such sound principles, such an enlargement of mind, such clear and sagacious sense, and such unshaken fortitude, as have bound me, as well as others much better than me, by an inviolable attachment to him from that time forward. Sir, Lord Rockingham very early in that summer received a strong representation from many weighty English merchants and manufacturers, from governors of provinces and commanders of men-of-war, against almost the whole of the American commercial regulations,— and particularly with regard to the total ruin which was threatened to the Spanish trade. I believe, Sir, the noble lord soon saw his way in this business. But he did not rashly determine against acts which it might be supposed were the result of much deliberation. However, Sir, he scarcely began to open the ground, when the whole veteran body of office took the alarm. A violent outcry of all (except those who knew and felt the mischief) was raised against any alteration. On one hand, his attempt was a direct violation of treaties and public law; on the other, the Act of Navigation and all the corps of trade-laws were drawn up in array against it.

The first step the noble lord took was, to have the opinion of his excellent, learned, and ever-lamented friend, the late Mr. Yorke, then Attorney-General, on the point of law. When he knew that formally and officially which in substance he had known before, he immediately dispatched orders to redress the grievance. But I will say it for the then minister, he is of that constitution of mind, that I know he would have issued, on the same critical occasion, the very same orders, if the acts of trade had been, as they were not, directly against him, and would have cheerfully submitted to the equity of Parliament for his indemnity.

On the conclusion of this business of the Spanish trade, the news of the troubles on account of the Stamp Act arrived in England. It was not until the end of October that these accounts were received. No sooner had the sound of that mighty tempest reached us in England, than the whole of the then opposition, instead of feeling humbled by the unhappy issue of their measures, seemed to be infinitely elated, and cried out, that the ministry, from envy to the glory of their predecessors, were prepared to repeal the Stamp Act. Near nine years after, the honorable gentleman takes quite opposite ground, and now challenges me to put my hand to my heart and say whether the ministry had resolved on the repeal till a considerable time after the meeting of Parliament. Though I do not very well know what the honorable gentleman wishes to infer from the admission or from the denial of this fact on which he so earnestly adjures me, I do put my hand on my heart and assure him that they did *not* come to a resolution directly to repeal. They weighed this matter as its difficulty and importance required. They considered maturely among themselves. They consulted with all who could give advice or information. It was not determined until a little before the meeting of Parliament; but it was determined, and the main lines of their own plan marked out, before that meeting. Two questions arose. (I hope I am not going into a narrative troublesome to the House.)

[A cry of "Go on, go on!"]

The first of the two considerations was, whether the repeal should be total, or whether only partial,—taking out everything burdensome and productive, and reserving only an empty acknowledgment, such as a stamp on cards or dice. The other question was, on what principle the act should be repealed. On this head also two principles were started. One, that the legislative rights of this country with regard to America were not entire, but had certain restrictions and limitations. The other principle was, that taxes of this kind were contrary to the fundamental principles of commerce on which the colonies were founded, and contrary to every idea of political equity,—by which equity we are bound as much as possible to extend the spirit and benefit of the British Constitution to every part of the British dominions. The option, both of the measure and of the principle of repeal, was made before the session; and I wonder how any one can read the king's speech at the opening of that session, without seeing in that speech both the repeal and the Declaratory Act very sufficiently crayoned out. Those who cannot see this can see nothing.

Surely the honorable gentleman will not think that a great deal less time than was then employed ought to have been spent in deliberation, when he considers that the news of the troubles did not arrive till towards the end of October. The Parliament sat to fill the vacancies on the 14th day of December, and on business the 14th of the following January.

Sir, a partial repeal, or, as the *bon-ton* of the court then was, a *modification,* would have satisfied a timid, unsystematic, procrastinating ministry, as such a measure has since done such a ministry. A modification is the constant resource of weak, undeciding minds. To repeal by a denial of our right to tax in the preamble (and this, too, did not want advisers) would have cut, in the heroic style, the Gordian knot with a sword. Either measure would have cost no more than a day's debate. But when the total repeal was adopted, and adopted on principles of policy, of equity, and of commerce, this plan made it necessary to enter into many and difficult measures. It became necessary to open a very large field of evidence commensurate to these extensive views. But then this labor did knights' service. It opened the eyes of several to the true state of the American affairs; it enlarged their ideas; it removed prejudices; and it conciliated the opinions and affections of men. The noble lord who then took the lead in administration, my honorable friend under me, and a right honorable gentleman (if he will not reject his share, and it was a large one, of this business) exerted the most laudable industry in bringing before you the fullest, most impartial, and least garbled body of evidence that ever was produced to this House. I think the inquiry lasted in the committee for six weeks; and at its conclusion, this House, by an independent, noble, spirited, and unexpected majority, by a majority that will redeem all the acts ever done by majorities in Parliament, in the teeth of all the old mercenary Swiss of state, in despite of all the speculators and augurs of political events, in defiance of the whole embattled legion of veteran pensioners and practised instruments of a court, gave a total repeal to the Stamp Act, and (if it had been so permitted) a lasting peace to this whole empire.

I state, Sir, these particulars, because this act of spirit and fortitude has lately been, in the circulation of the season, and in some hazarded declamations in this House, attributed to timidity. If, Sir, the conduct of ministry, in proposing the repeal, had arisen from timidity with regard to themselves, it would have been greatly to be condemned. Interested timidity disgraces as much in the cabinet as personal timidity does in the field. But timidity with regard to the well-being of our country is heroic virtue. The noble lord who then conducted affairs, and his worthy colleagues, whilst they trembled at the prospect of such distresses as you have since brought upon yourselves, were not afraid steadily to look in the face that glaring and dazzling influence at which the eyes of eagles have blenched.[9] He looked in the face one of the ablest, and let me say, not the most scrupulous oppositions, that perhaps ever was in this House; and withstood it, unaided by even one of the usual supports of administration. He did this, when he repealed the Stamp Act. He looked in the face a person he had long respected and regarded, and whose aid was then particularly wanting: I mean Lord Chatham. He did this when he passed the Declaratory Act.

It is now given out, for the usual purposes, by the usual emissaries, that Lord Rockingham did not consent to the repeal of this act until he was bullied into it by Lord Chatham; and the reporters have gone so far as publicly to assert, in an hundred companies, that the honorable gentleman under the gallery, who proposed the repeal in the American committee, had another set of resolutions in his pocket, directly the reverse of those he moved. These artifices of a desperate cause are at this time spread abroad, with incredible care, in every part of the town, from the highest to the lowest companies; as if the industry of the circulation were to make amends for the absurdity of the report.

Sir, whether the noble lord is of a complexion to be bullied by Lord Chatham, or by any man, I must submit to those who know him. I confess, when I look back to that time, I

---

[9] Burke refers to the "eagle eye" of the elder Pitt.

consider him as placed in one of the most trying situations in which, perhaps, any man ever stood. In the House of Peers there were very few of the ministry, out of the noble lord's own particular connection, (except Lord Egmont, who acted, as far as I could discern, an honorable and manly part,) that did not look to some other future arrangement, which warped his politics. There were in both Houses new and menacing appearances, that might very naturally drive any other than a most resolute minister from his measure or from his station. The household troops openly revolted. The allies of ministry (those, I mean, who supported some of their measures, but refused responsibility for any) endeavored to undermine their credit, and to take ground that must be fatal to the success of the very cause which they would be thought to countenance. The question of the repeal was brought on by ministry in the committee of this House in the very instant when it was known that more than one court negotiation was carrying on with the heads of the opposition. Everything, upon every side, was full of traps and mines. Earth below shook; heaven above menaced; all the elements of ministerial safety were dissolved. It was in the midst of this chaos of plots and counterplots, it was in the midst of this complicated warfare against public opposition and private treachery, that the firmness of that noble person was put to the proof. He never stirred from his ground: no, not an inch. He remained fixed and determined, in principle, in measure, and in conduct. He practised no managements. He secured no retreat. He sought no apology.

I will likewise do justice—I ought to do it—to the honorable gentleman who led us in this House. Far from the duplicity wickedly charged on him, he acted his part with alacrity and resolution. We all felt inspired by the example he gave us, down even to myself, the weakest in that phalanx. I declare for one, I knew well enough (it could not be concealed from anybody) the true state of things; but, in my life, I never came with so much spirits into this House. It was a time for a *man* to act in. We had powerful enemies; but we had faithful and determined friends, and a glorious cause. We had a great battle to fight; but we had the means of fighting: not as now, when our arms are tied behind us. We did fight that day, and conquer.

I remember, Sir, with a melancholy pleasure, the situation of the honorable gentleman who made the motion for the repeal: in that crisis, when the whole trading interest of this empire, crammed into your lobbies, with a trembling and anxious expectation, waited, almost to a winter's return of light, their fate from your resolutions. When at length you had determined in their favor, and your doors thrown open showed them the figure of their deliverer in the well-earned triumph of his important victory, from the whole of that grave multitude there arose an involuntary burst of gratitude and transport. They jumped upon him like children on a long absent father. They clung about him as captives about their redeemer. All England, all America, joined in his applause. Nor did he seem insensible to the best of all earthly rewards, the love and admiration of his fellow-citizens. *Hope elevated and joy brightened his crest.*[10] I stood near him; and his face, to use the expression of the Scripture of the first martyr, "his face was as if it had been the face of an angel." I do not know how others feel; but if I had stood in that situation, I never would have exchanged it for all that kings in their profusion could bestow. I did hope that that day's danger and honor would have been a bond to hold us all together forever. But, alas! that, with other pleasing visions, is long since vanished.

Sir, this act of supreme magnanimity has been represented as if it had been a measure of an administration that, having no scheme of their own, took a middle line, pilfered a bit

---

[10] *Paradise Lost*, IX. 633.

from one side and a bit from the other. Sir, they took *no* middle lines. They differed fundamentally from the schemes of both parties; but they preserved the objects of both. They preserved the authority of Great Britain; they preserved the equity of Great Britain. They made the Declaratory Act; they repealed the Stamp Act. They did both *fully:* because the Declaratory Act was *without qualification;* and the repeal of the Stamp Act *total.* This they did in the situation I have described.

Now, Sir, what will the adversary say to both these acts? If the principle of the Declaratory Act was not good, the principle we are contending for this day is monstrous. If the principle of the repeal was not good, why are we not at war for a real, substantial, effective revenue? If both were bad, why has this ministry incurred all the inconveniences of both and of all schemes? why have they enacted, repealed, enforced, yielded, and now attempt to enforce again?

Sir, I think I may as well now as at any other time speak to a certain matter of fact not wholly unrelated to the question under your consideration. We, who would persuade you to revert to the ancient policy of this kingdom, labor under the effect of this short current phrase, which the court leaders have given out to all their corps, in order to take away the credit of those who would prevent you from that frantic war you are going to wage upon your colonies. Their cant is this: "All the disturbances in America have been created by the repeal of the Stamp Act." I suppress for a moment my indignation at the falsehood, baseness, and absurdity of this most audacious assertion. Instead of remarking on the motives and character of those who have issued it for circulation, I will clearly lay before you the state of America, antecedently to that repeal, after the repeal, and since the renewal of the schemes of American taxation.

It is said, that the disturbances, if there were any before the repeal, were slight, and without difficulty or inconvenience might have been suppressed. For an answer to this assertion I will send you to the great author and patron of the Stamp Act, who, certainly meaning well to the authority of this country, and fully apprised of the state of that, made, before a repeal was so much as agitated in this House, the motion which is on your journals, and which, to save the clerk the trouble of turning to it, I will now read to you. It was for an amendment to the address of the 17th of December, 1765.

"To express our just resentment and indignation at the *outrageous tumults and insurrections* which have been excited and carried on in North America, and at the resistance given, by *open* and *rebellious* force, to the execution of the laws in that part of his Majesty's dominions; to assure his Majesty, that his faithful Commons, animated with the warmest duty and attachment to his royal person and government, ... will firmly and effectually support his Majesty in all such measures as shall be necessary for preserving and securing the legal dependence of the colonies upon this their mother country," &c., &c.

Here was certainly a disturbance preceding the repeal,— such a disturbance as Mr. Grenville thought necessary to qualify by the name of an *insurrection,* and the epithet of a *rebellious* force: terms much stronger than any by which those who then supported his motion have ever since thought proper to distinguish the subsequent disturbances in America. They were disturbances which seemed to him and his friends to justify as strong a promise of support as hath been usual to give in the beginning of a war with the most powerful and declared enemies. When the accounts of the American governors came before the House, they appeared stronger even than the warmth of public imagination had painted them: so much stronger, that the papers on your table bear me out in saying that all the late disturbances, which have been at one time the minister's motives for the repeal of five out of six of the new court taxes, and are now his pretences for refusing to repeal that sixth, did not amount—why do I compare them?—no, not to a tenth part of the tumults and violence which prevailed long before the repeal of that act.

Ministry cannot refuse the authority of the commander-in-chief, General Gage, who, in his letter of the 4th of November, from New York, thus represents the state of things:—

"It is difficult to say, from the *highest to the lowest,* who has not been *accessory* to this *insurrection,* either by writing, or *mutual agreements* to oppose the act, by what they are pleased to term all legal opposition to it. Nothing effectual has been proposed, either to prevent or quell the tumult. *The rest of the provinces are in the same situation,* as to a positive refusal to take the stamps, and threatening those who shall take them *to plunder and murder them;* and this affair stands *in all the provinces,* that, unless the act from its own nature enforce itself, nothing but a *very* considerable military force can do it."

It is remarkable, Sir, that the persons who formerly trumpeted forth the most loudly the violent resolutions of assemblies, the universal insurrections, the seizing and burning the stamped papers, the forcing stamp officers to resign their commissions under the gallows, the rifling and pulling down of the houses of magistrates, and the expulsion from their country of all who dared to write or speak a single word in defence of the powers of Parliament,—these very trumpeters are now the men that represent the whole as a mere trifle, and choose to date all the disturbances from the repeal of the Stamp Act, which put an end to them. Hear your officers abroad, and let them refute this shameless falsehood, who, in all their correspondence, state the disturbances as owing to their true causes, the discontent of the people from the taxes. You have this evidence in your own archives; and it will give you complete satisfaction, if you are not so far lost to all

Parliamentary ideas of information as rather to credit the lie of the day than the records of your own House.

Sir, this vermin of court reporters, when they are forced into day upon one point, are sure to burrow in another: but they shall have no refuge; I will make them bolt out of all their holes. Conscious that they must be baffled, when they attribute a precedent disturbance to a subsequent measure, they take other ground, almost as absurd, but very common in modern practice, and very wicked; which is, to attribute the ill effect of ill-judged conduct to the arguments which had been used to dissuade us from it. They say, that the opposition made in Parliament to the Stamp Act, at the time of its passing, encouraged the Americans to their resistance. This has even formally appeared in print in a regular volume from an advocate of that faction,—a Dr. Tucker. This Dr. Tucker is already a dean,[11] and his earnest labors in this vineyard will, I suppose, raise him to a bishopric. But this assertion, too, just like the rest, is false. In all the papers which have loaded your table, in all the vast crowd of verbal witnesses that appeared at your bar, witnesses which were indiscriminately produced from both sides of the House, not the least hint of such a cause of disturbance has ever appeared. As to the fact of a strenuous opposition to the Stamp Act, I sat as a stranger in your gallery when the act was under consideration. Far from anything inflammatory, I never heard a more languid debate in this House. No more than two or three gentlemen, as I remember, spoke against the act, and that with great reserve and remarkable temper. There was but one division in the whole progress of the bill; and the minority did not reach to more than 39 or 40. In the House of Lords I do not recollect that there was any debate or division at all. I am sure there was no protest. In fact, the affair passed

---

[11] Dr. Josiah Tucker (1711-99), Dean of Gloucester, noted for his works on political economy.

with so very, very little noise, that in town they scarcely knew
the nature of what you were doing. The opposition to the bill
in England never could have done this mischief, because there
scarcely ever was less of opposition to a bill of consequence.

Sir, the agents and distributors of falsehoods have, with
their usual industry, circulated another lie, of the same nature
with the former. It is this: that the disturbances arose from
the account which had been received in America of the
change in the ministry. No longer awed, it seems, with the
spirit of the former rulers, they thought themselves a match
for what our calumniators choose to qualify by the name of
so feeble a ministry as succeeded. Feeble in one sense these
men certainly may be called: for, with all their efforts, and
they have made many, they have not been able to resist the
distempered vigor and insane alacrity with which you are
rushing to your ruin. But it does so happen, that the falsity
of this circulation is (like the rest) demonstrated by indisputable dates and records.

So little was the change known in America, that the letters
of your governors, giving an account of these disturbances
long after they had arrived at their highest pitch, were all
directed to the *old ministry*, and particularly to the *Earl of
Halifax*, the Secretary of State corresponding with the colonies, without once in the smallest degree intimating the
slightest suspicion of any ministerial revolution whatsoever.
The ministry was not changed in England until the 10th day
of July, 1765. On the 14th of the preceding June, Governor
Fauquier, from Virginia, writes thus,—and writes thus to the
Earl of Halifax:—"Government is set at *defiance*, not having
strength enough in her hands to enforce obedience to the
laws of the community.—The private distress, which every
man feels, increases the *general dissatisfaction* at the duties
laid by the *Stamp Act*, which breaks out and shows itself
upon every trifling occasion." The general dissatisfaction had
produced some time before, that is, on the 29th of May,

several strong public resolves against the Stamp Act; and those resolves are assigned by Governor Bernard as the cause of the *insurrections* in Massachusetts Bay, in his letter of the 15th of August, still addressed to the Earl of Halifax; and he continued to address such accounts to that minister quite to the 7th of September of the same year. Similar accounts, and of as late a date, were sent from other governors, and all directed to Lord Halifax. Not one of these letters indicates the slightest idea of a change, either known or even apprehended.

Thus are blown away the insect race of courtly falsehoods! Thus perish the miserable inventions of the wretched runners for a wretched cause, which they have fly-blown into every weak and rotten part of the country, in vain hopes, that, when their maggots had taken wing, their importunate buzzing might sound something like the public voice!

Sir, I have troubled you sufficiently with the state of America before the repeal. Now I turn to the honorable gentleman who so stoutly challenges us to tell whether, after the repeal, the provinces were quiet. This is coming home to the point. Here I meet him directly, and answer most readily, *They were quiet.* And I, in my turn, challenge him to prove when, and where, and by whom, and in what numbers, and with what violence, the other laws of trade, as gentlemen assert, were violated in consequence of your concession, or that even your other revenue laws were attacked. But I quit the vantage-ground on which I stand, and where I might leave the burden of the proof upon him: I walk down upon the open plain, and undertake to show that they were not only quiet, but showed many unequivocal marks of acknowledgment and gratitude. And to give him every advantage, I select the obnoxious colony of Massachusetts Bay, which at this time (but without hearing her) is so heavily a culprit before Parliament: I will select their proceedings even under circumstances of no small irritation. For, a little imprudently,

I must say, Governor Bernard mixed in the administration of the lenitive of the repeal no small acrimony arising from matters of a separate nature. Yet see, Sir, the effect of that lenitive, though mixed with these bitter ingredients,—and how this rugged people can express themselves on a measure of concession.

"If it is not now in our power," (say they, in their address to Governor Bernard,) "in so full a manner as will be expected, to show our respectful gratitude to the mother country, or to make a dutiful, affectionate return to the indulgence of the King and Parliament, it shall be no fault of ours; for this we intend, and hope shall be able fully to effect."

Would to God that this temper had been cultivated, managed, and set in action! Other effects than those which we have since felt would have resulted from it. On the requisition for compensation to those who had suffered from the violence of the populace, in the same address they say,—"The recommendation enjoined by Mr. Secretary Conway's letter, and in consequence thereof made to us, we shall embrace the first convenient opportunity to consider and act upon." They did consider; they did act upon it. They obeyed the requisition. I know the mode has been chicaned upon; but it was substantially obeyed, and much better obeyed than I fear the Parliamentary requisition of this session will be, though enforced by all your rigor and backed with all your power. In a word, the damages of popular fury were compensated by legislative gravity. Almost every other part of America in various ways demonstrated their gratitude. I am bold to say, that so sudden a calm recovered after so violent a storm is without parallel in history. To say that no other disturbance should happen from any other cause is folly. But as far as appearances went, by the judicious sacrifice of one law you procured an acquiescence in all that remained. After this experience, nobody shall persuade me, when an whole people are concerned, that acts of lenity are not means of conciliation.

I hope the honorable gentleman has received a fair and full answer to his question.

I have done with the third period of your policy,—that of your repeal, and the return of your ancient system, and your ancient tranquillity and concord. Sir, this period was not as long as it was happy. Another scene was opened, and other actors appeared on the stage. The state, in the condition I have described it, was delivered into the hands of Lord Chatham, a great and celebrated name,—a name that keeps the name of this country respectable in every other on the globe. It may be truly called

> Clarum et venerabile nomen
> Gentibus, et multum nostræ quod proderat urbi.[12]

Sir, the venerable age of this great man, his merited rank, his superior eloquence, his splendid qualities, his eminent services, the vast space he fills in the eye of mankind, and, more than all the rest, his fall from power, which, like death, canonizes and sanctifies a great character, will not suffer me to censure any part of his conduct. I am afraid to flatter him; I am sure I am not disposed to blame him. Let those who have betrayed him by their adulation insult him with their malevolence. But what I do not presume to censure I may have leave to lament. For a wise man, he seemed to me at that time to be governed too much by general maxims. I speak with the freedom of history, and I hope without offence. One or two of these maxims, flowing from an opinion not the most indulgent to our unhappy species, and surely a little too general, led him into measures that were greatly mischievous to himself, and for that reason, among others, perhaps fatal to his country,—measures, the effects of which, I am afraid, are forever incurable. He made an administration

---

[12] Lucan, IX. 202.

so checkered and speckled, he put together a piece of joinery so crossly indented and whimsically dovetailed, a cabinet so variously inlaid, such a piece of diversified mosaic, such a tessellated pavement without cement,—here a bit of black stone and there a bit of white, patriots and courtiers, king's friends and republicans, Whigs and Tories, treacherous friends and open enemies,—that it was, indeed, a very curious show, but utterly unsafe to touch and unsure to stand on. The colleagues whom he had assorted at the same boards stared at each other, and were obliged to ask,—"Sir, your name?"— "Sir, you have the advantage of me."—"Mr. Such-a-one."— "I beg a thousand pardons."—I venture to say, it did so happen that persons had a single office divided between them, who had never spoke to each other in their lives, until they found themselves, they knew not how, pigging together, heads and points, in the same truckle-bed.[13]

Sir, in consequence of this arrangement, having put so much the larger part of his enemies and opposers into power, the confusion was such that his own principles could not possibly have any effect or influence in the conduct of affairs. If ever he fell into a fit of the gout, or if any other cause withdrew him from public cares, principles directly the contrary were sure to predominate. When he had executed his plan, he had not an inch of ground to stand upon. When he had accomplished his scheme of administration, he was no longer a minister.

When his face was hid but for a moment, his whole system was on a wide sea without chart or compass. The gentlemen, his particular friends, who, with the names of various departments of ministry, were admitted to seem as if they acted a part under him, with a modesty that becomes all men, and with a confidence in him which was justified even in its extravagance by his superior abilities, had never

---

[13] Supposedly Lord North and George Cooke, paymasters in the summer of 1766.

in any instance presumed upon any opinion of their own. Deprived of his guiding influence, they were whirled about, the sport of every gust, and easily driven into any port; and as those who joined with them in manning the vessel were the most directly opposite to his opinions, measures, and character, and far the most artful and most powerful of the set, they easily prevailed, so as to seize upon the vacant, unoccupied, and derelict minds of his friends, and instantly they turned the vessel wholly out of the course of his policy. As if it were to insult as well as to betray him, even long before the close of the first session of his administration, when everything was publicly transacted, and with great parade, in his name, they made an act declaring it highly just and expedient to raise a revenue in America. For even then, Sir, even before this splendid orb was entirely set, and while the western horizon was in a blaze with his descending glory, on the opposite quarter of the heavens arose another luminary, and for his hour became lord of the ascendant.

This light, too, is passed and set forever. You understand, to be sure, that I speak of Charles Townshend, officially the reproducer of this fatal scheme, whom I cannot even now remember without some degree of sensibility. In truth, Sir, he was the delight and ornament of this House, and the charm of every private society which he honored with his presence. Perhaps there never arose in this country, nor in any country, a man of a more pointed and finished wit, and (where his passions were not concerned) of a more refined, exquisite, and penetrating judgment. If he had not so great a stock as some have had, who flourished formerly, of knowledge long treasured up, he knew, better by far than any man I ever was acquainted with, how to bring together within a short time all that was necessary to establish, to illustrate, and to decorate that side of the question he supported. He stated his matter skilfully and powerfully. He particularly excelled in a most luminous explanation and display of his subject. His style of argument was neither trite and vulgar, nor subtle and abstruse. He hit the House just between wind and water. And not being troubled with too anxious a zeal for any matter in question, he was never more tedious or more earnest than the preconceived opinions and present temper of his hearers required, to whom he was always in perfect unison. He conformed exactly to the temper of the House; and he seemed to guide, because he was always sure to follow it.

I beg pardon, Sir, if, when I speak of this and of other great men, I appear to digress in saying something of their characters. In this eventful history of the revolutions of America, the characters of such men are of much importance. Great men are the guideposts and landmarks in the state. The credit of such men at court or in the nation is the sole cause of all the public measures. It would be an invidious thing (most foreign, I trust, to what you think my disposition) to remark the errors into which the authority of great names has brought the nation, without doing justice at the same time to the great qualities whence that authority arose. The subject is instructive to those who wish to form themselves on whatever of excellence has gone before them. There are many young members in the House (such of late has been the rapid succession of public men) who never saw that prodigy, Charles Townshend, nor of course know what a ferment he was able to excite in everything by the violent ebullition of his mixed virtues and failings. For failings he had undoubtedly,—many of us remember them; we are this day considering the effect of them. But he had no failings which were not owing to a noble cause,—to an ardent, generous, perhaps an immoderate passion for fame: a passion which is the instinct of all great souls. He worshipped that goddess, wheresoever she appeared; but he paid his particular devotions to her in her favorite habitation, in her chosen temple, the House of Commons. Besides the characters of the individuals that compose our body, it is impossible, Mr. Speaker, not to observe that this House has a collective character of its own. That character, too, however imperfect, is not unamiable. Like all great public collections of men, you possess a marked love of virtue and an abhorrence of vice. But among vices there is none which the House abhors in the same degree with *obstinacy*. Obstinacy, Sir, is certainly a great vice; and in the changeful state of political affairs it is frequently the cause of great mischief. It happens, however, very unfortunately, that almost the whole line of the great and masculine virtues, constancy, gravity, magnanimity, fortitude, fidelity, and firmness, are closely allied to this disagreeable quality, of which you have so just an abhorrence; and, in their excess, all these virtues very easily fall into it. He who paid such a punctilious attention to all your feelings certainly took care not to shock them by that vice which is the most disgustful to you.

That fear of displeasing those who ought most to be pleased betrayed him sometimes into the other extreme. He had voted, and, in the year 1765, had been an advocate for the Stamp Act. Things and the disposition of men's minds were changed. In short, the Stamp Act began to be no favorite in this House. He therefore attended at the private meeting in which the resolutions moved by a right honorable gentleman were settled: resolutions leading to the repeal. The next day he voted for that repeal; and he would have spoken for it, too, if an illness (not, as was then given out, a political, but, to my knowledge, a very real illness) had not prevented it.

The very next session, as the fashion of this world passeth away, the repeal began to be in as bad an odor in this House as the Stamp Act had been in the session before. To conform to the temper which began to prevail, and to prevail mostly amongst those most in power, he declared, very early in the winter, that a revenue must be had out of America. Instantly he was tied down to his engagements by some, who had no objection to such experiments, when made at the cost of persons for whom they had no particular regard. The whole body of courtiers drove him onward. They always talked as if the king stood in a sort of humiliated state, until something of the kind should be done.

Here this extraordinary man, then Chancellor of the Exchequer, found himself in great straits. To please universally was the object of his life; but to tax and to please, no more than to love and to be wise, is not given to men. However, he attempted it. To render the tax palatable to the partisans of American revenue, he made a preamble stating the necessity of such a revenue. To close with the American distinction, this revenue was *external* or port-duty; but again, to soften it to the other party, it was a duty of *supply*. To gratify the *colonists,* it was laid on British manufactures; to satisfy the *merchants of Britain,* the duty was trivial, and (except that on tea, which touched only the devoted East India Company) on none of the grand objects of commerce. To counter-work the American contraband, the duty on tea was reduced from a shilling to three-pence; but to secure the favor of those who would tax America, the scene of collection was changed, and, with the rest, it was levied in the colonies. What need I say more? This fine-spun scheme had the usual fate of all exquisite policy. But the original plan of the duties, and the mode of executing that plan, both arose singly and solely from a love of our applause. He was truly the child of the House. He never thought, did, or said anything, but with a view to you. He every day adapted himself to your disposition, and adjusted himself before it as at a looking-glass.

He had observed (indeed, it could not escape him) that several persons, infinitely his inferiors in all respects, had formerly rendered themselves considerable in this House by one method alone. They were a race of men (I hope in God the species is extinct) who, when they rose in their place, no man living could divine, from any known adherence to parties, to opinions, or to principles, from any order or system in their politics, or from any sequel or connection in their ideas, what part they were going to take in any debate. It is astonishing how much this uncertainty, especially at critical times, called the attention of all parties on such men. All eyes were fixed on them, all ears open to hear them; each party gaped, and looked alternately for their vote, almost to the end of their speeches. While the House hung in this uncertainty, now the *hear-hims* rose from this side, now they rebellowed from the other; and that party to whom they fell at length from their tremulous and dancing balance always received them in a tempest of applause. The fortune of such men was a temptation too great to be resisted by one to whom a single whiff of incense withheld gave much greater pain than he received delight in the clouds of it which daily rose about him from the prodigal superstition of innumerable admirers. He was a candidate for contradictory honors; and his great aim was, to make those agree in admiration of him who never agreed in anything else.

Hence arose this unfortunate act, the subject of this day's debate: from a disposition which, after making an American revenue to please one, repealed it to please others, and again revived it in hopes of pleasing a third, and of catching something in the ideas of all.

This revenue act of 1767 formed the fourth period of American policy. How we have fared since then: what woful variety of schemes have been adopted; what enforcing, and what repealing; what bullying, and what submitting; what doing, and undoing; what straining, and what relaxing; what assemblies dissolved for not obeying, and called again without obedience; what troops sent out to quell resistance, and, on meeting that resistance, recalled; what shiftings, and changes, and jumblings of all kinds of men at home, which left no possibility of order, consistency, vigor, or even so much as a decent unity of color, in any one public measure——It is a tedious, irksome task. My duty may call me to open it out some other time; on a former occasion[14] I tried your temper on a part of it; for the present I shall forbear.

After all these changes and agitations, your immediate situation upon the question on your paper is at length brought to this. You have an act of Parliament stating that "it is *expedient* to raise a revenue in America." By a partial repeal you annihilated the greatest part of that revenue which this preamble declares to be so expedient. You have substituted no other in the place of it. A Secretary of State has disclaimed, in the king's name, all thoughts of such a substitution in future. The principle of this disclaimer goes to what has been left, as well as what has been repealed. The tax which lingers after its companions (under a preamble declaring an American revenue expedient, and for the sole purpose of supporting the theory of that preamble) militates with the assurance authentically conveyed to the colonies, and is an exhaustless source of jealousy and animosity. On this state, which I take to be a fair one,—not being able to discern any grounds of honor, advantage, peace, or power, for adhering, either to the act or to the preamble, I shall vote for the question which leads to the repeal of both.

If you do not fall in with this motion, then secure something to fight for, consistent in theory and valuable in practice. If you must employ your strength, employ it to uphold you in some honorable right or some profitable wrong. If you are apprehensive that the concession recommended to you, though proper, should be a means of drawing on you further, but unreasonable claims,—why, then employ your force in supporting that reasonable concession against those unreasonable demands. You will employ it with more grace, with better

---

[14] In the Resolutions in May, 1770.

effect, and with great probable concurrence of all the quiet and rational people in the provinces, who are now united with and hurried away by the violent,—having, indeed, different dispositions, but a common interest. If you apprehend that on a concession you shall be pushed by metaphysical process to the extreme lines, and argued out of your whole authority, my advice is this: when you have recovered your old, your strong, your tenable position, then face about,—stop short,—do nothing more,—reason not at all,—oppose the ancient policy and practice of the empire as a rampart against the speculations of innovators on both sides of the question,—and you will stand on great, manly, and sure ground. On this solid basis fix your machines, and they will draw worlds towards you.

Your ministers, in their own and his Majesty's name, have already adopted the American distinction of internal and external duties. It is a distinction, whatever merit it may have, that was originally moved by the Americans themselves; and I think they will acquiesce in it, if they are not pushed with too much logic and too little sense, in all the consequences: that is, if external taxation be understood, as they and you understand it, when you please, to be not a distinction of geography, but of policy; that it is a power for regulating trade, and not for supporting establishments. The distinction, which is as nothing with regard to right, is of most weighty consideration in practice. Recover your old ground, and your old tranquillity; try it; I am persuaded the Americans will compromise with you. When confidence is once restored, the odious and suspicious *summum jus* will perish of course. The spirit of practicability, of moderation, and mutual convenience will never call in geometrical exactness as the arbitrator of an amicable settlement. Consult and follow your experience. Let not the long story with which I have exercised your patience prove fruitless to your interests.

For my part, I should choose (if I could have my wish) that the proposition of the honorable gentleman[15] for the repeal could go to America without the attendance of the penal bills. Alone I could almost answer for its success. I cannot be certain of its reception in the bad company it may keep. In such heterogeneous assortments, the most innocent person will lose the effect of his innocency. Though you should send out this angel of peace, yet you are sending out a destroying angel too; and what would be the effect of the conflict of these two adverse spirits, or which would predominate in the end, is what I dare not say: whether the lenient measures would cause American passion to subside, or the severe would increase its fury,—all this is in the hand of Providence. Yet now, even now, I should confide in the prevailing virtue and efficacious operation of lenity, though working in darkness and in chaos, in the midst of all this unnatural and turbid combination: I should hope it might produce order and beauty in the end.

Let us, Sir, embrace some system or other before we end this session. Do you mean to tax America, and to draw a productive revenue from thence? If you do, speak out: name, fix, ascertain this revenue; settle its quantity; define its objects; provide for its collection; and then fight, when you have something to fight for. If you murder, rob; if you kill, take possession; and do not appear in the character of madmen as well as assassins, violent, vindictive, bloody, and tyrannical, without an object. But may better counsels guide you!

Again, and again, revert to your old principles,—seek peace and ensue it,—leave America, if she has taxable matter in her, to tax herself. I am not here going into the distinctions of rights, nor attempting to mark their boundaries. I do not enter into these metaphysical distinctions; I hate the very sound of them. Leave the Americans as they anciently stood,

---

[15] Mr. Rose Fuller.

and these distinctions, born of our unhappy contest, will die along with it. They and we, and their and our ancestors, have been happy under that system. Let the memory of all actions in contradiction to that good old mode, on both sides, be extinguished forever. Be content to bind America by laws of trade: you have always done it. Let this be your reason for binding their trade. Do not burden them by taxes: you were not used to do so from the beginning. Let this be your reason for not taxing. These are the arguments of states and kingdoms. Leave the rest to the schools; for there only they may be discussed with safety. But if, intemperately, unwisely, fatally, you sophisticate and poison the very source of government, by urging subtle deductions, and consequences odious to those you govern, from the unlimited and illimitable nature of supreme sovereignty, you will teach them by these means to call that sovereignty itself in question. When you drive him hard, the boar will surely turn upon the hunters. If that sovereignty and their freedom cannot be reconciled, which will they take? They will cast your sovereignty in your face. Nobody will be argued into slavery. Sir, let the gentlemen on the other side call forth all their ability; let the best of them get up and tell me what one character of liberty the Americans have, and what one brand of slavery they are free from, if they are bound in their property and industry by all the restraints you can imagine on commerce, and at the same time are made pack-horses of every tax you choose to impose, without the least share in granting them. When they bear the burdens of unlimited monopoly, will you bring them to bear the burdens of unlimited revenue too? The Englishman in America will feel that this is slavery: that it is *legal* slavery will be no compensation either to his feelings or his understanding.

A noble lord,[16] who spoke some time ago, is full of the

---

[16] Lord Carmarthen.

fire of ingenuous youth; and when he has modelled the ideas of a lively imagination by further experience, he will be an ornament to his country in either House. He has said that the Americans are our children, and how can they revolt against their parent? He says, that, if they are not free in their present state, England is not free; because Manchester, and other considerable places, are not represented. So, then, because some towns in England are not represented, America is to have no representative at all. They are "our children"; but when children ask for bread, we are not to give a stone. Is it because the natural resistance of things, and the various mutations of time, hinders our government, or any scheme of government, from being any more than a sort of approximation to the right, is it therefore that the colonies are to recede from it infinitely? When this child of ours wishes to assimilate to its parent, and to reflect with a true filial resemblance the beauteous countenance of British liberty, are we to turn to them the shameful parts of our constitution? are we to give them our weakness for their strength, our opprobrium for their glory, and the slough of slavery, which we are not able to work off, to serve them for their freedom?

If this be the case, ask yourselves this question: Will they be content in such a state of slavery? If not, look to the consequences. Reflect how you are to govern a people who think they ought to be free, and think they are not. Your scheme yields no revenue; it yields nothing but discontent, disorder, disobedience: and such is the state of America, that, after wading up to your eyes in blood, you could only end just where you begun,—that is, to tax where no revenue is to be found, to——My voice fails me: my inclination, indeed, carries me no further; all is confusion beyond it.

Well, Sir, I have recovered a little, and before I sit down I must say something to another point with which gentlemen urge us. What is to become of the Declaratory Act, asserting the entireness of British legislative authority, if we abandon the practice of taxation?

For my part, I look upon the rights stated in that act exactly in the manner in which I viewed them on its very first proposition, and which I have often taken the liberty, with great humility, to lay before you. I look, I say, on the imperial rights of Great Britain, and the privileges which the colonists ought to enjoy under these rights, to be just the most reconcilable things in the world. The Parliament of Great Britain sits at the head of her extensive empire in two capacities. One as the local legislature of this island, providing for all things at home, immediately, and by no other instrument than the executive power. The other, and I think her nobler capacity, is what I call her *imperial character;* in which, as from the throne of heaven, she superintends all the several inferior legislatures, and guides and controls them all without annihilating any. As all these provincial legislatures are only coördinate to each other, they ought all to be subordinate to her; else they can neither preserve mutual peace, nor hope for mutual justice, nor effectually afford mutual assistance. It is necessary to coerce the negligent, to restrain the violent, and to aid the weak and deficient, by the overruling plenitude of her power. She is never to intrude into the place of the others, whilst they are equal to the common ends of their institution. But in order to enable Parliament to answer all these ends of provident and beneficent superintendence, her powers must be boundless. The gentlemen who think the powers of Parliament limited may please themselves to talk of requisitions. But suppose the requisitions are not obeyed? What! shall there be no reserved power in the empire, to supply a deficiency which may weaken, divide, and dissipate the whole? We are engaged in war,—the Secretary of State calls upon the colonies to contribute,—some would do it, I think most would cheerfully furnish whatever is demanded,—one or two, suppose, hang back, and, easing themselves, let the stress of the draft lie on the others,—surely it is proper that some authority might legally say, "Tax yourselves for the common supply, or Parliament will do it for you." This backwardness was, as I am told, actually the case of Pennsylvania for some short time towards the beginning of the last war, owing to some internal dissensions in the colony. But whether the fact were so or otherwise, the case is equally to be provided for by a competent sovereign power. But then this ought to be no ordinary power, nor ever used in the first instance. This is what I meant, when I have said, at various times, that I consider the power of taxing in Parliament as an instrument of empire, and not as a means of supply.

Such, Sir, is my idea of the Constitution of the British Empire, as distinguished from the Constitution of Britain; and on these grounds I think subordination and liberty may be sufficiently reconciled through the whole,—whether to serve a refining speculatist or a factious demagogue I know not, but enough surely for the ease and happiness of man.

Sir, whilst we held this happy course, we drew more from the colonies than all the impotent violence of despotism ever could extort from them. We did this abundantly in the last war; it has never been once denied; and what reason have we to imagine that the colonies would not have proceeded in supplying government as liberally, if you had not stepped in and hindered them from contributing, by interrupting the channel in which their liberality flowed with so strong a course,—by attempting to take, instead of being satisfied to receive? Sir William Temple says, that Holland has loaded itself with ten times the impositions which it revolted from Spain rather than submit to. He says true. Tyranny is a poor provider. It knows neither how to accumulate nor how to extract.

I charge, therefore, to this new and unfortunate system the

loss not only of peace, of union, and of commerce, but even of revenue, which its friends are contending for. It is morally certain that we have lost at least a million of free grants since the peace. I think we have lost a great deal more; and that those who look for a revenue from the provinces never could have pursued, even in that light, a course more directly repugnant to their purposes.

Now, Sir, I trust I have shown, first on that narrow ground which the honorable gentleman measured, that you are like to lose nothing by complying with the motion, except what you have lost already. I have shown afterwards, that in time of peace you flourished in commerce, and, when war required it, had sufficient aid from the colonies, while you pursued your ancient policy; that you threw everything into confusion, when you made the Stamp Act; and that you restored everything to peace and order, when you repealed it. I have shown that the revival of the system of taxation has produced the very worst effects; and that the partial repeal has produced, not partial good, but universal evil. Let these considerations, founded on facts, not one of which can be denied, bring us back to our reason by the road of our experience.

I cannot, as I have said, answer for mixed measures: but surely this mixture of lenity would give the whole a better chance of success. When you once regain confidence, the way will be clear before you. Then you may enforce the Act of Navigation, when it ought to be enforced. You will yourselves open it, where it ought still further to be opened. Proceed in what you do, whatever you do, from policy, and not from rancor. Let us act like men, let us act like statesmen. Let us hold some sort of consistent conduct. It is agreed that a revenue is not to be had in America. If we lose the profit, let us get rid of the odium.

On this business of America, I confess I am serious, even to sadness. I have had but one opinion concerning it, since

I sat, and before I sat in Parliament. The noble lord [17] will, as usual, probably, attribute the part taken by me and my friends in this business to a desire of getting his places. Let him enjoy this happy and original idea. If I deprived him of it, I should take away most of his wit, and all his argument. But I had rather bear the brunt of all his wit, and indeed blows much heavier, than stand answerable to God for embracing a system that tends to the destruction of some of the very best and fairest of His works. But I know the map of England as well as the noble lord, or as any other person; and I know that the way I take is not the road to preferment. My excellent and honorable friend under me on the floor has trod that road with great toil for upwards of twenty years together. He is not yet arrived at the noble lord's destination. However, the tracks of my worthy friend are those I have ever wished to follow; because I know they lead to honor. Long may we tread the same road together, whoever may accompany us, or whoever may laugh at us on our journey! I honestly and solemnly declare, I have in all seasons adhered to the system of 1766 for no other reason than that I think it laid deep in your truest interests,—and that, by limiting the exercise, it fixes on the firmest foundations a real, consistent, well-grounded authority in Parliament. Until you come back to that system, there will be no peace for England.

---

[17] Lord North.

Speech on Moving His Resolutions for Conciliation with the Colonies

(MARCH 22, 1775)

---

hope, Sir, that, notwithstanding the austerity of the Chair, your good-nature will incline you to some degree of indulgence towards human frailty. You will not think it unnatural, that those who have an object depending, which strongly engages their hopes and fears, should be somewhat inclined to superstition. As I came into the House, full of anxiety about the event of my motion, I found, to my infinite surprise, that the grand penal bill by which we had passed sentence on the trade and sustenance of America is to be returned to us from the other House.[1] I do confess, I could not help looking on this event as a fortunate omen. I look upon it as a sort of Providential favor by which we are put once more in possession of our deliberative capacity, upon a business so very questionable in its nature, so very uncertain in its issue. By the return of this bill, which seemed to have

[1] The act to restrain the trade and commerce of the provinces of Massachusetts Bay and New Hampshire, and colonies of Connecticut and Rhode Island and Providence Plantation, in North America, to Great Britain, Ireland, and the British Islands in the West Indies; and to prohibit such provinces and colonies from carrying on any fishery on the banks of Newfoundland, and other places therein mentioned, under certain conditions and limitations.

taken its flight forever, we are at this very instant nearly as free to choose a plan for our American government as we were on the first day of the session. If, Sir, we incline to the side of conciliation, we are not at all embarrassed (unless we please to make ourselves so) by any incongruous mixture of coercion and restraint. We are therefore called upon, as it were by a superior warning voice, again to attend to America, —to attend to the whole of it together,—and to review the subject with an unusual degree of care and calmness.

Surely it is an awful subject,—or there is none so on this side of the grave. When I first had the honor of a seat in this House, the affairs of that continent pressed themselves upon us as the most important and most delicate object of Parliamentary attention. My little share in this great deliberation oppressed me. I found myself a partaker in a very high trust; and having no sort of reason to rely on the strength of my natural abilities for the proper execution of that trust, I was obliged to take more than common pains to instruct myself in everything which relates to our colonies. I was not less under the necessity of forming some fixed ideas concerning the general policy of the British empire. Something of this sort seemed to be indispensable, in order, amidst so vast a fluctuation of passions and opinions, to concentre my thoughts, to ballast my conduct, to preserve me from being blown about by every wind of fashionable doctrine. I really did not think it safe or manly to have fresh principles to seek upon every fresh mail which should arrive from America.

At that period I had the fortune to find myself in perfect concurrence with a large majority in this House. Bowing under that high authority, and penetrated with the sharpness and strength of that early impression, I have continued ever since, without the least deviation, in my original sentiments. Whether this be owing to an obstinate perseverance in error, or to a religious adherence to what appears to me truth and reason, it is in your equity to judge.

Sir, Parliament, having an enlarged view of objects, made, during this interval, more frequent changes in their sentiments and their conduct than could be justified in a particular person upon the contracted scale of private information. But though I do not hazard anything approaching to a censure on the motives of former Parliaments to all those alterations, one fact is undoubted,—that under them the state of America has been kept in continual agitation. Everything administered as remedy to the public complaint, if it did not produce, was at least followed by, an heightening of the distemper, until, by a variety of experiments, that important country has been brought into her present situation,—a situation which I will not miscall, which I dare not name, which I scarcely know how to comprehend in the terms of any description.

In this posture, Sir, things stood at the beginning of the session. About that time, a worthy member,[2] of great Parliamentary experience, who in the year 1766 filled the chair of the American Committee with much ability, took me aside, and, lamenting the present aspect of our politics, told me, things were come to such a pass that our former methods of proceeding in the House would be no longer tolerated,—that the public tribunal (never too indulgent to a long and unsuccessful opposition) would now scrutinize our conduct with unusual severity,—that the very vicissitudes and shiftings of ministerial measures, instead of convicting their authors of inconstancy and want of system, would be taken as an occasion of charging us with a predetermined discontent which nothing could satisfy, whilst we accused every measure of vigor as cruel and every proposal of lenity as weak and irresolute. The public, he said, would not have patience to see us play the game out with our adversaries; we must produce our hand. It would be expected that those who for many years had been active in such affairs should show that

---

[2] Mr. Rose Fuller.

they had formed some clear and decided idea of the principles of colony government, and were capable of drawing out something like a platform of the ground which might be laid for future and permanent tranquillity.

I felt the truth of what my honorable friend represented; but I felt my situation, too. His application might have been made with far greater propriety to many other gentlemen. No man was, indeed, ever better disposed, or worse qualified, for such an undertaking, than myself. Though I gave so far into his opinion, that I immediately threw my thoughts into a sort of Parliamentary form, I was by no means equally ready to produce them. It generally argues some degree of natural impotence of mind, or some want of knowledge of the world, to hazard plans of government, except from a seat of authority. Propositions are made, not only ineffectually, but somewhat disreputably, when the minds of men are not properly disposed for their reception; and for my part, I am not ambitious of ridicule, not absolutely a candidate for disgrace.

Besides, Sir, to speak the plain truth, I have in general no very exalted opinion of the virtue of paper government, nor of any politics in which the plan is to be wholly separated from the execution. But when I saw that anger and violence prevailed every day more and more, and that things were hastening towards an incurable alienation of our colonies, I confess my caution gave way. I felt this as one of those few moments in which decorum yields to an higher duty. Public calamity is a mighty leveller; and there are occasions when any, even the slightest, chance of doing good must be laid hold on, even by the most inconsiderable person.

To restore order and repose to an empire so great and so distracted as ours is, merely in the attempt, an undertaking that would ennoble the flights of the highest genius, and obtain pardon for the efforts of the meanest understanding. Struggling a good while with these thoughts, by degrees I felt myself more firm. I derived, at length, some confidence from what in other circumstances usually produces timidity. I grew less anxious, even from the idea of my own insignificance. For, judging of what you are by what you ought to be, I persuaded myself that you would not reject a reasonable proposition because it had nothing but its reason to recommend it. On the other hand, being totally destitute of all shadow of influence, natural or adventitious, I was very sure, that, if my proposition were futile or dangerous, if it were weakly conceived or improperly timed, there was nothing exterior to it of power to awe, dazzle, or delude you. You will see it just as it is, and you will treat it just as it deserves.

The proposition is peace. Not peace through the medium of war; not peace to be hunted through the labyrinth of intricate and endless negotiations; not peace to arise out of universal discord, fomented from principle, in all parts of the empire; not peace to depend on the juridical determination of perplexing questions, or the precise marking the shadowy boundaries of a complex government. It is simple peace, sought in its natural course and in its ordinary haunts. It is peace sought in the spirit of peace, and laid in principles purely pacific. I propose, by removing the ground of the difference, and by restoring the *former unsuspecting con fidence of the colonies in the mother country,* to give permanent satisfaction to your people,—and (far from a scheme of ruling by discord) to reconcile them to each other in the same act and by the bond of the very same interest which reconciles them to British government.

My idea is nothing more. Refined policy ever has been the parent of confusion,—and ever will be so, as long as the world endures. Plain good intention, which is as easily discovered at the first view as fraud is surely detected at last, is, let me say, of no mean force in the government of mankind. Genuine simplicity of heart is an healing and cementing principle. My plan, therefore, being formed upon the most simple grounds imaginable, may disappoint some people, when they hear it. It has nothing to recommend it to the pruriency of curious ears. There is nothing at all new and captivating in it. It has nothing of the splendor of the project which has been lately laid upon your table by the noble lord in the blue riband.[3] It does not propose to fill your lobby with squabbling colony agents, who will require the interposition of your mace at every instant to keep the peace amongst them. It does not institute a magnificent auction of finance, where captivated provinces come to general ransom by bidding against each other, until you knock down the hammer, and determine a proportion of payments beyond all the powers of algebra to equalize and settle.

The plan which I shall presume to suggest derives, however, one great advantage from the proposition and registry of that noble lord's project. The idea of conciliation is admissible. First, the House, in accepting the resolution moved by the noble lord, has admitted, notwithstanding the menacing front of our address, notwithstanding our heavy bill of pains and penalties, that we do not think ourselves precluded from all ideas of free grace and bounty.

The House has gone farther: it has declared conciliation admissible *previous* to any submission on the part of America. It has even shot a good deal beyond that mark, and has admitted that the complaints of our former mode of exerting the right of taxation were not wholly unfounded. That right thus exerted is allowed to have had something reprehensible in it,—something unwise, or something grievous; since, in the midst of our heat and resentment, we, of ourselves, have proposed a capital alteration, and, in order to get rid of what

---

[3] Lord North, who about three weeks before (27 February, 1775) had made the resolution, passed by the House, not to tax any colony that contributed voluntarily to the imperial revenue. The approval of Parliament was to be merely discretionary, and the means of raising the sum left entirely to the Colonial assemblies.

seemed so very exceptionable, have instituted a mode that is altogether new,—one that is, indeed, wholly alien from all the ancient methods and forms of Parliament.

The *principle* of this proceeding is large enough for my purpose. The means proposed by the noble lord for carrying his ideas into execution, I think, indeed, are very indifferently suited to the end; and this I shall endeavor to show you before I sit down. But, for the present, I take my ground on the admitted principle. I mean to give peace. Peace implies reconciliation; and where there has been a material dispute, reconciliation does in a manner always imply concession on the one part or on the other. In this state of things I make no difficulty in affirming that the proposal ought to originate from us. Great and acknowledged force is not impaired, either in effect or in opinion, by an unwillingness to exert itself. The superior power may offer peace with honor and with safety. Such an offer from such a power will be attributed to magnanimity. But the concessions of the weak are the concessions of fear. When such a one is disarmed, he is wholly at the mercy of his superior; and he loses forever that time and those chances which, as they happen to all men, are the strength and resources of all inferior power.

The capital leading questions on which you must this day decide are these two: First, whether you ought to concede; and secondly, what your concession ought to be. On the first of these questions we have gained (as I have just taken the liberty of observing to you) some ground. But I am sensible that a good deal more is still to be done. Indeed, Sir, to enable us to determine both on the one and the other of these great questions with a firm and precise judgment, I think it may be necessary to consider distinctly the true nature and the peculiar circumstances of the object which we have before us: because, after all our struggle, whether we will or not, we must govern America according to that nature and to those circumstances, and not according to our own imaginations, not according to abstract ideas of right, by no means according to mere general theories of government, the resort to which appears to me, in our present situation, no better than arrant trifling. I shall therefore endeavor, with your leave, to lay before you some of the most material of these circumstances in as full and as clear a manner as I am able to state them.

The first thing that we have to consider with regard to the nature of the object is the number of people in the colonies. I have taken for some years a good deal of pains on that point. I can by no calculation justify myself in placing the number below two millions of inhabitants of our own European blood and color,—besides at least 500,000 others, who form no inconsiderable part of the strength and opulence of the whole. This, Sir, is, I believe, about the true number. There is no occasion to exaggerate, where plain truth is of so much weight and importance. But whether I put the present numbers too high or too low is a matter of little moment. Such is the strength with which population shoots in that part of the world, that, state the numbers as high as we will, whilst the dispute continues, the exaggeration ends. Whilst we are discussing any given magnitude, they are grown to it. Whilst we spend our time in deliberating on the mode of governing two millions, we shall find we have millions more to manage. Your children do not grow faster from infancy to manhood than they spread from families to communities, and from villages to nations.

I put this consideration of the present and the growing numbers in the front of our deliberation, because, Sir, this consideration will make it evident to a blunter discernment than yours, that no partial, narrow, contracted, pinched, occasional system will be at all suitable to such an object. It will show you that it is not to be considered as one of those *minima* which are out of the eye and consideration of the law,—not a paltry excrescence of the state,—not a mean dependant, who may be neglected with little damage and provoked with little danger. It will prove that some degree of care and caution is required in the handling such an object; it will show that you ought not, in reason, to trifle with so large a mass of the interests and feelings of the human race. You could at no time do so without guilt; and be assured you will not be able to do it long with impunity.

But the population of this country, the great and growing population, though a very important consideration, will lose much of its weight, if not combined with other circumstances. The commerce of your colonies is out of all proportion beyond the numbers of the people. This ground of their commerce, indeed, has been trod some days ago, and with great ability, by a distinguished person,[4] at your bar. This gentleman, after thirty-five years,—it is so long since he first appeared at the same place to plead for the commerce of Great Britain,— has come again before you to plead the same cause, without any other effect of time than that to the fire of imagination and extent of erudition, which even then marked him as one of the first literary characters of his age, he has added a consummate knowledge in the commercial interest of his country, formed by a long course of enlightened and dis- criminating experience.

Sir, I should be inexcusable in coming after such a person with any detail, if a great part of the members who now fill the House had not the misfortune to be absent when he appeared at your bar. Besides, Sir, I propose to take the matter at periods of time somewhat different from his. There is, if I mistake not, a point of view from whence, if you will look at this subject, it is impossible that it should not make an impression upon you.

I have in my hand two accounts: one a comparative state of the export trade of England to its colonies, as it stood in

---

[4] Richard Glover (1712-85).

the year 1704, and as it stood in the year 1772; the other a
state of the export trade of this country to its colonies alone,
as it stood in 1772, compared with the whole trade of England to all parts of the world (the colonies included) in the
year 1704. They are from good vouchers: the latter period
from the accounts on your table; the earlier from an original
manuscript of Davenant, who first established the Inspector-
General's office, which has been ever since his time so
abundant a source of Parliamentary information.

The export trade to the colonies consists of three great
branches: the African, which, terminating almost wholly in
the colonies, must be put to the account of their commerce;
the West Indian; and the North American. All these are so
interwoven, that the attempt to separate them would tear to
pieces the contexture of the whole, and, if not entirely
destroy, would very much depreciate, the value of all the
parts. I therefore consider these three denominations to be,
what in effect they are, one trade.

The trade to the colonies, taken on the export side, at the
beginning of this century, that is, in the year 1704, stood
thus:—

Exports to North America and the West Indies	£483,265
To Africa	86,665
	£569,930

In the year 1772, which I take as a middle year between
the highest and lowest of those lately laid on your table, the
account was as follows:—

To North America and the West Indies	£4,791,734
To Africa	866,398
To which if you add the export trade from Scotland, which had in 1704 no existence	364,000
	£6,022,132

From five hundred and odd thousand, it has grown to six millions. It has increased no less than twelvefold. This is the state of the colony trade, as compared with itself at these two periods, within this century;—and this is matter for meditation. But this is not all. Examine my second account. See how the export trade to the colonies alone in 1772 stood in the other point of view, that is, as compared to the whole trade of England in 1704.

The whole export trade of England, including that to the colonies, in 1704	£ 6,509,000
Export to the colonies alone, in 1772	6,024,000
Difference	£ 485,000

The trade with America alone is now within less than 500,000*l.* of being equal to what this great commercial nation, England, carried on at the beginning of this century with the whole world! If I had taken the largest year of those on your table, it would rather have exceeded. But, it will be said, is not this American trade an unnatural protuberance, that has drawn the juices from the rest of the body? The reverse. It is the very food that has nourished every other part into its present magnitude. Our general trade has been greatly augmented, and augmented more or less in almost every part to which it ever extended, but with this material difference: that of the six millions which in the beginning of the century constituted the whole mass of our export commerce the colony trade was but one twelfth part; it is now (as a part of sixteen millions) considerably more than a third of the whole. This is the relative proportion of the importance of the colonies at these two periods: and all reasoning concerning our mode of treating them must have this proportion as its basis, or it is a reasoning weak, rotten, and sophistical.

Mr. Speaker, I cannot prevail on myself to hurry over this great consideration. It is good for us to be here. We stand

where we have an immense view of what is, and what is past.
Clouds indeed, and darkness, rest upon the future. Let us,
however, before we descend from this noble eminence, reflect
that this growth of our national prosperity has happened within the short period of the life of man. It has happened within
sixty-eight years. There are those alive whose memory might
touch the two extremities. For instance, my Lord Bathurst
might remember all the stages of the progress. He was in
1704 of an age at least to be made to comprehend such
things. He was then old enough *acta parentum jam legere, et
quæ sit poterit cognoscere virtus.*[5] Suppose, Sir, that the
angel of this auspicious youth, foreseeing the many virtues
which made him one of the most amiable, as he is one of the
most fortunate men of his age, had opened to him in vision,
that, when, in the fourth generation, the third prince of the
House of Brunswick had sat twelve years on the throne of
that nation which (by the happy issue of moderate and healing councils) was to be made Great Britain, he should see his
son, Lord Chancellor of England, turn back the current of
hereditary dignity to its fountain, and raise him to an higher
rank of peerage, whilst he enriched the family with a new one,
—if, amidst these bright and happy scenes of domestic honor
and prosperity, that angel should have drawn up the curtain,
and unfolded the rising glories of his country, and whilst he
was gazing with admiration on the then commercial grandeur
of England, the genius should point out to him a little speck,
scarce visible in the mass of the national interest, a small
seminal principle rather than a formed body, and should tell
him,—"Young man, there is America,—which at this day
serves for little more than to amuse you with stories of savage
men and uncouth manners, yet shall, before you taste of
death, show itself equal to the whole of that commerce which
now attracts the envy of the world. Whatever England has

---

[5] Virgil, *Eclogues,* IV. 26.

been growing to by a progressive increase of improvement, brought in by varieties of people, by succession of civilizing conquests and civilizing settlements in a series of seventeen hundred years, you shall see as much added to her by America in the course of a single life!" If this state of his country had been foretold to him, would it not require all the sanguine credulity of youth, and all the fervid glow of enthusiasm, to make him believe it? Fortunate man, he has lived to see it! Fortunate indeed, if he lives to see nothing that shall vary the prospect, and cloud the setting of his day!

Excuse me, Sir, if, turning from such thoughts, I resume this comparative view once more. You have seen it on a large scale; look at it on a small one. I will point out to your attention a particular instance of it in the single province of Pennsylvania. In the year 1704, that province called for 11,459*l.* in value of your commodities, native and foreign. This was the whole. What did it demand in 1772? Why, nearly fifty times as much; for in that year the export to Pennsylvania was 507,909*l.*, nearly equal to the export to all the colonies together in the first period.

I choose, Sir, to enter into these minute and particular details; because generalities, which in all other cases are apt to heighten and raise the subject, have here a tendency to sink it. When we speak of the commerce with our colonies, fiction lags after truth, invention is unfruitful, and imagination cold and barren.

So far, Sir, as to the importance of the object in the view of its commerce, as concerned in the exports from England. If I were to detail the imports, I could show how many enjoyments they procure which deceive the burden of life, how many materials which invigorate the springs of national industry and extend and animate every part of our foreign and domestic commerce. This would be a curious subject indeed, —but I must prescribe bounds to myself in a matter so vast and various.

I pass, therefore, to the colonies in another point of view,—
their agriculture. This they have prosecuted with such a spirit,
that, besides feeding plentifully their own growing multitude,
their annual export of grain, comprehending rice, has some
years ago exceeded a million in value. Of their last harvest, I
am persuaded, they will export much more. At the beginning
of the century some of these colonies imported corn from the
mother country. For some time past the Old World has been
fed from the New. The scarcity which you have felt would
have been a desolating famine, if this child of your old age,
with a true filial piety, with a Roman charity, had not put the
full breast of its youthful exuberance to the mouth of its exhausted parent.

As to the wealth which the colonies have drawn from the
sea by their fisheries, you had all that matter fully opened at
your bar. You surely thought those acquisitions of value, for
they seemed even to excite your envy; and yet the spirit by
which that enterprising employment has been exercised ought
rather, in my opinion, to have raised your esteem and admiration. And pray, Sir, what in the world is equal to it? Pass by
the other parts, and look at the manner in which the people of
New England have of late carried on the whale-fishery. Whilst
we follow them among the tumbling mountains of ice, and
behold them penetrating into the deepest frozen recesses of
Hudson's Bay and Davis's Straits, whilst we are looking for
them beneath the arctic circle, we hear that they have pierced
into the opposite region of polar cold, that they are at the
antipodes, and engaged under the frozen serpent of the South.
Falkland Island, which seemed too remote and romantic an
object for the grasp of national ambition,[6] is but a stage and
resting-place in the progress of their victorious industry. Nor
is the equinoctial heat more discouraging to them than the
accumulated winter of both the poles. We know, that, whilst

---

[6] England had abandoned its post in the remote Falkland Islands
(Port Egmont, West Falkland) in 1773.

some of them draw the line and strike the harpoon on the coast of Africa, others run the longitude, and pursue their gigantic game along the coast of Brazil. No sea but what is vexed by their fisheries. No climate that is not witness to their toils. Neither the perseverance of Holland, nor the activity of France, nor the dexterous and firm sagacity of English enterprise, ever carried this most perilous mode of hardy industry to the extent to which it has been pushed by this recent people,—a people who are still, as it were, but in the gristle, and not yet hardened into the bone of manhood. When I contemplate these things,—when I know that the colonies in general owe little or nothing to any care of ours, and that they are not squeezed into this happy form by the constraint of watchful and suspicious government, but that, through a wise and salutary neglect, a generous nature has been suffered to take her own way to perfection,—when I reflect upon these effects, when I see how profitable they have been to us, I feel all the pride of power sink, and all presumption in the wisdom of human contrivances melt and die away within me,— my rigor relents,—I pardon something to the spirit of liberty.

I am sensible, Sir, that all which I have asserted in my detail is admitted in the gross, but that quite a different conclusion is drawn from it. America, gentlemen say, is a noble object,—it is an object well worth fighting for. Certainly it is, if fighting a people be the best way of gaining them. Gentlemen in this respect will be led to their choice of means by their complexions and their habits. Those who understand the military art will of course have some predilection for it. Those who wield the thunder of the state may have more confidence in the efficacy of arms. But I confess, possibly for want of this knowledge, my opinion is much more in favor of prudent management than of force,—considering force not as an odious, but a feeble instrument, for preserving a people so numerous, so active, so growing, so spirited as this, in a profitable and subordinate connection with us.

First, Sir, permit me to observe, that the use of force alone is but *temporary*. It may subdue for a moment; but it does not remove the necessity of subduing again: and a nation is not governed which is perpetually to be conquered.

My next objection is its *uncertainty*. Terror is not always the effect of force, and an armament is not a victory. If you do not succeed, you are without resource: for, conciliation failing, force remains; but, force failing, no further hope of reconciliation is left. Power and authority are sometimes bought by kindness; but they can never be begged as alms by an impoverished and defeated violence.

A further objection to force is, that you *impair the object* by your very endeavors to preserve it. The thing you fought for is not the thing which you recover, but depreciated, sunk, wasted, and consumed in the contest. Nothing less will content me than *whole America*. I do not choose to consume its strength along with our own; because in all parts it is the British strength that I consume. I do not choose to be caught by a foreign enemy at the end of this exhausting conflict, and still less in the midst of it. I may escape, but I can make no insurance against such an event. Let me add, that I do not choose wholly to break the American spirit; because it is the spirit that has made the country.

Lastly, we have no sort of *experience* in favor of force as an instrument in the rule of our colonies. Their growth and their utility has been owing to methods altogether different. Our ancient indulgence has been said to be pursued to a fault. It may be so; but we know, if feeling is evidence, that our fault was more tolerable than our attempt to mend it, and our sin far more salutary than our penitence.

These, Sir, are my reasons for not entertaining that high opinion of untried force by which many gentlemen, for whose sentiments in other particulars I have great respect, seem to be so greatly captivated. But there is still behind a third consideration concerning this object, which serves to determine my opinion on the sort of policy which ought to be pursued in the management of America, even more than its population and its commerce: I mean its *temper and character*.

In this character of the Americans a love of freedom is the predominating feature which marks and distinguishes the whole: and as an ardent is always a jealous affection, your colonies become suspicious, restive, and untractable, whenever they see the least attempt to wrest from them by force, or shuffle from them by chicane, what they think the only advantage worth living for. This fierce spirit of liberty is stronger in the English colonies, probably, than in any other people of the earth, and this from a great variety of powerful causes; which, to understand the true temper of their minds, and the direction which this spirit takes, it will not be amiss to lay open somewhat more largely.

First, the people of the colonies are descendants of Englishmen. England, Sir, is a nation which still, I hope, respects, and formerly adored, her freedom. The colonists emigrated from you when this part of your character was most predominant; and they took this bias and direction the moment they parted from your hands. They are therefore not only devoted to liberty, but to liberty according to English ideas and on English principles. Abstract liberty, like other mere abstractions, is not to be found. Liberty inheres in some sensible object; and every nation has formed to itself some favorite point, which by way of eminence becomes the criterion of their happiness. It happened, you know, Sir, that the great contests for freedom in this country were from the earliest times chiefly upon the question of taxing. Most of the contests in the ancient commonwealths turned primarily on the right of election of magistrates, or on the balance among the several orders of the state. The question of money was not with them so immediate. But in England it was otherwise. On this point of taxes the ablest pens and most eloquent tongues have been exercised, the greatest spirits have acted and suffered. In order to give the fullest satisfaction concerning the importance of this point, it was not only necessary for those who in argument defended the excellence of the English Constitution to insist on this privilege of granting money as a dry point of fact, and to prove that the right had been acknowledged in ancient parchments and blind usages to reside in a certain body called an House of Commons: they went much further: they attempted to prove, and they succeeded, that in theory it ought to be so, from the particular nature of a House of Commons, as an immediate representative of the people, whether the old records had delivered this oracle or not. They took infinite pains to inculcate, as a fundamental principle, that in all monarchies the people must in effect themselves, mediately or immediately, possess the power of granting their own money, or no shadow of liberty could subsist. The colonies draw from you, as with their life-blood, these ideas and principles. Their love of liberty, as with you, fixed and attached on this specific point of taxing. Liberty might be safe or might be endangered in twenty other particulars without their being much pleased or alarmed. Here they felt its pulse; and as they found that beat, they thought themselves sick or sound. I do not say whether they were right or wrong in applying your general arguments to their own case. It is not easy, indeed, to make a monopoly of theorems and corollaries. The fact is, that they did thus apply those general arguments; and your mode of governing them, whether through lenity or indolence, through wisdom or mistake, confirmed them in the imagination, that they, as well as you, had an interest in these common principles.

They were further confirmed in this pleasing error by the form of their provincial legislative assemblies. Their governments are popular in an high degree: some are merely popular; in all, the popular representative is the most weighty; and this share of the people in their ordinary government never fails to inspire them with lofty sentiments, and with a strong aversion from whatever tends to deprive them of their chief importance.

If anything were wanting to this necessary operation of the form of government, religion would have given it a complete effect. Religion, always a principle of energy, in this new people is no way worn out or impaired; and their mode of professing it is also one main cause of this free spirit. The people are Protestants, and of that kind which is the most adverse to all implicit submission of mind and opinion. This is a persuasion not only favorable to liberty, but built upon it. I do not think, Sir, that the reason of this averseness in the dissenting churches from all that looks like absolute government is so much to be sought in their religious tenets as in their history. Every one knows that the Roman Catholic religion is at least coeval with most of the governments where it prevails, that it has generally gone hand in hand with them, and received great favor and every kind of support from authority. The Church of England, too, was formed from her cradle under the nursing care of regular government. But the dissenting interests have sprung up in direct opposition to all the ordinary powers of the world, and could justify that opposition only on a strong claim to natural liberty. Their very existence depended on the powerful and unremitted assertion of that claim. All Protestantism, even the most cold and passive, is a sort of dissent. But the religion most prevalent in our northern colonies is a refinement on the principle of resistance: it is the dissidence of dissent, and the protestantism of the Protestant religion. This religion, under a variety of denominations agreeing in nothing but in the communion of the spirit of liberty, is predominant in most of the northern provinces, where the Church of England, notwithstanding its legal rights, is in reality no more than a sort of private sect, not composing, most probably, the tenth of the people. The colonists left England when this spirit was high, and in the emigrants was the highest of all; and even that stream of foreigners which has been constantly flowing into these colonies has, for the greatest part, been composed of dissenters from the establishments of their several countries, and have brought with them a temper and character far from alien to that of the people with whom they mixed.

Sir, I can perceive, by their manner, that some gentlemen object to the latitude of this description, because in the southern colonies the Church of England forms a large body, and has a regular establishment. It is certainly true. There is, however, a circumstance attending these colonies, which, in my opinion, fully counterbalances this difference, and makes the spirit of liberty still more high and haughty than in those to the northward. It is, that in Virginia and the Carolinas they have a vast multitude of slaves. Where this is the case in any part of the world, those who are free are by far the most proud and jealous of their freedom. Freedom is to them not only an enjoyment, but a kind of rank and privilege. Not seeing there, that freedom, as in countries where it is a common blessing, and as broad and general as the air, may be united with much abject toil, with great misery, with all the exterior of servitude, liberty looks, amongst them, like something that is more noble and liberal. I do not mean, Sir, to commend the superior morality of this sentiment, which has at least as much pride as virtue in it; but I cannot alter the nature of man. The fact is so; and these people of the southern colonies are much more strongly, and with an higher and more stubborn spirit, attached to liberty, than those to the northward. Such were all the ancient commonwealths; such were our Gothic ancestors; such in our days were the Poles; and such will be all masters of slaves, who are not slaves themselves. In such a people, the haughtiness of domination combines with the spirit of freedom, fortifies it, and renders it invincible.

Permit me, Sir, to add another circumstance in our colonies, which contributes no mean part towards the growth and effect of this untractable spirit: I mean their education. In no country, perhaps, in the world is the law so general a study. The profession itself is numerous and powerful, and in most provinces it takes the lead. The greater number of the deputies sent to the Congress were lawyers. But all who read, and most do read, endeavor to obtain some smattering in that science. I have been told by an eminent bookseller, that in no branch of his business, after tracts of popular devotion, were so many books as those on the law exported to the plantations. The colonists have now fallen into the way of printing them for their own use. I hear that they have sold nearly as many of Blackstone's "Commentaries" in America as in England. General Gage marks out this disposition very particularly in a letter on your table. He states, that all the people in his government are lawyers, or smatterers in law,—and that in Boston they have been enabled, by successful chicane, wholly to evade many parts of one of your capital penal constitutions. The smartness of debate will say, that this knowledge ought to teach them more clearly the rights of legislature, their obligations to obedience, and the penalties of rebellion. All this is mighty well. But my honorable and learned friend [7] on the floor, who condescends to mark what I say for animadversion, will disdain that ground. He has heard, as well as I, that, when great honors and great emoluments do not win over this knowledge to the service of the state, it is a formidable adversary to government. If the spirit be not tamed and broken by these happy methods, it is stubborn and litigious. *Abeunt studia in mores.* [8] This study renders men acute, inquisitive, dexterous, prompt in attack, ready in defence, full of resources. In other countries, the people, more simple, and of a less mercurial cast, judge of an ill principle in government only by an actual grievance; here they anticipate the evil, and judge of the pressure of the grievance by the badness of the principle. They augur mis-

---

[7] The Attorney-General.
[8] Ovid, *Heroid.*, Ep. XV. 83.

government at a distance, and snuff the approach of tyranny in every tainted breeze.

The last cause of this disobedient spirit in the colonies is hardly less powerful than the rest, as it is not merely moral, but laid deep in the natural constitution of things. Three thousand miles of ocean lie between you and them. No contrivance can prevent the effect of this distance in weakening government. Seas roll, and months pass, between the order and the execution; and the want of a speedy explanation of a single point is enough to defeat an whole system. You have, indeed, winged ministers of vengeance, who carry your bolts in their pounces to the remotest verge of the sea: but there a power steps in, that limits the arrogance of raging passions and furious elements, and says, "So far shalt thou go, and no farther." Who are you, that should fret and rage, and bite the chains of Nature? Nothing worse happens to you than does to all nations who have extensive empire; and it happens in all the forms into which empire can be thrown. In large bodies, the circulation of power must be less vigorous at the extremities. Nature has said it. The Turk cannot govern Egypt, and Arabia, and Kurdistan, as he governs Thrace; nor has he the same dominion in Crimea and Algiers which he has at Brusa and Smyrna. Despotism itself is obliged to truck and huckster. The Sultan gets such obedience as he can. He governs with a loose rein, that he may govern at all; and the whole of the force and vigor of his authority in his centre is derived from a prudent relaxation in all his borders. Spain, in her provinces, is perhaps not so well obeyed as you are in yours. She complies, too; she submits; she watches times. This is the immutable condition, the eternal law, of extensive and detached empire.

Then, Sir, from these six capital sources, of descent, of form of government, of religion in the northern provinces, of manners in the southern, of education, of the remoteness of situation from the first mover of government,—from all these causes a fierce spirit of liberty has grown up. It has grown with the growth of the people in your colonies, and increased with the increase of their wealth: a spirit, that, unhappily meeting with an exercise of power in England, which, however lawful, is not reconcilable to any ideas of liberty, much less with theirs, has kindled this flame that is ready to consume us.

I do not mean to commend either the spirit in this excess, or the moral causes which produce it. Perhaps a more smooth and accommodating spirit of freedom in them would be more acceptable to us. Perhaps ideas of liberty might be desired more reconcilable with an arbitrary and boundless authority. Perhaps we might wish the colonists to be persuaded that their liberty is more secure when held in trust for them by us (as their guardians during a perpetual minority) than with any part of it in their own hands. But the question is not, whether their spirit deserves praise or blame,—what, in the name of God, shall we do with it? You have before you the object, such as it is,—with all its glories, with all its imperfections on its head. You see the magnitude, the importance, the temper, the habits, the disorders. By all these considerations we are strongly urged to determine something concerning it. We are called upon to fix some rule and line for our future conduct, which may give a little stability to our politics, and prevent the return of such unhappy deliberations as the present. Every such return will bring the matter before us in a still more untractable form. For what astonishing and incredible things have we not seen already! What monsters have not been generated from this unnatural contention! Whilst every principle of authority and resistance has been pushed, upon both sides, as far as it would go, there is nothing so solid and certain, either in reasoning or in practice, that has not been shaken. Until very lately, all authority in America seemed to be nothing but an emanation from yours. Even the popular part of the colony constitution derived all its activity, and its first vital movement, from the pleasure of the crown. We thought, Sir, that the utmost which the discontented colonists could do was to disturb authority; we never dreamt they could of themselves supply it, knowing in general what an operose business it is to establish a government absolutely new. But having, for our purposes in this contention, resolved that none but an obedient assembly should sit, the humors of the people there, finding all passage through the legal channel stopped, with great violence broke out another way. Some provinces have tried their experiment, as we have tried ours; and theirs has succeeded. They have formed a government sufficient for its purposes, without the bustle of a revolution, or the troublesome formality of an election. Evident necessity and tacit consent have done the business in an instant. So well they have done it, that Lord Dunmore (the account is among the fragments on your table) tells you that the new institution is infinitely better obeyed than the ancient government ever was in its most fortunate periods. Obedience is what makes government, and not the names by which it is called: not the name of Governor, as formerly, or Committee, as at present. This new government has originated directly from the people, and was not transmitted through any of the ordinary artificial media of a positive constitution. It was not a manufacture ready formed, and transmitted to them in that condition from England. The evil arising from hence is this: that the colonists having once found the possibility of enjoying the advantages of order in the midst of a struggle for liberty, such struggles will not henceforward seem so terrible to the settled and sober part of mankind as they had appeared before the trial.

Pursuing the same plan of punishing by the denial of the exercise of government to still greater lengths, we wholly abrogated the ancient government of Massachusetts. We were confident that the first feeling, if not the very prospect of anarchy, would instantly enforce a complete submission. The experiment was tried. A new, strange, unexpected face of things appeared. Anarchy is found tolerable. A vast province has now subsisted, and subsisted in a considerable degree of health and vigor, for near a twelvemonth, without governor, without public council, without judges, without executive magistrates. How long it will continue in this state, or what may arise out of this unheard-of situation, how can the wisest of us conjecture? Our late experience has taught us that many of those fundamental principles formerly believed infallible are either not of the importance they were imagined to be, or that we have not at all adverted to some other far more important and far more powerful principles which entirely overrule those we had considered as omnipotent. I am much against any further experiments which tend to put to the proof any more of these allowed opinions which contribute so much to the public tranquillity. In effect, we suffer as much at home by this loosening of all ties, and this concussion of all established opinions, as we do abroad. For, in order to prove that the Americans have no right to their liberties, we are every day endeavoring to subvert the maxims which preserve the whole spirit of our own. To prove that the Americans ought not to be free, we are obliged to depreciate the value of freedom itself; and we never seem to gain a paltry advantage over them in debate, without attacking some of those principles, or deriding some of those feelings, for which our ancestors have shed their blood.

But, Sir, in wishing to put an end to pernicious experiments, I do not mean to preclude the fullest inquiry. Far from it. Far from deciding on a sudden or partial view, I would patiently go round and round the subject, and survey it minutely in every possible aspect. Sir, if I were capable of engaging you to an equal attention, I would state, that, as far as I am capable of discerning, there are but three ways of proceeding relative to this stubborn spirit which prevails in your colonies and disturbs your government. These are,—to change that spirit, as inconvenient, by removing the causes,—to prosecute it, as criminal,—or to comply with it, as necessary. I would not be guilty of an imperfect enumeration; I can think of but these three. Another has, indeed been started,—that of giving up the colonies; but it met so slight a reception that I do not think myself obliged to dwell a great while upon it. It is nothing but a little sally of anger, like the frowardness of peevish children, who, when they cannot get all they would have, are resolved to take nothing.

The first of these plans—to change the spirit, as inconvenient, by removing the causes—I think is the most like a systematic proceeding. It is radical in its principle; but it is attended with great difficulties: some of them little short, as I conceive, of impossibilities. This will appear by examining into the plans which have been proposed.

As the growing population of the colonies is evidently one cause of their resistance, it was last session mentioned in both Houses, by men of weight, and received not without applause, that, in order to check this evil, it would be proper for the crown to make no further grants of land. But to this scheme there are two objections. The first, that there is already so much unsettled land in private hands as to afford room for an immense future population, although the crown not only withheld its grants, but annihilated its soil. If this be the case, then the only effect of this avarice of desolation, this hoarding of a royal wilderness, would be to raise the value of the possessions in the hands of the great private monopolists, without any adequate check to the growing and alarming mischief of population.

But if you stopped your grants, what would be the consequence? The people would occupy without grants. They have already so occupied in many places. You cannot station garrisons in every part of these deserts. If you drive the people from one place, they will carry on their annual tillage, and remove with their flocks and herds to another. Many of the people in the back settlements are already little attached to particular situations. Already they have topped the Appalachian mountains. From thence they behold before them an immense plain, one vast, rich, level meadow: a square of five hundred miles. Over this they would wander without a possibility of restraint; they would change their manners with the habits of their life; would soon forget a government by which they were disowned; would become hordes of English Tartars, and, pouring down upon your unfortified frontiers a fierce and irresistible cavalry, become masters of your governors and your counsellors, your collectors and comptrollers, and of all the slaves that adhered to them. Such would, and, in no long time, must be, the effect of attempting to forbid as a crime, and to suppress as an evil, the command and blessing of Providence, "Increase and multiply." Such would be the happy result of an endeavor to keep as a lair of wild beasts that earth which God by an express charter has given to the children of men. Far different, and surely much wiser, has been our policy hitherto. Hitherto we have invited our people, by every kind of bounty, to fixed establishments. We have invited the husbandman to look to authority for his title. We have taught him piously to believe in the mysterious virtue of wax and parchment. We have thrown each tract of land, as it was peopled, into districts, that the ruling power should never be wholly out of sight. We have settled all we could; and we have carefully attended every settlement with government.

Adhering, Sir, as I do, to this policy, as well as for the reasons I have just given, I think this new project of hedging in population to be neither prudent nor practicable.

To impoverish the colonies in general, and in particular to arrest the noble course of their marine enterprises, would be a more easy task. I freely confess it. We have shown a disposition to a system of this kind,—a disposition even to continue the restraint after the offence,—looking on ourselves as rivals to our colonies, and persuaded that of course we must gain all that they shall lose. Much mischief we may certainly do. The power inadequate to all other things is often more than sufficient for this. I do not look on the direct and immediate power of the colonies to resist our violence as very formidable. In this, however, I may be mistaken. But when I consider that we have colonies for no purpose but to be serviceable to us, it seems to my poor understanding a little preposterous to make them unserviceable, in order to keep them obedient. It is, in truth, nothing more than the old, and, as I thought, exploded problem of tyranny, which proposes to beggar its subjects into submission. But remember, when you have completed your system of impoverishment, that Nature still proceeds in her ordinary course; that discontent will increase with misery; and that there are critical moments in the fortune of all states, when they who are too weak to contribute to your prosperity may be strong enough to complete your ruin. *Spoliatis arma supersunt.*[9]

The temper and character which prevail in our colonies are, I am afraid, unalterable by any human art. We cannot, I fear, falsify the pedigree of this fierce people, and persuade them that they are not sprung from a nation in whose veins the blood of freedom circulates. The language in which they would hear you tell them this tale would detect the imposition; your speech would betray you. An Englishman is the unfittest person on earth to argue another Englishman into slavery.

I think it is nearly as little in our power to change their republican religion as their free descent, or to substitute the Roman Catholic as a penalty, or the Church of England as an improvement. The mode of inquisition and dragooning is going out of fashion in the Old World, and I should not confide much to their efficacy in the New. The education of

---

[9] Juvenal, VIII. 124.

the Americans is also on the same unalterable bottom with their religion. You cannot persuade them to burn their books of curious science,[10] to banish their lawyers from their courts of law, or to quench the lights of their assemblies by refusing to choose those persons who are best read in their privileges. It would be no less impracticable to think of wholly annihilating the popular assemblies in which these lawyers sit. The army, by which we must govern in their place, would be far more chargeable to us, not quite so effectual, and perhaps, in the end, full as difficult to be kept in obedience.

With regard to the high aristocratic spirit of Virginia and the southern colonies, it has been proposed, I know, to reduce it by declaring a general enfranchisement of their slaves. This project has had its advocates and panegyrists; yet I never could argue myself into any opinion of it. Slaves are often much attached to their masters. A general wild offer of liberty would not always be accepted. History furnishes few instances of it. It is sometimes as hard to persuade slaves to be free as it is to compel freemen to be slaves; and in this auspicious scheme we should have both these pleasing tasks on our hands at once. But when we talk of enfranchisement, do we not perceive that the American master may enfranchise, too, and arm servile hands in defence of freedom?—a measure to which other people have had recourse more than once, and not without success, in a desperate situation of their affairs.

Slaves as these unfortunate black people are, and dull as all men are from slavery, must they not a little suspect the offer of freedom from that very nation which has sold them to their present masters,—from that nation, one of whose causes of quarrel with those masters is their refusal to deal any more in that inhuman traffic? An offer of freedom from England would come rather oddly, shipped to them in an African vessel, which is refused an entry into the ports of

---

[10] Acts, XIX. 19.

Virginia or Carolina, with a cargo of three hundred Angola negroes. It would be curious to see the Guinea captain attempting at the same instant to publish his proclamation of liberty and to advertise his sale of slaves.

But let us suppose all these moral difficulties got over. The ocean remains. You cannot pump this dry; and as long as it continues in its present bed, so long all the causes which weaken authority by distance will continue.

> "Ye Gods! annihilate but space and time,
> And make two lovers happy," [11]

was a pious and passionate prayer,—but just as reasonable as many of the serious wishes of very grave and solemn politicians.

If, then, Sir, it seems almost desperate to think of any alternative course for changing the moral causes (and not quite easy to remove the natural) which produce prejudices irreconcilable to the late exercise of our authority, but that the spirit infallibly will continue, and, continuing, will produce such effects as now embarrass us,—the second mode under consideration is, to prosecute that spirit in its overt acts, as *criminal*.

At this proposition I must pause a moment. The thing seems a great deal too big for my ideas of jurisprudence. It should seem, to my way of conceiving such matters, that there is a very wide difference, in reason and policy, between the mode of proceeding on the irregular conduct of scattered individuals, or even of bands of men, who disturb order within the state, and the civil dissensions which may, from time to time, on great questions, agitate the several communities which compose a great empire. It looks to me to be narrow and pedantic to apply the ordinary ideas of criminal justice to this great public contest. I do not know the method of drawing up an indictment against an whole people. I cannot

---

[11] Martinus Scriblerus, "Art of Sinking in Poetry."

insult and ridicule the feelings of millions of my fellow-creatures as Sir Edward Coke insulted one excellent individual (Sir Walter Raleigh) at the bar. I am not ripe to pass sentence on the gravest public bodies, intrusted with magistracies of great authority and dignity, and charged with the safety of their fellow-citizens, upon the very same title that I am. I really think that for wise men this is not judicious, for sober men not decent, for minds tinctured with humanity not mild and merciful.

Perhaps, Sir, I am mistaken in my idea of an empire, as distinguished from a single state or kingdom. But my idea of it is this: that an empire is the aggregate of many states under one common head, whether this head be a monarch or a presiding republic. It does, in such constitutions, frequently happen (and nothing but the dismal, cold, dead uniformity of servitude can prevent its happening) that the subordinate parts have many local privileges and immunities. Between these privileges and the supreme common authority the line may be extremely nice. Of course disputes, often, too, very bitter disputes, and much ill blood, will arise. But though every privilege is an exemption (in the case) from the ordinary exercise of the supreme authority, it is no denial of it. The claim of a privilege seems rather, *ex vi termini,* to imply a superior power: for to talk of the privileges of a state or of a person who has no superior is hardly any better than speaking nonsense. Now in such unfortunate quarrels among the component parts of a great political union of communities, I can scarcely conceive anything more completely imprudent than for the head of the empire to insist, that if any privilege is pleaded against his will or his acts, that his whole authority is denied,—instantly to proclaim rebellion, to beat to arms, and to put the offending provinces under the ban. Will not this, Sir, very soon teach the provinces to make no distinctions on their part? Will it not teach them that the government against which a claim of liberty is tantamount to high treason is a government to which submission is equivalent to slavery? It may not always be quite convenient to impress dependent communities with such an idea.

We are, indeed, in all disputes with the colonies, by the necessity of things, the judge. It is true, Sir. But I confess that the character of judge in my own cause is a thing that frightens me. Instead of filling me with pride, I am exceedingly humbled by it. I cannot proceed with a stern, assured judicial confidence, until I find myself in something more like a judicial character. I must have these hesitations as long as I am compelled to recollect, that, in my little reading upon such contests as these, the sense of mankind has at least as often decided against the superior as the subordinate power. Sir, let me add, too, that the opinion of my having some abstract right in my favor would not put me much at my ease in passing sentence, unless I could be sure that there were no rights which, in their exercise under certain circumstances, were not the most odious of all wrongs and the most vexatious of all injustice. Sir, these considerations have great weight with me, when I find things so circumstanced that I see the same party at once a civil litigant against me in a point of right and a culprit before me, while I sit as criminal judge on acts of his whose moral quality is to be decided upon the merits of that very litigation. Men are every now and then put, by the complexity of human affairs, into strange situations; but justice is the same, let the judge be in what situation he will.

There is, Sir, also a circumstance which convinces me that this mode of criminal proceeding is not (at least in the present stage of our contest) altogether expedient,—which is nothing less than the conduct of those very persons who have seemed to adopt that mode, by lately declaring a rebellion in Massachusetts Bay, as they had formerly addressed to have traitors brought hither, under an act of Henry the Eighth, for trial. For, though rebellion is declared, it is not proceeded against as such; nor have any steps been taken towards the apprehension or conviction of any individual offender, either on our late or our former address; but modes of public coercion have been adopted, and such as have much more resemblance to a sort of qualified hostility towards an independent power than the punishment of rebellious subjects. All this seems rather inconsistent; but it shows how difficult it is to apply these juridical ideas to our present case.

In this situation, let us seriously and coolly ponder. What is it we have got by all our menaces, which have been many and ferocious? What advantage have we derived from the penal laws we have passed, and which, for the time, have been severe and numerous? What advances have we made towards our object, by the sending of a force, which, by land and sea, is no contemptible strength? Has the disorder abated? Nothing less.—When I see things in this situation, after such confident hopes, bold promises, and active exertions, I cannot, for my life, avoid a suspicion that the plan itself is not correctly right.

If, then, the removal of the causes of this spirit of American liberty be, for the greater part, or rather entirely, impracticable,—if the ideas of criminal process be inapplicable, or, if applicable, are in the highest degree inexpedient, what way yet remains? No way is open, but the third and last,—to comply with the American spirit as necessary, or, if you please, to submit to it as a necessary evil.

If we adopt this mode, if we mean to conciliate and concede, let us see of what nature the concession ought to be. To ascertain the nature of our concession, we must look at their complaint. The colonies complain that they have not the characteristic mark and seal of British freedom. They complain that they are taxed in a Parliament in which they are not represented. If you mean to satisfy them at all, you must satisfy them with regard to this complaint. If you mean to please any people, you must give them the boon which they ask,—not what you may think better for them, but of a kind totally different. Such an act may be a wise regulation, but it is no concession; whereas our present theme is the mode of giving satisfaction.

Sir, I think you must perceive that I am resolved this day to have nothing at all to do with the question of the right of taxation. Some gentlemen startle,—but it is true: I put it totally out of the question. It is less than nothing in my consideration. I do not indeed wonder, nor will you, Sir, that gentlemen of profound learning are fond of displaying it on this profound subject. But my consideration is narrow, confined, and wholly limited to the policy of the question. I do not examine whether the giving away a man's money be a power excepted and reserved out of the general trust of government, and how far all mankind, in all forms of polity, are entitled to an exercise of that right by the charter of Nature, —or whether, on the contrary, a right of taxation is necessarily involved in the general principle of legislation, and inseparable from the ordinary supreme power. These are deep questions, where great names militate against each other, where reason is perplexed, and an appeal to authorities only thickens the confusion: for high and reverend authorities lift up their heads on both sides, and there is no sure footing in the middle. This point is the *great Serbonian bog, betwixt Damiata and Mount Casius old, where armies whole have sunk.*[12] I do not intend to be overwhelmed in that bog, though in such respectable company. The question with me is, not whether you have a right to render your people miserable, but whether it is not your interest to make them happy. It is not what a lawyer tells me I *may* do, but what humanity, reason, and justice tell me I ought to do. Is a politic act the worse for being a generous one? Is no concession proper, but that which is made from your want of right to keep what you grant? Or does it lessen the grace or dignity of relaxing in the

---

[12] Paradise Lost, II. 592.

exercise of an odious claim, because you have your evidence-room full of titles, and your magazines stuffed with arms to enforce them? What signify all those titles and all those arms? Of what avail are they, when the reason of the thing tells me that the assertion of my title is the loss of my suit, and that I could do nothing but wound myself by the use of my own weapons?

Such is steadfastly my opinion of the absolute necessity of keeping up the concord of this empire by a unity of spirit, though in a diversity of operations, that, if I were sure the colonists had, at their leaving this country, sealed a regular compact of servitude, that they had solemnly abjured all the rights of citizens, that they had made a vow to renounce all ideas of liberty for them and their posterity to all generations, yet I should hold myself obliged to conform to the temper I found universally prevalent in my own day, and to govern two million of men, impatient of servitude, on the principles of freedom. I am not determining a point of law; I am restoring tranquillity: and the general character and situation of a people must determine what sort of government is fitted for them. That point nothing else can or ought to determine.

My idea, therefore, without considering whether we yield as matter of right or grant as matter of favor, is, *to admit the people of our colonies into an interest in the Constitution,* and, by recording that admission in the journals of Parliament, to give them as strong an assurance as the nature of the thing will admit that we mean forever to adhere to that solemn declaration of systematic indulgence.

Some years ago, the repeal of a revenue act, upon its understood principle, might have served to show that we intended an unconditional abatement of the exercise of a taxing power. Such a measure was then sufficient to remove all suspicion and to give perfect content. But unfortunate events since that time may make something further necessary,—and not more necessary for the satisfaction of the colonies than for the dignity and consistency of our own future proceedings.

I have taken a very incorrect measure of the disposition of the House, if this proposal in itself would be received with dislike. I think, Sir, we have few American financiers. But our misfortune is, we are too acute, we are too exquisite in our conjectures of the future, for men oppressed with such great and present evils. The more moderate among the opposers of Parliamentary concession freely confess that they hope no good from taxation; but they apprehend the colonists have further views, and if this point were conceded, they would instantly attack the trade laws. These gentlemen are convinced that this was the intention from the beginning, and the quarrel of the Americans with taxation was no more than a cloak and cover to this design. Such has been the language even of a gentleman of real moderation, and of a natural temper well adjusted to fair and equal government. I am, however, Sir, not a little surprised at this kind of discourse, whenever I hear it; and I am the more surprised on account of the arguments which I constantly find in company with it, and which are often urged from the same mouths and on the same day.

For instance, when we allege that it is against reason to tax a people under so many restraints in trade as the Americans, the noble lord [13] in the blue riband shall tell you that the restraints on trade are futile and useless, of no advantage to us, and of no burden to those on whom they are imposed,—that the trade to America is not secured by the Acts of Navigation, but by the natural and irresistible advantage of a commercial preference.

Such is the merit of the trade laws in this posture of the debate. But when strong internal circumstances are urged against the taxes,—when the scheme is dissected,—when

---

[13] Lord North.

experience and the nature of things are brought to prove, and do prove, the utter impossibility of obtaining an effective revenue from the colonies,—when these things are pressed, or rather press themselves, so as to drive the advocates of colony taxes to a clear admission of the futility of the scheme,—then, Sir, the sleeping trade laws revive from their trance, and this useless taxation is to be kept sacred, not for its own sake, but as a counter-guard and security of the laws of trade.

Then, Sir, you keep up revenue laws which are mischievous in order to preserve trade laws that are useless. Such is the wisdom of our plan in both its members. They are separately given up as of no value; and yet one is always to be defended for the sake of the other. But I cannot agree with the noble lord, nor with the pamphlet from whence he seems to have borrowed these ideas concerning the inutility of the trade laws. For, without idolizing them, I am sure they are still, in many ways, of great use to us; and in former times they have been of the greatest. They do confine, and they do greatly narrow, the market for the Americans. But my perfect conviction of this does not help me in the least to discern how the revenue laws form any security whatsoever to the commercial regulations,—or that these commercial regulations are the true ground of the quarrel,—or that the giving way, in any one instance, of authority is to lose all that may remain unconceded.

One fact is clear and indisputable: the public and avowed origin of this quarrel was on taxation. This quarrel has, indeed, brought on new disputes on new questions, but certainly the least bitter, and the fewest of all, on the trade laws. To judge which of the two be the real, radical cause of quarrel, we have to see whether the commercial dispute did, in order of time, precede the dispute on taxation. There is not a shadow of evidence for it. Next, to enable us to judge whether at this moment a dislike to the trade laws be the real cause of quarrel, it is absolutely necessary to put the taxes out of the question by a repeal. See how the Americans act in this position, and then you will be able to discern correctly what is the true object of the controversy, or whether any controversy at all will remain. Unless you consent to remove this cause of difference, it is impossible, with decency, to assert that the dispute is not upon what it is avowed to be. And I would, Sir, recommend to your serious consideration, whether it be prudent to form a rule for punishing people, not on their own acts, but on your conjectures. Surely it is preposterous, at the very best. It is not justifying your anger by their misconduct, but it is converting your ill-will into their delinquency.

But the colonies will go further.—Alas! alas! when will this speculating against fact and reason end? What will quiet these panic fears which we entertain of the hostile effect of a conciliatory conduct? Is it true that no case can exist in which it is proper for the sovereign to accede to the desires of his discontented subjects? Is there anything peculiar in this case, to make a rule for itself? Is all authority of course lost, when it is not pushed to the extreme? Is it a certain maxim, that, the fewer causes of dissatisfaction are left by government, the more the subject will be inclined to resist and rebel?

All these objections being in fact no more than suspicions, conjectures, divinations, formed in defiance of fact and experience, they did not, Sir, discourage me from entertaining the idea of a conciliatory concession, founded on the principles which I have just stated.

In forming a plan for this purpose, I endeavored to put myself in that frame of mind which was the most natural and the most reasonable, and which was certainly the most probable means of securing me from all error. I set out with a perfect distrust of my own abilities, a total renunciation of every speculation of my own, and with a profound reverence for the wisdom of our ancestors, who have left us the inheritance of so happy a Constitution and so flourishing an empire, and, what is a thousand times more valuable, the treasury of the maxims and principles which formed the one and obtained the other.

During the reigns of the kings of Spain of the Austrian family, whenever they were at a loss in the Spanish councils, it was common for their statesmen to say that they ought to consult the genius of Philip the Second. The genius of Philip the Second might mislead them; and the issue of their affairs showed that they had not chosen the most perfect standard. But, Sir, I am sure that I shall not be misled, when, in a case of constitutional difficulty, I consult the genius of the English Constitution. Consulting at that oracle, (it was with all due humility and piety,) I found four capital examples in a similar case before me: those of Ireland, Wales, Chester, and Durham.

Ireland, before the English conquest, though never governed by a despotic power, had no Parliament. How far the English Parliament itself was at that time modelled according to the present form is disputed among antiquarians. But we have all the reason in the world to be assured, that a form of Parliament, such as England then enjoyed, she instantly communicated to Ireland; and we are equally sure that almost every successive improvement in constitutional liberty, as fast as it was made here, was transmitted thither. The feudal baronage, and the feudal knighthood, the roots of our primitive Constitution, were early transplanted into that soil, and grew and flourished there. Magna Charta, if it did not give us originally the House of Commons, gave us at least an House of Commons of weight and consequence. But your ancestors did not churlishly sit down alone to the feast of Magna Charta. Ireland was made immediately a partaker. This benefit of English laws and liberties, I confess, was not at first extended to *all* Ireland. Mark the consequence. English authority and English liberty had exactly the same boundaries. Your standard could never be advanced an inch before your privileges. Sir John Davies [14] shows beyond a doubt, that the refusal of a general communication of these rights was the true cause why Ireland was five hundred years in subduing; and after the vain projects of a military government, attempted in the reign of Queen Elizabeth, it was soon discovered that nothing could make that country English, in civility and allegiance, but your laws and your forms of legislature. It was not English arms, but the English Constitution, that conquered Ireland. From that time, Ireland has ever had a general Parliament, as she had before a partial Parliament. You changed the people, you altered the religion, but you never touched the form or the vital substance of free government in that kingdom. You deposed kings; you restored them; you altered the succession to theirs, as well as to your own crown; but you never altered their Constitution, the principle of which was respected by usurpation, restored with the restoration of monarchy, and established, I trust, forever by the glorious Revolution. This has made Ireland the great and flourishing kingdom that it is, and, from a disgrace and a burden intolerable to this nation, has rendered her a principal part of our strength and ornament. This country cannot be said to have ever formally taxed her. The irregular things done in the confusion of mighty troubles, and on the hinge of great revolutions, even if all were done that is said to have been done, form no example. If they have any effect in argument, they make an exception to prove the rule. None of your own liberties could stand a moment, if the casual deviations from them, at such times, were suffered to be used as proofs of their nullity. By the lucrative amount of such casual breaches in the Constitution, judge what the

---

[14] Who wrote "Discoverie of the true Causes why Ireland was never entirely subdued until the beginning of his Majestie's happy reign" (1604).

stated and fixed rule of supply has been in that kingdom. Your Irish pensioners would starve, if they had no other fund to live on than taxes granted by English authority. Turn your eyes to those popular grants from whence all your great supplies are come, and learn to respect that only source of public wealth in the British empire.

My next example is Wales. This country was said to be reduced by Henry the Third. It was said more truly to be so by Edward the First. But though then conquered, it was not looked upon as any part of the realm of England. Its old Constitution, whatever that might have been, was destroyed; and no good one was substituted in its place. The care of that tract was put into the hands of Lords Marchers: a form of government of a very singular kind; a strange, hetero-geneous monster, something between hostility and govern-ment: perhaps it has a sort of resemblance, according to the modes of those times, to that of commander-in-chief at pres-ent, to whom all civil power is granted as secondary. The manners of the Welsh nation followed the genius of the government: the people were ferocious, restive, savage, and uncultivated; sometimes composed, never pacified. Wales, within itself, was in perpetual disorder; and it kept the frontier of England in perpetual alarm. Benefits from it to the state there were none. Wales was only known to England by incursion and invasion.

Sir, during that state of things, Parliament was not idle. They attempted to subdue the fierce spirit of the Welsh by all sorts of rigorous laws. They prohibited by statute the sending all sorts of arms into Wales, as you prohibit by proclamation (with something more of doubt on the legality) the sending arms to America. They disarmed the Welsh by statute, as you attempted (but still with more question on the legality) to disarm New England by an instruction. They made an act to drag offenders from Wales into England for trial, as you have done (but with more hardship) with regard to America. By another act, where one of the parties was an Englishman, they ordained that his trial should be always by English. They made acts to restrain trade, as you do; and they prevented the Welsh from the use of fairs and markets, as you do the Americans from fisheries and foreign ports. In short, when the statute-book was not quite so much swelled as it is now, you find no less than fifteen acts of penal regulation on the subject of Wales.

Here we rub our hands,—A fine body of precedents for the authority of Parliament and the use of it!—I admit it fully; and pray add likewise to these precedents, that all the while Wales rid this kingdom like an *incubus;* that it was an unprofitable and oppressive burden; and that an Englishman travelling in that country could not go six yards from the highroad without being murdered.

The march of the human mind is slow. Sir, it was not until after two hundred years discovered, that, by an eternal law, Providence had decreed vexation to violence, and poverty to rapine. Your ancestors did, however, at length open their eyes to the ill husbandry of injustice. They found that the tyranny of a free people could of all tyrannies the least be endured, and that laws made against an whole nation were not the most effectual methods for securing its obedience. Accordingly, in the twenty-seventh year of Henry the Eighth the course was entirely altered. With a preamble stating the entire and perfect rights of the crown of England, it gave to the Welsh all the rights and privileges of English subjects. A political order was established; the military power gave way to the civil; the marches were turned into counties. But that a nation should have a right to English liberties, and yet no share at all in the fundamental security of these liberties,— the grant of their own property,—seemed a thing so incongruous, that eight years after, that is, in the thirty-fifth of that reign, a complete and not ill-proportioned representation by counties and boroughs was bestowed upon Wales by act of Parliament. From that moment, as by a charm, the tumults subsided; obedience was restored; peace, order, and civilization followed in the train of liberty. When the day-star of the English Constitution had arisen in their hearts, all was harmony within and without:—

> Simul alba nautis
> Stella refulsit,
> Defluit saxis agitatus humor,
> Concidunt venti, fugiuntque nubes,
> Et minax (quod sic voluere) ponto
> Unda recumbit.[15]

The very same year the County Palatine of Chester received the same relief from its oppressions, and the same remedy to its disorders. Before this time Chester was little less distempered than Wales. The inhabitants, without rights themselves, were the fittest to destroy the rights of others; and from thence Richard the Second drew the standing army of archers with which for a time he oppressed England. The people of Chester applied to Parliament in a petition penned as I shall read to you.

"To the king our sovereign lord, in most humble wise shown unto your most excellent Majesty, the inhabitants of your Grace's County Palatine of Chester: That where the said County Palatine of Chester is and hath been alway hitherto exempt, excluded, and separated out and from your high court of Parliament, to have any knights and burgesses within the said court; by reason whereof the said inhabitants have hitherto sustained manifold disherisons, losses, and damages, as well in their lands, goods, and bodies, as in the good, civil, and politic governance and maintenance of the common wealth of their said country: And forasmuch as the

---

[15] Horace, *Odes*, I. 12. 27.

said inhabitants have always hitherto been bound by the acts and statutes made and ordained by your said Highness, and your most noble progenitors, by authority of the said court, as far forth as other counties, cities, and boroughs have been, that have had their knights and burgesses within your said court of Parliament, and yet have had neither knight ne burgess there for the said County Palatine; the said inhabitants, for lack thereof, have been oftentimes touched and grieved with acts and statutes made within the said court, as well derogatory unto the most ancient jurisdictions, liberties, and privileges of your said County Palatine, as prejudicial unto the common wealth, quietness, rest, and peace of your Grace's most bounden subjects inhabiting within the same."

What did Parliament with this audacious address?—Reject it as a libel? Treat it as an affront to government? Spurn it as a derogation from the rights of legislature? Did they toss it over the table? Did they burn it by the hands of the common hangman?—They took the petition of grievance, all rugged as it was, without softening or temperament, unpurged of the original bitterness and indignation of complaint; they made it the very preamble to their act of redress, and consecrated its principle to all ages in the sanctuary of legislation.

Here is my third example. It was attended with the success of the two former. Chester, civilized as well as Wales, has demonstrated that freedom, and not servitude, is the cure of anarchy; as religion, and not atheism, is the true remedy for superstition. Sir, this pattern of Chester was followed in the reign of Charles the Second with regard to the County Palatine of Durham, which is my fourth example. This county had long lain out of the pale of free legislation. So scrupulously was the example of Chester followed, that the style of the preamble is nearly the same with that of the Chester act; and, without affecting the abstract extent of the authority of Parliament, it recognizes the equity of not suffering any considerable district, in which the British subjects may act as a body, to be taxed without their own voice in the grant.

Now if the doctrines of policy contained in these preambles, and the force of these examples in the acts of Parliament, avail anything, what can be said against applying them with regard to America? Are not the people of America as much Englishmen as the Welsh? The preamble of the act of Henry the Eighth says, the Welsh speak a language no way resembling that of his Majesty's English subjects. Are the Americans not as numerous? If we may trust the learned and accurate Judge Barrington's account of North Wales, and take that as a standard to measure the rest, there is no comparison. The people cannot amount to above 200,000: not a tenth part of the number in the colonies. Is America in rebellion? Wales was hardly ever free from it. Have you attempted to govern America by penal statutes? You made fifteen for Wales. But your legislative authority is perfect with regard to America: was it less perfect in Wales, Chester, and Durham? But America is virtually represented. What! does the electric force of virtual representation more easily pass over the Atlantic than pervade Wales, which lies in your neighborhood? or than Chester and Durham, surrounded by abundance of representation that is actual and palpable? But, Sir, your ancestors thought this sort of virtual representation, however ample, to be totally insufficient for the freedom of the inhabitants of territories that are so near, and comparatively so inconsiderable. How, then, can I think it sufficient for those which are infinitely greater, and infinitely more remote?

You will now, Sir, perhaps imagine that I am on the point of proposing to you a scheme for a representation of the colonies in Parliament. Perhaps I might be inclined to entertain some such thought; but a great flood stops me .in my course. *Opposuit Natura.*[16] I cannot remove the eternal barriers of the creation. The thing, in that mode, I do not know to be possible. As I meddle with no theory, I do not absolutely assert the impracticability of such a representation; but I do not see my way to it; and those who have been more confident have not been more successful. However, the arm of public benevolence is not shortened; and there are often several means to the same end. What Nature has disjoined in one way wisdom may unite in another. When we cannot give the benefit as we would wish, let us not refuse it altogether. If we cannot give the principal, let us find a substitute. But how? where? what substitute?

Fortunately, I am not obliged, for the ways and means of this substitute, to tax my own unproductive invention. I am not even obliged to go to the rich treasury of the fertile framers of imaginary commonwealths: not to the Republic of Plato, not to the Utopia of More, not to the Oceana of Harrington. It is before me,—it is at my feet,—

> "And the rude swain
> Treads daily on it with his clouted shoon." [17]

I only wish you to recognize, for the theory, the ancient constitutional policy of this kingdom with regard to representation, as that policy has been declared in acts of Parliament,—and as to the practice, to return to that mode which an uniform experience has marked out to you as best, and in which you walked with security, advantage, and honor, until the year 1763.

My resolutions, therefore, mean to establish the equity and justice of a taxation of America by *grant,* and not by *imposition;* to mark the *legal competency* of the colony assemblies for the support of their government in peace, and

---

[16] Juvenal, X. 152.
[17] Milton, *Comus,* I. 683.

for public aids in time of war; to acknowledge that this legal competency has had *a dutiful and beneficial exercise,* and that experience has shown *the benefit of their grants,* and *the futility of Parliamentary taxation, as a method of supply.*

These solid truths compose six fundamental propositions. There are three more resolutions corollary to these. If you admit the first set, you can hardly reject the others. But if you admit the first, I shall be far from solicitous whether you accept or refuse the last. I think these six massive pillars will be of strength sufficient to support the temple of British concord. I have no more doubt than I entertain of my existence, that, if you admitted these, you would command an immediate peace, and, with but tolerable future management, a lasting obedience in America. I am not arrogant in this confident assurance. The propositions are all mere matters of fact; and if they are such facts as draw irresistible conclusions even in the stating, this is the power of truth, and not any management of mine.

Sir, I shall open the whole plan to you together, with such observations on the motions as may tend to illustrate them, where they may want explanation.

The first is a resolution,—"That the colonies and plantations of Great Britain in North America, consisting of fourteen separate governments, and containing two millions and upwards of free inhabitants, have not had the liberty and privilege of electing and sending any knights and burgesses, or others, to represent them in the high court of Parliament."

This is a plain matter of fact, necessary to be laid down, and (excepting the description) it is laid down in the language of the Constitution; it is taken nearly *verbatim* from acts of Parliament.

The second is like unto the first,—"That the said colonies and plantations have been made liable to, and bounden by, several subsidies, payments, rates, and taxes, given and granted by Parliament, though the said colonies and plantations have not their knights and burgesses in the said high court of Parliament, of their own election, to represent the condition of their country; by lack whereof they have been oftentimes touched and grieved by subsidies, given, granted, and assented to, in the said court, in a manner prejudicial to the common wealth, quietness, rest, and peace of the subjects inhabiting within the same."

Is this description too hot or too cold, too strong or too weak? Does it arrogate too much to the supreme legislature? Does it lean too much to the claims of the people? If it runs into any of these errors, the fault is not mine. It is the language of your own ancient acts of Parliament.

> Non meus hic sermo, sed quæ præcepit Ofellus
> Rusticus, abnormis sapiens.[18]

It is the genuine produce of the ancient, rustic, manly, home-bred sense of this country. I did not dare to rub off a particle of the venerable rust that rather adorns and preserves than destroys the metal. It would be a profanation to touch with a tool the stones which construct the sacred altar of peace. I would not violate with modern polish the ingenuous and noble roughness of these truly constitutional materials. Above all things, I was resolved not to be guilty of tampering,—the odious vice of restless and unstable minds. I put my foot in the tracks of our forefathers, where I can neither wander nor stumble. Determining to fix articles of peace, I was resolved not to be wise beyond what was written; I was resolved to use nothing else than the form of sound words, to let others abound in their own sense, and carefully to abstain from all expressions of my own. What the law has said, I say. In all things else I am silent. I have no organ but for her words. This, if it be not ingenious, I am sure is safe.

There are, indeed, words expressive of grievance in this

---

[18] Horace, *Serm.*, II. 2. 3.

second resolution, which those who are resolved always to be in the right will deny to contain matter of fact, as applied to the present case; although Parliament thought them true with regard to the Counties of Chester and Durham. They will deny that the Americans were ever "touched and grieved" with the taxes. If they consider nothing in taxes but their weight as pecuniary impositions, there might be some pretence for this denial. But men may be sorely touched and deeply grieved in their privileges, as well as in their purses Men may lose little in property by the act which takes away all their freedom. When a man is robbed of a trifle on the highway, it is not the twopence lost that constitutes the capital outrage. This is not confined to privileges. Even ancient indulgences withdrawn, without offence on the part of those who enjoyed such favors, operate as grievances. But were the Americans, then, not touched and grieved by the taxes, in some measure, merely as taxes? If so, why were they almost all either wholly repealed or exceedingly reduced? Were they not touched and grieved even by the regulating duties of the sixth of George the Second? Else why were the duties first reduced to one third in 1764, and afterwards to a third of that third in the year 1766? Were they not touched and grieved by the Stamp Act? I shall say they were, until that tax is revived. Were they not touched and grieved by the duties of 1767, which were likewise repealed, and which Lord Hillsborough tells you (for the ministry) were laid contrary to the true principle of commerce? Is not the assurance given by that noble person to the colonies of a resolution to lay no more taxes on them an admission that taxes would touch and grieve them? Is not the resolution of the noble lord in the blue riband, now standing on your journals, the strongest of all proofs that Parliamentary subsidies really touched and grieved them? Else why all these changes, modifications, repeals, assurances, and resolutions?

The next proposition is,—"That, from the distance of the

said colonies, and from other circumstances, no method hath hitherto been devised for procuring a representation in Parliament for the said colonies."

This is an assertion of a fact. I go no further on the paper; though, in my private judgment, an useful representation is impossible; I am sure it is not desired by them, nor ought it, perhaps, by us: but I abstain from opinions.

The fourth resolution is,—"That each of the said colonies hath within itself a body, chosen, in part or in the whole, by the freemen, freeholders, or other free inhabitants thereof, commonly called the General Assembly, or General Court, with powers legally to raise, levy, and assess, according to the several usages of such colonies, duties and taxes towards defraying all sorts of public services."

This competence in the colony assemblies is certain. It is proved by the whole tenor of their acts of supply in all the assemblies, in which the constant style of granting is, "An aid to his Majesty"; and acts granting to the crown have regularly, for near a century, passed the public offices without dispute. Those who have been pleased paradoxically to deny this right, holding that none but the British Parliament can grant to the crown, are wished to look to what is done, not only in the colonies, but in Ireland, in one uniform, unbroken tenor, every session. Sir, I am surprised that this doctrine should come from some of the law servants of the crown. I say, that if the crown could be responsible, his Majesty,—but certainly the ministers, and even these law officers themselves, through whose hands the acts pass biennially in Ireland, or annually in the colonies, are in an habitual course of committing impeachable offences. What habitual offenders have been all Presidents of the Council, all Secretaries of State, all First Lords of Trade, all Attorneys and all Solicitors General! However, they are safe, as no one impeaches them; and there is no ground of charge against them, except in their own unfounded theories.

The fifth resolution is also a resolution of fact,—"That the said general assemblies, general courts, or other bodies legally qualified as aforesaid, have at sundry times freely granted several large subsidies and public aids for his Majesty's service, according to their abilities, when required thereto by letter from one of his Majesty's principal Secretaries of State; and that their right to grant the same, and their cheerfulness and sufficiency in the said grants, have been at sundry times acknowledged by Parliament."

To say nothing of their great expenses in the Indian wars, and not to take their exertion in foreign ones, so high as the supplies in the year 1695, not to go back to their public contributions in the year 1710, I shall begin to travel only where the journals give me light,—resolving to deal in nothing but fact authenticated by Parliamentary record, and to build myself wholly on that solid basis.

On the 4th of April, 1748, a committee of this House came to the following resolution:—

"*Resolved,* That it is the opinion of this committee, *that it is just and reasonable,* that the several provinces and colonies of Massachusetts Bay, New Hampshire, Connecticut, and Rhode Island be reimbursed the expenses they have been at in taking and securing to the crown of Great Britain the island of Cape Breton and its dependencies."

These expenses were immense for such colonies. They were above 200,000*l.* sterling: money first raised and advanced on their public credit.

On the 28th of January, 1756, a message from the king came to us, to this effect:—"His Majesty, being sensible of the zeal and vigor with which his faithful subjects of certain colonies in North America have exerted themselves in defence of his Majesty's just rights and possessions, recommends it to this House to take the same into their consideration, and to enable his Majesty to give them such assistance as may be a *proper reward and encouragement.*"

On the 3d of February, 1756, the House came to a suitable resolution, expressed in words nearly the same as those of the message; but with the further addition, that the money then voted was as an *encouragement* to the colonies to exert themselves with vigor. It will not be necessary to go through all the testimonies which your own records have given to the truth of my resolutions. I will only refer you to the places in the journals:—

Vol. XXVII.—16th and 19th May, 1757.
Vol. XXVIII.—June 1st, 1758,—April 26th and 30th, 1759, —March 26th and 31st, and April 28th, 1760,—Jan. 9th and 20th, 1761.
Vol. XXIX.—Jan. 22d and 26th, 1762,—March 14th and 17th, 1763.

Sir, here is the repeated acknowledgment of Parliament, that the colonies not only gave, but gave to satiety. This nation has formally acknowledged two things: first, that the colonies had gone beyond their abilities, Parliament having thought it necessary to reimburse them; secondly, that they had acted legally and laudably in their grants of money, and their maintenance of troops, since the compensation is expressly given as reward and encouragement. Reward is not bestowed for acts that are unlawful; and encouragement is not held out to things that deserve reprehension. My resolution, therefore, does nothing more than collect into one proposition what is scattered through your journals. I give you nothing but your own; and you cannot refuse in the gross what you have so often acknowledged in detail. The admission of this, which will be so honorable to them and to you, will, indeed, be mortal to all the miserable stories by which the passions of the misguided people have been engaged in an unhappy system. The people heard, indeed, from the beginning of these disputes, one thing continually dinned in their ears: that reason and justice demanded, that the Americans, who paid no taxes, should be compelled to contribute. How did that fact, of their paying nothing, stand, when the taxing system began? When Mr. Grenville began to form his system of American revenue, he stated in this House that the colonies were then in debt two million six hundred thousand pounds sterling money, and was of opinion they would discharge that debt in four years. On this state, those untaxed people were actually subject to the payment of taxes to the amount of six hundred and fifty thousand a year. In fact, however, Mr. Grenville was mistaken. The funds given for sinking the debt did not prove quite so ample as both the colonies and he expected. The calculation was too sanguine: the reduction was not completed till some years after, and at different times in different colonies. However, the taxes after the war continued too great to bear any *addition, with prudence or propriety; and when the burdens imposed in consequence of former requisitions were discharged, our tone became too high to resort again to requisition. No colony, since that time, ever has had any requisition whatsoever made to it.

We see the sense of the crown, and the sense of Parliament, on the productive nature of a *revenue by grant*. Now search the same journals for the produce of the *revenue by imposition*. Where is it?—let us know the volume and the page. What is the gross, what is the net produce? To what service is it applied? How have you appropriated its surplus? —What! can none of the many skilful index-makers that we are now employing find any trace of it?—Well, let them and that rest together.—But are the journals, which say nothing of the revenue, as silent on the discontent?—Oh, no! a child may find it. It is the melancholy burden and blot of every page.

I think, then, I am, from those journals, justified in the sixth and last resolution, which is,—"That it hath been found by experience, that the manner of granting the said supplies and aids by the said general assemblies hath been more agreeable to the inhabitants of the said colonies, and more beneficial and conducive to the public service, than the mode of giving and granting aids and subsidies in Parliament, to be raised and paid in the said colonies."

This makes the whole of the fundamental part of the plan. The conclusion is irresistible. You cannot say that you were driven by any necessity to an exercise of the utmost rights of legislature. You cannot assert that you took on yourselves the task of imposing colony taxes, from the want of another legal body that is competent to the purpose of supplying the exigencies of the state without wounding the prejudices of the people. Neither is it true that the body so qualified, and having that competence, had neglected the duty.

The question now, on all this accumulated matter, is,— Whether you will choose to abide by a profitable experience or a mischievous theory? whether you choose to build on imagination or fact? whether you prefer enjoyment or hope? satisfaction in your subjects, or discontent?

If these propositions are accepted, everything which has been made to enforce a contrary system must, I take it for granted, fall along with it. On that ground, I have drawn the following resolution, which, when it comes to be moved, will naturally be divided in a proper manner:—"That it may be proper to repeal an act, made in the seventh year of the reign of his present Majesty, intituled, 'An act for granting certain duties in the British colonies and plantations in America; for allowing a drawback of the duties of customs, upon the exportation from this kingdom, of coffee and cocoa-nuts, of the produce of the said colonies or plantations; for discontinuing the drawbacks payable on China earthen ware exported to America; and for more effectually preventing the clandestine running of goods in the said colonies and plantations.'—And also, that it may be proper to repeal an act, made in the fourteenth year of the reign of his present

Majesty, intituled, 'An act to discontinue, in such manner and for such time as are therein mentioned, the landing and discharging, lading or shipping, of goods, wares, and merchandise, at the town and within the harbor of Boston, in the province of Massachusetts Bay, in North America.'—And also, that it may be proper to repeal an act, made in the fourteenth year of the reign of his present Majesty, intituled, 'An act for the impartial administration of justice, in the cases of persons questioned for any acts done by them, in the execution of the law, or for the suppression of riots and tumults, in the province of the Massachusetts Bay, in New England.'—And also, that it may be proper to repeal an act, made in the fourteenth year of the reign of his present Majesty, intituled, 'An act for the better regulating the government of the province of the Massachusetts Bay, in New England.'—And also, that it may be proper to explain and amend an act, made in the thirty-fifth year of the reign of King Henry the Eighth, intituled, 'An act for the trial of treasons committed out of the king's dominions.' "

I wish, Sir, to repeal the Boston Port Bill, because (independently of the dangerous precedent of suspending the rights of the subject during the king's pleasure) it was passed, as I apprehend, with less regularity, and on more partial principles, than it ought. The corporation of Boston was not heard before it was condemned. Other towns, full as guilty as she was, have not had their ports blocked up. Even the Restraining Bill of the present session does not go to the length of the Boston Port Act. The same ideas of prudence, which induced you not to extend equal punishment to equal guilt, even when you were punishing, induce me, who mean not to chastise, but to reconcile, to be satisfied with the punishment already partially inflicted.

Ideas of prudence and accomodation to circumstances prevent you from taking away the charters of Connecticut and Rhode Island, as you have taken away that of Massachusetts

Colony, though the crown has far less power in the two former provinces than it enjoyed in the latter, and though the abuses have been full as great and as flagrant in the exempted as in the punished. The same reasons of prudence and accommodation have weight with me in restoring the charter of Massachusetts Bay. Besides, Sir, the act which changes the charter of Massachusetts is in many particulars so exceptionable, that, if I did not wish absolutely to repeal, I would by all means desire to alter it; as several of its provisions tend to the subversion of all public and private justice. Such, among others, is the power in the governor to change the sheriff at his pleasure, and to make a new returning officer for every special cause. It is shameful to behold such a regulation standing among English laws.

The act for bringing persons accused of committing murder under the orders of government to England for trial is but temporary. That act has calculated the probable duration of our quarrel with the colonies, and is accommodated to that supposed duration. I would hasten the happy moment of reconciliation, and therefore must, on my principle, get rid of that most justly obnoxious act.

The act of Henry the Eighth for the trial of treasons I do not mean to take away, but to confine it to its proper bounds and original intention: to make it expressly for trial of treasons (and the greatest treasons may be committed) in places where the jurisdiction of the crown does not extend.

Having guarded the privileges of local legislature, I would next secure to the colonies a fair and unbiased judicature; for which purpose, Sir, I propose the following resolution:—
"That, from the time when the general assembly, or general court, of any colony or plantation in North America shall have appointed, by act of assembly duly confirmed, a settled salary to the offices of the chief justice and other judges of the superior courts, it may be proper that the said chief justice and other judges of the superior courts of such colony

shall hold his and their office and offices during their good behavior, and shall not be removed therefrom, but when the said removal shall be adjudged by his Majesty in council, upon a hearing on complaint from the general assembly, or on a complaint from the governor, or the council, or the house of representatives, severally, of the colony in which the said chief justice and other judges have exercised the said offices."

The next resolution relates to the courts of admiralty. It is this:—"That it may be proper to regulate the courts of admiralty or vice-admiralty, authorized by the 15th chapter of the 4th George the Third, in such a manner as to make the same more commodious to those who sue or are sued in the said courts, and to provide for the more decent maintenance of the judges of the same."

These courts I do not wish to take away: they are in themselves proper establishments. This court is one of the capital securities of the Act of Navigation. The extent of its jurisdiction, indeed, has been increased; but this is altogether as proper, and is, indeed, on many accounts, more eligible, where new powers were wanted, than a court absolutely new. But courts incommodiously situated, in effect, deny justice; and a court partaking in the fruits of its own condemnation is a robber. The Congress complain, and complain justly, of this grievance.

These are the three consequential propositions. I have thought of two or three more; but they come rather too near detail, and to the province of executive government, which I wish Parliament always to superintend, never to assume. If the first six are granted, congruity will carry the latter three. If not, the things that remain unrepealed will be, I hope, rather unseemly incumbrances on the building than very materially detrimental to its strength and stability.

Here, Sir, I should close, but that I plainly perceive some objections remain, which I ought, if possible, to remove. The first will be, that, in resorting to the doctrine of our ancestors, as contained in the preamble to the Chester act, I prove too much: that the grievance from a want of representation, stated in that preamble, goes to the whole of legislation as well as to taxation; and that the colonies, grounding themselves upon that doctrine, will apply it to all parts of legislative authority.

To this objection, with all possible deference and humility, and wishing as little as any man living to impair the smallest particle of our supreme authority, I answer, that *the words are the words of Parliament, and not mine;* and that all false and inconclusive inferences drawn from them are not mine; for I heartily disclaim any such inference. I have chosen the words of an act of Parliament, which Mr. Grenville, surely a tolerably zealous and very judicious advocate for the sovereignty of Parliament, formerly moved to have read at your table in confirmation of his tenets. It is true that Lord Chatham considered these preambles as declaring strongly in favor of his opinions. He was a no less powerful advocate for the privileges of the Americans. Ought I not from hence to presume that these preambles are as favorable as possible to both, when properly understood: favorable both to the rights of Parliament, and to the privilege of the dependencies of this crown? But, Sir, the object of grievance in my resolution I have not taken from the Chester, but from the Durham act, which confines the hardship of want of representation to the case of subsidies, and which therefore falls in exactly with the case of the colonies. But whether the unrepresented counties were *de jure* or *de facto* bound the preambles do not accurately distinguish; nor, indeed, was it necessary: for, whether *de jure* or *de facto,* the legislature thought the exercise of the power of taxing, as of right, or as of fact without right, equally a grievance, and equally oppressive.

I do not know that the colonies have, in any general way, or in any cool hour, gone much beyond the demand of immunity in relation to taxes. It is not fair to judge of the temper or dispositions of any man or any set of men, when they are composed and at rest, from their conduct or their expressions in a state of disturbance and irritation. It is, besides, a very great mistake to imagine that mankind follow up practically any speculative principle, either of government or of freedom, as far as it will go in argument and logical illation. We Englishmen stop very short of the principles upon which we support any given part of our Constitution, or even the whole of it together. I could easily, if I had not already tired you, give you very striking and convincing instances of it. This is nothing but what is natural and proper. All government, indeed every human benefit and enjoyment, every virtue and every prudent act, is founded on compromise and barter. We balance inconveniences; we give and take; we remit some rights, that we may enjoy others; and we choose rather to be happy citizens than subtle disputants. As we must give away some natural liberty, to enjoy civil advantages, so we must sacrifice some civil liberties, for the advantages to be derived from the communion and fellowship of a great empire. But, in all fair dealings, the thing bought must bear some proportion to the purchase paid. None will barter away the immediate jewel of his soul. Though a great house is apt to make slaves haughty, yet it is purchasing a part of the artificial importance of a great empire too dear, to pay for it all essential rights, and all the intrinsic dignity of human nature. None of us who would not risk his life rather than fall under a government purely arbitrary. But although there are some amongst us who think our Constitution wants many improvements to make it a complete system of liberty, perhaps none who are of that opinion would think it right to aim at such improvement by disturbing his country and risking everything that is dear to him. In every arduous enterprise, we consider what we are to lose, as well as what we are to gain; and the more and better stake of liberty every people possess, the less they will hazard in a vain attempt to make it more. These are *the cords of man*. Man acts from adequate motives relative to his interest, and not on metaphysical speculations. Aristotle, the great master of reasoning, cautions us, and with great weight and propriety, against this species of delusive geometrical accuracy in moral arguments, as the most fallacious of all sophistry.

The Americans will have no interest contrary to the grandeur and glory of England, when they are not oppressed by the weight of it; and they will rather be inclined to respect the acts of a superintending legislature, when they see them the acts of that power which is itself the security, not the rival, of their secondary importance. In this assurance my mind most perfectly acquiesces, and I confess I feel not the least alarm from the discontents which are to arise from putting people at their ease; nor do I apprehend the destruction of this empire from giving, by an act of free grace and indulgence, to two millions of my fellow-citizens some share of those rights upon which I have always been taught to value myself.

It is said, indeed, that this power of granting, vested in American assemblies, would dissolve the unity of the empire, —which was preserved entire, although Wales, and Chester, and Durham were added to it. Truly, Mr. Speaker, I do not know what this unity means; nor has it ever been heard of, that I know, in the constitutional policy of this country. The very idea of subordination of parts excludes this notion of simple and undivided unity. England is the head; but she is not the head and the members too. Ireland has ever had from the beginning a separate, but not an independent legislature, which, far from distracting, promoted the union of the whole. Everything was sweetly and harmoniously disposed through both islands for the conservation of English dominion and the communication of English liberties. I do not see that the same principles might not be carried into twenty islands, and with the same good effect. This is my model with regard to America, as far as the internal circumstances of the two countries are the same. I know no other unity of this empire than I can draw from its example during these periods, when it seemed to my poor understanding more united than it is now, or than it is likely to be by the present methods.

But since I speak of these methods, I recollect, Mr. Speaker, almost too late, that I promised, before I finished, to say something of the proposition of the noble lord [19] on the floor, which has been so lately received, and stands on your journals. I must be deeply concerned, whenever it is my misfortune to continue a difference with the majority of this House. But as the reasons for that difference are my apology for thus troubling you, suffer me to state them in a very few words. I shall compress them into as small a body as I possibly can, having already debated that matter at large, when the question was before the committee.

First, then, I cannot admit that proposition of a ransom by auction,—because it is a mere project. It is a thing new, unheard of, supported by no experience, justified by no analogy, without example of our ancestors, or root in the Constitution. It is neither regular Parliamentary taxation nor colony grant. *Experimentum in corpore vili* is a good rule, which will ever make me adverse to any trial of experiments on what is certainly the most valuable of all subjects, the peace of this empire.

Secondly, it is an experiment which must be fatal in the end to our Constitution. For what is it but a scheme for taxing the colonies in the antechamber of the noble lord and his successors? To settle the quotas and proportions in this House is clearly impossible. You, Sir, may flatter your-

---

[19] Lord North.

self you shall sit a state auctioneer, with your hammer in your hand, and knock down to each colony as it bids. But to settle (on the plan laid down by the noble lord) the true proportional payment for four or five and twenty governments, according to the absolute and the relative wealth of each, and according to the British proportion of wealth and burden, is a wild and chimerical notion. This new taxation must therefore come in by the back-door of the Constitution. Each quota must be brought to this House ready formed. You can neither add nor alter. You must register it. You can do nothing further. For on what grounds can you deliberate either before or after the proposition? You cannot hear the counsel for all these provinces, quarrelling each on its own quantity of payment, and its proportion to others. If you should attempt it, the Committee of Provincial Ways and Means, or by whatever other name it will delight to be called, must swallow up all the time of Parliament.

Thirdly, it does not give satisfaction to the complaint of the colonies. They complain that they are taxed without their consent. You answer, that you will fix the sum at which they shall be taxed. That is, you give them the very grievance for the remedy. You tell them, indeed, that you will leave the mode to themselves. I really beg pardon; it gives me pain to mention it; but you must be sensible that you will not perform this part of the compact. For suppose the colonies were to lay the duties which furnished their contingent upon the importation of your manufactures; you know you would never suffer such a tax to be laid. You know, too, that you would not suffer many other modes of taxation. So that, when you come to explain yourself, it will be found that you will neither leave to themselves the quantum nor the mode, nor indeed anything. The whole is delusion, from one end to the other.

Fourthly, this method of ransom by auction, unless it be *universally* accepted, will plunge you into great and inextricable difficulties. In what year of our Lord are the proportions of payments to be settled? To say nothing of the impossibility that colony agents should have general powers of taxing the colonies at their discretion, consider, I implore you, that the communication by special messages and orders between these agents and their constituents on each variation of the case, when the parties come to contend together, and to dispute on their relative proportions, will be a matter of delay, perplexity, and confusion, that never can have an end.

If all the colonies do not appear at the outcry, what is the condition of those assemblies who offer, by themselves or their agents, to tax themselves up to your ideas of their proportion? The refractory colonies, who refuse all composition, will remain taxed only to your old impositions, which, however grievous in principle, are trifling as to production. The obedient colonies in this scheme are heavily taxed; the refractory remain unburdened. What will you do? Will you lay new and heavier taxes by Parliament on the disobedient? Pray consider in what way you can do it. You are perfectly convinced, that, in the way of taxing, you can do nothing but at the ports. Now suppose it is Virginia that refuses to appear at your auction, while Maryland and North Carolina bid handsomely for their ransom, and are taxed to your quota, how will you put these colonies on a par? Will you tax the tobacco of Virginia? If you do, you give its death-wound to your English revenue at home, and to one of the very greatest articles of your own foreign trade. If you tax the import of that rebellious colony, what do you tax but your own manufactures, or the goods of some other obedient and already well-taxed colony? Who has said one word on this labyrinth of detail, which bewilders you more and more as you enter into it? Who has presented, who can present, you with a clew to lead you out of it? I think, Sir, it is impossible that you should not recollect that the colony **bounds are so** implicated in one another (you know it by your other experiments in the bill for prohibiting the New England fishery) that you can lay no possible restraints on almost any of them which may not be presently eluded, if you do not confound the innocent with the guilty, and burden those whom upon every principle you ought to exonerate. He must be grossly ignorant of America, who thinks, that, without falling into this confusion of all rules of equity and policy, you can restrain any single colony, especially Virginia and Maryland, the central, and most important of them all.

Let it also be considered, that either in the present confusion you settle a permanent contingent, which will and must be trifling, and then you have no effectual revenue,— or you change the quota at every exigency, and then on every new repartition you will have a new quarrel.

Reflect besides, that, when you have fixed a quota for every colony, you have not provided for prompt and punctual payment. Suppose one, two, five, ten years' arrears. You cannot issue a Treasury extent against the failing colony. You must make new Boston port bills, new restraining laws, new acts for dragging men to England for trial. You must send out new fleets, new armies. All is to begin again. From this day forward the empire is never to know an hour's tranquillity. An intestine fire will be kept alive in the bowels of the colonies, which one time or other must consume this whole empire. I allow, indeed, that the Empire of Germany raises her revenue and her troops by quotas and contingents; but the revenue of the Empire and the army of the Empire is the worst revenue and the worst army in the world.

Instead of a standing revenue, you will therefore have a perpetual quarrel. Indeed, the noble lord who proposed this project of a ransom by auction seemed himself to be of that opinion. His project was rather designed for breaking the union of the colonies than for establishing a revenue. He confessed he apprehended that his proposal would not be to *their taste*. I say, this scheme of disunion seems to be at the bottom of the project; for I will not suspect that the noble lord meant nothing but merely to delude the nation by an airy phantom which he never intended to realize. But whatever his views may be, as I propose the peace and union of the colonies as the very foundation of my plan, it cannot accord with one whose foundation is perpetual discord.

Compare the two. This I offer to give you is plain and simple: the other full of perplexed and intricate mazes. This is mild: that harsh. This is found by experience effectual for its purposes: the other is a new project. This is universal: the other calculated for certain colonies only. This is immediate in its conciliatory operation: the other remote, contingent, full of hazard. Mine is what becomes the dignity of a ruling people: gratuitous, unconditional, and not held out as matter of bargain and sale. I have done my duty in proposing it to you. I have, indeed, tired you by a long discourse; but this is the misfortune of those to whose influence nothing will be conceded, and who must win every inch of their ground by argument. You have heard me with goodness. May you decide with wisdom! For my part, I feel my mind greatly disburdened by what I have done to-day. I have been the less fearful of trying your patience, because on this subject I mean to spare it altogether in future. I have this comfort,—that, in every stage of the American affairs, I have steadily opposed the measures that have produced the confusion, and may bring on the destruction, of this empire. I now go so far as to risk a proposal of my own. If I cannot give peace to my country, I give it to my conscience.

But what (says the financier) is peace to us without money? Your plan gives us no revenue.—No! But it does: for it secures to the subject the power of REFUSAL,—the first of all revenues. Experience is a cheat, and fact a liar, if this power in the subject, of proportioning his grant, or of not granting at all, has not been found the richest mine of revenue ever discovered by the skill or by the fortune of man. It does not, indeed, vote you £152,750: 11: 2¾ths, nor any other paltry limited sum; but it gives the strong-box itself, the fund, the bank, from whence only revenues can arise amongst a people sensible of freedom: *Posita luditur arca.*[20] Cannot you in England, cannot you at this time of day, cannot you, an House of Commons, trust to the principle which has raised so mighty a revenue, and accumulated a debt of near 140 millions in this country? Is this principle to be true in England and false everywhere else? Is it not true in Ireland? Has it not hitherto been true in the colonies? Why should you presume, that, in any country, a body duly constituted for any function will neglect to perform its duty, and abdicate its trust? Such a presumption would go against all government in all modes. But, in truth, this dread of penury of supply from a free assembly has no foundation in Nature. For first observe, that, besides the desire which all men have naturally of supporting the honor of their own government, that sense of dignity, and that security to property, which ever attends freedom, has a tendency to increase the stock of the free community. Most may be taken where most is accumulated. And what is the soil or climate where experience has not uniformly proved that the voluntary flow of heaped-up plenty, bursting from the weight of its own rich luxuriance, has ever run with a more copious stream of revenue than could be squeezed from the dry husks of oppressed indigence by the straining of all the politic machinery in the world?

Next, we know that parties must ever exist in a free country. We know, too, that the emulations of such parties, their contradictions, their reciprocal necessities, their hopes, and their fears, must send them all in their turns to him that holds the balance of the state. The parties are the gamesters;

---

[20] Juvenal, I. 90.

but government keeps the table, and is sure to be the winner in the end. When this game is played, I really think it is more to be feared that the people will be exhausted than that government will not be supplied. Whereas whatever is got by acts of absolute power ill obeyed because odious, or by contracts ill kept because constrained, will be narrow, feeble, uncertain, and precarious.

> "Ease would retract
> Vows made in pain, as violent and void." [21]

I, for one, protest against compounding our demands: I declare against compounding, for a poor limited sum, the immense, ever-growing, eternal debt which is due to generous government from protected freedom. And so may I speed in the great object I propose to you, as I think it would not only be an act of injustice, but would be the worst economy in the world, to compel the colonies to a sum certain, either in the way of ransom, or in the way of compulsory compact.

But to clear up my ideas on this subject,—a revenue from America transmitted hither. Do not delude yourselves: you can never receive it,—no, not a shilling. We have experience that from remote countries it is not to be expected. If, when you attempted to extract revenue from Bengal, you were obliged to return in loan what you had taken in imposition, what can you expect from North America? For, certainly, if ever there was a country qualified to produce wealth, it is India; or an institution fit for the transmission, it is the East India Company. America has none of these aptitudes. If America gives you taxable objects on which you lay your duties here, and gives you at the same time a surplus by a foreign sale of her commodities to pay the duties on these objects which you tax at home, she has performed her part to the British revenue. But with regard to her own internal establishments, she may, I doubt not she will, contribute in

---

[21] *Paradise Lost,* IV. 96.

moderation. I say in moderation; for she ought not to be permitted to exhaust herself. She ought to be reserved to a war; the weight of which, with the enemies that we are most likely to have, must be considerable in her quarter of the globe. There she may serve you, and serve you essentially.

For that service, for all service, whether of revenue, trade, or empire, my trust is in her interest in the British Constitution. My hold of the colonies is in the close affection which grows from common names, from kindred blood, from similar privileges, and equal protection. These are ties which, though light as air, are as strong as links of iron. Let the colonies always keep the idea of their civil rights associated with your government,—they will cling and grapple to you, and no force under heaven will be of power to tear them from their allegiance. But let it be once understood that your government may be one thing and their privileges another, that these two things may exist without any mutual relation,—the cement is gone, the cohesion is loosened, and everything hastens to decay and dissolution. As long as you have the wisdom to keep the sovereign authority of this country as the sanctuary of liberty, the sacred temple consecrated to our common faith, wherever the chosen race and sons of England worship freedom, they will turn their faces towards you. The more they multiply, the more friends you will have; the more ardently they love liberty, the more perfect will be their obedience. Slavery they can have anywhere. It is a weed that grows in every soil. They may have it from Spain, they may have it from Prussia. But, until you become lost to all feeling of your true interest and your natural dignity, freedom they can have from none but you. This is the commodity of price, of which you have the monopoly. This is the true Act of Navigation, which binds to you the commerce of the colonies, and through them secures to you the wealth of the world. Deny them this participation of freedom, and you break that sole bond which originally made, and must still preserve, the unity of the empire. Do not entertain so weak an imagination as that your registers and your bonds, your affidavits and your sufferances, your cockets and your clearances, are what form the great securities of your commerce. Do not dream that your letters of office, and your instructions, and your suspending clauses are the things that hold together the great contexture of this mysterious whole. These things do not make your government. Dead instruments, passive tools as they are, it is the spirit of the English communion that gives all their life and efficacy to them. It is the spirit of the English Constitution, which, infused through the mighty mass, pervades, feeds, unites, invigorates, vivifies every part of the empire, even down to the minutest member.

Is it not the same virtue which does everything for us here in England? Do you imagine, then, that it is the Land-Tax Act which raises your revenue? that it is the annual vote in the Committee of Supply which gives you your army? or that it is the Mutiny Bill which inspires it with bravery and discipline? No! surely, no! It is the love of the people; it is their attachment to their government, from the sense of the deep stake they have in such a glorious institution, which gives you your army and your navy, and infuses into both that liberal obedience without which your army would be a base rabble and your navy nothing but rotten timber.

All this, I know well enough, will sound wild and chimerical to the profane herd of those vulgar and mechanical politicians who have no place among us: a sort of people who think that nothing exists but what is gross and material, —and who, therefore, far from being qualified to be directors of the great movement of empire, are not fit to turn a wheel in the machine. But to men truly initiated and rightly taught, these ruling and master principles, which in the opinion of such men as I have mentioned have no substantial existence, are in truth everything, and all in all. Magnanimity in politics

is not seldom the truest wisdom; and a great empire and little
minds go ill together. If we are conscious of our situation,
and glow with zeal to fill our place as becomes our station
and ourselves, we ought to auspicate all our public proceedings on America with the old warning of the Church,
Sursum corda! We ought to elevate our minds to the greatness
of that trust to which the order of Providence has called us.
By adverting to the dignity of this high calling our ancestors
have turned a savage wilderness into a glorious empire, and
have made the most extensive and the only honorable conquests, not by destroying, but by promoting the wealth, the
number, the happiness of the human race. Let us get an
American revenue as we have got an American empire.
English privileges have made it all that it is; English privileges
alone will make it all it can be.

In full confidence of this unalterable truth, I now (*quod
felix faustumque sit!*) lay the first stone of the Temple of
Peace; and I move you,—

"That the colonies and plantations of Great Britain in
North America, consisting of fourteen separate governments,
and containing two millions and upwards of free inhabitants,
have not had the liberty and privilege of electing and sending
any knights and burgesses, or others, to represent them in
the high court of Parliament."

[Upon this Resolution, the previous question was put, and
carried;—for the previous question 270, against it, 78.
The first four motions and the last had the previous question
put on them. The others were negatived.]

Letter to the Sheriffs of Bristol[1]

Gentlemen,—I have the honor of sending you the two last acts which have been passed with regard to the troubles in America. These acts are similar to all the rest which have been made on the same subject. They operate by the same principle, and they are derived from the very same policy. I think they complete the number of this sort of statutes to nine. It affords no matter for very pleasing reflection to observe that our subjects diminish as our laws increase.

If I have the misfortune of differing with some of my fellow-citizens on this great and arduous subject, it is no small consolation to me that I do not differ from you. With you I am perfectly united. We are heartily agreed in our detestation of a civil war. We have ever expressed the most unqualified disapprobation of all the steps which have led to it, and of all those which tend to prolong it. And I have no doubt that we feel exactly the same emotions of grief and shame on all its miserable consequences, whether they appear, on the one side or the other, in the shape of victories or defeats, of captures made from the English on the continent or from the English in these islands, of legislative regulations which subvert the liberties of our brethren or which undermine our own.

Of the first of these statutes (that for the letter of marque) I shall say little. Exceptionable as it may be, and as I think it is in some particulars, it seems the natural, perhaps neces-

---

[1] "Letter to John Farr and John Harris, Esqrs. (Sheriffs of the City of Bristol) on the Affairs of America" (1777).

sary, result of the measures we have taken and the situation we are in. The other (for a partial suspension of the *Habeas Corpus*) appears to me of a much deeper malignity. During its progress through the House of Commons, it has been amended, so as to express, more distinctly than at first it did, the avowed sentiments of those who framed it; and the main ground of my exception to it is, because it does express, and does carry into execution, purposes which appear to me so contradictory to all the principles, not only of the constitutional policy of Great Britain, but even of that species of hostile justice which no asperity of war wholly extinguishes in the minds of a civilized people.

It seems to have in view two capital objects: the first, to enable administration to confine, as long as it shall think proper, those whom that act is pleased to qualify by the name of *pirates*. Those so qualified I understand to be the commanders and mariners of such privateers and ships of war belonging to the colonies as in the course of this unhappy contest may fall into the hands of the crown. They are therefore to be detained in prison, under the criminal description of piracy, to a future trial and ignominious punishment, whenever circumstances shall make it convenient to execute vengeance on them, under the color of that odious and infamous offence.

To this first purpose of the law I have no small dislike, because the act does not (as all laws and all equitable transactions ought to do) fairly describe its object. The persons who make a naval war upon us, in consequence of the present troubles, may be rebels; but to call and treat them as pirates is confounding not only the natural distinction of things, but the order of crimes,—which, whether by putting them from a higher part of the scale to the lower or from the lower to the higher, is never done without dangerously disordering the whole frame of jurisprudence. Though piracy may be, in the eye of the law, a *less* offence than treason, yet, as both are, in effect, punished with the same death, the same forfeiture, and the same corruption of blood, I never would take from any fellow-creature whatever any sort of advantage which he may derive to his safety from the pity of mankind, or to his reputation from their general feelings, by degrading his offence, when I cannot soften his punishment. The general sense of mankind tells me that those offences which may possibly arise from mistaken virtue are not in the class of infamous actions. Lord Coke, the oracle of the English law, conforms to that general sense, where he says that "those things which are of the highest criminality may be of the least disgrace." The act prepares a sort of masked proceeding, not honorable to the justice of the kingdom, and by no means necessary for its safety. I cannot enter into it. If Lord Balmerino,[2] in the last rebellion, had driven off the cattle of twenty clans, I should have thought it would have been a scandalous and low juggle, utterly unworthy of the manliness of an English judicature, to have tried him for felony as a stealer of cows.

Besides, I must honestly tell you that I could not vote for, or countenance in any way, a statute which stigmatizes with the crime of piracy these men whom an act of Parliament had previously put out of the protection of the law. When the legislature of this kingdom had ordered all their ships and goods, for the mere new-created offence of exercising trade, to be divided as a spoil among the seamen of the navy,— to consider the necessary reprisal of an unhappy, proscribed, interdicted people, as the crime of piracy, would have appeared, in any other legislature than ours, a strain of the most insulting and most unnatural cruelty and injustice. I assure you I never remember to have heard of anything like it in any time or country.

The second professed purpose of the act is to detain in

---

[2] Arthur Elphinstone (1688-1746), beheaded for treason.

England for trial those who shall commit high treason in America.

That you may be enabled to enter into the true spirit of the present law, it is necessary, Gentlemen, to apprise you that there is an act, made so long ago as in the reign of Henry the Eighth, before the existence or thought of any English colonies in America, for the trial in this kingdom of treasons committed out of the realm. In the year 1769 Parliament thought proper to acquaint the crown with their construction of that act in a formal address, wherein they entreated his Majesty to cause persons charged with high treason in America to be brought into this kingdom for trial. By this act of Henry the Eighth, *so construed and so applied,* almost all that is substantial and beneficial in a trial by jury is taken away from the subject in the colonies. This is, however, saying too little; for to try a man under that act is, in effect, to condemn him unheard. A person is brought hither in the dungeon of a ship's hold; thence he is vomited into a dungeon on land, loaded with irons, unfurnished with money, unsupported by friends, three thousand miles from all means of calling upon or confronting evidence, where no one local circumstance that tends to detect perjury can possibly be judged of;—such a person may be executed according to form, but he can never be tried according to justice.

I therefore could never reconcile myself to the bill I send you, which is expressly provided to remove all inconveniences from the establishment of a mode of trial which has ever appeared to me most unjust and most unconstitutional. Far from removing the difficulties which impede the execution of so mischievous a project, I would heap new difficulties upon it, if it were in my power. All the ancient, honest, juridical principles and institutions of England are so many clogs to check and retard the headlong course of violence and oppression. They were invented for this one good purpose, that what was not just should not be convenient. Convinced of this, I would leave things as I found them. The old, <u>cool-headed,</u> general law is as good as any deviation dictated by present <u>heat.</u> *Patience is necessity of good government.*

I could see no fair, justifiable expedience pleaded to favor this new suspension of the liberty of the subject. If the English in the colonies can support the independency to which they have been unfortunately driven, I suppose nobody has such a fanatical zeal for the criminal justice of Henry the Eighth that he will contend for executions which must be retaliated tenfold on his own friends, or who has conceived so strange an idea of English dignity as to think the defeats in America compensated by the triumphs at Tyburn. If, on the *Practical* contrary, the colonies are reduced to the obedience of the crown, there must be, under that authority, tribunals in the country itself fully competent to administer justice on all offenders. But if there are not, and that we must suppose a thing so humiliating to our government as that all this vast continent should unanimously concur in thinking that no ill fortune can convert resistance to the royal authority into a criminal act, we may call the effect of our victory peace, or obedience, or what we will, but the war is not ended; the hostile mind continues in full vigor, and it continues under a worse form. <u>If your peace be nothing more than a sullen pause from arms, if their quiet be nothing but the meditation of revenge, where smitten pride smarting from its wounds festers into new rancor, neither the act of Henry the Eighth nor its handmaid of this reign will answer any wise end of policy or justice.</u> For, if the bloody fields which they saw and felt are not sufficient to subdue the reason of America, (to use the expressive phrase of a great lord in office,) it is not the judicial slaughter which is made in another hemisphere against their universal sense of justice that will ever reconcile them to the British government.

I take it for granted, Gentlemen, that we sympathize in a

proper horror of all punishment further than as it serves for an example. To whom, then, does the example of an execution in England for this American rebellion apply? Remember, you are told every day, that the present is a contest between the two countries, and that we in England are at war for *our own* dignity against our rebellious children. Is this true? If it be, it is surely among such rebellious children that examples for disobedience should be made, to be in any degree instructive: for who ever thought of teaching parents their duty by an example from the punishment of an undutiful son? As well might the execution of a fugitive negro in the plantations be considered as a lesson to teach masters humanity to their slaves. Such executions may, indeed, satiate our revenge; they may harden our hearts, and puff us up with pride and arrogance. Alas! this is not instruction.

If anything can be drawn from such examples by a parity of the case, it is to show how deep their crime and how heavy their punishment will be, who shall at any time dare to resist a distant power actually disposing of their property without their voice or consent to the disposition, and overturning their franchises without charge or hearing. God forbid that England should ever read this lesson written in the blood of *any* of her offspring!

War is at present carried on between the king's natural and foreign troops, on one side, and the English in America, on the other, upon the usual footing of other wars; and accordingly an exchange of prisoners has been regularly made from the beginning. If, notwithstanding this hitherto equal procedure, upon some prospect of ending the war with success (which, however, may be delusive) administration prepares to act against those as *traitors* who remain in their hands at the end of the troubles, in my opinion we shall exhibit to the world as indecent a piece of injustice as ever civil fury has produced. If the prisoners who have been exchanged have not by that exchange been *virtually pardoned,* the cartel (whether avowed or understood) is a cruel fraud; for you have received the life of a man, and you ought to return a life for it, or there is no parity or fairness in the transaction.

If, on the other hand, we admit that they who are actually exchanged are pardoned, but contend that you may justly reserve for vengeance those who remain unexchanged, then this unpleasant and unhandsome consequence will follow: that you judge of the delinquency of men merely by the time of their guilt, and not by the heinousness of it; and you make fortune and accidents, and not the moral qualities of human action, the rule of your justice.

These strange incongruities must ever perplex those who confound the unhappiness of civil dissension with the crime of treason. Whenever a rebellion really and truly exists, which is as easily known in fact as it is difficult to define in words, government has not entered into such military conventions, but has ever declined all intermediate treaty which should put rebels in possession of the law of nations with regard to war. Commanders would receive no benefits at their hands, because they could make no return for them. Who has ever heard of capitulation, and parole of honor, and exchange of prisoners in the late rebellions in this kingdom? The answer to all demands of that sort was, "We can engage for nothing; you are at the king's pleasure." We ought to remember, that, if our present enemies be in reality and truth rebels, the king's generals have no right to release them upon any conditions whatsoever; and they are themselves answerable to the law, and as much in want of a pardon, for doing so, as the rebels whom they release.

Lawyers, I know, cannot make the distinction for which I contend; because they have their strict rule to go by. But legislators ought to do what lawyers cannot; for they have no other rules to bind them but the great principles of reason and equity and the general sense of mankind. These they are bound to obey and follow; and rather to enlarge and en-

lighten law by the liberality of legislative reason than to fetter
and bind their higher capacity by the narrow constructions
of subordinate, artificial justice. If we had adverted to this,
we never could consider the convulsions of a great empire,
not disturbed by a little disseminated faction, but divided by
whole communities and provinces, and entire legal representatives of a people, as fit matter of discussion under a commission of Oyer and Terminer. It is as opposite to reason and
prudence as it is to humanity and justice.

This act, proceeding on these principles, that is, preparing
to end the present troubles by a trial of one sort of hostility
under the name of piracy, and of another by the name of
treason, and executing the act of Henry the Eighth according
to a new and unconstitutional interpretation, I have thought
evil and dangerous, even though the instruments of effecting
such purposes had been merely of a neutral quality.

But it really appears to me, that the means which this act
employs are, at least, as exceptionable as the end. Permit me
to open myself a little upon this subject, because it is of importance to me, when I am obliged to submit to the power
without acquiescing in the reason of an act of legislature,
that I should justify my dissent by such arguments as may be
supposed to have weight with a sober man.

The main operative regulation of the act is to suspend the
common law, and the statute *Habeas Corpus* (the sole securities either for liberty or justice), with regard to all those
who have been out of the realm, or on the high seas, within
a given time. The rest of the people, as I understand, are to
continue as they stood before.

I confess, Gentlemen, that this appears to me as bad in the
principle, and far worse in its consequence, than an universal
suspension of the *Habeas Corpus* Act; and the limiting qualification, instead of taking out the sting, does in my humble
opinion sharpen and envenom it to a greater degree. Liberty.

Means of Act

for all men

if I understand it at all, is a *general* principle, and the clear right of all the subjects within the realm or of none. Partial freedom seems to me a most invidious mode of slavery. But, unfortunately, it is the kind of slavery the most easily admitted in times of civil discord; for parties are but too apt to forget their own future safety in their desire of sacrificing their enemies. People without much difficulty admit the entrance of that injustice of which they are not to be the immediate victims. In times of high proceeding it is never the faction of the predominant power that is in danger; for no tyranny chastises its own instruments. It is the obnoxious and the suspected who want the protection of law; and there is nothing to bridle the partial violence of state factions but this: "that whenever an act is made for a cessation of law and justice, the whole people should be universally subjected to the same suspension of their franchises." The alarm of such a proceeding would then be universal. It would operate as a sort of *call of the nation*. It would become every man's immediate and instant concern to be made very sensible of *the absolute necessity* of this total eclipse of liberty. They would more carefully advert to every renewal, and more powerfully resist it. These great determined measures are not commonly so dangerous to freedom. They are marked with too strong lines to slide into use. No plea, nor pretence, of *inconvenience or evil example* (which must in their nature be daily and ordinary incidents) can be admitted as a reason for such mighty operations. But the true danger is, when liberty is nibbled away, for expedients, and by parts. The *Habeas Corpus* Act supposes, contrary to the genius of most other laws, that the lawful magistrate may see particular men with a malignant eye, and it provides for that identical case. But when men, in particular descriptions, marked out by the magistrate himself, are delivered over by Parliament to this possible malignity, it is not the *Habeas Corpus* that is oc-

Weak-ness

casionally suspended, but its spirit that is mistaken, and its principle that is subverted. Indeed nothing is security to any individual but the common interest of all.

This act, therefore, has this distinguished evil in it, that it is the first *partial* suspension of the *Habeas Corpus* that has been made. The precedent, which is always of very great importance, is now established. For the first time a distinction is made among the people within this realm. Before this act, every man putting his foot on English ground, every stranger owing only a local and temporary allegiance, even negro slaves who had been sold in the colonies and under an act of Parliament, became as free as every other man who breathed the same air with them. Now a line is drawn, which may be advanced farther and farther at pleasure on the same argument of mere expedience on which it was first described. There is no equality among us; we are not fellow-citizens, if the mariner who lands on the quay does not rest on as firm legal ground as the merchant who sits in his counting-house. Other laws may injure the community, this dissolves it. As things now stand, every man in the West Indies, every one inhabitant of three unoffending provinces on the continent, every person coming from the East Indies, every gentleman who has travelled for his health or education, every mariner who has navigated the seas, is, for no other offence, under a temporary proscription. Let any of these facts (now become presumptions of guilt) be proved against him, and the bare suspicion of the crown puts him out of the law. It is even by no means clear to me whether the negative proof does not lie upon the person apprehended on suspicion to the subversion of all justice.

I have not debated against this bill in its progress through the House, because it would have been vain to oppose and impossible to correct it. It is some time since I have been clearly convinced that in the present state of things all opposition to any measures proposed by ministers, where the name of America appears, is vain and frivolous. You may be sure that I do not speak of my opposition, which in all circumstances must be so, but that of men of the greatest wisdom and authority in the nation. Everything proposed against America is supposed of course to be in favor of Great Britain. Good and ill success are equally admitted as reasons for persevering in the present methods. Several very prudent and very well-intentioned persons were of opinion that during the prevalence of such dispositions, all struggle rather inflamed than lessened the distemper of the public councils. Finding such resistance to be considered as factious by most withindoors, and by very many without, I cannot conscientiously support what is against my opinion, nor prudently contend with what I know is irresistible. Preserving my principles unshaken, I reserve my activity for rational endeavors; and I hope that my past conduct has given sufficient evidence that if I am a single day from my place, it is not owing to indolence or love of dissipation. The slightest hope of doing good is sufficient to recall me to what I quitted with regret. In declining for some time my usual strict attendance, I do not in the least condemn the spirit of those gentlemen who, with a just confidence in their abilities (in which I claim a sort of share from my love and admiration of them), were of opinion that their exertions in this desperate case might be of some service. They thought that by contracting the sphere of its application they might lessen the malignity of an evil principle. Perhaps they were in the right. But when my opinion was so very clearly to the contrary, for the reasons I have just stated, I am sure *my* attendance would have been ridiculous.

I must add in further explanation of my conduct that, far from softening the features of such a principle, and thereby removing any part of the popular odium or natural terrors attending it, I should be sorry that anything framed in contradiction to the spirit of our Constitution did not instantly produce, in fact, the grossest of the evils with which it was pregnant in its nature. It is by lying dormant a long time, or being at first very rarely exercised, that arbitrary power steals upon a people. On the next unconstitutional act, all the fashionable world will be ready to say——Your prophecies are ridiculous, your fears are vain, you see how little of the mischiefs which you formerly foreboded are come to pass. Thus, by degrees, that artful softening of all arbitrary power, the alleged infrequency or narrow extent of its operation, will be received as a sort of aphorism——and Mr. *Hume* will not be singular in telling us that the felicity of mankind is no more disturbed by it than by earthquakes or thunder or the other more unusual accidents of nature.

The act of which I speak is among the fruits of the American war; a war in my humble opinion productive of many mischiefs of a kind which distinguish it from all others. Not only our policy is deranged, and our empire distracted, but our laws and our legislative spirit appear to have been totally perverted by it. We have made war on our colonies, not by arms only, but by laws. As hostility and law are not very concordant ideas, every step we have taken in this business has been made by trampling on some maxim of justice, or some capital principle of wise government. What precedents were established, and what principles overturned (I will not say of English privilege, but of general justice), in the Boston Port, the Massachusetts Charter, the Military Bill, and all that long array of hostile acts of Parliament by which the war with America has been begun and supported! Had the principles of any of these acts been first exerted on English ground they would probably have expired as soon as they touched it. But by being removed from our persons they have rooted in our laws, and the latest posterity will taste the fruits of them.

Nor is it the worst effect of this unnatural contention, that our *laws* are corrupted. Whilst *manners* remain entire, they will correct the vices of law, and soften it at length to their own temper. But we have to lament that in most of the late proceedings we see very <u>few traces</u> of that <u>generosity, humanity, and dignity of mind which</u> formerly characterized this nation. War suspends the rules of moral obligation, and what is long suspended is in danger of being totally abrogated. Civil wars strike deepest of all into the manners of the people. They vitiate their politics; they corrupt their morals; they pervert even the natural taste and relish of equity and justice. By teaching us to consider our fellow-citizens in an hostile light, the whole body of our nation becomes gradually less dear to us. The very names of affection and kindred, which were the bond of charity whilst we agreed, become new incentives to hatred and rage, when the communion of our country is dissolved. We may flatter ourselves that we shall not fall into this misfortune. But we have no charter of exemption, that I know of, from the ordinary frailties of our nature.

What but that <u>blindness of heart</u> which arises from the frenzy of civil contention could have made any persons conceive the present situation of the British affairs as an object of triumph to themselves, or of congratulation to their sovereign? Nothing surely could be more lamentable to those who remember the flourishing days of this kingdom than to see the insane joy of several unhappy people, amidst the sad spectacle which our affairs and conduct exhibit to the scorn of Europe. We behold (and it seems some people rejoice in beholding) our native land, which used to sit the envied arbiter of all her neighbors, reduced to a servile dependence on their mercy,—acquiescing in assurances of friendship which she does not trust,—complaining of hostilities which she dares not resent,—deficient to her allies, lofty to her subjects, and submissive to her enemies,—whilst the liberal government of this free nation is supported by the hireling sword of German boors and vassals, and three millions of the subjects of Great Britain are seeking for protection to English privileges in the arms of France!

These circumstances appear to me more like shocking

prodigies than natural changes in human affairs. Men of firmer minds may see them without staggering or astonishment. Some may think them matters of congratulation and complimentary addresses; but I trust your candor will be so indulgent to my weakness as not to have the worse opinion of me for my declining to participate in this joy, and my rejecting all share whatsoever in such a triumph. I am too old, too stiff in my inveterate partialities, to be ready at all the fashionable evolutions of opinion. I scarcely know how to adapt my mind to the feelings with which the Court Gazettes mean to impress the people. It is not instantly that I can be brought to rejoice, when I hear of the slaughter and captivity of long lists of those names which have been familiar to my ears from my infancy, and to rejoice that they have fallen under the sword of strangers, whose barbarous appellations I scarcely know how to pronounce. The glory acquired at the White Plains by Colonel Rahl has no charms for me, and I fairly acknowledge that I have not yet learned to delight in finding Fort Kniphausen in the heart of the British dominions.

It might be some consolation for the loss of our old regards, if our reason were enlightened in proportion as our honest prejudices are removed. Wanting feelings for the honor of our country, we might then in cold blood be brought to think a little of our interests as individual citizens and our private conscience as moral agents.

Indeed, our affairs are in a bad condition. I do assure those gentlemen who have prayed for war, and obtained the blessing they have sought, that they are at this instant in very great straits. The abused wealth of this country continues a little longer to feed its distemper. As yet they, and their German allies of twenty hireling states, have contended only with the unprepared strength of our own infant colonies. But America is not subdued. Not one unattacked village which was originally adverse throughout that vast continent has yet submitted from love or terror. You have the ground you encamp on, and you have no more. The cantonments of your troops and your dominions are exactly of the same extent. You spread devastation, but you do not enlarge the sphere of authority.

The events of this war are of so much greater magnitude than those who either wished or feared it ever looked for, that this alone ought to fill every considerate mind with anxiety and diffidence. Wise men often tremble at the very things which fill the thoughtless with security. For many reasons I do not choose to expose to public view all the particulars of the state in which you stood with regard to foreign powers during the whole course of the last year. Whether you are yet wholly out of danger from them is more than I know, or than your rulers can divine. But even if I were certain of my safety, I could not easily forgive those who had brought me into the most dreadful perils, because by accidents, unforeseen by them or me, I have escaped.

Believe me, Gentlemen, the way still before you is intricate, dark, and full of perplexed and treacherous mazes. Those who think they have the clew may lead us out of this labyrinth. We may trust them as amply as we think proper; but as they have most certainly a call for all the reason which their stock can furnish, why should we think it proper to disturb its operation by inflaming their passions? I may be unable to lend an helping hand to those who direct the state; but I should be ashamed to make myself one of a noisy multitude to halloo and hearten them into doubtful and dangerous courses. A conscientious man would be cautious how he dealt in blood. He would feel some apprehension at being called to a tremendous account for engaging in so deep a play without any sort of knowledge of the game. It is no excuse for presumptuous ignorance, that it is directed by insolent passion. The poorest being that crawls on earth, contending to save itself from injustice and oppression, is an object respectable in the eyes of God and man. But I cannot conceive any exist-

The worst possible man ence under heaven (which in the depths of its wisdom tolerates all sorts of things) that is more truly odious and disgusting than an impotent, helpless creature, without civil wisdom or military skill, without a consciousness of any other qualification for power but his servility to it, bloated with pride and arrogance, calling for battles which he is not to fight, contending for a violent dominion which he can never exercise, and satisfied to be himself mean and miserable, in order to render others contemptible and wretched.

If you and I find our talents not of the great and ruling kind, our conduct, at least, is conformable to our faculties. No man's life pays the forfeit of our rashness. No desolate widow weeps tears of blood over our ignorance. Scrupulous and sober in a well-grounded distrust of ourselves, we would keep in the port of peace and security; and perhaps in recommending to others something of the same diffidence, we should show ourselves more charitable to their welfare than injurious to their abilities.

There are many circumstances in the zeal shown for civil war which seem to discover but little of real magnanimity. The addressers offer their own persons, and they are satisfied with hiring Germans. They promise their private fortunes, and they mortgage their country. They have all the merit of volunteers, without risk of person or charge of contribution; and when the unfeeling arm of a foreign soldiery pours out their kindred blood like water, they exult and triumph as if they themselves had performed some notable exploit. I am really ashamed of the fashionable language which has been held for some time past, which, to say the best of it, is full of levity. You know that I allude to the general cry against the cowardice of the Americans, as if we despised them for not making the king's soldiery purchase the advantage they have obtained at a dearer rate. It is not, Gentlemen, it is not to respect the dispensations of Providence, nor to provide any decent retreat in the mutability of human affairs. It leaves no medium between insolent victory and infamous defeat. It tends to alienate our minds further and further from our natural regards, and to make an eternal rent and schism in the British nation. Those who do not wish for such a separation would not dissolve that cement of reciprocal esteem and regard which can alone bind together the parts of this great fabric. It ought to be our wish, as it is our duty, not only to forbear this style of outrage ourselves, but to make every one as sensible as we can of the impropriety and unworthiness of the tempers which give rise to it, and which designing men are laboring with such malignant industry to diffuse amongst us. It is our business to counteract them, if possible,—if possible, to awake our natural regards, and to revive the old partiality to the English name. Without something of this kind I do not see how it is ever practicable really to reconcile with those whose affection, after all, must be the surest hold of our government, and which is a thousand times more worth to us than the mercenary zeal of all the circles of Germany.

I can well conceive a country completely overrun, and miserably wasted, without approaching in the least to settlement. In my apprehension, as long as English government is attempted to be supported over Englishmen by the sword alone, things will thus continue. I anticipate in my mind the moment of the final triumph of foreign military force. When that hour arrives, (for it may arrive,) then it is that all this mass of weakness and violence will appear in its full light. If we should be expelled from America, the delusion of the partisans of military government might still continue. They might still feed their imaginations with the possible good consequences which might have attended success. Nobody could prove the contrary by facts. But in case the sword should do all that the sword can do, the success of their arms and the defeat of their policy will be one and the same thing. You will never see any revenue from America. Some increase of the means of corruption, without ease of the public burdens, is the very best that can happen. Is it for this that we are at war,—and in such a war?

As to the difficulties of laying once more the foundations of that government which, for the sake of conquering what was our own, has been voluntarily and wantonly pulled down by a court faction here, I tremble to look at them. Has any of these gentlemen who are so eager to govern all mankind shown himself possessed of the first qualification towards government, some knowledge of the object, and of the difficulties which occur in the task they have undertaken?

I assure you, that, on the most prosperous issue of your arms, you will not be where you stood when you called in war to supply the defects of your political establishment. Nor would any disorder or disobedience to government which could arise from the most abject concession on our part ever equal those which will be felt after the most triumphant violence. You have got all the intermediate evils of war into the bargain.

I think I know America,—if I do not, my ignorance is incurable, for I have spared no pains to understand it,—and I do most solemnly assure those of my constituents who put any sort of confidence in my industry and integrity, that everything that has been done there has arisen from a total misconception of the object: that our means of originally holding America, that our means of reconciling with it after quarrel, of recovering it after separation, of keeping it after victory, did depend, and must depend, in their several stages and periods, upon a total renunciation of that unconditional submission which has taken such possession of the minds of violent men. The whole of those maxims upon which we have made and continued this war must be abandoned. Nothing, indeed, (for I would not deceive you,) can place us in our former situation. That hope must be laid aside. But there is a difference between bad and the worst of all. Terms relative

America misunderstood (Not submission, but conciliation)

what we should go,

to the cause of the war ought to be offered by the authority of Parliament. An arrangement at home promising some security for them ought to be made. By doing this, without the least impairing of our strength, we add to the credit of our moderation, which, in itself, is always strength more or less.

I know many have been taught to think that moderation in a case like this is a sort of treason,—and that all arguments for it are sufficiently answered by railing at rebels and rebellion, and by charging all the present or future miseries which we may suffer on the resistance of our brethren. But I would wish them, in this grave matter, and if peace is not wholly removed from their hearts, to consider seriously, first, that to criminate and recriminate never yet was the road to reconciliation, in any difference amongst men. In the next place, it would be right to reflect that the American English (whom they may abuse, if they think it honorable to revile the absent) can, as things now stand, neither be provoked at our railing or bettered by our instruction. All communication is cut off between us. But this we know with certainty, that, though we cannot reclaim them, we may reform ourselves. If measures of peace are necessary, they must begin somewhere; and a conciliatory temper must precede and prepare every plan of reconciliation. Nor do I conceive that we suffer anything by thus regulating our own minds. We are not disarmed by being disencumbered of our passions. Declaiming on rebellion never added a bayonet or a charge of powder to your military force; but I am afraid that it has been the means of taking up many muskets against you.

This outrageous language, which has been encouraged and kept alive by every art, has already done incredible mischief. For a long time, even amidst the desolations of war, and the insults of hostile laws daily accumulated on one another, the American leaders seem to have had the greatest difficulty in bringing up their people to a declaration of total independ-

ence. But the Court Gazette accomplished what the abettors
of independence had attempted in vain. When that disin-
genuous compilation and strange medley of railing and
flattery was adduced as a proof of the united sentiments of
the people of Great Britain, there was a great change throughout all America. The tide of popular affection, which had
still set towards the parent country, began immediately to
turn, and to flow with great rapidity in a contrary course.
Far from concealing these wild declarations of enmity, the
author of the celebrated pamphlet which prepared the minds
of the people for independence[3] insists largely on the multitude and the spirit of these addresses; and he draws an argument from them, which, if the fact were as he supposes, must
be irresistible. For I never knew a writer on the theory of
government so partial to authority as not to allow that the
hostile mind of the rulers to their people did fully justify a
change of government; nor can any reason whatever be given
why one people should voluntarily yield any degree of pre-
ëminence to another but on a supposition of great affection
and benevolence towards them. Unfortunately, your rulers,
trusting to other things, took no notice of this great principle
of connection. From the beginning of this affair, they have
done all they could to alienate your minds from your own
kindred; and if they could excite hatred enough in one of the
parties towards the other, they seemed to be of opinion that
they had gone half the way towards reconciling the quarrel.

I know it is said, that your kindness is only alienated on
account of their resistance, and therefore, if the colonies surrender at discretion, all sort of regard, and even much indulgence, is meant towards them in future. But can those who
are partisans for continuing a war to enforce such a surrender
be responsible (after all that has passed) for such a future
use of a power that is bound by no compacts and restrained

---

[3] Thomas Paine's *Common Sense*.

by no terror? Will they tell us what they call indulgences? Do they not at this instant call the present war and all its horrors a lenient and merciful proceeding?

No conqueror that I ever heard of has *professed* to make a cruel, harsh, and insolent use of his conquest. No! The man of the most declared pride scarcely dares to trust his own heart with this dreadful secret of ambition. But it will appear in its time; and no man who professes to reduce another to the insolent mercy of a foreign arm ever had any sort of good-will towards him. The profession of kindness, with that sword in his hand, and that demand of surrender, is one о_ the most provoking acts of his hostility. I shall be told that all this is lenient as against rebellious adversaries. But are the leaders of their faction more lenient to those who submit? Lord Howe and General Howe have powers, under an act of Parliament, to restore to the king's peace and to free trade any men or district which shall submit. Is this done? We have been over and over informed by the authorized gazette, that the city of New York and the countries of Staten and Long Island have submitted voluntarily and cheerfully, and that many are very full of zeal to the cause of administration. Were they instantly restored to trade? Are they yet restored to it? Is not the benignity of two commissioners, naturally most humane and generous men, some way fettered by instructions, equally against their dispositions and the spirit of Parliamentary faith, when Mr. Tryon, vaunting of the fidelity of the city in which he is governor, is obliged to apply to ministry for leave to protect the king's loyal subjects, and to grant to them, not the disputed rights and privileges of freedom, but the common rights of men, by the name of *graces?* Why do not the commissioners restore them on the spot? Were they not named as commissioners for that express purpose? But we see well enough to what the whole leads. The trade of America is to be dealt out in *private indulgences and graces,*—that is, in jobs to recompense the incendiaries of war. They will be informed of the proper time in which to send out their merchandise. From a national, the American trade is to be turned into a personal monopoly, and one set of merchants are to be rewarded for the pretended zeal of which another set are the dupes; and thus, between craft and credulity, the voice of reason is stifled, and all the misconduct, all the calamities of the war are covered and continued.

If I had not lived long enough to be little surprised at anything, I should have been in some degree astonished at the continued rage of several gentlemen, who, not satisfied with carrying fire and sword into America, are animated nearly with the same fury against those neighbors of theirs whose only crime it is, that they have charitably and humanely wished them to entertain more reasonable sentiments, and not always to sacrifice their interest to their passion. All this rage against unresisting dissent convinces me, that, at bottom, they are far from satisfied they are in the right. For what is it they would have? A war? They certainly have at this moment the blessing of something that is very like one; and if the war they enjoy at present be not sufficiently hot and extensive, they may shortly have it as warm and as spreading as their hearts can desire. Is it the force of the kingdom they call for? They have it already; and if they choose to fight their battles in their own person, nobody prevents their setting sail to America in the next transports. Do they think that the service is stinted for want of liberal supplies? Indeed they complain without reason. The table of the House of Commons will glut them, let their appetite for expense be never so keen. And I assure them further, that those who think with them in the House of Commons are full as easy in the control as they are liberal in the vote of these expenses. If this be not supply or confidence sufficient, let them open their own private purse-strings, and give, from what is left to them, as largely and with as little care as they think proper.

Tolerated in their passions, let them learn not to persecute the moderation *a virtue* of their fellow-citizens. If all the world joined them in a full cry against rebellion, and were as hotly inflamed against the whole theory and enjoyment of freedom as those who are the most factious for servitude, it could not, in my opinion, answer any one end whatsoever in this contest. The leaders of this war could not hire (to gratify their friends) one German more than they do, or inspire him with less feeling for the persons or less value for the privileges of their revolted brethren. If we all adopted their sentiments to a man, their allies, the savage Indians, could not be more ferocious than they are: they could not murder one more helpless woman or child, or with more exquisite refinements of cruelty torment to death one more of their English flesh and blood, than they do already. The public money is given to purchase this alliance;—and they have their bargain.

They are continually boasting of unanimity, or calling for it. But before this unanimity can be matter either of wish or congratulation, we ought to be pretty sure that we are engaged in a rational pursuit. Frenzy does not become a slighter distemper on account of the number of those who may be infected with it. Delusion and weakness produce not one mischief the less because they are universal. I declare that I cannot discern the least advantage which could accrue to us, if we were able to persuade our colonies that they had not a single friend in Great Britain. On the contrary, if the affections and opinions of mankind be not exploded as principles of connection, I conceive it would be happy for us, if they were taught to believe that there was even a formed American party in England, to whom they could always look for support. Happy would it be for us, if, in all tempers, they might turn their eyes to the parent state, so that their very turbulence and sedition should find vent in no other place than this! I believe there is not a man (except those who prefer the interest of some paltry faction to the very being of their country) who would not wish that the Americans should from

time to time carry many points, and even some of them not
quite reasonable, by the aid of any denomination of men
here, rather than they should be driven to seek for protection
against the fury of foreign mercenaries and the waste of savages in the arms of France.

When any community is subordinately connected with another, the great danger of the connection is the extreme pride
and self-complacency of the superior, which in all matters of
controversy will probably decide in its own favor. It is a
powerful corrective to such a very rational cause of fear, if
the inferior body can be made to believe that the party inclination or political views of several in the principal state will
induce them in some degree to counteract this blind and tyrannical partiality. There is no danger that any one acquiring
consideration or power in the presiding state should carry
this leaning to the inferior too far. The fault of human nature
is not of that sort. Power, in whatever hands, is rarely guilty
of too strict limitations on itself. But one great advantage to
the support of authority attends such an amicable and protecting connection: that those who have conferred favors obtain influence, and from the foresight of future events can
persuade men who have received obligations sometimes to return them. Thus, by the mediation of those healing principles,
(call them good or evil,) troublesome discussions are brought
to some sort of adjustment, and every hot controversy is not a
civil war.

But, if the colonies (to bring the general matter home to
us) could see that in Great Britain the mass of the people is
melted into its government, and that every dispute with the
ministry must of necessity be always a quarrel with the nation, they can stand no longer in the equal and friendly relation of fellow-citizens to the subjects of this kingdom.
Humble as this relation may appear to some, when it is
once broken, a strong tie is dissolved. Other sort of connec-

tions will be sought. For there are very few in the world who will not prefer an useful ally to an insolent master.

Such discord has been the effect of the unanimity into which so many have of late been seduced or bullied, or into the appearance of which they have sunk through mere despair. They have been told that their dissent from violent measures is an encouragement to rebellion. Men of great presumption and little knowledge will hold a language which is contradicted by the whole course of history. *General* rebellions and revolts of an whole people never were *encouraged*, now or at any time. They are always *provoked*. But if this unheard-of doctrine of the encouragement of rebellion were true, if it were true that an assurance of the friendship of numbers in this country towards the colonies could become an encouragement to them to break off all connection with it, what is the inference? Does anybody seriously maintain, that, charged with my share of the public councils, I am obliged not to resist projects which I think mischievous, lest men who suffer should be encouraged to resist? The very tendency of such projects to produce rebellion is one of the chief reasons against them. Shall that reason not be given? Is it, then, a rule, that no man in this nation shall open his mouth in favor of the colonies, shall defend their rights, or complain of their sufferings,—or when war finally breaks out, no man shall express his desires of peace? Has this been the law of our past, or is it to be the terms of our future connection? Even looking no further than ourselves, can it be true loyalty to any government, or true patriotism towards any country, to degrade their solemn councils into servile drawing-rooms, to flatter their pride and passions rather than to enlighten their reason, and to prevent them from being cautioned against violence lest others should be encouraged to resistance? By such acquiescence great kings and mighty nations have been undone; and if any are at this day in a perilous situation from rejecting truth and listening to flattery, it would rather become them to reform the errors under which they suffer than to reproach those who forewarned them of their danger.

But the rebels looked for assistance from this country.— They did so, in the beginning of this controversy, most certainly; and they sought it by earnest supplications to government, which dignity rejected, and by a suspension of commerce, which the wealth of this nation enabled you to despise. When they found that neither prayers nor menaces had any sort of weight, but that a firm resolution was taken to reduce them to unconditional obedience by a military force, they came to the last extremity. Despairing of us, they trusted in themselves. Not strong enough themselves, they sought succor in France. In proportion as all encouragement here lessened, their distance from this country increased. The encouragement is over; the alienation is complete.

In order to produce this favorite unanimity in delusion, and to prevent all possibility of a return to our ancient happy concord, arguments for our continuance in this course are drawn from the wretched situation itself into which we have been betrayed. It is said, that, being at war with the colonies, whatever our sentiments might have been before, all ties between us are now dissolved, and all the policy we have left is to strengthen the hands of government to reduce them. On the principle of this argument, the more mischiefs we suffer from any administration, the more our trust in it is to be confirmed. Let them but once get us into a war, and then their power is safe, and an act of oblivion passed for all their misconduct.

But is it really true that government is always to be strengthened with the instruments of war, but never furnished with the means of peace? In former times, ministers, I allow, have been sometimes driven by the popular voice to assert by arms the national honor against foreign powers. But the wisdom of the nation has been far more clear, when those ministers have been compelled to consult its interests by treaty. We all know that the sense of the nation obliged the court of Charles the Second to abandon the *Dutch war:* a war, next to the present, the most impolitic which we ever carried on. The good people of England considered Holland as a sort of dependency on this kingdom; they dreaded to drive it to the protection or subject it to the power of France by their own inconsiderate hostility. They paid but little respect to the court jargon of that day; nor were they inflamed by the pretended rivalship of the Dutch in trade,—by the massacre at Amboyna, acted on the stage to provoke the public vengeance,—nor by declamations against the ingratitude of the United Provinces for the benefits England had conferred upon them in their infant state. They were not moved from their evident interest by all these arts; nor was it enough to tell them, they were at war, that they must go through with it, and that the cause of the dispute was lost in the consequences. The people of England were then, as they are now, called upon to make government strong. They thought it a great deal better to make it wise and honest.

When I was amongst my constituents at the last summer assizes, I remember that men of all descriptions did then express a very strong desire for peace, and no slight hopes of attaining it from the commission sent out by my Lord Howe. And it is not a little remarkable, that, in proportion as every person showed a zeal for the court measures, he was then earnest in circulating an opinion of the extent of the supposed powers of that commission. When I told them that Lord Howe had no powers to treat, or to promise satisfaction on any point whatsoever of the controversy, I was hardly credited,—so strong and general was the desire of terminating this war by the method of accommodation. As far as I could discover, this was the temper then prevalent through the kingdom. The king's forces, it must be observed, had at that time been obliged to evacuate Boston. The superiority of the former campaign rested wholly with the colonists. If such powers of treaty were to be wished whilst success was very doubtful, how came they to be less so, since his Majesty's arms have been crowned with many considerable advantages? Have these successes induced us to alter our mind, as thinking the season of victory not the time for treating with honor or advantage? Whatever changes have happened in the national character, it can scarcely be our wish that terms of accommodation never should be proposed to our enemy, except when they must be attributed solely to our fears. It has happened, let me say unfortunately, that we read of his Majesty's commission for making peace, and his troops evacuating his last town in the Thirteen Colonies, at the same hour and in the same gazette. It was still more unfortunate that no commission went to America to settle the troubles there, until several months after an act had been passed to put the colonies out of the protection of this government, and to divide their trading property, without a possibility of restitution, as spoil among the seamen of the navy. The most abject submission on the part of the colonies could not redeem them. There was no man on that whole continent, or within three thousand miles of it, qualified by law to follow allegiance with protection or submission with pardon. A proceeding of this kind has no example in history. Independency, and independency with an enmity, (which, putting ourselves out of the question, would be called natural and much provoked,) was the inevitable consequence. How this came to pass the nation may be one day in an humor to inquire.

All the attempts made this session to give fuller powers of peace to the commanders in America were stifled by the fatal confidence of victory and the wild hopes of unconditional submission. There was a moment favorable to the king's arms, when, if any powers of concession had existed on the other side of the Atlantic, even after all our errors, peace in all probability might have been restored. But calamity is unhappily the usual season of reflection; and the pride of men will not often suffer reason to have any scope, until it can be no longer of service.

I have always wished, that as the dispute had its apparent origin from things done in Parliament, and as the acts passed there had provoked the war, that the foundations of peace should be laid in Parliament also. I have been astonished to find that those whose zeal for the dignity of our body was so hot as to light up the flames of civil war should even publicly declare that these delicate points ought to be wholly left to the crown. Poorly as I may be thought affected to the authority of Parliament, I shall never admit that our constitutional rights can ever become a matter of ministerial negotiation.

I am charged with being an American. If warm affection towards those over whom I claim any share of authority be a crime, I am guilty of this charge. But I do assure you, (and they who know me publicly and privately will bear witness to me,) that, if ever one man lived more zealous than another for the supremacy of Parliament and the rights of this imperial crown, it was myself. Many others, indeed, might be more knowing in the extent of the foundation of these rights. I do not pretend to be an antiquary, a lawyer, or qualified for the chair of professor in metaphysics. I never ventured to put your solid interests upon speculative grounds. My having constantly declined to do so has been attributed to my incapacity for such disquisitions; and I am inclined to believe it is partly the cause. I never shall be ashamed to confess, that, where I am ignorant, I am diffident. I am, indeed, not very solicitous to clear myself of this imputed incapacity; because men even less conversant than I am in this kind of subtleties, and placed in stations to which I ought not to aspire, have, by the mere force of civil discretion, often conducted the affairs of great nations with distinguished felicity and glory.

When I first came into a public trust, I found your Parliament in possession of an unlimited legislative power over the colonies. I could not open the statute-book without seeing the actual exercise of it, more or less, in all cases whatsoever. This possession passed with me for a title. It does so in all human affairs. No man examines into the defects of his title to his paternal estate or to his established government. Indeed, common sense taught me that a legislative authority not actually limited by the express terms of its foundation, or by its own subsequent acts, cannot have its powers parcelled out by argumentative distinctions, so as to enable us to say that here they can and there they cannot bind. Nobody was so obliging as to produce to me any record of such distinctions, by compact or otherwise, either at the successive formation of the several colonies or during the existence of any of them. If any gentlemen were able to see how one power could be given up (merely on abstract reasoning) without giving up the rest, I can only say that they saw further than I could. Nor did I ever presume to condemn any one for being clear-sighted when I was blind. I praise their penetration and learning, and hope that their practice has been correspondent to their theory.

I had, indeed, very earnest wishes to keep the whole body of this authority perfect and entire as I found it,—and to keep it so, not for our advantage solely, but principally for the sake of those on whose account all just authority exists: I mean the people to be governed. For I thought I saw that many cases might well happen in which the exercise of every power comprehended in the broadest idea of legislature might become, in its time and circumstances, not a little expedient for the peace and union of the colonies amongst themselves, as well as for their perfect harmony with Great Britain. Thinking so, (perhaps erroneously, but being honestly of that opinion,) I was at the same time very sure that the authority of which I was so jealous could not, under the actual circumstances of our plantations, be at all preserved in any of its members, but by the greatest reserve in its application, particularly in those delicate points in which the feelings of mankind are the most irritable. They who thought otherwise have found a few more difficulties in their work than (I hope) they were thoroughly aware of, when they undertook the present business. I must beg leave to observe, that it is not only the invidious branch of taxation that will be resisted, but that no other given part of legislative rights can be exercised, without regard to the general opinion of those who are to be governed. That general opinion is the vehicle and organ of legislative omnipotence. Without this, it may be a theory to entertain the mind, but it is nothing in the direction of affairs. The completeness of the legislative authority of Parliament *over this kingdom* is not questioned; and yet many things indubitably included in the abstract idea of that power, and which carry no absolute injustice in themselves, yet being contrary to the opinions and feelings of the people, can as little be exercised as if Parliament in that case had been possessed of no right at all. I see no abstract reason, which can be given, why the same power which made and repealed the High Commission Court and the Star-Chamber might not revive them again; and these courts, warned by their former fate, might possibly exercise their powers with some degree of justice. But the madness would be as unquestionable as the competence of that Parliament which should attempt such things. If anything can be supposed out of the power of human legislature, it is religion; I admit, however, that the established religion of this country has been three or four times altered by act of Parliament, and therefore that a statute binds even in that case. But we may very safely affirm, that, notwithstanding this apparent omnipotence, it would be now found as impossible for King and Parliament to alter the established religion of this country as it was to King James alone, when he attempted to make such an alteration without a Parliament. In effect, to follow, not to force, the public inclination,—to give a direction, a form, a technical dress, and a specific sanction, to the general sense of the community, is the true end of legislature.

It is so with regard to the exercise of all the powers which our Constitution knows in any of its parts, and indeed to the substantial existence of any of the parts themselves. The king's negative to bills is one of the most indisputed of the royal prerogatives; and it extends to all cases whatsoever. I am far from certain, that if several laws, which I know, had fallen under the stroke of that sceptre, that the public would have had a very heavy loss. But it is not the *propriety* of the exercise which is in question. The exercise itself is wisely forborne. Its repose may be the preservation of its existence; and its existence may be the means of saving the Constitution itself, on an occasion worthy of bringing it forth.

As the disputants whose accurate and logical reasonings have brought us into our present condition think it absurd that powers or members of any constitution should exist, rarely, if ever, to be exercised, I hope I shall be excused in mentioning another instance that is material. We know that the Convocation of the Clergy had formerly been called, and sat with nearly as much regularity to business as Parliament itself. It is now called for form only. It sits for the purpose of making some polite ecclesiastical compliments to the king, and, when that grace is said, retires and is heard of no more. It is, however, *a part of the Constitution,* and may be called out into act and energy, whenever there is occasion, and whenever those who conjure up that spirit will choose to abide the consequences. It is wise to permit its legal existence: it is much wiser to continue it a legal existence only. So truly has prudence (constituted as the god of this lower world) the entire dominion over every exercise of power committed into its hands! And yet I have lived to see prudence and conformity to circumstances wholly set at nought in our late controversies, and treated as if they were the most contemptible and irrational of all things. I have heard it an hundred times very gravely alleged, that, in order to keep power in wind, it was necessary, by preference, to exert it in those very points in which it was most likely to be resisted and the least likely to be productive of any advantage.

These were the considerations, Gentlemen, which led me early to think, that, in the comprehensive dominion which the Divine Providence had put into our hands, instead of troubling our understandings with speculations concerning the unity of empire and the identity or distinction of legislative powers, and inflaming our passions with the heat and pride of controversy, it was our duty, in all soberness, to conform our government to the character and circumstances of the several people who composed this mighty and strangely diversified mass. I never was wild enough to conceive that one method would serve for the whole, that the natives of Hindostan and those of Virginia could be ordered in the same manner, or that the Cutchery court and the grand jury of Salem could be regulated on a similar plan. I was persuaded that government was a practical thing made for the happiness of mankind, and not to furnish out a spectacle of uniformity to gratify the schemes of visionary politicians. Our business was to rule, not to wrangle; and it would have been a poor compensation that we had triumphed in a dispute, whilst we lost an empire.

If there be one fact in the world perfectly clear, it is this, —"that the disposition of the people of America is wholly averse to any other than a free government"; and this is indication enough to any honest statesman how he ought to adapt whatever power he finds in his hands to their case. If any ask me what a free government is, I answer, that, for any practical purpose, it is what the people think so,—and that they, and not I, are the natural, lawful, and competent judges of this matter. If they practically allow me a greater degree of authority over them than is consistent with any correct ideas of perfect freedom, I ought to thank them for so great

a trust, and not to endeavor to prove from thence that they
have reasoned amiss, and that, having gone so far, by analogy
they must hereafter have no enjoyment but by my pleasure.

If we had seen this done by any others, we should have
concluded them far gone in madness. It is melancholy, as
well as ridiculous, to observe the kind of reasoning with
which the public has been amused, in order to divert our
minds from the common sense of our American policy.
There are people who have split and anatomized the doctrine
of free government, as if it were an abstract question concerning metaphysical liberty and necessity, and not a matter
of moral prudence and natural feeling. They have disputed
whether liberty be a positive or a negative idea; whether it
does not consist in being governed by laws, without considering what are the laws, or who are the makers; whether
man has any rights by Nature; and whether all the property
he enjoys be not the alms of his government, and his life
itself their favor and indulgence. Others, corrupting religion
as these have perverted philosophy, contend that Christians
are redeemed into captivity, and the blood of the Saviour
of mankind has been shed to make them the slaves of a few
proud and insolent sinners. These shocking extremes provoking
to extremes of another kind, speculations are let loose as
destructive to all authority as the former are to all freedom;
and every government is called tyranny and usurpation which
is not formed on their fancies. In this manner the stirrers-up
of this contention, not satisfied with distracting our dependencies and filling them with blood and slaughter, are corrupting
our understandings: they are endeavoring to tear up, along
with practical liberty, all the foundations of human society,
all equity and justice, religion and order.

Civil freedom, Gentlemen, is not, as many have endeavored
to persuade you, a thing that lies hid in the depth of abstruse
science. It is a blessing and a benefit, not an abstract speculation: and all the just reasoning that can be upon it is of so

coarse a texture as perfectly to suit the ordinary capacities of those who are to enjoy, and of those who are to defend it. Far from any resemblance to those propositions in geometry and metaphysics which admit no medium, but must be true or false in all their latitude, social and civil freedom, like all other things in common life, are variously mixed and modified, enjoyed in very different degrees, and shaped into an infinite diversity of forms, according to the temper and circumstances of every community. The *extreme* of liberty (which is its abstract perfection, but its real fault) obtains nowhere, nor ought to obtain anywhere; because extremes, as we all know, in every point which relates either to our duties or satisfactions in life, are destructive both to virtue and enjoyment. Liberty, too, must be limited in order to be possessed. The degree of restraint it is impossible in any case to settle precisely. But it ought to be the constant aim of every wise public counsel to find out by cautious experiments, and rational, cool endeavors, with how little, not how much, of this restraint the community can subsist: for liberty is a good to be improved, and not an evil to be lessened. It is not only a private blessing of the first order, but the vital spring and energy of the state itself, which has just so much life and vigor as there is liberty in it. But whether liberty be advantageous or not, (for I know it is a fashion to decry the very principle,) none will dispute that peace is a blessing; and peace must, in the course of human affairs, be frequently bought by some indulgence and toleration at least to liberty: for, as the Sabbath (though of divine institution) was made for man, not man for the Sabbath, government, which can claim no higher origin or authority, in its exercise at least, ought to conform to the exigencies of the time, and the temper and character of the people with whom it is concerned, and not always to attempt violently to bend the people to their theories of subjection. The bulk of mankind, on their part, are not excessively curious concerning any theories whilst they are really happy; and one sure symptom of an ill-conducted state is the propensity of the people to resort to them.

But when subjects, by a long course of such ill conduct, are once thoroughly _inflamed_, and the state itself violently distempered, the people must have some satisfaction to their feelings more solid than a sophistical speculation on law and government. Such was our situation: and such a satisfaction was necessary to prevent recourse to arms; it was necessary towards laying them down; it will be necessary to prevent the taking them up again and again. Of what nature this satisfaction ought to be I wish it had been the disposition of Parliament seriously to consider. It was certainly a deliberation that called for the exertion of all their wisdom.

I am, and ever have been, deeply sensible of the difficulty of reconciling the strong presiding power, that is so useful towards the conservation of a vast, disconnected, infinitely diversified empire, with that liberty and safety of the provinces which they must enjoy, (in opinion and practice at least,) or they will not be provinces at all. I know, and have long felt, the difficulty of reconciling the unwieldy haughtiness of a great ruling nation, habituated to command, pampered by enormous wealth, and confident from a long course of prosperity and victory, to the high spirit of free dependencies, animated with the first glow and activity of juvenile heat, and assuming to themselves, as their birthright, some part of that very pride which oppresses them. They who perceive no difficulty in reconciling these tempers (which, however, to make peace, must some way or other be reconciled) are much above my capacity, or much below the magnitude of the business. Of one thing I am perfectly clear: that it is not by deciding the suit, but by compromising the difference, that peace can be restored or kept. They who would put an end to such quarrels by declaring roundly in favor of the whole demands of either party have mistaken, in my humble opinion, the office of a mediator.

The war is now of full two years' standing: the controversy of many more. In different periods of the dispute, different methods of reconciliation were to be pursued. I mean to trouble you with a short state of things at the most important of these periods, in order to give you a more distinct idea of our policy with regard to this most delicate of all objects. The colonies were from the beginning subject to the legislature of Great Britain on principles which they never examined; and we permitted to them many local privileges, without asking how they agreed with that legislative authority. Modes of administration were formed in an insensible and very unsystematic manner. But they gradually adapted themselves to the varying condition of things. What was first a single kingdom stretched into an empire; and an imperial superintendency, of some kind or other, became necessary. Parliament, from a mere representative of the people, and a guardian of popular privileges for its own immediate constituents, grew into a mighty sovereign. Instead of being a control on the crown on its own behalf, it communicated a sort of strength to the royal authority, which was wanted for the conservation of a new object, but which could not be safely trusted to the crown alone. On the other hand, the colonies, advancing by equal steps, and governed by the same necessity, had formed within themselves, either by royal instruction or royal charter, assemblies so exceedingly resembling a parliament, in all their forms, functions, and powers, that it was impossible they should not imbibe some opinion of a similar authority.

At the first designation of these assemblies, they were probably not intended for anything more (nor perhaps did they think themselves much higher) than the municipal corporations within this island, to which some at present love to compare them. But nothing in (progression) can rest on its original plan. We may as well think of rocking a grown man in the cradle of an infant. Therefore, as the colonies prospered and increased to a numerous and mighty people, spreading over a very great tract of the globe, it was natural that they should attribute to assemblies so respectable in their formal constitution some part of the dignity of the great nations which they represented. No longer tied to by-laws, these assemblies made acts of all sorts and in all cases whatsoever. They levied money, not for parochial purposes, but upon regular grants to the crown, following all the rules and principles of a parliament, to which they approached every day more and more nearly. Those who think themselves wiser than Providence and stronger than the course of Nature may complain of all this variation, on the one side or the other, as their several humors and prejudices may lead them. But things could not be otherwise; and English colonies must be had on these terms, or not had at all. In the mean time neither party felt any inconvenience from this double legislature, to which they had been formed by imperceptible habits, and old custom, the great support of all the governments in the world. Though these two legislatures were sometimes found perhaps performing the very same functions, they did not very grossly or systematically clash. In all likelihood this arose from mere neglect, possibly from the natural operation of things, which, left to themselves, generally fall into their proper order. But whatever was the cause, it is certain that a regular revenue, by the authority of Parliament, for the support of civil and military establishments, seems not to have been thought of until the colonies were too proud to submit, too strong to be forced, too enlightened not to see all the consequences which must arise from such a system.

If ever this scheme of taxation was to be pushed against the inclinations of the people, it was evident that discussions must arise, which would let loose all the elements that composed this double constitution, would show how much each of their members had departed from its original principles, and would discover contradictions in each legislature, as well to its own first principles as to its relation to the other, very difficult, if not absolutely impossible, to be reconciled.

Therefore, at the first fatal opening of this contest, the wisest course seemed to be to put an end as soon as possible to the immediate causes of the dispute, and to quiet a discussion, not easily settled upon clear principles, and arising from claims which pride would permit neither party to abandon, by resorting as nearly as possible to the old, successful course. A mere repeal of the obnoxious tax, with a declaration of the legislative authority of this kingdom, was then fully sufficient to procure peace to *both sides*. Man is a creature of habit, and, the first breach being of very short continuance, the colonies fell back exactly into their ancient state. The Congress has used an expression with regard to this pacification which appears to me truly significant. After the repeal of the Stamp Act, "the colonies fell," says this assembly, "into their ancient state of *unsuspecting confidence in the mother country*." This unsuspecting confidence is the true centre of gravity amongst mankind, about which all the parts are at rest. It is this *unsuspecting confidence* that removes all difficulties, and reconciles all the contradictions which occur in the complexity of all ancient puzzled political establishments. Happy are the rulers which have the secret of preserving it!

The whole empire has reason to remember with eternal gratitude the wisdom and temper of that man and his excellent associates, who, to recover this confidence, formed a plan of pacification in 1766. That plan, being built upon the nature of man, and the circumstances and habits of the two countries, and not on any visionary speculations, perfectly answered its end, as long as it was thought proper to adhere to it. Without giving a rude shock to the dignity (well or ill understood) of this Parliament, they gave perfect content to our dependencies. Had it not been for the mediatorial spirit and talents of that great man between such clashing pretensions and passions, we should then have rushed headlong (I know what I say) into the calamities of that civil war in which, by departing from his system, we are at length involved; and we should have been precipitated into that war at a time when circumstances both at home and abroad were far, very far, more unfavorable unto us than they were at the breaking out of the present troubles.

I had the happiness of giving my first votes in Parliament for that pacification. I was one of those almost unanimous members who, in the necessary concessions of Parliament, would as much as possible have preserved its authority and respected its honor. I could not at once tear from my heart prejudices which were dear to me, and which bore a resemblance to virtue. I had then, and I have still, my partialities. What Parliament gave up I wished to be given as of grace and favor and affection, and not as a restitution of stolen goods. High dignity relented as it was soothed; and a benignity from old acknowledged greatness had its full effect on our dependencies. Our unlimited declaration of legislative authority produced not a single murmur. If this undefined power has become odious since that time, and full of horror to the colonies, it is because the *unsuspicious confidence* is lost, and the parental affection, in the bosom of whose boundless authority they reposed their privileges, is become estranged and hostile.

It will be asked, if such was then my opinion of the mode of pacification, how I came to be the very person who moved, not only for a repeal of all the late coercive statutes, but for mutilating, by a positive law, the entireness of the legislative power of Parliament, and cutting off from it the whole right of taxation. I answer, Because a different state of things requires a different conduct. When the dispute had gone to these last extremities, (which no man labored more to prevent than I did,) the concessions which had satisfied in the beginning could satisfy no longer; because the violation of tacit faith required explicit security. The same cause which has introduced all formal compacts and covenants among men made it necessary: I mean habits of soreness, jealousy, and distrust. I parted with it as with a limb, but as a limb to save the body; and I would have parted with more, if more had been necessary; anything rather than a fruitless, hopeless, unnatural civil war. This mode of yielding would, it is said, give way to independency without a war. I am persuaded, from the nature of things, and from every information, that it would have had a directly contrary effect. But if it had this effect, I confess that I should prefer independency without war to independency with it; and I have so much trust in the inclinations and prejudices of mankind, and so little in anything else, that I should expect ten times more benefit to this kingdom from the affection of America, though under a separate establishment, than from her perfect submission to the crown and Parliament, accompanied with her terror, disgust, and abhorrence. Bodies tied together by so unnatural a bond of union as mutual hatred are only connected to their ruin.

One hundred and ten respectable members of Parliament voted for that concession. Many not present when the motion was made were of the sentiments of those who voted. I knew it would then have made peace. I am not without hopes that it would do so at present, if it were adopted. No benefit, no revenue, could be lost by it; something might possibly be gained by its consequences. For be fully assured, that, of all the phantoms that ever deluded the fond hopes of a credulous world, a Parliamentary revenue in the colonies is the most perfectly chimerical. Your breaking them to any subjection, far from relieving your burdens, (the pretext for this war,) will never pay that military force which will be kept up to the destruction of their liberties and yours. I risk nothing in this prophecy.

Gentlemen, you have my opinions on the present state of public affairs. Mean as they may be in themselves, your partiality has made them of some importance. Without troubling myself to inquire whether I am under a formal obligation to it, I have a pleasure in accounting for my conduct to my constituents. I feel warmly on this subject, and I express myself as I feel. If I presume to blame any public proceeding, I cannot be supposed to be personal. Would to God I could be suspected of it! My fault might be greater, but the public calamity would be less extensive. If my conduct has not been able to make any impression on the warm part of that ancient and powerful party with whose support I was not honored at my election, on my side, my respect, regard, and duty to them is not at all lessened. I owe the gentlemen who compose it my most humble service in everything. I hope that whenever any of them were pleased to command me, that they found me perfectly equal in my obedience. But flattery and friendship are very different things; and to mislead is not to serve them. I cannot purchase the favor of any man by concealing from him what I think his ruin.

By the favor of my fellow-citizens, I am the representative of an honest, well-ordered, virtuous city,—of a people who preserve more of the original English simplicity and purity of manners than perhaps any other. You possess among you several men and magistrates of large and cultivated understandings, fit for any employment in any sphere. I do, to the best of my power, act so as to make myself worthy of so honorable a choice. If I were ready, on any call of my own vanity or interest, or to answer any election purpose, to forsake principles (whatever they are) which I had formed at a mature age, on full reflection, and which had been confirmed by long experience, I should forfeit the only thing which makes you pardon so many errors and imperfections in me.

Not that I think it fit for any one to rely too much on his own understanding, or to be filled with a presumption not becoming a Christian man in his own personal stability and rectitude. I hope I am far from that vain confidence which almost always fails in trial. I know my weakness in all respects, as much at least as any enemy I have; and I attempt to take security against it. The only method which has ever been found effectual to preserve any man against the corruption of nature and example is an habit of life and communication of councils with the most virtuous and public-spirited men of the age you live in. Such a society cannot be kept without advantage, or deserted without shame. For this rule of conduct I may be called in reproach a *party man;* but I am little affected with such aspersions. In the way which they call party I worship the Constitution of your fathers; and I shall never blush for my political company. All reverence to honor, all idea of what it is, will be lost out of the world, before it can be imputed as a fault to any man, that he has been closely connected with those incomparable persons, living and dead, with whom for eleven years I have constantly thought and acted. If I have wandered out of the paths of rectitude into those of interested faction, it was in company with the Saviles, the Dowdeswells, the Wentworths, the Bentincks; with the Lenoxes, the Manchesters, the Keppels, the Saunderses; with the temperate, permanent, hereditary virtue of the whole house of Cavendish: names, among which, some have extended your fame and empire in arms, and all have fought the battle of your liberties in fields not less glorious. These, and many more like these, grafting public principles on private honor, have redeemed the present age, and would have adorned the most splendid period in your history. Where could any man, conscious of his own inability to act alone, and willing to act as he ought to do, have arranged himself better? If any one thinks this kind of society to be taken up as the best method of gratifying low personal pride or ambitious interest, he is mistaken, and knows nothing of the world.

Preferring this connection, I do not mean to detract in the slightest degree from others. There are some of those whom I admire at something of a greater distance, with whom I have had the happiness also perfectly to agree, in almost all the particulars in which I have differed with some successive administrations; and they are such as it never can be reputable to any government to reckon among its enemies.

I hope there are none of you corrupted with the doctrine taught by wicked men for the worst purposes, and received by the malignant credulity of envy and ignorance, which is, that the men who act upon the public stage are all alike, all equally corrupt, all influenced by no other views than the sordid lure of salary and pension. The thing I know by experience to be false. Never expecting to find perfection in men, and not looking for divine attributes in created beings, in my commerce with my contemporaries I have found much human virtue. I have seen not a little public spirit, a real subordination of interest to duty, and a decent and regulated sensibility to honest fame and reputation. The age unquestionably produces (whether in a greater or less number than former times I know not) daring profligates and insidious hypocrites. What then? Am I not to avail myself of whatever good is to be found in the world, because of the mixture of evil that will always be in it? The smallness of the quantity in currency only heightens the value. They who raise suspicions on the good on account of the behavior of ill men are of the party of the latter. The common cant is no justification for taking this party. I have been deceived, say they, by *Titius* and *Mævius;* I have been the dupe of this pretender or of that mountebank; and I can trust appearances no longer. But my credulity and want of discernment cannot, as I conceive, amount to a fair presumption against any man's integrity. A conscientious person would rather doubt his own judgment than condemn his species. He would say, "I have observed without attention, or judged upon erroneous maxims; I trusted to profession, when I ought to have attended to conduct." Such a man will grow wise, not malignant, by his acquaintance with the world. But he that accuses all mankind of corruption ought to remember that he is sure to convict only one. In truth, I should much rather admit those whom at any time I have disrelished the most to be patterns of perfection than seek a consolation to my own unworthiness in a general communion of depravity with all about me.

That this ill-natured doctrine should be preached by the missionaries of a court I do not wonder. It answers their purpose. But that it should be heard among those who pretend to be strong assertors of liberty is not only surprising, but hardly natural. This moral levelling is a *servile principle*. It leads to practical passive obedience far better than all the doctrines which the pliant accommodation of theology to power has ever produced. It cuts up by the roots, not only all idea of forcible resistance, but even of civil opposition. It disposes men to an abject submission, not by opinion, which may be shaken by argument or altered by passion, but by the strong ties of public and private interest. For, if all men who act in a public situation are equally selfish, corrupt, and venal, what reason can be given for desiring any sort of change, which, besides the evils which must attend all changes, can be productive of no possible advantage? The active men in the state are true samples of the mass. If they are universally depraved, the commonwealth itself is not sound. We may amuse ourselves with talking as much as we please of the virtue of middle or humble life; that is, we may place our confidence in the virtue of those who have never been tried. But if the persons who are continually emerging out of that sphere be no better than those whom birth has placed above it, what hopes are there in the remainder of the body which is to furnish the perpetual succession of the state? All who have ever written on government are unanimous, that among a people generally corrupt liberty cannot long exist. And, indeed, how is it possible, when those who are to make the laws, to guard, to enforce, or to obey them, are, by a tacit confederacy of manners, indisposed to the spirit of all generous and noble institutions?

I am aware that the age is not what we all wish. But I am sure that the only means of checking its precipitate degeneracy is heartily to concur with whatever is the best in our time, and to have some more correct standard of judging what that best is than the transient and uncertain favor of a court. If once we are able to find, and can prevail on ourselves to strengthen an union of such men, whatever accidentally becomes indisposed to ill-exercised power, even by the ordinary operation of human passions, must join with that society, and cannot long be joined without in some degree assimilating to it. Virtue will catch as well as vice by contact; and the public stock of honest, manly principle will daily accumulate. We are not too nicely to scrutinize motives as long as action is irreproachable. It is enough (and for a worthy man perhaps too much) to deal out its infamy to convicted guilt and declared apostasy.

This, Gentlemen, has been from the beginning the rule of my conduct; and I mean to continue it, as long as such a body as I have described can by any possibility be kept together; for I should think it the most dreadful of all offences, not only towards the present generation, but to all the future, if I were to do anything which could make the minutest breach in this great conservatory of free principles. Those who perhaps have the same intentions, but are separated by some little political animosities, will, I hope, discern at last how little conducive it is to any rational purpose to lower its reputation. For my part, Gentlemen, from much experience, from no little thinking, and from comparing a great variety of things, I am thoroughly per suaded that the last hopes of preserving the spirit of the English Constitution, or of reuniting the dissipated members of the English race upon a common plan of tranquillity and liberty, does entirely depend on their firm and lasting union, and above all on their keeping themselves from that despair which is so very apt to fall on those whom a violence of character and a mixture of ambitious views do not support through a long, painful, and unsuccessful struggle.

There never, Gentlemen, was a period in which the steadfastness of some men has been put to so sore a trial. It is not very difficult for well-formed minds to abandon their interest; but the separation of fame and virtue is an harsh divorce. Liberty is in danger of being made unpopular to Englishmen. Contending for an imaginary power, we begin to acquire the spirit of domination, and to lose the relish of honest equality. The principles of our forefathers become suspected to us, because we see them animating the present opposition of our children. The faults which grow out of the luxuriance of freedom appear much more shocking to us than the base vices which are generated from the rankness of servitude. Accordingly, the least resistance to power appears more inexcusable in our eyes than the greatest abuses of authority. All dread of a standing military force is looked upon as a superstitious panic. All shame of calling in foreigners and savages in a civil contest is worn off. We grow indifferent to the consequences inevitable to ourselves from the plan of ruling half the empire by a mercenary sword. We are taught to believe that a desire of domineering over our countrymen is love to our country, that those who hate civil war abet rebellion, and that the amiable and conciliatory virtues of lenity, moderation, and tenderness to the privileges of those who depend on this kingdom are a sort of treason to the state.

It is impossible that we should remain long in a situation which breeds such notions and dispositions without some great alteration in the national character. Those ingenuous and feeling minds who are so fortified against all other things, and so unarmed to whatever approaches in the shape of disgrace, finding these principles, which they considered as sure means of honor, to be grown into disrepute, will retire disheartened and disgusted. Those of a more robust make, the bold, able, ambitious men, who pay some of their court to power through the people, and substitute the voice of transient opinion in the place of true glory, will give into the general mode; and those superior understandings which ought to correct vulgar prejudice will confirm and aggravate its errors. Many things have been long operating towards a gradual change in our principles; but this American war has done more in a very few years than all the other causes could have effected in a century. It is therefore not on its own separate account, but because of its attendant circumstances, that I consider its continuance, or its ending in any way but that of an honorable and liberal accommodation, as the greatest evils which can befall us. For that reason I have troubled you with this long letter. For that reason I entreat you, again and again, neither to be persuaded, shamed, or frighted out of the principles that have hitherto led so many of you to abhor the war, its cause, and its consequences. Let us not be amongst the first who renounce the maxims of our forefathers.

I have the honor to be,

Gentlemen,

Your most obedient and faithful humble servant,

Edmund Burke.

Beaconsfield, April 3, 1777.

P. S.　You may communicate this letter in any manner you think proper to my constituents.

II CATHOLICISM AND IRELAND

FROM *Tract on the Popery Laws*[1]

The system which we have just reviewed, and the manner in which religious influence on the public is made to operate upon the laws concerning property in Ireland, is in its nature very singular, and differs, I apprehend, essentially, and perhaps to its disadvantage, from any scheme of religious persecution now existing in any other country in Europe, or which has prevailed in any time or nation with which history has made us acquainted. I believe it will not be difficult to show that it is unjust, impolitic, and inefficacious; that it has the most unhappy influence on the prosperity, the morals, and the safety of that country; that this influence is not accidental, but has flowed as the necessary and direct consequence of the laws themselves, first on account of the object which they affect, and next by the quality of the greatest part of the instruments they employ. Upon all these points, first upon the general, and then on the particular, this question will be considered with as much order as can be followed in a matter of itself as involved and intricate as it is important.

The first and most capital consideration with regard to

[1] Consisting of Chap. III (Pt. 1), with some omissions. The *Tract on the Popery Laws* (written soon after 1765) was left unfinished and published posthumously.

this, as to every object, is the extent of it. And here it is necessary to premise, this system of penalty and incapacity has for its object no small sect or obscure party, but a very numerous body of men,—a body which comprehends at least two thirds of that whole nation: it amounts to 2,800,000, souls, a number sufficient for the materials constituent of a great people. Now it is well worthy of a serious and dispassionate examination, whether such a system, respecting such an object, be in reality agreeable to any sound principles of legislation or any authorized definition of law; for if our reasons or practices differ from the general informed sense of mankind, it is very moderate to say that they are at least suspicious.

This consideration of the magnitude of the object ought to attend us through the whole inquiry: if it does not always affect the reason, it is always decisive on the importance of the question. It not only makes in itself a more leading point, but complicates itself with every other part of the matter, giving every error, minute in itself, a character and significance from its application. It is therefore not to be wondered at, if we perpetually recur to it in the course of this essay.

In the making of a new law it is undoubtedly the duty of the legislator to see that no injustice be done even to an individual: for there is then nothing to be unsettled, and the matter is under his hands to mould it as he pleases; and if he finds it untractable in the working, he may abandon it without incurring any new inconvenience. But in the question concerning the repeal of an old one, the work is of more difficulty; because laws, like houses, lean on one another, and the operation is delicate, and should be necessary: the objection, in such a case, ought not to arise from the natural infirmity of human institutions, but from substantial faults which contradict the nature and end of law itself,—faults not arising from the imperfection, but from the misapplication and abuse of our reason. As no legislators can regard the *minima* of equity, a law may in some instances be a just subject of censure without being at all an object of repeal. But if its transgressions against common right and the ends of just government should be considerable in their nature and spreading in their effects, as this objection goes to the root and principle of the law, it renders it void in its obligatory quality on the mind, and therefore determines it as the proper object of abrogation and repeal, so far as regards its civil existence. The objection here is, as we observed, by no means on account of the imperfection of the law; it is on account of its erroneous principle: for if this be fundamentally wrong, the more perfect the law is made, the worse it becomes. It cannot be said to have the properties of genuine law, even in its imperfections and defects. The true weakness and opprobrium of our best general constitutions is, that they cannot provide beneficially for every particular case, and thus fill, adequately to their intentions, the circle of universal justice. But where the principle is faulty, the erroneous part of the law is the beneficial, and justice only finds refuge in those holes and corners which had escaped the sagacity and inquisition of the legislator. The happiness or misery of multitudes can never be a thing indifferent. A law against the majority of the people is in substance a law against the people itself; its extent determines its invalidity; it even changes its character as it enlarges its operation: it is not particular injustice, but general oppression; and can no longer be considered as a private hardship, which might be borne, but spreads and grows up into the unfortunate importance of a national calamity.

Now as a law directed against the mass of the nation has not the nature of a reasonable institution, so neither has it the authority: for in all forms of government the people is the true legislator; and whether the immediate and instrumental cause of the law be a single person or many, the remote and efficient cause is the consent of the people, either actual or implied; and such consent is absolutely essential to its validity. To the solid establishment of every law two things are essentially requisite: first, a proper and sufficient human power to declare and modify the matter of the law; and next, such a fit and equitable constitution as they have a right to declare and render binding. With regard to the first requisite, the human authority, it is their judgment they give up, not their right. The people, indeed, are presumed to consent to whatever the legislature ordains for their benefit; and they are to acquiesce in it, though they do not clearly see into the propriety of the means by which they are conducted to that desirable end. This they owe as an act of homage and just deference to a reason which the necessity of government has made superior to their own. But though the means, and indeed the nature, of a public advantage may not always be evident to the understanding of the subject, no one is so gross and stupid as not to distinguish between a benefit and an injury. No one can imagine, then, an exclusion of a great body of men, not from favors, privileges, and trusts, but from the common advantages of society, can ever be a thing intended for their good, or can ever be ratified by any implied consent of theirs. If, therefore, at least an implied human consent is necessary to the existence of a law, such a constitution cannot in propriety be a law at all.

But if we could suppose that such a ratification was made, not virtually, but actually, by the people, not representatively, but even collectively, still it would be null and void. They have no right to make a law prejudicial to the whole community, even though the delinquents in making such an act should be themselves the chief sufferers by it; because it would be made against the principle of a superior law, which it is not in the power of any community, or of the whole race of man, to alter,—I mean the will of Him who gave us our nature, and in giving impressed an invariable law upon it. It would be hard to point out any error more truly subversive of all the order and beauty, of all the peace and happiness of human society, than the position, that any body of men have a right to make what laws they please,— or that laws can derive any authority from their institution merely, and independent of the quality of the subject-matter. No arguments of policy, reason of state, or preservation of the constitution can be pleaded in favor of such a practice. They may, indeed, impeach the frame of that constitution, but can never touch this immovable principle. This seems to be, indeed, the doctrine which Hobbes broached in the last century, and which was then so frequently and so ably refuted. Cicero exclaims with the utmost indignation and contempt against such a notion:[2] he considers it not only as unworthy of a philosopher, but of an illiterate peasant; that of all things this was the most truly absurd, to fancy that the rule of justice was to be taken from the constitutions of commonwealths, or that laws derived their authority from the statutes of the people, the edicts of princes, or the decrees of judges. If it be admitted that it is not the black-letter and the king's arms that makes the law, we are to look for it elsewhere.

In reality there are two, and only two, foundations of law; and they are both of them conditions without which nothing can give it any force: I mean equity and utility. . . .

Partiality and law are contradictory terms. Neither the merits nor the ill deserts, neither the wealth and importance nor the indigence and obscurity, of the one part or of the other, can make any alteration in this fundamental truth. On any other scheme, I defy any man living to settle a correct standard which may discriminate between equitable

---

[2] Cicero, *De Legibus*, Lib. I. 14, 15 et 16.—"O rem dignam, in qua non modo docti, verum etiam agrestes erubescant! Jam vero illud stultissimum existimare omnia justa esse, quæ scita sint in populorum institutis aut legibus," etc. "Quod si populorum jussis, si principum decretis, si sententiis judicum jura constituerentur, jus esset latrocinari, jus adulterare, jus testamenta falsa supponere, si hæc suffragiis aut scitis multitudinis probarentur." [Burke]

rule and the most direct tyranny. For if we can once prevail upon ourselves to depart from the strictness and integrity of this principle in favor even of a considerable party, the argument will hold for one that is less so; and thus we shall go on, narrowing the bottom of public right, until step by step we arrive, though after no very long or very forced deduction, at what one of our poets calls the *enormous faith,* —the faith of the many, created for the advantage of a single person. I cannot see a glimmering of distinction to evade it; nor is it possible to allege any reason for the proscription of so large a part of the kingdom, which would not hold equally to support, under parallel circumstances, the proscription of the whole.

I am sensible that these principles, in their abstract light, will not be very strenuously opposed. Reason is never inconvenient, but when it comes to be applied. Mere general truths interfere very little with the passions. They can, until they are roused by a troublesome application, rest in great tranquillity, side by side with tempers and proceedings the most directly opposite to them. Men want to be reminded, who do not want to be taught; because those original ideas of rectitude, to which the mind is compelled to assent when they are proposed, are not always as present to it as they ought to be. When people are gone, if not into a denial, at least into a sort of oblivion of those ideas, when they know them only as barren speculations, and not as practical motives for conduct, it will be proper to press, as well as to offer them to the understanding; and when one is attacked by prejudices which aim to intrude themselves into the place of law, what is left for us but to vouch and call to warranty those principles of original justice from whence alone our title to everything valuable in society is derived? Can it be thought to arise from a superfluous, vain parade of displaying general and uncontroverted maxims, that we should revert at this time to the first principles of law, when we have directly

under our consideration a whole body of statutes, which, I
say, are so many contradictions, which their advocates allow
to be so many exceptions from those very principles? Take
them in the most favorable light, every exception from the
original and fixed rule of equality and justice ought surely to
be very well authorized in the reason of their deviation, and
very rare in their use. For, if they should grow to be frequent,
in what would they differ from an abrogation of the rule
itself? By becoming thus frequent, they might even go
further, and, establishing themselves into a principle, convert the rule into the exception. It cannot be dissembled
that this is not at all remote from the case before us, where
the great body of the people are excluded from all valuable
property,—where the greatest and most ordinary benefits of
society are conferred as privileges, and not enjoyed on the
footing of common rights.

The clandestine manner in which those in power carry on
such designs is a sufficient argument of the sense they inwardly entertain of the true nature of their proceedings.
Seldom is the title or preamble of the law of the same import
with the body and enacting part; but they generally place
some other color uppermost, which differs from that which
is afterwards to appear, or at least one that is several shades
fainter. Thus, the penal laws in question are not called laws
to oblige men baptized and educated in Popery to renounce
their religion or their property, but are called laws to prevent
the growth of Popery; as if their purpose was only to prevent
conversions to that sect, and not to persecute a million of
people already engaged in it. But of all the instances of this
sort of legislative artifice, and of the principles that produced
it, I never met with any which made a stronger impression on
me than that of Louis the Fourteenth, in the revocation of
the Edict of Nantes. That monarch had, when he made that
revocation, as few measures to keep with public opinion as
any man. In the exercise of the most unresisted authority at

home, in a career of uninterrupted victory abroad, and in a course of flattery equal to the circumstances of his greatness in both these particulars, he might be supposed to have as little need as disposition to render any sort of account to the world of his procedure towards his subjects. But the persecution of so vast a body of men as the Huguenots was too strong a measure even for the law of pride and power. It was too glaring a contradiction even to those principles upon which persecution itself is supported. Shocked at the naked attempt, he had recourse, for a palliation of his conduct, to an unkingly denial of the fact which made against him. In the preamble, therefore, to his Act of Revocation, he sets forth that the Edict of Nantes was no longer necessary, as the object of it (the Protestants of his kingdom) were then reduced to a very small number. The refugees in Holland cried out against this misrepresentation. They asserted, I believe with truth, that this revocation had driven two hundred thousand of them out of their country, and that they could readily demonstrate there still remained six hundred thousand Protestants in France. If this were the fact, (as it was undoubtedly,) no argument of policy could have been strong enough to excuse a measure by which eight hundred thousand men were despoiled, at one stroke, of so many of their rights and privileges. Louis the Fourteenth confessed, by this sort of apology, that, if the number had been large, the revocation had been unjust. But, after all, is it not most evident that this act of injustice, which let loose on that monarch such a torrent of invective and reproach, and which threw so dark a cloud over all the splendor of a most illustrious reign, falls far short of the case in Ireland? The privileges which the Protestants of that kingdom enjoyed antecedent to this revocation were far greater than the Roman Catholics of Ireland ever aspired to under a contrary establishment. The number of their sufferers, if considered absolutely, is not half of ours; if considered relatively to the body of each community, it is not perhaps a twentieth part. And then the penalties and incapacities which grew from that revocation are not so grievous in their nature, nor so certain in their execution, nor so ruinous by a great deal to the civil prosperity of the state, as those which we have established for a perpetual law in our unhappy country. It cannot be thought to arise from affectation, that I call it so. What other name can be given to a country which contains so many hundred thousands of human creatures reduced to a state of the most abject servitude? . . .

Let me add, that the great inlet by which a color for oppression has entered into the world is by one man's pretending to determine concerning the happiness of another, and by claiming a right to use what means he thinks proper in order to bring him to a sense of it. It is the ordinary and trite sophism of oppression. But there is not yet such a convenient ductility in the human understanding as to make us capable of being persuaded that men can possibly mean the ultimate good of the whole society by rendering miserable for a century together the greater part of it,—or that any one has such a reversionary benevolence as seriously to intend the remote good of a late posterity, who can give up the present enjoyment which every honest man must have in the happiness of his contemporaries. Everybody is satisfied that a conservation and secure enjoyment of our natural rights is the great and ultimate purpose of civil society, and that therefore all forms whatsoever of government are only good as they are subservient to that purpose to which they are entirely subordinate. Now to aim at the establishment of any form of government by sacrificing what is the substance of it, to take away or at least to suspend the rights of Nature in order to [have] an approved system for the protection of them, and for the sake of that about which men must dispute forever to postpone those things about which they have no controversy at all, and this not in minute and subordinate, but large and principal objects, is a procedure as preposterous and absurd in argument as it is oppressive and cruel in its effect. For the Protestant religion, nor (I speak it with reverence, I am sure) the truth of our common Christianity, is not so clear as this proposition,—that all men, at least the majority of men in the society, ought to enjoy the common advantages of it. You fall, therefore, into a double error: first, you incur a certain mischief for an advantage which is comparatively problematical, even though you were sure of obtaining it; secondly, whatever the proposed advantage may be, were it of a certain nature, the attainment of it is by no means certain; and such deep gaming for stakes so valuable ought not to be admitted: the risk is of too much consequence to society. If no other country furnished examples of this risk, yet our laws and our country are enough fully to demonstrate the fact: Ireland, after almost a century of persecution, is at this hour full of penalties and full of Papists. This is a point which would lead us a great way; but it is only just touched here, having much to say upon it in its proper place. So that you have incurred a certain and an immediate inconvenience for a remote and for a doubly uncertain benefit. —Thus far as to the argument which would sanctify the injustice of these laws by the benefits which are proposed to arise from them, and as to that liberty which, by a new political chemistry, was to be extracted out of a system of oppression.

Now as to the other point, that the objects of these laws suffer voluntarily: this seems to me to be an insult rather than an argument. For, besides that it totally annihilates every characteristic and therefore every faulty idea of persecution, just as the former does, it supposes, what is false in fact, that it is in a man's moral power to change his religion whenever his convenience requires it. If he be beforehand satisfied that your opinion is better than his, he will voluntarily come over to you, and without compulsion, and then your law would be unnecessary; but if he is not so convinced, he must know that it is his duty in this point to sacrifice his interest here to his opinion of his eternal happiness, else he could have in reality no religion at all. In the former case, therefore, as your law would be unnecessary, in the latter it would be persecuting: that is, it would put your penalty and his ideas of duty in the opposite scales; which is, or I know not what is, the precise idea of persecution. If, then, you require a renunciation of his conscience, as a preliminary to his admission to the rights of society, you annex, morally speaking, an impossible condition to it. In this case, in the language of reason and jurisprudence, the condition would be void, and the gift absolute; as the practice runs, it is to establish the condition, and to withhold the benefit. The suffering is, then, not voluntary. And I never heard any other argument, drawn from the nature of laws and the good of human society, urged in favor of those proscriptive statutes, except those which have just been mentioned.

FROM *Letters to Gentlemen in Bristol*[1]

Sir,—I am honored with your letter of the 13th, in answer to mine, which accompanied the resolutions of the House relative to the trade of Ireland.

You will be so good as to present my best respects to the Society, and to assure them that it was altogether unnecessary to remind me of the interest of the constituents. I have never regarded anything else since I had a seat in Parliament. Having frequently and maturely considered that interest, and stated it to myself in almost every point of view, I am persuaded, that, under the present circumstances, I cannot more effectually pursue it than by giving all the support in my power to the propositions which I lately transmitted to the Hall.

The fault I find in the scheme is, that it falls extremely short of that liberality in the commercial system which I trust will one day be adopted. If I had not considered the present resolutions merely as preparatory to better things, and as a means of showing, experimentally, that justice to others is not always folly to ourselves, I should have contented myself with receiving them in a cold and silent acquiescence.

[1] "Letters to Samuel Span, Esq., Master of the Society of Merchants Adventurers of Bristol" (1778). The following selection consists of the bulk of the first of these two letters.

238

Separately considered, they are matters of no very great importance. But they aim, however imperfectly, at a right principle. I submit to the restraint to appease prejudice; I accept the enlargement, so far as it goes, as the result of reason and of sound policy.

We cannot be insensible of the calamities which have been brought upon this nation by an obstinate adherence to narrow and restrictive plans of government. I confess, I cannot prevail on myself to take them up precisely at a time when the most decisive experience has taught the rest of the world to lay them down. The propositions in question did not originate from me, or from my particular friends. But when things are so right in themselves, I hold it my duty not to inquire from what hands they come. I opposed the American measures upon the very same principle on which I support those that relate to Ireland. I was convinced that the evils which have arisen from the adoption of the former would be infinitely aggravated by the rejection of the latter. . . .

After all, what are the matters we dispute with so much warmth? Do we in these resolutions *bestow* anything upon Ireland? Not a shilling. We only consent to *leave* to them, in two or three instances, the use of the natural faculties which God has given to them, and to all mankind. Is Ireland united to the crown of Great Britain for no other purpose than that we should counteract the bounty of Providence in her favor? and in proportion as that bounty has been liberal, that we are to regard it as an evil, which is to be met with in every sort of corrective? To say that Ireland interferes with us, and therefore must be checked, is, in my opinion, a very mistaken and a very dangerous principle. I must beg leave to repeat, what I took the liberty of suggesting to you in my last letter, that Ireland is a country in the same climate and of the same natural qualities and productions with this, and has consequently no other means of growing wealthy in herself, or, in other words, of being useful to us, but by doing the very same things which we do for the same purposes. I hope that in Great Britain we shall always pursue, without exception, *every* means of prosperity, and, of course, that Ireland *will* interfere with us in something or other: for either, in order to *limit* her, we *must restrain* ourselves, or we must fall into that shocking conclusion, that we are to keep our yet remaining dependency under a general and indiscriminate restraint for the mere purpose of oppression. Indeed, Sir, England and Ireland may flourish together. The world is large enough for us both. Let it be our care not to make ourselves too little for it.

I know it is said, that the people of Ireland do not pay the same taxes, and therefore ought not in equity to enjoy the same benefits with this. I had hopes that the unhappy phantom of a compulsory *equal taxation* had haunted us long enough. I do assure you, that, until it is entirely banished from our imaginations, (where alone it has, or can have, any existence,) we shall never cease to do ourselves the most substantial injuries. To that argument of equal taxation I can only say, that Ireland pays as many taxes as those who are the best judges of her powers are of opinion she can bear. To bear more, she must have more ability; and, in the order of Nature, the advantage must *precede* the charge. This disposition of things being the law of God, neither you nor I *can* alter it. So that, if you will have more help from Ireland, you must *previously* supply her with more means. I believe it will be found, that, if men are suffered freely to cultivate their natural advantages, a virtual equality of contribution will come in its own time, and will flow by an easy descent through its own proper and natural channels. An attempt to disturb that course, and to force Nature, will only bring on universal discontent, distress, and confusion.

You tell me, Sir, that you prefer an union with Ireland to the little regulations which are proposed in Parliament. This union is a great question of state, to which, when it comes properly before me in my Parliamentary capacity, I shall give an honest and unprejudiced consideration. However, it is a settled rule with me, to make the most of my *actual situation,* and not to refuse to do a proper thing because there is something else more proper which I am not able to do. This union is a business of difficulty, and, on the principles of your letter, a business impracticable. Until it can be matured into a feasible and desirable scheme, I wish to have as close an union of interest and affection with Ireland as I can have; and that, I am sure, is a far better thing than any nominal union of government.

France, and indeed most extensive empires, which by various designs and fortunes have grown into one great mass, contain many provinces that are very different from each other in privileges and modes of government; and they raise their supplies in different ways, in different proportions, and under different authorities: yet none of them are for this reason curtailed of their natural rights; but they carry on trade and manufactures with perfect equality. In some way or other the true balance is found; and all of them are properly poised and harmonized. How much have you lost by the participation of Scotland in all your commerce? The external trade of England has more than doubled since that period; and I believe your internal (which is the most advantageous) has been augmented at least fourfold. Such virtue there is in liberality of sentiment, that you have grown richer even by the partnership of poverty.

If you think that this participation was a loss, commercially considered, but that it has been compensated by the share which Scotland has taken in defraying the public charge, I believe you have not very carefully looked at the public accounts. Ireland, Sir, pays a great deal more than Scotland, and is perhaps as much and as effectually united to England as Scotland is. But if Scotland, instead of paying little, had paid nothing at all, we should be gainers, not losers, by acquiring the hearty coöperation of an active, intelligent people towards the increase of the common stock, instead of our being employed in watching and counteracting them, and their being employed in watching and counteracting us, with the peevish and churlish jealousy of rivals and enemies on both sides.

I am sure, Sir, that the commercial experience of the merchants of Bristol will soon disabuse them of the prejudice, that they can trade no longer, if countries more lightly taxed are permitted to deal in the same commodities at the same markets. You know, that, in fact, you trade very largely where you are met by the goods of all nations. You even pay high duties on the import of your goods, and afterwards undersell nations less taxed, at their own markets, and where goods of the same kind are not charged at all. If it were otherwise, you could trade very little. You know that the price of all sorts of manufacture is not a great deal enhanced (except to the domestic consumer) by any taxes paid in this country. This I might very easily prove.

The same consideration will relieve you from the apprehension you express with relation to sugars, and the difference of the duties paid here and in Ireland. Those duties affect the interior consumer only, and for obvious reasons, relative to the interest of revenue itself, they must be proportioned to his ability of payment; but in all cases in which sugar can be an *object of commerce,* and therefore (in this view) of rivalship, you are sensible that you are at least on a par with Ireland. As to your apprehensions concerning the more advantageous situation of Ireland for some branches of commerce, (for it is so but for some,) I trust you will not find them more serious. Milford Haven, which is at your door, may serve to show you that the mere advantage of ports is not the thing which shifts the seat of commerce from one part of the world to the other. If I thought you inclined to take up this matter on local considerations, I should state to you, that I do not know any part of the kingdom so well situated for an advantageous commerce with Ireland as Bristol, and that none would be so likely to profit of its prosperity as our city. But your profit and theirs must concur. Beggary and bankruptcy are not the circumstances which invite to an intercourse with that or with any country; and I believe it will be found invariably true, that the superfluities of a rich nation furnish a better object of trade than the necessities of a poor one. It is the interest of the commercial world that wealth should be found everywhere.

The true ground of fear, in my opinion, is this: that Ireland, from the vicious system of its internal polity, will be a long time before it can derive any benefit from the liberty now granted, or from anything else. But, as I do not vote advantages in hopes that they may not be enjoyed, I will not lay any stress upon this consideration. I rather wish that the Parliament of Ireland may, in its own wisdom, remove these impediments, and put their country in a condition to avail itself of its natural advantages. If they do not, the fault is with them, and not with us.

I have written this long letter in order to give all possible satisfaction to my constituents with regard to the part I have taken in this affair. It gave me inexpressible concern to find that my conduct had been a cause of uneasiness to any of them. Next to my honor and conscience, I have nothing so near and dear to me as their approbation. However, I had much rather run the risk of displeasing than of injuring them, —if I am driven to make such an option. You obligingly lament that you are not to have me for your advocate; but if I had been capable of acting as an advocate in opposition to a plan so perfectly consonant to my known principles, and to the opinions I had publicly declared on an hundred occasions, I should only disgrace myself, without supporting, with the smallest degree of credit or effect, the cause you wished me to undertake. I should have lost the only thing which can make such abilities as mine of any use to the world now or hereafter: I mean that authority which is derived from an opinion that a member speaks the language of truth and sincerity, and that he is not ready to take up or lay down a great political system for the convenience of the hour, that he is in Parliament to support his opinion of the public good, and does not form his opinion in order to get into Parliament, or to continue in it. It is in a great measure for your sake that I wish to preserve this character. Without it, I am sure, I should be ill able to discharge, by any service, the smallest part of that debt of gratitude and affection which I owe you for the great and honorable trust you have reposed in me.

I am, with the highest regard and esteem, Sir,

Your most obedient and humble servant,

E. B.

BEACONSFIELD, 23rd April, 1778.

III ECONOMIC REFORM

FROM *On the Plan for Economical Reform*[1]

Mr. Speaker,—I rise, in acquittal of my engagement to the House, in obedience to the strong and just requisition of my constituents, and, I am persuaded, in conformity to the unanimous wishes of the whole nation, to submit to the wisdom of Parliament "A Plan of Reform in the Constitution of Several Parts of the Public Economy."

I have endeavored that this plan should include, in its execution, a considerable reduction of improper expense; that it should effect a conversion of unprofitable titles into a productive estate; that it should lead to, and indeed almost compel, a provident administration of such sums of public money as must remain under discretionary trusts; that it should render the incurring debts on the civil establishment (which must ultimately affect national strength and national credit) so very difficult as to become next to impracticable.

But what, I confess, was uppermost with me, what I bent the whole force of my mind to, was the reduction of that corrupt influence which is itself the perennial spring of all prodigality and of all disorder,—which loads us more than millions of debt,—which takes away vigor from our arms,

---

[1] Excerpts from "Speech on Presenting to the House of Commons (on the 11th February, 1780) A Plan for the Better Security of the Independence of Parliament, and the Economical Reformation of the Civil and Other Establishments." The omitted portions consist of a detailed analysis of the offices Burke sought to reform.

wisdom from our councils, and every shadow of authority
and credit from the most venerable parts of our Constitution.

Sir, I assure you very solemnly, and with a very clear
conscience, that nothing in the world has led me to such an
undertaking but my zeal for the honor of this House, and
the settled, habitual, systematic affection I bear to the cause
and to the principles of government.

I enter perfectly into the nature and consequences of my
attempt, and I advance to it with a tremor that shakes me
to the inmost fibre of my frame. I feel that I engage in a
business, in itself most ungracious, totally wide of the course
of prudent conduct, and, I really think, the most completely
adverse that can be imagined to the natural turn and temper
of my own mind. I know that all parsimony is of a quality
approaching to unkindness, and that (on some person or
other) every reform must operate as a sort of punishment.
Indeed, the whole class of the severe and restrictive virtues
are at a market almost too high for humanity. What is worse,
there are very few of those virtues which are not capable of
being imitated, and even outdone in many of their most
striking effects, by the worst of vices. Malignity and envy will
carve much more deeply, and finish much more sharply, in
the work of retrenchment, than frugality and providence. I
do not, therefore, wonder that gentlemen have kept away
from such a task, as well from good-nature as from prudence.
Private feeling might, indeed, be overborne by legislative
reason; and a man of a long-sighted and a strong-nerved
humanity might bring himself not so much to consider from
whom he takes a superfluous enjoyment as for whom in the
end he may preserve the absolute necessaries of life. . . .

I do most seriously put it to administration to consider the
wisdom of a timely reform. Early reformations are amicable
arrangements with a friend in power; late reformations are
terms imposed upon a conquered enemy: early reformations
are made in cool blood; late reformations are made under a

state of inflammation. In that state of things the people behold in government nothing that is respectable. They see the abuse, and they will see nothing else. They fall into the temper of a furious populace provoked at the disorder of a house of ill-fame; they never attempt to correct or regulate; they go to work by the shortest way: they abate the nuisance, they pull down the house.

This is my opinion with regard to the true interest of government. But as it is the interest of government that reformation should be early, it is the interest of the people that it should be temperate. It is their interest, because a temperate reform is permanent, and because it has a principle of growth. Whenever we improve, it is right to leave room for a further improvement. It is right to consider, to look about us, to examine the effect of what we have done. Then we can proceed with confidence, because we can proceed with intelligence. Whereas in hot reformations, in what men more zealous than considerate call *making clear work,* the whole is generally so crude, so harsh, so indigested, mixed with so much imprudence and so much injustice, so contrary to the whole course of human nature and human institutions, that the very people who are most eager for it are among the first to grow disgusted at what they have done. Then some part of the abdicated grievance is recalled from its exile in order to become a corrective of the correction. Then the abuse assumes all the credit and popularity of a reform. The very idea of purity and disinterestedness in politics falls into disrepute, and is considered as a vision of hot and inexperienced men; and thus disorders become incurable, not by the virulence of their own quality, but by the unapt and violent nature of the remedies. A great part, therefore, of my idea of reform is meant to operate gradually: some benefits will come at a nearer, some at a more remote period. We must no more make haste to be rich by parsimony than by intemperate acquisition. . . .

Sir, before I proceed further, I will lay these principles fairly before you, that afterwards you may be in a condition to judge whether every object of regulation, as I propose it, comes fairly under its rule. This will exceedingly shorten all discussion between us, if we are perfectly in earnest in establishing a system of good management. I therefore lay down to myself seven fundamental rules: they might, indeed, be reduced to two or three simple maxims; but they would be too general, and their application to the several heads of the business before us would not be so distinct and visible. I conceive, then,

First, That all jurisdictions which furnish more matter of expense, more temptation to oppression, or more means and instruments of corrupt influence, than advantage to justice or political administration, ought to be abolished.

Secondly, That all public estates which are more subservient to the purposes of vexing, overawing, and influencing those who hold under them, and to the expense of perception and management, than of benefit to the revenue, ought, upon every principle both of revenue and of freedom, to be disposed of.

Thirdly, That all offices which bring more charge than proportional advantage to the state, that all offices which may be engrafted on others, uniting and simplifying their duties, ought, in the first case, to be taken away, and, in the second, to be consolidated.

Fourthly, That all such offices ought to be abolished as obstruct the prospect of the general superintendent of finance, which destroy his superintendency, which disable him from foreseeing and providing for charges as they may occur, from preventing expense in its origin, checking it in its progress, or securing its application to its proper purposes. A minister, under whom expenses can be made without his knowledge, can never say what it is that he can spend, or what it is that he can save.

Fifthly, That it is proper to establish an invariable order in all payments, which will prevent partiality, which will give preference to services, not according to the importunity of the demandant, but the rank and order of their utility or their justice.

Sixthly, That it is right to reduce every establishment and every part of an establishment (as nearly as possible) to certainty, the life of all order and good management.

Seventhly, That all subordinate treasuries, as the nurseries of mismanagement, and as naturally drawing to themselves as much money as they can, keeping it as long as they can, and accounting for it as late as they can, ought to be dissolved. They have a tendency to perplex and distract the public accounts, and to excite a suspicion of government even beyond the extent of their abuse.

Under the authority and with the guidance of those principles I proceed,—wishing that nothing in any establishment may be changed, where I am not able to make a strong, direct, and solid application of those principles, or of some one of them. An economical constitution is a necessary basis for an economical administration.

First, with regard to the sovereign jurisdictions, I must observe, Sir, that whoever takes a view of this kingdom in a cursory manner will imagine that he beholds a solid, compacted, uniform system of monarchy, in which all inferior jurisdictions are but as rays diverging from one centre. But on examining it more nearly, you find much eccentricity and confusion. It is not a *monarchy* in strictness. But, as in the Saxon times this country was an heptarchy, it is now a strange sort of *pentarchy.* It is divided into five several distinct principalities, besides the supreme. There is, indeed, this difference from the Saxon times,—that, as in the itinerant exhibitions of the stage, for want of a complete company, they are obliged to throw a variety of parts on their chief performer, so our sovereign condescends himself to act not only

the principal, but all the subordinate parts in the play.
He condescends to dissipate the royal character, and to trifle
with those light, subordinate, lacquered sceptres in those
hands that sustain the ball representing the world, or which
wield the trident that commands the ocean. Cross a brook,
and you lose the King of England; but you have some
comfort in coming again under his Majesty, though "shorn
of his beams," and no more than Prince of Wales. Go to
the north, and you find him dwindled to a Duke of Lancaster;
turn to the west of that north, and he pops upon you in the
humble character of Earl of Chester. Travel a few miles on,
the Earl of Chester disappears, and the king surprises you
again as Count Palatine of Lancaster. If you travel beyond
Mount Edgecombe, you find him once more in his incognito,
and he is Duke of Cornwall. So that, quite fatigued and
satiated with this dull variety, you are infinitely refreshed
when you return to the sphere of his proper splendor, and
behold your amiable sovereign in his true, simple, undisguised, native character of Majesty.

In every one of these five principalities, duchies, palati-
nates, there is a regular establishment of considerable expense
and most domineering influence. As his Majesty submits to
appear in this state of subordination to himself, his loyal peers
and faithful commons attend his royal transformations, and
are not so nice as to refuse to nibble at those crumbs of
emoluments which console their petty metamorphoses. Thus
every one of those principalities has the apparatus of a
kingdom for the jurisdiction over a few private estates, and
the formality and charge of the Exchequer of Great Britain
for collecting the rents of a country squire. Cornwall is the
best of them; but when you compare the charge with the
receipt, you will find that it furnishes no exception to the
general rule. The Duchy and County Palatine of Lancaster
do not yield, as I have reason to believe, on an average of
twenty years, four thousand pounds a year clear to the crown.

As to Wales, and the County Palatine of Chester, I have my doubts whether their productive exchequer yields any returns at all. . . .

When a government is rendered complex, (which in itself is no desirable thing,) it ought to be for some political end which cannot be answered otherwise. Subdivisions in government are only admissible in favor of the dignity of inferior princes and high nobility, or for the support of an aristocratic confederacy under some head, or for the conservation of the franchises of the people in some privileged province. For the two former of these ends, such are the subdivisions in favor of the electoral and other princes in the Empire;[2] for the latter of these purposes are the jurisdictions of the Imperial cities and the Hanse towns. For the latter of these ends are also the countries of the States (*Pays d'États*) and certain cities and orders in France. These are all regulations with an object, and some of them with a very good object. But how are the principles of any of these subdivisions applicable in the case before us?

Do they answer any purpose to the king? The Principality of Wales was given by patent to Edward the Black Prince on the ground on which it has since stood. Lord Coke sagaciously observes upon it, "That in the charter of creating the Black Prince Edward Prince of Wales there is a *great mystery:* for *less* than an estate of inheritance so *great* a prince *could* not have, and an *absolute estate of inheritance* in so *great* a principality as Wales (this principality being *so dear* to him) he *should* not have; and therefore it was made *sibi et heredibus suis regibus Angliæ,* that by his decease, or attaining to the crown, it might be extinguished in the crown."

For the sake of this foolish *mystery,* of what a great prince *could* not have *less* and *should* not have *so much,* of a principality which was too *dear* to be given and too *great*

---

[2] The Holy Roman Empire.

to be kept,—and for no other cause that ever I could find,—
this form and shadow of a principality, without any substance, has been maintained. That you may judge in this
instance (and it serves for the rest) of the difference between
a great and a little economy, you will please to recollect, Sir,
that Wales may be about the tenth part of England in size
and population, and certainly not a hundredth part in
opulence. Twelve judges perform the whole of the business,
both of the stationary and the itinerant justice of this kingdom; but for Wales there are eight judges. There is in Wales
an exchequer, as well as in all the duchies, according to the
very best and most authentic absurdity of form. There are
in all of them a hundred more difficult trifles and laborious
fooleries, which serve no other purpose than to keep alive
corrupt hope and servile dependence.

These principalities are so far from contributing to the
ease of the king, to his wealth, or his dignity, that they render
both his supreme and his subordinate authority perfectly
ridiculous. It was but the other day, that that pert, factious
fellow, the Duke of Lancaster, presumed to fly in the face
of his liege lord, our gracious sovereign, and, *associating*
with a parcel of lawyers as factious as himself, to the
destruction of *all law and order,* and *in committees leading
directly to rebellion,* presumed to go to law with the king.
The object is neither your business nor mine. Which of the
parties got the better I really forget. I think it was (as it ought
to be) the king. The material point is, that the suit cost about
fifteen thousand pounds. But as the Duke of Lancaster is but
a sort of *Duke Humphrey,* and not worth a groat, our
sovereign was obliged to pay the costs of both. Indeed, this
art of converting a great monarch into a little prince, this
royal masquerading, is a very dangerous and expensive amusement, and one of the king's *menus plaisirs,* which ought to be
reformed. This duchy, which is not worth four thousand

pounds a year at best to *revenue,* is worth forty or fifty thousand to *influence.* . . .

If, therefore, we aim at regulating this household, the question will be, whether we ought to economize by *detail* or by *principle.* The example we have had of the success of an attempt to economize by detail, and under establishments adverse to the attempt, may tend to decide this question.

At the beginning of his Majesty's reign, Lord Talbot came to the administration of a great department in the household.[3] I believe no man ever entered into his Majesty's service, or into the service of any prince, with a more clear integrity, or with more zeal and affection for the interest of his master, and, I must add, with abilities for a still higher service. Economy was then announced as a maxim of the reign. This noble lord, therefore, made several attempts towards a reform. In the year 1777, when the king's civil list debts came last to be paid, he explained very fully the success of his undertaking. He told the House of Lords that he had attempted to reduce the charges of the king's tables and his kitchen. The thing, Sir, was not below him. He knew that there is nothing interesting in the concerns of men whom we love and honor, that is beneath our attention. "Love," says one of our old poets, "esteems no office mean,"—and with still more spirit, "Entire affection scorneth nicer hands." Frugality, Sir, is founded on the principle, that all riches have limits. A royal household, grown enormous, even in the meanest departments, may weaken and perhaps destroy all energy in the highest offices of the state. The gorging a royal kitchen may stint and famish the negotiations of a kingdom. Therefore the object was worthy of his, was worthy of any man's attention.

In consequence of this noble lord's resolution, (as he told

---

[3] That of Lord Steward.

the other House,) he reduced several tables, and put the persons entitled to them upon board wages, much to their own satisfaction. But, unluckily, subsequent duties requiring constant attendance, it was not possible to prevent their being fed where they were employed: and thus this first step towards economy doubled the expense.

There was another disaster far more doleful than this. I shall state it, as the cause of that misfortune lies at the bottom of almost all our prodigality. Lord Talbot attempted to reform the kitchen; but such, as he well observed, is the consequence of having duty done by one person whilst another enjoys the emoluments, that he found himself frustrated in all his designs. On that rock his whole adventure split, his whole scheme of economy was dashed to pieces. His department became more expensive than ever; the civil list debt accumulated. Why? It was truly from a cause which, though perfectly adequate to the effect, one would not have instantly guessed. It was because *the turnspit in the king's kitchen was a member of Parliament!* The king's domestic servants were all undone, his tradesmen remained unpaid and became bankrupt,—*because the turnspit of the king's kitchen was a member of Parliament.* His Majesty's slumbers were interrupted, his pillow was stuffed with thorns, and his peace of mind entirely broken,—*because the king's turnspit was a member of Parliament.* The judges were unpaid, the justice of the kingdom bent and gave way, the foreign ministers remained inactive and unprovided, the system of Europe was dissolved, the chain of our alliances was broken, all the wheels of government at home and abroad were stopped,—*because the king's turnspit was a member of Parliament.*

Such, Sir, was the situation of affairs, and such the cause of that situation, when his Majesty came a second time to Parliament to desire the payment of those debts which the employment of its members in various offices, visible and invisible, had occasioned. I believe that a like fate will attend every attempt at economy by detail, under similar circumstances, and in every department. A complex, operose office of account and control is, in itself, and even if members of Parliament had nothing to do with it, the most prodigal of all things. The most audacious robberies or the most subtle frauds would never venture upon such a waste as an over-careful detailed guard against them will infallibly produce. In our establishments, we frequently see an office of account of an hundred pounds a year expense, and another office of an equal expense to control that office, and the whole upon a matter that is not worth twenty shillings.

To avoid, therefore, this minute care, which produces the consequences of the most extensive neglect, and to oblige members of Parliament to attend to public cares, and not to the servile offices of domestic management, I propose, Sir, to *economize by principle* . . .

Sir, I think myself bound to give you my reasons as clearly and as fully for stopping in the course of reformation as for proceeding in it. My limits are the rules of law, the rules of policy, and the service of the state. This is the reason why I am not able to intermeddle with another article, which seems to be a specific object in several of the petitions: I mean the reduction of exorbitant emoluments to efficient offices. If I knew of any real efficient office which did possess exorbitant emoluments, I should be extremely desirous of reducing them. Others may know of them: I do not. I am not possessed of an exact common measure between real service and its reward. I am very sure that states do sometimes receive services which is hardly in their power to reward according to their worth. If I were to give my judgment with regard to this country, I do not think the great efficient offices of the state to be overpaid. The service of the public is a thing which cannot be put to auction and struck down to those who will agree to execute it the cheapest. When the proportion between reward and service is our object, we must always consider of what nature the service is, and what sort of men they are that must perform it. What is just payment for one kind of labor, and full encouragement for one kind of talents, is fraud and discouragement to others. Many of the great offices have much duty to do, and much expense of representation to maintain. A Secretary of State, for instance, must not appear sordid in the eyes of the ministers of other nations; neither ought our ministers abroad to appear contemptible in the courts where they reside. In all offices of duty, there is almost necessarily a great neglect of all domestic affairs. A person in high office can rarely take a view of his family-house. If he sees that the state takes no detriment, the state must see that his affairs should take as little.

I will even go so far as to affirm, that, if men were willing to serve in such situations without salary, they ought not to be permitted to do it. Ordinary service must be secured by the motives to ordinary integrity. I do not hesitate to say that that state which lays its foundation in rare and heroic virtues will be sure to have its superstructure in the basest profligacy and corruption. An honorable and fair profit is the best security against avarice and rapacity; as in all things else, a lawful and regulated enjoyment is the best security against debauchery and excess. For as wealth is power, so all power will infallibly draw wealth to itself by some means or other; and when men are left no way of ascertaining their profits but by their means of obtaining them, those means will be increased to infinity. This is true in all the parts of administration, as well as in the whole. If any individual were to decline his appointments, it might give an unfair advantage to ostentatious ambition over unpretending service; it might breed invidious comparisons; it might tend to destroy whatever little unity and agreement may be found among ministers. And, after all, when an ambitious man had run down his competitors by a fallacious show of disinterestedness, and fixed himself in power by that means, what security is there that he would not change his course, and claim as an indemnity ten times more than he has given up?

This rule, like every other, may admit its exceptions. When a great man has some one great object in view to be achieved in a given time, it may be absolutely necessary for him to walk out of all the common roads, and, if his fortune permits it, to hold himself out as a splendid example. I am told that something of this kind is now doing in a country near us. But this is for a short race, the training for a heat or two, and not the proper preparation for the regular stages of a methodical journey. I am speaking of establishments, and not of men.

It may be expected, Sir, that, when I am giving my reasons why I limit myself in the reduction of employments, or of their profits, I should say something of those which seem of eminent inutility in the state: I mean the number of officers who, by their places, are attendant on the person of the king. Considering the commonwealth merely as such, and considering those officers only as relative to the direct purposes of the state, I admit that they are of no use at all. But there are many things in the constitution of establishments, which appear of little value on the first view, which in a secondary and oblique manner produce very material advantages. It was on full consideration that I determined not to lessen any of the offices of honor about the crown, in their number or their emoluments. These emoluments, except in one or two cases, do not much more than answer the charge of attendance. Men of condition naturally love to be about a court; and women of condition love it much more. But there is in all regular attendance so much of constraint, that, if it were a mere charge, without any compensation, you would soon have the court deserted by all the nobility of the kingdom.

Sir, the most serious mischiefs would follow from such a desertion. Kings are naturally lovers of low company. They are so elevated above all the rest of mankind that they must look upon all their subjects as on a level. They are rather

apt to hate than to love their nobility, on account of the occasional resistance to their will which will be made by their
virtue, their petulance, or their pride. It must, indeed, be admitted that many of the nobility are as perfectly willing to act
the part of flatterers, tale-bearers, parasites, pimps, and buf-
foons, as any of the lowest and vilest of mankind can possibly
be. But they are not properly qualified for this object of their
ambition. The want of a regular education, and early habits,
and some lurking remains of their dignity, will never permit
them to become a match for an Italian eunuch, a mountebank,
a fiddler, a player, or any regular practitioner of that tribe.
The Roman emperors, almost from the beginning, threw
themselves into such hands; and the mischief increased every
day till the decline and final ruin of the empire. It is therefore
of very great importance (provided the thing is not overdone)
to contrive such an establishment as must, almost whether a
prince will or not, bring into daily and hourly offices about his
person a great number of his first nobility; and it is rather an
useful prejudice that gives them a pride in such a servitude.
Though they are not much the better for a court, a court will
be much the better for them. I have therefore not attempted
to reform any of the offices of honor about the king's
person. . . .

Sir, I move for leave to bring in a bill, "For the better
regulation of his Majesty's civil establishments, and of certain
public offices; for the limitation of pensions, and the suppression of sundry useless, expensive, and inconvenient places,
and for applying the moneys saved thereby to the public service."

IV INDIA

VI

FROM *Speech on Fox's East India Bill*[1]

. . . It is now to be determined whether the three years of laborious Parliamentary research, whether the twenty years of patient Indian suffering, are to produce a substantial reform in our Eastern administration; or whether our knowledge of the grievances has abated our zeal for the correction of them, and our very inquiry into the evil was only a pretext to elude the remedy which is demanded from us by humanity, by justice, and by every principle of true policy. Depend upon it, this business cannot be indifferent to our fame. It will turn out a matter of great disgrace or great glory to the whole British nation. We are on a conspicuous stage, and the world marks our demeanor.

I am therefore a little concerned to perceive the spirit and temper in which the debate has been all along pursued upon one side of the House. The declamation of the gentlemen who oppose the bill has been abundant and vehement; but they have been reserved and even silent about the fitness or unfitness of the plan to attain the direct object it has in view. By

---

[1] From Burke's "Speech (December 1, 1783) upon the Question for the Speaker's Leaving the Chair in Order for the House to Resolve Itself into a Committee on Mr. Fox's East India Bill." Approximately one third of the total speech is offered here, the omitted portion consisting mainly of a detailed bill of particulars on the misgovernment by the East India Company.

some gentlemen it is taken up (by way of exercise, I presume) as a point of law, on a question of private property and corporate franchise; by others it is regarded as the petty intrigue of a faction at court, and argued merely as it tends to set this man a little higher or that a little lower in situation and power. All the void has been filled up with invectives against coalition, with allusions to the loss of America, with the activity and inactivity of ministers. The total silence of these gentlemen concerning the interest and well-being of the people of India, and concerning the interest which this nation has in the commerce and revenues of that country, is a strong indication of the value which they set upon these objects.

It has been a little painful to me to observe the intrusion into this important debate of such company as *quo warranto,* and *mandamus,* and *certiorari:* as if we were on a trial about mayors and aldermen and capital burgesses, or engaged in a suit concerning the borough of Penryn, or Saltash, or St. Ives, or St. Mawes. Gentlemen have argued with as much heat and passion as if the first things in the world were at stake; and their topics are such as belong only to matter of the lowest and meanest litigation. It is not right, it is not worthy of us, in this manner to depreciate the value, to degrade the majesty, of this grave deliberation of policy and empire.

For my part, I have thought myself bound, when a matter of this extraordinary weight came before me, not to consider (as some gentlemen are so fond of doing) whether the bill originated from a Secretary of State for the Home Department or from a Secretary for the Foreign, from a minister of influence or a minister of the people, from Jacob or from Esau. I asked myself, and I ask myself nothing else, what part it was fit for a member of Parliament, who has supplied a mediocrity of talents by the extreme of diligence, and who has thought himself obliged by the research of years to wind himself into the inmost recesses and labyrinths of the Indian detail,—what part, I say, it became such a member of Parliament to take, when a minister of state, in conformity to a recommendation from the throne, has brought before us a system for the better government of the territory and commerce of the East. In this light, and in this only, I will trouble you with my sentiments.

It is not only agreed, but demanded, by the right honorable gentleman,[2] and by those who act with him, that a *whole* system ought to be produced; that it ought not to be an *half-measure;* that it ought to be no *palliative,* but a legislative provision, vigorous, substantial, and effective.—I believe that no man who understands the subject can doubt for a moment that those must be the conditions of anything deserving the name of a reform in the Indian government; that anything short of them would not only be delusive, but, in this matter, which admits no medium, noxious in the extreme.

To all the conditions proposed by his adversaries the mover of the bill perfectly agrees; and on his performance of them he rests his cause. On the other hand, not the least objection has been taken with regard to the efficiency, the vigor, or the completeness of the scheme. I am therefore warranted to assume, as a thing admitted, that the bills accomplish what both sides of the House demand as essential. The end is completely answered, so far as the direct and immediate object is concerned.

But though there are no direct, yet there are various collateral objections made: objections from the effects which this plan of reform for Indian administration may have on the privileges of great public bodies in England; from its probable influence on the constitutional rights, or on the freedom and integrity, of the several branches of the legislature.

Before I answer these objections, I must beg leave to observe, that, if we are not able to contrive some method of governing India *well,* which will not of necessity become the means of governing Great Britain *ill,* a ground is laid for their

---

[2] William Pitt.

eternal separation, but none for sacrificing the people of that country to our Constitution. I am, however, far from being persuaded that any such incompatibility of interest does at all exist. On the contrary, I am certain that every means effectual to preserve India from oppression is a guard to preserve the British Constitution from its worst corruption. To show this, I will consider the objections, which, I think, are four.

1st, That the bill is an attack on the chartered rights of men.

2ndly, That it increases the influence of the crown.

3rdly, That it does *not* increase, but diminishes, the influence of the crown, in order to promote the interests of certain ministers and their party.

4thly, That it deeply affects the national credit.

As to the first of these objections, I must observe that the phrase of "the chartered rights *of men*" is full of affectation, and very unusual in the discussion of privileges conferred by charters of the present description. But it is not difficult to discover what end that ambiguous mode of expression, so often reiterated, is meant to answer.

The rights of *men*—that is to say, the natural rights of mankind—are indeed sacred things; and if any public measure is proved mischievously to affect them, the objection ought to be fatal to that measure, even if no charter at all could be set up against it. If these natural rights are further affirmed and declared by express covenants, if they are clearly defined and secured against chicane, against power and authority, by written instruments and positive engagements, they are in a still better condition: they partake not only of the sanctity of the object so secured, but of that solemn public faith itself which secures an object of such importance. Indeed, this formal recognition, by the sovereign power, of an original right in the subject, can never be subverted, but by rooting up the holding radical principles of government, and even of society itself. The charters which we call by distinction *great* are public instruments of this nature: I mean the charters of King John and King Henry the Third. The things secured by these instruments may, without any deceitful ambiguity, be very fitly called *the chartered rights of men.*

These charters have made the very name of a charter dear to the heart of every Englishman. But, Sir, there may be, and there are, charters, not only different in nature, but formed on principles *the very reverse* of those of the Great Charter. Of this kind is the charter of the East India Company. *Magna Charta* is a charter to restrain power and to destroy monopoly. The East India charter is a charter to establish monopoly and to create power. Political power and commercial monopoly are *not* the rights of men; and the rights to them derived from charters it is fallacious and sophistical to call "the chartered rights of men." These chartered rights (to speak of such charters and of their effects in terms of the greatest possible moderation) do at least suspend the natural rights of mankind at large, and in their very frame and constitution are liable to fall into a direct violation of them.

It is a charter of this latter description (that is to say, a charter of power and monopoly) which is affected by the bill before you. The bill, Sir, does without question affect it: it does affect it essentially and substantially. But, having stated to you of what description the chartered rights are which this bill touches, I feel no difficulty at all in acknowledging the existence of those chartered rights in their fullest extent. They belong to the Company in the surest manner, and they are secured to that body by every sort of public sanction. They are stamped by the faith of the king; they are stamped by the faith of Parliament: they have been bought for money, for money honestly and fairly paid; they have been bought for valuable consideration, over and over again.

I therefore freely admit to the East India Company their claim to exclude their fellow-subjects from the commerce of

half the globe. I admit their claim to administer an annual
territorial revenue of seven millions sterling, to command an
army of sixty thousand men, and to dispose (under the control of a sovereign, imperial discretion, and with the due observance of the natural and local law) of the lives and fortunes
of thirty millions of their fellow-creatures. All this they possess
by charter, and by Acts of Parliament, (in my opinion,)
without a shadow of controversy.

Those who carry the rights and claims of the Company the
furthest do not contend for more than this; and all this I
freely grant. But, granting all this, they must grant to me, in
my turn, that all political power which is set over men, and
that all privilege claimed or exercised in exclusion of them,
being wholly artificial, and for so much a derogation from
the natural equality of mankind at large, ought to be some
way or other exercised ultimately for their benefit.

If this is true with regard to every species of political
dominion and every description of commercial privilege, none
of which can be original, self-derived rights, or grants for the
mere private benefit of the holders, then such rights, or privileges, or whatever else you choose to call them, are all in the
strictest sense *a trust:* and it is of the very essence of every
trust to be rendered *accountable,*—and even totally to *cease,*
when it substantially varies from the purposes for which alone
it could have a lawful existence.

This I conceive, Sir, to be true of trusts of power vested
in the highest hands, and of such as seem to hold of no human creature. But about the application of this principle to
subordinate *derivative* trusts I do not see how a controversy
can be maintained. To whom, then, would I make the East
India Company accountable? Why, to Parliament, to be sure,
—to Parliament, from whom their trust was derived,—to
Parliament, which alone is capable of comprehending the
magnitude of its object, and its abuse, and alone capable of
an effectual legislative remedy. The very charter, which is

held out to exclude Parliament from correcting malversation with regard to the high trust vested in the Company, is the very thing which at once gives a title and imposes a duty on us to interfere with effect, wherever power and authority originating from ourselves are perverted from their purposes, and become instruments of wrong and violence. . . .

I ground myself, therefore, on this principle:—that, if the abuse is proved, the contract is broken, and we reënter into all our rights, that is, into the exercise of all our duties. Our own authority is, indeed, as much a trust originally as the Company's authority is a trust derivatively; and it is the use we make of the resumed power that must justify or condemn us in the resumption of it. When we have perfected the plan laid before us by the right honorable mover, the world will then see what it is we destroy, and what it is we create. By that test we stand or fall; and by that test I trust that it will be found, in the issue, that we are going to supersede a charter abused to the full extent of all the powers which it could abuse, and exercised in the plenitude of despotism, tyranny, and corruption,—and that in one and the same plan we provide a real chartered security for *the rights of men,* cruelly violated under that charter.

This bill, and those connected with it, are intended to form the *Magna Charta* of Hindostan. Whatever the Treaty of Westphalia is to the liberty of the princes and free cities of the Empire, and to the three religions there professed,—whatever the Great Charter, the Statute of Tallage, the Petition of Right, and the Declaration of Right are to Great Britain, these bills are to the people of India. Of this benefit I am certain their condition is capable: and when I know that they are capable of more, my vote shall most assuredly be for our giving to the full extent of their capacity of receiving; and no charter of dominion shall stand as a bar in my way to their charter of safety and protection.

The strong admission I have made of the Company's rights

(I am conscious of it) binds me to do a great deal. I do not presume to condemn those who argue *a priori* against the propriety of leaving such extensive political powers in the hands of a company of merchants. I know much is, and much more may be, said against such a system. But, with my particular ideas and sentiments, I cannot go that way to work. I feel an insuperable reluctance in giving my hand to destroy any established institution of government, upon a theory, however plausible it may be. My experience in life teaches me nothing clear upon the subject. I have known merchants with the sentiments and the abilities of great statesmen, and I have seen persons in the rank of statesmen with the conceptions and character of peddlers. Indeed, my observation has furnished me with nothing that is to be found in any habits of life or education, which tends wholly to disqualify men for the functions of government, but that by which the power of exercising those functions is very frequently obtained: I mean a spirit and habits of low cabal and intrigue; which I have never, in one instance, seen united with a capacity for sound and manly policy.

To justify us in taking the administration of their affairs out of the hands of the East India Company, on my principles, I must see several conditions. 1st, The object affected by the abuse should be great and important. 2nd, The abuse affecting this great object ought to be a great abuse. 3d, It ought to be habitual, and not accidental. 4th, It ought to be utterly incurable in the body as it now stands constituted. All this ought to be made as visible to me as the light of the sun, before I should strike off an atom of their charter. A right honorable gentleman[3] has said, and said, I think, but once, and that very slightly, (whatever his original demand for a plan might seem to require,) that "there are abuses in the Company's government." If that were all, the scheme of the

---

[3] William Pitt.

mover of this bill, the scheme of his learned friend, and his own scheme of reformation, (if he has any,) are all equally needless. There are, and must be, abuses in all governments. It amounts to no more than a nugatory proposition. But before I consider of what nature these abuses are, of which the gentleman speaks so very lightly, permit me to recall to your recollection the map of the country which this abused chartered right affects. This I shall do, that you may judge whether in that map I can discover anything like the first of my conditions: that is, whether the object affected by the abuse of the East India Company's power be of importance sufficient to justify the measure and means of reform applied to it in this bill.

With very few, and those inconsiderable intervals, the British dominion, either in the Company's name, or in the names of princes absolutely dependent upon the Company, extends from the mountains that separate India from Tartary to Cape Comorin, that is, one-and-twenty degrees of latitude!

In the northern parts it is a solid mass of land, about eight hundred miles in length, and four or five hundred broad. As you go southward, it becomes narrower for a space. It afterwards dilates; but, narrower or broader, you possess the whole eastern and northeastern coast of that vast country, quite from the borders of Pegu.[4]—Bengal, Bahar, and Orissa, with Benares, (now unfortunately in our immediate possession,) measure 161,978 square English miles: a territory considerably larger than the whole kingdom of France. Oude, with its dependent provinces, is 53,286 square miles: not a great deal less than England. The Carnatic, with Tanjore and the Circars, is 65,948 square miles: very considerably larger than England. And the whole of the Company's dominions, comprehending Bombay and Salsette, amounts to 281,412 square miles: which forms a territory larger than any European

---

[4] Southern Burma.

dominion, Russia and Turkey excepted. Through all that vast
extent of country there is not a man who eats a mouthful of
rice but by permission of the East India Company.

So far with regard to the extent. The population of this
great empire is not easy to be calculated. When the countries
of which it is composed came into our possession, they were
all eminently peopled, and eminently productive,—though at
that time considerably declined from their ancient prosperity.
But since they are come into our hands!——! However, if we
make the period of our estimate immediately before the utter
desolation of the Carnatic, and if we allow for the havoc
which our government had even then made in these regions,
we cannot, in my opinion, rate the population at much less
than thirty millions of souls: more than four times the number of persons in the island of Great Britain.

My next inquiry to that of the number is the quality and
description of the inhabitants. This multitude of men does not
consist of an abject and barbarous populace; much less of
gangs of savages, like the Guaranies and Chiquitos, who
wander on the waste borders of the River of Amazons or the
Plate; but a people for ages civilized and cultivated,—cultivated by all the arts of polished life, whilst we were yet in
the woods. There have been (and still the skeletons remain)
princes once of great dignity, authority, and opulence. There
are to be found the chiefs of tribes and nations. There is to be
found an ancient and venerable priesthood, the depository
of their laws, learning, and history, the guides of the people
whilst living and their consolation in death; a nobility of great
antiquity and renown; a multitude of cities, not exceeded in
population and trade by those of the first class in Europe;
merchants and bankers, individual houses of whom have
once vied in capital with the Bank of England, whose credit
had often supported a tottering state, and preserved their
governments in the midst of war and desolation; millions of
ingenious manufacturers and mechanics; millions of the most

diligent, and not the least intelligent, tillers of the earth. Here are to be found almost all the religions professed by men,— the Braminical, the Mussulman, the Eastern and the Western Christian.

If I were to take the whole aggregate of our possessions there, I should compare it, as the nearest parallel I can find, with the Empire of Germany. Our immediate possessions I should compare with the Austrian dominions: and they would not suffer in the comparison. The Nabob of Oude might stand for the King of Prussia; the Nabob of Arcot I would compare, as superior in territory, and equal in revenue, to the Elector of Saxony. Cheit Sing, the Rajah of Benares, might well rank with the Prince of Hesse, at least; and the Rajah of Tanjore (though hardly equal in extent of dominion, superior in revenue) to the Elector of Bavaria. The polygars and the Northern zemindars, and other great chiefs, might well class with the rest of the princes, dukes, counts, marquises, and bishops in the Empire; all of whom I mention to honor, and surely without disparagement to any or all of those most respectable princes and grandees.

All this vast mass, composed of so many orders and classes of men, is again infinitely diversified by manners, by religion, by hereditary employment, through all their possible combinations. This renders the handling of India a matter in an high degree critical and delicate. But, oh, it has been handled rudely indeed! Even some of the reformers seem to have forgot that they had anything to do but to regulate the tenants of a manor, or the shopkeepers of the next county town.

It is an empire of this extent, of this complicated nature, of this dignity and importance, that I have compared to Germany and the German government,—not for an exact resemblance, but as a sort of a middle term, by which India might be approximated to our understandings, and, if possible, to our feelings, in order to awaken something of sympathy for the unfortunate natives, of which I am afraid we are not perfectly susceptible, whilst we look at this very remote object through a false and cloudy medium.

My second condition necessary to justify me in touching the charter is, whether the Company's abuse of their trust with regard to this great object be an abuse of great atrocity. I shall beg your permission to consider their conduct in two lights: first the political, and then the commercial. . . .[5]

The several irruptions of Arabs, Tartars, and Persians into India were, for the greater part, ferocious, bloody, and wasteful in the extreme: our entrance into the dominion of that country was, as generally, with small comparative effusion of blood,—being introduced by various frauds and delusions, and by taking advantage of the incurable, blind, and senseless animosity which the several country powers bear towards each other, rather than by open force. But the difference in favor of the first conquerors is this. The Asiatic conquerors very soon abated of their ferocity, because they made the conquered country their own. They rose or fell with the rise or fall of the territory they lived in. Fathers there deposited the hopes of their posterity; and children there beheld the monuments of their fathers. Here their lot was finally cast; and it is the natural wish of all that their lot should not be cast in a bad land. Poverty, sterility, and desolation are not a recreating prospect to the eye of man; and there are very few who can bear to grow old among the curses of a whole people. If their passion or their avarice drove the Tartar lords to acts of rapacity or tyranny, there was time enough, even in the short life of man, to bring round the ill effects of an abuse of power upon the power itself. If hoards were made by violence and tyranny, they were still domestic hoards; and domestic profusion, or the rapine of a more powerful and prodigal hand, restored them to the people. With many dis-

---

[5] Burke here presents a detailed discussion of wrongs and mismanagement committed by representatives of the East India Company, including Warren Hastings.

orders, and with few political checks upon power, Nature had still fair play; the sources of acquisition were not dried up; and therefore the trade, the manufactures, and the commerce of the country flourished. Even avarice and usury itself operated both for the preservation and the employment of national wealth. The husbandman and manufacturer paid heavy interest, but then they augmented the fund from whence they were again to borrow. Their resources were dearly bought, but they were sure; and the general stock of the community grew by the general effort.

But under the English government all this order is reversed. The Tartar invasion was mischievous; but it is our protection that destroys India. It was their enmity; but it is our friendship. Our conquest there, after twenty years, is as crude as it was the first day. The natives scarcely know what it is to see the gray head of an Englishman. Young men (boys almost) govern there, without society and without sympathy with the natives. They have no more social habits with the people than if they still resided in England,—nor, indeed, any species of intercourse, but that which is necessary to making a sudden fortune, with a view to a remote settlement. Animated with all the avarice of age and all the impetuosity of youth, they roll in one after another, wave after wave; and there is nothing before the eyes of the natives but an endless, hopeless prospect of new flights of birds of prey and passage, with appetites continually renewing for a food that is continually wasting. Every rupee of profit made by an Englishman is lost forever to India. With us are no retributory superstitions, by which a foundation of charity compensates, through ages, to the poor, for the rapine and injustice of a day. With us no pride erects stately monuments which repair the mischiefs which pride had produced, and which adorn a country out of its own spoils. England has erected no churches, no hospitals, no palaces, no schools; England has built no bridges, made no high-roads, cut no navigations, dug out no reservoirs.

Every other conqueror of every other description has left some
monument, either of state or beneficence, behind him. Were
we to be driven out of India this day, nothing would remain
to tell that it had been possessed, during the inglorious period
of our dominion, by anything better than the orangoutang or
the tiger.

There is nothing in the boys we send to India worse than
in the boys whom we are whipping at school, or that we see
trailing a pike or bending over a desk at home. But as English
youth in India drink the intoxicating draught of authority and
dominion before their heads are able to bear it, and as they
are full grown in fortune long before they are ripe in principle, neither Nature nor reason have any opportunity to exert
themselves for remedy of the excesses of their premature
power. The consequences of their conduct, which in good
minds (and many of theirs are probably such) might produce
penitence or amendment, are unable to pursue the rapidity
of their flight. Their prey is lodged in England; and the cries
of India are given to seas and winds, to be blown about, in
every breaking up of the monsoon, over a remote and un-
hearing ocean. In India all the vices operate by which sudden
fortune is acquired: in England are often displayed, by the
same persons, the virtues which dispense hereditary wealth.
Arrived in England, the destroyers of the nobility and gentry
of a whole kingdom will find the best company in this nation
at a board of elegance and hospitality. Here the manufacturer
and husbandman will bless the just and punctual hand that in
India has torn the cloth from the loom, or wrested the
scanty portion of rice and salt from the peasant of Bengal, or
wrung from him the very opium in which he forgot his oppressions and his oppressor. They marry into your families;
they enter into your senate; they ease your estates by loans;
they raise their value by demand; they cherish and protect
your relations which lie heavy on your patronage; and there
is scarcely an house in the kingdom that does not feel some

concern and interest that makes all reform of our Eastern
government appear officious and disgusting, and, on the whole,
a most discouraging attempt. In such an attempt you hurt
those who are able to return kindness or to resent injury. If
you succeed, you save those who cannot so much as give you
thanks. All these things show the difficulty of the work we
have on hand: but they show its necessity, too. Our Indian
government is in its best state a grievance. It is necessary that
the correctives should be uncommonly vigorous, and the
work of men sanguine, warm, and even impassioned in the
cause. But it is an arduous thing to plead against abuses of a
power which originates from your own country, and affects
those whom we are used to consider as strangers.

I shall certainly endeavor to modulate myself to this temper; though I am sensible that a cold style of describing
actions, which appear to me in a very affecting light, is equally
contrary to the justice due to the people and to all genuine
human feelings about them. I ask pardon of truth and Nature
for this compliance. But I shall be very sparing of epithets
either to persons or things. It has been said, (and, with regard
to one of them, with truth,) that Tacitus and Machiavel, by
their cold way of relating enormous crimes, have in some sort
appeared not to disapprove them; that they seem a sort of professors of the art of tyranny; and that they corrupt the minds of
their readers by not expressing the detestation and horror that
naturally belong to horrible and detestable proceedings. But
we are in general, Sir, so little acquainted with Indian details,
the instruments of oppression under which the people suffer
are so hard to be understood, and even the very names of the
sufferers are so uncouth and strange to our ears, that it is
very difficult for our sympathy to fix upon these objects. I
am sure that some of us have come down stairs from the com-
mittee-room with impressions on our minds which to us were
the inevitable results of our discoveries, yet, if we should venture to express ourselves in the proper language of our senti-

ments to other gentlemen not at all prepared to enter into the
cause of them, nothing could appear more harsh and disso-
nant, more violent and unaccountable, than our language and
behavior. All these circumstances are not, I confess, very
favorable to the idea of our attempting to govern India at all.
But there we are; there we are placed by the Sovereign Disposer; and we must do the best we can in our situation. The
situation of man is the preceptor of his duty. . . .[6]

It is now more than two years, that upon account of the
gross abuses and ruinous situation of the Company's affairs,
(which occasioned the cry of the whole world long before it
was taken up here,) that we instituted two committees to inquire into the mismanagements by which the Company's
affairs had been brought to the brink of ruin. These inquiries
had been pursued with unremitting diligence, and a great body
of facts was collected and printed for general information.
In the result of those inquiries, although the committees con-
sisted of very different descriptions, they were unanimous.
They joined in censuring the conduct of the Indian administration, and enforcing the responsibility upon two men, whom
this House, in consequence of these reports, declared it to be
the duty of the Directors to remove from their stations, and
recall to Great Britain,—*"because they had acted in a manner
repugnant to the honor and policy of this nation, and thereby
brought great calamities on India and enormous expenses on
the East India Company."*

Here was no attempt on the charter. Here was no question
of their privileges. To vindicate their own honor, to support
their own interests, to enforce obedience to their own orders,
—these were the sole object of the monitory resolution of
this House. But as soon as the General Court could assemble,
they assembled to demonstrate who they really were. Re-
gardless of the proceedings of this House, they ordered the

---

[6] In the omitted portions that follow, Burke again turns to a detailed
indictment of the representatives of the Company.

Directors not to carry into effect any resolution they might come to for the removal of Mr. Hastings and Mr. Hornby. The Directors, still retaining some shadow of respect to this House, instituted an inquiry themselves, which continued from June to October, and, after an attentive perusal and full consideration of papers, resolved to take steps for removing the persons who had been the objects of our resolution, but not without a violent struggle against evidence. Seven Directors went so far as to enter a protest against the vote of their court. Upon this the General Court takes the alarm: it reassembles; it orders the Directors to rescind their resolution, that is, not to recall Mr. Hastings and Mr. Hornby, and to despise the resolution of the House of Commons. Without so much as the pretence of looking into a single paper, without the formality of instituting any committee of inquiry, they superseded all the labors of their own Directors and of this House.

It will naturally occur to ask, how it was possible that they should not attempt some sort of examination into facts, as a color for their resistance to a public authority proceeding so very deliberately, and exerted, apparently at least, in favor of their own. The answer, and the only answer which can be given, is, that they were afraid that their true relation should be mistaken. They were afraid that their patrons and masters in India should attribute their support of them to an opinion of their cause, and not to an attachment to their power. They were afraid it should be suspected that they did not mean blindly to support them in the use they made of that power. They determined to show that they at least were set against reformation: that they were firmly resolved to bring the territories, the trade, and the stock of the Company to ruin, rather than be wanting in fidelity to their nominal servants and real masters, in the ways they took to their private fortunes. . . .

It has been said, If you violate this charter, what security has the charter of the Bank, in which public credit is so deeply concerned, and even the charter of London, in which the rights of so many subjects are involved? I answer, In the like case they have no security at all,—no, no security at all. If the Bank should, by every species of mismanagement, fall into a state similar to that of the East India Company,—if it should be oppressed with demands it could not answer, engagements which it could not perform, and with bills for which it could not procure payment,—no charter should protect the mismanagement from correction, and such public grievances from redress. If the city of London had the means and will of destroying an empire, and of cruelly oppressing and tyrannizing over millions of men as good as themselves, the charter of the city of London should prove no sanction to such tyranny and such oppression. Charters are kept, when their purposes are maintained: they are violated, when the privilege is supported against its end and its object.

Now, Sir, I have finished all I proposed to say, as my reasons for giving my vote to this bill. If I am wrong, it is not for want of pains to know what is right. This pledge, at least, of my rectitude I have given to my country.

And now, having done my duty to the bill, let me say a word to the author. I should leave him to his own noble sentiments, if the unworthy and illiberal language with which he has been treated, beyond all example of Parliamentary liberty, did not make a few words necessary,—not so much in justice to him as to my own feelings. I must say, then, that it will be a distinction honorable to the age, that the rescue of the greatest number of the human race that ever were so grievously oppressed from the greatest tyranny that was ever exercised has fallen to the lot of abilities and dispositions equal to the task,—that it has fallen to one who has the enlargement to comprehend, the spirit to undertake, and the eloquence to support so great a measure of hazardous benevolence. His spirit is not owing to his ignorance of the state of men and things: he well knows what snares are spread about his path, from personal animosity, from court intrigues, and possibly from popular delusion. But he has put to hazard his ease, his security, his interest, his power, even his darling popularity, for the benefit of a people whom he has never seen. This is the road that all heroes have trod before him. He is traduced and abused for his supposed motives. He will remember that obloquy is a necessary ingredient in the composition of all true glory: he will remember that it was not only in the Roman customs, but it is in the nature and constitution of things, that calumny and abuse are essential parts of triumph. These thoughts will support a mind which only exists for honor under the burden of temporary reproach. He is doing, indeed, a great good,—such as rarely falls to the lot, and almost as rarely coincides with the desires, of any man. Let him use his time. Let him give the whole length of the reins to his benevolence. He is now on a great eminence, where the eyes of mankind are turned to him. He may live long, he may do much; but here is the summit: he never can exceed what he does this day. . . .

I have spoken what I think, and what I feel, of the mover of this bill. An honorable friend of mine, speaking of his merits, was charged with having made a studied panegyric. I don't know what his was. Mine, I am sure, is a studied panegyric,—the fruit of much meditation, the result of the observation of near twenty years. For my own part, I am happy that I have lived to see this day; I feel myself overpaid for the labors of eighteen years, when, at this late period, I am able to take my share, by one humble vote, in destroying a tyranny that exists to the disgrace of this nation and the destruction of so large a part of the human species.

FROM *Speech in Opening the Impeachment of Warren Hastings, Fourth Day*

(FEBRUARY 19, 1788)[1]

. . . I therefore charge Mr. Hastings with having destroyed, for private purposes, the whole system of government by the six Provincial Councils, which he had no right to destroy.

I charge him with having delegated to others that power which the act of Parliament had directed him to preserve unalienably in himself.

I charge him with having formed a committee to be mere instruments and tools, at the enormous expense of 62,000*l.* per annum.

I charge him with having appointed a person their dewan

---

[1] Burke's great "Speech in Opening the Impeachment," planned as a general introduction to all the charges, lasted four full days (February 15 to 19, 1788). The above selection concludes the fourth and final day. Hereafter Sheridan and others took over the introduction to the specific charges, with Burke, a year later, giving the massive introductory "Speech on the Sixth Article of Charge," which also lasted four days (during the period from April 21 to May 7, 1789).

to whom these Englishmen were to be subservient tools,—whose name, to his own knowledge, was, by the general voice of India, by the general recorded voice of the Company, by recorded official transactions, by everything that can make a man known, abhorred, and detested, stamped with infamy; and with giving him the whole power which he had thus separated from the Council-General, and from the Provincial Councils.

I charge him with taking bribes of Gunga Govind Sing.

I charge him with not having done that bribe-service which fidelity even in iniquity requires at the hands of the worst of men.

I charge him with having robbed those people of whom he took the bribes.

I charge him with having fraudulently alienated the fortunes of widows.

I charge him with having, without right, title, or purchase, taken the lands of orphans, and given them to wicked persons under him.

I charge him with having removed the natural guardians of a minor Rajah, and with having given that trust to a stranger, Debi Sing, whose wickedness was known to himself and all the world, and by whom the Rajah, his family, and dependants were cruelly oppressed.

I charge him with having committed to the management of Debi Sing three great provinces; and thereby with having wasted the country, ruined the landed interest, cruelly harassed the peasants, burnt their houses, seized their crops, tortured and degraded their persons, and destroyed the honor of the whole female race of that country.

In the name of the Commons of England, I charge all this villany upon Warren Hastings, in this last moment of my application to you.

My Lords, what is it that we want here to a great act of national justice? Do we want a cause, my Lords? You have the cause of oppressed princes, of undone women of the first rank, of desolated provinces, and of wasted kingdoms.

Do you want a criminal, my Lords? When was there so much iniquity ever laid to the charge of any one? No, my Lords, you must not look to punish any other such delinquent from India. Warren Hastings has not left substance enough in India to nourish such another delinquent.

My Lords, is it a prosecutor you want? You have before you the Commons of Great Britain as prosecutors; and I believe, my Lords, that the sun, in his beneficent progress round the world, does not behold a more glorious sight than that of men, separated from a remote people by the material bounds and barriers of Nature, united by the bond of a social and moral community,—all the Commons of England resenting, as their own, the indignities and cruelties that are offered to all the people of India.

Do we want a tribunal? My Lords, no example of antiquity, nothing in the modern world, nothing in the range of human imagination, can supply us with a tribunal like this. My Lords, here we see virtually, in the mind's eye, that sacred majesty of the crown, under whose authority you sit, and whose power you exercise. We see in that invisible authority, what we all feel in reality and life, the beneficent powers and protecting justice of his Majesty. We have here the heir-apparent to the crown, such as the fond wishes of the people of England wish an heir-apparent of the crown to be. We have here all the branches of the royal family, in a situation between majesty and subjection, between the sovereign and the subject,—offering a pledge in that situation for the support of the rights of the crown and the liberties of the people, both which extremities they touch. My Lords, we have a great hereditary peerage here,—those who have their own honor, the honor of their ancestors and of their posterity to guard, and who will justify, as they have always justified, that provision in the Constitution by which justice is made an hereditary office. My Lords, we have here a new nobility, who have risen and exalted themselves by various merits,—by great military services which have extended the fame of this country from the rising to the setting sun. We have those who, by various civil merits and various civil talents, have been exalted to a situation which they well deserve, and in which they will justify the favor of their sovereign, and the good opinion of their fellow-subjects, and make them rejoice to see those virtuous characters that were the other day upon a level with them now exalted above them in rank, but feeling with them in sympathy what they felt in common with them before. We have persons exalted from the practice of the law, from the place in which they administered high, though subordinate, justice, to a seat here, to enlighten with their knowledge and to strengthen with their votes those principles which have distinguished the courts in which they have presided.

My Lords, you have here also the lights of our religion, you have the bishops of England. My Lords, you have that true image of the primitive Church, in its ancient form, in its ancient ordinances, purified from the superstitions and the vices which a long succession of ages will bring upon the best institutions. You have the representatives of that religion which says that their God is love, that the very vital spirit of their institution is charity,—a religion which so much hates oppression, that, when the God whom we adore appeared in human form, He did not appear in a form of greatness and majesty, but in sympathy with the lowest of the people, and thereby made it a firm and ruling principle that their welfare was the object of all government, since the Person who was the Master of Nature chose to appear Himself in a subordinate situation. These are the considerations which influence them, which animate them, and will animate them, against all oppression,—knowing that He who is called first

among them, and first among us all, both of the flock that is
fed and of those who feed it, made Himself "the servant of
all."

My Lords, these are the securities which we have in all the
constituent parts of the body of this House. We know them,
we reckon, we rest upon them, and commit safely the interests
of India and of humanity into your hands. Therefore it is
with confidence, that, ordered by the Commons,

I impeach Warren Hastings, Esquire, of high crimes and
misdemeanors.

I impeach him in the name of the Commons of Great Britain in Parliament assembled, whose Parliamentary trust he
has betrayed.

I impeach him in the name of all the Commons of Great
Britain, whose national character he has dishonored.

I impeach him in the name of the people of India, whose
laws, rights, and liberties he has subverted, whose properties
he has destroyed, whose country he has laid waste and desolate.

I impeach him in the name and by virtue of those eternal
laws of justice which he has violated.

I impeach him in the name of human nature itself, which
he has cruelly outraged, injured, and oppressed, in both sexes,
in every age, rank, situation, and condition of life.

Impeachment of Warren Hastings: Speech in General Reply, Ninth Day

(JUNE 16, 1794)[1]

My Lords,—I should think it necessary to make an apology to your Lordships for appearing before you one day more, if I were inclined to measure this business either by the standard of my own ability, or by my own impatience, or by any supposed impatience of yours. I know no measure, in such a case, but the nature of the subject, and the duty which we owe to it. You will therefore, my Lords, permit me, in a few words, to lead you back to what we did yesterday, that you may the better comprehend the manner in which I mean to conclude the business to-day.

My Lords, we took the liberty of stating to you the condition of Bengal before our taking possession of it, and of the several classes of its inhabitants. We first brought before you the Mahometan inhabitants, who had the judicial authority of the country in their hands; and we proved to you the utter

---

[1] Six years and a quarter after his "Speech in Opening the Impeachment," Burke concluded his great effort on behalf of India with his "Speech in General Reply" (during the period from May 28 to June 16, 1794). The above gives entire the ninth and final day, with its famous peroration.

ruin of that body of people, and with them of the justice
of the country, by their being, both one and the other, sold
to an infamous woman called Munny Begum. We next showed
you, that the whole landed interest, the zemindars, or Hindoo
gentry of the country, was likewise ruined by its being given
over, by letting it on a five years' lease, to infamous farmers,
and giving it up to their merciless exactions,—and afterwards
by subjecting the rank of those zemindars, their title-deeds,
and all their pecuniary affairs, to the minutest scrutiny, under
pain of criminal punishment, by a commission granted to a
nefarious villain called Gunga Govind Sing. We lastly showed
you that the remaining third class, that of the English, was
partly corrupted, or had its authority dissolved, and that the
whole superintending English control was subverted or subdued,—that the products of the country were diminished, and
that the revenues of the Company were dilapidated, by an
overcharge of expenses, in four years, to the amount of
500,000*l.*, in consequence of these corrupt, dangerous, and
mischievous projects.

We have farther stated, that the Company's servants were
corrupted by contracts and jobs; we proved that those that
were not so corrupted were removed from their stations or
reduced to a state of abject dependence; we showed you the
destruction of the Provincial Councils, the destruction of the
Council-General, and the formation of a committee for no
other ends whatever but for the purposes of bribery, concealment, and corruption. We next stated some of the most
monstrous instances of that bribery; and though we were of
opinion that in none of them any satisfactory defence worth
mentioning had been made, yet we have thought that this
should not hinder us from recalling to your Lordships' recollection the peculiar nature and circumstances of one of those
proceedings.

The proceedings to which we wish to call your attention
are those belonging to the second bribe given by the Nabob

of Oude to Mr. Hastings. Mr. Hastings's own knowledge and opinion that that money was set apart for his use, either in bills or assets, I have before stated; and I now wish to call your Lordships' minute recollection to the manner in which the fraudulent impeachment of Mr. Middleton, for the purpose of stifling an inquiry into that business, was carried on. Your Lordships will remember that I proved to you, upon the face of that proceeding, the collusive nature of the accusation, and that the real state of the case was not charged,—and that Mr. Hastings acquitted the party accused of one article of the charge, not upon the evidence of the case, contrary to his own avowed, declared, moral certainty of his guilt, but upon a pretended appeal to the conscience of the man accused. He did not, however, give him a complete, formal, official acquittal, but referred the matter to the Court of Directors, who could not possibly know anything of the matter, without one article of evidence whatever produced at the time or transmitted. We lastly proved to you, that, after finding him guilty of five charges, and leaving the other to the Court of Directors, Mr. Hastings, without any reason assigned, appointed him to a great office in the Company's service.

These proceedings were brought before you for two purposes: first, to show the corrupt principle of the whole proceeding; next, to show the manner in which the Company's servants are treated. They are accused and persecuted, until they are brought to submit to whatever terms it may be thought proper to impose upon them; they are then formally, indeed, acquitted of the most atrocious crimes charged against them, but virtually condemned upon some articles, with the scourge hung over them,—and in some instances rewarded by the greatest, most honorable, and most lucrative situations in the Company's service. My Lords, it is on the same ground of the wicked, pernicious, and ruinous principles of Mr. Hastings's government, that I have charged this with everything that is chargeable against him, namely, that, if your Lordships should ratify those principles by your acquittal of him, they become principles of government,—rejected, indeed, by the Commons, but adopted by the Peerage of Great Britain.

There is another article which I have just touched but which I must do more than barely notice, upon account of the evil example of it: I mean the taking great sums of money, under pretence of an entertainment. Your Lordships will recollect, that, when this business was charged against him in India, Mr. Hastings neither affirmed nor denied the fact. Confession could not be there extorted from him. He next appeared before the House of Commons, and he still evaded a denial or a confession of it. He lastly appeared before your Lordships, and in his answer to our charge he in the same manner evaded either a confession or a denial. He forced us to employ a great part of a session in endeavoring to establish what we have at last established, the receipt of the sums first charged, and of seven lacs more, by him. At length the proof could not be evaded; and after we had fought through all the difficulties which the law could interpose in his defence, and of which he availed himself with a degree of effrontery that has, I believe, no example in the world, he confesses, avows, and justifies his conduct. If the custom alleged be well founded, and be an honorable and a proper and just practice, why did he not avow it in every part and progress of our proceedings here? Why should he have put us to the necessity of wasting so many months in the proof of the fact? And why, after we have proved it, and not before, did he confess it, avow it, and even glory in it?

I must remind your Lordships that the sum charged to be so taken by way of entertainment made only a part, a single article, of the bribes charged by Nundcomar to have been received by Mr. Hastings; and when we find him confessing, what he could not deny, that single article, and evading all explanation respecting the others, and not giving any reason whatever why one was received and the others rejected, your Lordships will judge of the strong presumption of his having taken them all, even if we had given no other proofs of it. We think, however, that we have proved the whole very satisfactorily. But whether we have or not, the proof of a single present received is sufficient; because the principle to be established respecting these bribes is this,— whether or not a Governor-General, paying a visit to any of the poor, miserable, dependent creatures called sovereign princes in that country, (men whom Mr. Hastings has himself declared to be nothing but phantoms, and that they had no one attribute of sovereignty about them,) whether, I say, he can consider them to be such sovereign princes as to justify his taking from them great sums of money by way of a present. The Nabob, in fact, was not a sovereign prince, nor a country power, in any sense but that which the Company meant to exempt from the custom of making presents. It was their design to prevent their servants from availing themselves of the real dependence of the nominal native powers to extort money from them under the pretence of their sovereignty. Such presents, so far from being voluntary, were in reality obtained from their weakness, their hopeless and unprotected condition; and you are to decide whether or not this custom, which is insisted upon by the prisoner's counsel, with great triumph, to be a thing which he could not evade, without breaking through all the usages of the country, and violating principles established by the most clear law of India, is to be admitted as his justification.

It was on this very account, namely, the extortion suffered by these people, under the name or pretence of presents, that the Company first bound their servants by a covenant, which your Lordships shall now hear read.

"That they shall not take any grant of lands, or rents or revenues issuing out of lands, or any territorial possession, jurisdiction, dominion, power, or authority whatsoever, from any of the Indian princes, sovereigns, subahs, or nabobs, or any of their ministers, servants, or agents, for any service or services, or upon any account or pretence whatsoever, without the license or consent of the Court of Directors."

This clause in the covenant had doubtless a regard to Lord Clive, and to Sir Hector Munro, and to some others, who had received gifts, and grants of jaghires, and other territorial revenues, that were confirmed by the Company. But though this confirmation might be justifiable at a time when we had no real sovereignty in the country, yet the Company very wisely provided afterwards, that under no pretence whatever should their servants have the means of extorting from the sovereigns or pretended sovereigns of the country any of their lands or possessions. Afterwards it appeared that there existed abuses of a similar nature, and particularly (as was proved before us in the year 1773, and reported to our House, upon the evidence of Mahomed Reza Khân) the practice of frequently visiting the princes, and of extorting, under pretence of such visits, great sums of money. All their servants, and the Governor-General particularly, were therefore obliged to enter into the following covenant:—

"That they shall not, directly or indirectly, accept, take, or receive, or agree to accept, take, or receive, any gift, reward, gratuity, allowance, donation, or compensation, in money, effects, jewels, or otherwise howsoever, from any of the Indian princes, sovereigns, subahs, or nabobs, or any of their ministers, servants, or agents, exceeding the value of four thousand rupees, for any service or services performed or to be performed by them in India, or upon any other account or pretence whatsoever."

By this covenant, my Lords, Mr. Hastings is forbidden to accept, upon any pretence and under any name whatsoever, any sum above four thousand rupees,—that is to say, any sum above four hundred pounds. Now the sum that was here received is eighteen thousand pounds sterling, by way of a present, under the name of an allowance for an entertainment, which is the precise thing which his covenant was made to prevent. The covenant suffered him to receive four hundred pounds: if he received more than that money, he became a criminal, he had broken his covenant, and forfeited the obligation he had made with his masters. Think with yourselves, my Lords, what you will do, if you acquit the prisoner of this charge. You will avow the validity, you will sanction the principle of his defence: for, as the fact is avowed, there is an end of that.

Good God! my Lords, where are we? If they conceal their gifts and presents, they are safe by their concealment; if they avow them, they are still safer. They plead the customs of the country, or rather, the customs which we have introduced into the country,—customs which have been declared to have their foundation in a system of the most abominable corruption, the most flagitious extortion, the most dreadful oppression,—those very customs which their covenant is made to abolish. Think where your Lordships are. You have before you a covenant declaring that he should take under no name whatever (I do not know how words could be selected in the English language more expressive) any sum more than four hundred pounds. He says, "I have taken eighteen thousand pounds." He makes his counsel declare, and he desires your Lordships to confirm their declaration, that he is not only justifiable in so doing, but that he ought to do so,—that he ought to break his covenant, and act in direct contradiction to it. He does not even pretend to say that this money was intended, either inwardly or outwardly, avowedly or covertly, for the Company's service. He put absolutely into his own pocket eighteen thousand pounds, besides his salary.

Consider, my Lords, the consequences of this species of iniquity. If any servant of the Company, high in station, chooses to make a visit from Calcutta to Moorshedabad, which Moorshedabad was then the residence of our principal revenue government,—if he should choose to take an airing for his health, if he has a fancy to make a little voyage for pleasure as far as Moorshedabad, in one of those handsome barges or budgeros of which you have heard so much in his charge against Nundcomar, he can put twenty thousand pounds into his pocket any day he pleases, in defiance of all our acts of Parliament, covenants, and regulations.

Do you make your laws, do you make your covenants, for the very purpose of their being evaded? Is this the purpose for which a British tribunal sits here, to furnish a subject for an epigram, or a tale for the laughter of the world? Believe me, my Lords, the world is not to be thus trifled with. But, my Lords, you will never trifle with your duty. You have a gross, horrid piece of corruption before you,—impudently confessed, and more impudently defended. But you will not suffer Mr. Hastings to say, "I have only to go to Moorshedabad, or to order the Nabob to meet me half way, and I can set aside and laugh at all your covenants and acts of Parliament." Is this all the force and power of the covenant by which you would prevent the servants of the Company from committing acts of fraud and oppression, that they have nothing to do but to amuse themselves with a tour of pleasure to Moorshedabad in order to put any sum of money in their pocket that they please?

But they justify themselves by saying, such things have been practised before. No doubt they have; and these covenants were made that they should not be practised any more. But your Lordships are desired to say, that the very custom which the covenant is made to destroy, the very grievance itself, may be pleaded; the abuse shall be admitted to destroy the law made to prevent it. It is impossible, I venture to say, that your Lordships should act thus. The conduct of the criminal is not half so abhorrent as the justification is affronting to justice, whilst it tends to vilify and degrade the dignity of the Peerage and the character of the Commons of Great Britain, before the former and against the latter of which such a justification is produced in the face of the world.

At the same time that we call for your justice upon this man, we beseech you to remember the severest justice upon him is the tenderest pity towards the innocent victims of his crimes. Consider what was at that time the state of the people from whom, in direct defiance of his covenant, he took this sum of money. Were they at this time richer, were they more opulent, was the state of the country more flourishing than when Mr. Sumner, when Mr. Vansittart, in short, than when the long line of Mr. Hastings's predecessors visited that country? No, they were not. Mr. Hastings at this very time had reduced the Nabob's income from 450,000*l.* [400,000*l.*?] sterling a year, exclusive of other considerable domains and revenues, to 160,000*l.* He was, indeed, an object of compassion. His revenues had not only been reduced during his state of minority, but they were reduced when he afterwards continued in a state in which he could do no one valid act; and yet, in this state, he was made competent to give away, under the name of compensation for entertainments, the sum of 18,000*l.*,—perhaps at that time nearly all he had in the world.

Look at your minutes, and you will find Mr. Hastings had just before this time said that the bread of ten thousand persons, many of them of high rank, depended upon the means possessed by the Nabob for their support,—that his heart was cut and afflicted to see himself obliged to ruin and starve so many of the Mahometan nobility, the greatest part of whose yet remaining miserable allowances were now taken away. You know, and you will forgive me again remarking, that it is the nature of the eagles and more generous birds of prey to fall upon living, healthy victims, but that vultures and carrion crows, and birds of that base and degenerate kind, always prey upon dead or dying carcases. It is upon ruined houses, it is upon decayed families, it is upon extinguished nobility, that Mr. Hastings chooses to prey, and to justify his making them his prey.

But again we hear, my Lords, that it is a custom, upon ceremonial and complimentary visits, to receive these presents. Do not let us deceive ourselves. Mr. Hastings was there upon no visit either of ceremony or politics. He was a member, at that time, of the Committee of Circuit, which went to Moorshedabad for the purpose of establishing a system of revenue in the country. He went up upon that business only, as a member of the Committee of Circuit, for which business he was, like other members of the Committee of Circuit, amply paid, in addition to his emoluments as Governor, which amounted to about 30,000*l.* a year. Not satisfied with those emoluments, and without incurring new known expense of any kind or sort, he was paid for the extra expenses of his journey, as appears in your minutes, like other members of the Committee of Circuit. In fact, he was on no visit there at all. He was merely executing his duty in the settlement of the revenue, as a member of the Committee of Circuit. I do not mean to praise the Committee of Circuit in any way: God forbid I should!—for we know that it was a committee of robbers. He was there as one of that committee, which I am pretty well justified in describing as I have done, because the Court of Directors, together with the Board of Control, did, in the year 1786, declare that the five years' settlement (which originated in that committee) was a thing bought and sold: your Lordships may read it whenever you please, in the 80th paragraph of their letter.

Your Lordships are now fully in possession of all the facts upon which we charge the prisoner with peculation, by extorting or receiving large sums of money, upon pretence of visits, or in compensation of entertainments. I appeal to your Lordships' consciences for a serious and impartial consideration of our charge. This is a business not to be hurried over in the mass, as amongst the acts of a great man, who may have his little errors among his great services; no, you cannot, as a judicial body, huddle all this into a hotchpotch, and decide upon it in a heap. You will have to ask yourselves,—Is this justifiable by his covenant? Is this justifiable by law? Is this justifiable, under the circumstances of the case, by an enlarged discretion? Is it to be justified under any principles of humanity? Would it be justifiable by local customs, if such were applicable to the case in question? and even if it were, is it a practice fit for an English Governor-General to follow?

I dwell the longer upon this, because the fact is avowed; the whole is an issue of law between us,—whether a Governor-General, in such a case, ought to take such money; and therefore, before I finally dismiss it, I beg leave to restate it briefly once more for your Lordships' consideration.

First I wish to leave fixed in your Lordships' minds, what is distinctly fixed, and shall never go out of ours, that his covenant did not allow him to take above four hundred pounds as a present, upon any pretence whatsoever.

Your Lordships will observe we contend, that, if there was a custom, this covenant puts an end to that custom. It was declared and intended so to do. The fact is, that, if such custom existed at all, it was a custom applicable only to an ambassador or public minister sent on a necessary complimentary visit to a sovereign prince. We deny, positively, that there is any such general custom. We say, that he never was any such minister, or that he ever went upon any such complimentary visit. We affirm, that, when he took this money, he was doing an act of quite another nature, and came upon that business only to Moorshedabad, the residence of the prince of the country. Now do you call a man who is going to execute a commission, a commission more severe than those issued against bankrupts, a commission to take away half a man's income, and to starve a whole body of people dependent upon that income,—do you call this a complimentary visit? Is this a visit for which a man is to have great entertainments given him? No, the pretence for taking this money is worse than the act itself. When a man is going to execute upon another such harsh cruelty, when he is going upon a service at which he himself says his mind must revolt, is that precisely the time when he is to take from his undone host a present, as if he was upon a visit of compliment, or about to confer some honor or benefit upon him,—to augment his revenues, to add to his territories, or to conclude some valuable treaty with him? Was this a proper time to take at all from an helpless minor so large a sum of money?

And here I shall leave this matter for your Lordships' consideration, after reminding you that this poor Nabob is still at Moorshedabad, and at the mercy of any English gentleman who may choose to take 18,000*l.*, or any other given sum of money from him, after the example of the prisoner at your bar, if it should be sanctioned by your connivance. Far different was the example set him by General Clavering. In page 1269 your Lordships will find the most honorable testimony to the uprightness and fidelity of this meritorious servant of the Company. It runs thus: "Conceiving it to be the intention of the legislature that the Governor-General and members of the Council should receive no presents, either from the Indian powers or any persons whatever, he [General Clavering] has strictly complied, since his arrival here, both with the spirit and the letter of the act of Parliament, and has accordingly returned all the presents which have been made to him." I have dwelt thus long upon this subject, not merely upon account if its own corrupt character, which has been sufficiently stigmatized by my honorable colleague, but upon account of the principle that is laid down by the prisoner, in his defence of his conduct;— a principle directly leading to a continuance of the same iniquitous practice, and subversive of every attempt to check or control it.

I must beg leave to recall your Lordships' attention to another, but similar instance of his peculation, another and new mode of taking presents: I mean, the present which Mr. Hastings took, through Gunga Govind Sing, from those farmers of the revenues amongst whom he had distributed the pillage of the whole country. This scandalous breach of his covenant he attempts to justify by the inward intention of his own mind to apply the money so taken to the public service. Upon this, my Lords, I shall only observe, that this plea of an inward intention in his own mind may, if admitted, justify any evil act whatever of this kind. You have seen how presents from the Nabob are justified; you have seen how the taking a sum of money or allowance for entertainment, directly contrary to the covenant, how that is attempted to be justified; you see in what manner he justifies this last-mentioned act of peculation; and your Lordships will now have to decide upon the validity of these pleas.

There still remains, unobserved upon, an instance of his malversation, wholly new in its kind, to which I will venture to desire your Lordships very seriously to turn your attention. In all the causes of peculation or malversation in office that ever have been tried before this high court, or before any lower court of judicature, in all the judicial records of modern crimes, or of antiquity, you will not find anything in any degree like it. We have all, in our early education, read the Verrine Orations. We read them not merely to instruct us, as they will do, in the principles of eloquence, and to acquaint us with the manners, customs, and laws of the ancient Romans, of which they are an abundant repository, but we may read them from a much higher motive. We may read them from a motive which the great author had doubtless in his view, when by publishing them he left to the world and to the latest posterity a monument by which it might be seen what course a great public accuser in a great public cause ought to pursue, and, as connected with it, what course judges ought to pursue in deciding upon such a cause. In these orations you will find almost every instance of rapacity and peculation which we charge upon Mr. Hastings. Undoubtedly, many Roman and English governors have received corrupt gifts and bribes, under various pretences. But in the cause before your Lordships there is one species of disgrace, in the conduct of the party accused, which I defy you to find in Verres, or in the whole tribe of Roman peculators, in any governor-general, proconsul, or viceroy. I desire you to consider it not included in any other class of crimes, but as a species apart by itself. It is an individual, a single case; but it is like the phœnix,— it makes a class or species by itself: I mean the business of Nobkissin. The money taken from him was not money pretended to be received in lieu of entertainment; it was not money taken from a farmer-general of revenue, out of an idea that his profits were unreasonable, and greater than government ought to allow; it was not a donation from a great man, as an act of his bounty. No, it was a sum of money taken from a private individual,—or rather, as has been proved to you by Mr. Larkins, his own book-keeper, money borrowed, for which he had engaged to give his bond. That he had actually deposited his bond for this money Mr. Larkins has proved to you,—and that the bond was carried to Nobkissin's credit, in his account with the government. But Mr. Hastings, when he was called upon for the money, withdraws the bond; he will not pay the money; he refused to pay it upon the applications made to him both in India and here at home; and he now comes to your Lordships and says, "I borrowed this money, I intended to give my bond for it, as has been proved before you; but I must have it for my own use." We have heard of governors being everything that is bad and wicked; but a governor putting himself in the situation of a common cheat, of a common swindler, never was, I believe, heard of since the creation of the world to this day. This does not taste of the common oppressions of power; this does not taste of the common abuses of office; but it in no way differs from one of those base swindling cases that come to be tried and heavily punished in the King's Bench every day. This is neither more nor less than a plain, barefaced cheat.

Now, my Lords, let us see how it is justified. To justify openly and directly a cheat, to justify a fraud upon an individual, is reserved for our times. But, good Heavens, what a justification have we here! Oh, my Lords, consider into what a state Indian corruption has brought us in this country, when any person can be found to come to the bar of the House of Lords and say, "I did cheat, I did defraud; I did promise, and gave my bond; I have now withdrawn it, but I will account for it to you as to a gang of robbers concerned with me in the transaction. I confess I robbed this man; but I have acted as trustee for the gang. Observe what I have done for the gang. Come forward, Mr. Auriol, and prove what handsome budgeros I gave the company: were not they elegantly painted, beautifully gilt, charming and commodious? I made use of them as long as I had occasion; and though they are little worse for wear, and would hardly suffer the least percentage deduction from prime cost upon them, I gave them to the company. Oh, I did not put the money into my own pocket. I provided for myself and wore a suit of lace clothes, when I was Jew bail for some of this company: it will turn, for it is hardly the worse for wear, though I appeared two or three times, in different characters, as bail

for you on such and such an occasion. I therefore set off
these items against this money which I gained by swindling
on your account. It is true I also picked such a one's pocket
of a watch; here it is; I have worn it as long as it was
convenient; now I give the watch to the company, and let
them send it to the pawnbroker for what it will bring. Besides
all this, I maintained aide-de-camps for you, and gave them
house-rent." (By the way, my Lords, what sort of aide-de-
camps were these? Who made him a military man, and to
have such a legion of aide-de-camps?) "But," says he, "I paid
house-rent for them; that is, in other words, I paid, at night-
cellars and houses in Saint Giles's, sixpence a week for some
of the gang." (This, my Lords, is the real spirit of the whole
proceeding, and more especially of the last item in it.)
"Then," says he, "I was the gang's schoolmaster, and taught
lessons on their account. I founded a Mahometan school."
(Your Lordships have already heard something of this shameful affair, of this scene of iniquity,—I think of such iniquity
as the world never yet had to blush at.) "I founded a
Mahometan college for your use; and I bore the expense of
it from September, 1780, when I placed a professor there,
called Mudjed-o-Din."—This Mudjed-o-Din was to perfect
men, by contract, in all the arts and sciences, in about six
months; and the chief purpose of the school was, as Mr.
Hastings himself tells you, to breed theologians, magistrates,
and moulavies, that is to say, judges and doctors of law, who
were to be something like our masters in chancery, the
assessors of judges, to assist them in their judgments. Such
was the college founded by Mr. Hastings, and he soon afterwards appropriated one of the Company's estates, (I am
speaking of matters of public notoriety,) worth 3,000*l.* a
year, for its support. Heaven be praised, that Mr. Hastings,
when he was resolved to be pious and munificent, and to be
a great founder, chose a Mahometan rather than a Christian
foundation, so that our religion was not disgraced by such a
foundation!

Observe how he charges the expense of the foundation to the Company twice over. He first makes them set aside an estate of 3,000*l*. a year for its support. In what manner this income was applied during Mr. Hastings's stay in India no man living knows; but we know, that, at his departure, one of the last acts he did was to desire it should be put into the hands of Mudjed-o-Din. He afterwards, as you have seen, takes credit to himself with the Company for the expenses relative to this college.

I must now introduce your Lordships to the last visitation that was made of this college. It was visited by order of Lord Cornwallis in the year 1788, upon the complaints made against it which I have already mentioned to your Lordships, —that it was a sink of filth, vermin, and misery. Mr. Chapman, who was the visitor, and the friend of Mr. Hastings, declares that he could not sit in it even for a few minutes; his words are,—"The wretched, squalid figures that from every part ran out upon me appeared to be more like anything else than students." In fact, a universal outcry was raised by the whole city against it, not only as a receptacle of every kind of abuse, not only of filth and excrements which made it stink in the natural nostrils, but of worse filth, which made it insufferably offensive to the moral nostrils of every inhabitant. Such is the account given of a college supported at an expense of 3,000*l*. a year, (a handsome foundation for a college,) and for building which the Company was charged 5,000*l*.: though no vouchers of its expenditure were ever given by Mr. Hastings. But this is not all. When Lord Cornwallis came to inquire into it, he found that Mudjed-o-Din had sunk the income of the estate from 3,000*l*. to 2,000*l*. a year,—in short, that it had been a scene of peculation, both by the masters and scholars, as well as of abandonment to every kind of vicious and licentious courses; and all this without the shadow of any benefit having been derived from it. The visitors expressly inquired whether there was any good mixed with all this evil; and they found it was all bad and mischievous, from one end to the other. Your Lordships will remark, that the greatest part of this disgusting business must have been known to Mr. Hastings when he gave to Mudjed-o-Din the disposal of 3,000*l.* a year. And now, my Lords, can you vote this money, expended in the manner which I have stated to you, to be a set-off in his favor, in an account for money which was itself swindled from a private individual?

But there still remains behind another more serious matter belonging to this affair; and I hope you will not think that I am laying too much stress upon it, when I declare, that, if I were to select from the whole of his conduct one thing more dishonorable than another to the British nation, it would be that which I am now about to mention. I will leave your Lordships to judge of the sincerity of this declaration, when you shall have heard read a paper produced by the prisoner in justification of conduct such as I have stated his to have been. It is the *razinama,* or attestation, of Munny Begum (the woman whom Mr. Hastings placed in the seat of justice in that country) concerning this college, made precisely at the time of this inquisition by Lord Cornwallis into the management of it. Your Lordships will see what sort of things attestations are from that country: that they are attestations procured in diametrical contradiction to the certain knowledge of the party attesting. It is in page 2350 of your Minutes. Indeed, my Lords, these are pages which, unless they are effaced by your judgment, will rise up in judgment against us, some day or other.

"He [Mr. Hastings] respected the learned and wise men, and, in order for the propagation of learning, he built a college, and endowed it with a provision for the maintenance of the students, insomuch that thousands reaping the benefits thereof offer up their prayers for the prosperity of the King of England, and for the success of the Company."

I must here remind your Lordships of another attestation of the same character, and to the same effect. It comes from Mahomed Reza Khân, who, as your Lordships will remember, had been reduced by Mr. Hastings from a situation of the highest rank and authority, with an income of suitable magnitude, to one of comparative insignificance, with a small salary annexed. This man is made to disgrace himself, and to abet the disgrace and injury done to his country, by bearing his testimony to the merits of this very college.

I hope your Lordships will never lose sight of this aggravating circumstance of the prisoner's criminality,—namely, that you never find any wicked, fraudulent, and criminal act, in which you do not find the persons who suffered by it, and must have been well acquainted with it, to be the very persons who are brought to attest in its favor. O Heaven! but let shame for one moment veil its face, let indignation suppress its feelings, whilst I again call upon you to view all this as a mere swindling transaction, in which the prisoner was attempting to defraud the Company.

Mr. Hastings has declared, and you will find it upon the Company's records, that this institution (which cost the Company not less than 40,000*l.* in one way or other) did not commence before October in the year 1780; and he brings it before the board in April, 1781,—that is, about six months after its foundation. Now look at his other account, in which he makes it to begin in the year 1779, and in which he has therefore overcharged the expenses of it a whole year.— But Mr. Larkins, who kept this latter account for him, may have been inaccurate.—Good Heavens! where are we? Mr. Hastings, who was bred an accountant, who was bred in all sorts of trade and business, declares that he keeps no accounts. Then comes Mr. Larkins, who keeps an account for him; but he keeps a false account. Indeed, all the accounts from India, from one end to another, are nothing but a series of fraud, while Mr. Hastings was concerned in them. Mr. Larkins, who keeps his private account just as his master kept the public accounts, has swindled from the Company a whole year's expenses of this college. I should not thus repeatedly dwell upon this transaction, but because I wish your Lordships to be cautious how you admit such accounts at all to be given in evidence, into the truth of which you cannot penetrate in any regular way. Upon the face of the two accounts there is a gross fraud. It is no matter which is true or false, as it is an account which you are in no situation to decide upon. I lay down this as a fixed judicial rule, that no judge ought to receive an account (which is as serious a part of a judicial proceeding as can be) the correctness of which he has no means of ascertaining, but must depend upon the sole word of the accountant.

Having stated, therefore, the nature of the offence, which differs nothing from a common dog-trot fraud, such as we see amongst the meanest of mankind, your Lordships will be cautious how you admit these, or any other of his pretended services, to be set off against his crimes. These stand on record confessed before you; the former, of which you can form no just estimate, and into which you cannot enter, rest for their truth upon his own assertions, and they all are found, upon the very face of them, to carry marks of fraud as well as of wickedness.

I have only further to observe to your Lordships, that this Mudjed-o-Din, who, under the patronage of Mr. Hastings, was to do all these wonders, Lord Cornwallis turned out of his office with every mark of disgrace, when he attempted to put into some more respectable state that establishment which Mr. Hastings had made a sink of abuse.

I here conclude all that I have to say upon this business, trusting that your Lordships will feel yourselves more offended, and justice more insulted, by the defence than by the criminal acts of the prisoner at your bar; and that your Lordships will concur with us in thinking, that to make this unhappy people make these attestations, knowing the direct contrary of every word which they say to be the truth, is a shocking aggravation of his guilt. I say they must know it; for Lord Cornwallis tells you it is notorious; and if you think fit to inquire into it, you will find that it was unusually notorious.

My Lords, we have now brought to a conclusion our observations upon the effects produced by that mass of oppression which we have stated and proved before your Lordships,—namely, its effects upon the revenues, and upon the public servants of the Company. We have shown you how greatly the former were diminished, and in what manner the latter were reduced to the worst of all bad states, a state of subserviency to the will of the Governor-General. I have shown your Lordships that in this state they were not only rendered incapable of performing their own duty, but were fitted for the worst of all purposes, coöperation with him in the perpetration of his criminal acts, and collusion with him in the concealment of them. I have lastly to speak of these effects as they regard the general state and welfare of the country. And here your Lordships will permit me to read the evidence given by Lord Cornwallis, a witness called by the prisoner at your bar, Mr. Hastings himself.

The Evidence of Lord Cornwallis. Page 2721.

"*Q.* Whether your Lordship recollects an account that you have given to the Court of Directors, in your letter of the 2d of August, 1789, concerning the state of those provinces? —*A.* I really could not venture to be particular as to any letter I may have written so long since, as I have brought no copies of my letters with me from India, having left them at Bengal when I went to the coast.—*Q.* Whether your Lordship recollects, in any letter that you wrote about the 2d of August, 1789, paragraph 18, any expressions to this effect, namely: 'I am sorry to be obliged to say, that agriculture and internal commerce have for many years been gradually declining, and that at present, excepting the class of shroffs and banians, who reside almost entirely in great towns, the inhabitants of these provinces are advancing hastily to a general state of poverty and wretchedness':—whether your Lordship recollects that you have written a letter to that effect?—*A.* I cannot take upon me to recollect the words of a letter that I have written five years ago, but I conclude I must have written to that effect.—*Q.* Whether your Lordship recollects that in the immediately following paragraph, the 19th, you wrote to this effect: 'In this description' (namely, the foregone description) 'I must even include almost every zemindar in the Company's territories, which, though it may have been partly occasioned by their own indolence and extravagance, I am afraid must also be in a great measure attributed to the defects of our former system of management.' (Paragraph 20.) 'The settlement, in conformity to your orders, will only be made for ten years certain, with the notification of its being your intention to declare it a perpetual, an unalterable assessment of these provinces, if the amount and the principles upon which it has been made should meet with your approbation':—whether your Lordship recollects to have written something to the effect of these two last paragraphs, as well as of the first?—*A.* I do recollect that I did write it; but in that letter I alluded to the former system of annual assessments.—*Q.* Whether your Lordship recollects that you wrote, on or about the 18th of September, 1789, in one of your minutes, thus: 'I may safely assert that one third of the Company's territory in Hindostan is now a jungle, inhabited only by wild beasts: will a ten years' lease induce any proprietor to clear away that jungle, and encourage the ryot to come and cultivate his lands, when at the end of that lease he must either submit to be taxed *ad libitum* for the newly cultivated lands, or lose all hopes of deriving any benefit from his labor, for which perhaps by that time he will hardly be repaid?'—whether your Lordship recollects a minute to that effect?—*A.* I perfectly recollect to have written that minute.—*Q.* Now with respect to a letter, dated November the 3d, 1788, paragraph 38, containing the following sentiments: 'I shall therefore only remark in general, that, from frequent changes of system or other reasons, much is wanting to establish good order and regulations in the internal business of the country, and that, from various causes, by far the greatest part of the zemindars, and other landholders and renters, are fallen into a state much below that of wealth and affluence. This country, however, when the fertility of its soil, and the industry and ingenuity of its numerous inhabitants are taken into consideration, must unquestionably be admitted to be one of the finest in the world; and, with the uniform attention of government to moderation in exaction, and to a due administration of justice, may long prove a source of great riches both to the Company and to Britain.' (Paragraph 39.) 'I am persuaded, that, by a train of judicious measures, the land revenue of these provinces is capable in time of being increased; but, consistent with the principles of humanity, and even those of your own interest, it is only by adopting measures for the gradual cultivation and improvement of these waste lands, and by a gentle and cautious plan for the resumption of lands that have been fraudulently alienated, that it ought ever to be attempted to be accomplished. Men of speculative and sanguine dispositions, and others, either from ignorance of the subject, or with views of recommending themselves to your favor, may confidently hold forth specious grounds to encourage you to hope that a great and immediate accession to that branch of your revenue might be practicable. My public duty obliges me to caution you, in the most serious manner, against listening to propositions which recommend this attempt; because I am clearly con-

vinced, that, if carried into execution, they would be attended
with the most baneful consequences.' (Paragraph 40.) 'Desperate adventurers, without fortune or character, would undoubtedly be found, as has already been too often experienced, to rent the different districts of the country at the
highest rates that could be put upon them; that [but?] the
delusion would be of a short duration, and the impolicy and
inhumanity of the plan would, when perhaps too late for
effectual remedy, become apparent by the complaints of the
people and the disappointments at the treasury in the payments of the revenue, and would probably terminate in the
ruin and depopulation of the unfortunate country':—whether
your Lordship recollects to have written anything to that
effect about that time?—*A*. I perfectly recollect having
written the extracts that have been read."

My Lords, Lord Cornwallis has been called, he has been
examined before you. We stopped our proceedings ten days
for the purpose of taking his evidence. We do not regret this
delay. And he has borne the testimony which you have heard
to the effects of Mr. Hastings's government of a country
once the most fertile and cultivated, of a people the most
industrious, flourishing, and happy,—that the one was wasted
and desolated, the other reduced to a condition of want and
misery, and that the zemindars, that is, the nobility and
gentry of the country, were so beggared as not to be able to
give even a common decent education to their children, notwithstanding the foundation of Mr. Hastings's colleges. You
have heard this noble person, who had been an eye-witness of
what he relates, supplicating for their relief, and expressly
stating that most of the complicated miseries, and perhaps
the cruelest of the afflictions they endured, arose from the
management of the country having been taken out of the
hands of its natural rulers, and given up to Mr. Hastings's
farmers, namely, the banians of Calcutta. These are the

things that ought to go to your Lordships' hearts. You see a country wasted and desolated. You see a third of it become a jungle for wild beasts. You see the other parts oppressed by persons in the form and shape of men, but with all the character and disposition of beasts of prey. This state of the country is brought before you, and by the most unexceptionable evidence,—being brought forward through Mr. Hastings himself. This evidence, whatever opinion you may entertain of the effrontery or of the impudence of the criminal who has produced it, is of double and treble force. And yet at the very time when Lord Cornwallis is giving this statement of the country and its inhabitants, at the very time when he is calling for pity upon their condition, are these people brought forward to bear testimony to the benign and auspicious government of Mr. Hastings, directed, as your Lordships know it was, by the merciful and upright Gunga Govind Sing.

My Lords, you have now the evidence of Lord Cornwallis on the one hand, and the razinamas of India on the other. But before I dismiss this part of my subject, I must call your Lordships' attention to another authority,—to a declaration, strictly speaking, *legal,* of the state to which our Indian provinces were reduced, and of the oppressions which they have suffered, during the government of Mr. Hastings: I speak of the act 24 Geo. III. cap. 25, intituled, "An act for the better regulation and management of the affairs of the East India Company, and of the British possessions in India, and for establishing a court of judicature for the more speedy and effectual trial of persons accused of offences committed in the East Indies," § 39.

My Lords, here is an act of Parliament; here are regulations enacted in consequence of an inquiry which had been directed to be made into the grievances of India, for the redress of them. This act of Parliament declares the existence of oppressions in the country. What oppressions were they?

The oppressions which it suffered by being let out to the farmers of the Company's revenues. Who was the person that sold these revenues to the farmers? Warren Hastings. By whom were these oppressions notified to the Court of Directors? By Lord Cornwallis. Upon what occasion were these letters written by my Lord Cornwallis? They were answers to inquiries made by the Court of Directors, and ordered by an act of Parliament to be made. The existence, then, of the grievances, and the cause of them, are expressly declared in an act of Parliament. It orders an inquiry; and Lord Cornwallis, in consequence of that inquiry, transmits to the Court of Directors this very information; he gives you this identical state of the country: so that it is consolidated, mixed, and embodied with an act of Parliament itself, which no power on earth, I trust, but the power that made it, can shake. I trust, I say, that neither we, the Commons, nor you, the Lords, nor his Majesty, the sovereign of this country, can shake one word of this act of Parliament,—can invalidate the truth of its declaration, or the authority of the persons, men of high honor and character, that made that inquiry and this report. Your Lordships must repeal this act in order to acquit Mr. Hastings.

But Mr. Hastings and his counsel have produced evidence against this act of Parliament, against the order of the Court of Directors by which an inquiry and report were made under that act, against Lord Cornwallis's return to that inquiry; and now, once for all, hear what the miserable wretches are themselves made to say, to invalidate the act of Parliament, to invalidate the authority of the Court of Directors, to invalidate the evidence of an official return of Lord Cornwallis under the act. Pray hear what these miserable creatures describe as an elysium, speaking with rapture of their satisfaction under the government of Mr. Hastings.

"All we zemindars, chowdries, and talookdars of the district of Akbarnagur, commonly called Rajamahal, in the kingdom of Bengal, have heard that the gentlemen in England are displeased with Mr. Hastings, on suspicion that he oppressed us inhabitants of this place, took our money by deceit and force, and ruined the country; therefore we, upon the strength of our religion and religious tenets, which we hold as a duty upon us, and in order to act conformable to the duties of God in delivering evidence, relate the praiseworthy actions, full of prudence and rectitude, friendship and politeness, of Mr. Hastings, possessed of great abilities and understanding, and, by representing facts, remove the doubts that have possessed the minds of the gentlemen in England;—that Mr. Hastings distributed protection and security to religion, and kindness and peace to all; he is free from the charge of embezzlement and fraud, and that his heart is void of covetousness and avidity; during the period of his government, no one experienced from him other than protection and justice, never having felt hardships from him, nor did the poor ever know the weight of an oppressive hand from him; our characters and reputations have always been guarded in quiet from attack by the vigilance of his power and foresight, and preserved by the terror of his justice; he never omitted the smallest instance of kindness and goodness towards us and those entitled to it, but always applied by soothings and mildness the salve of comfort to the wounds of affliction, not allowing a single person to be overwhelmed by despair; he displayed his friendship and kindness to all; he destroyed the power of the enemies and wicked men by the strength of his terror; he tied the hands of tyrants and oppressors by his justice, and by this conduct he secured happiness and joy to us; he reëstablished the foundation of justice, and we at all times, during his government, lived in comfort and passed our days in peace; we are many, many of us satisfied and pleased with him. As Mr. Hastings was perfectly well acquainted with the manners and customs of these countries, he was always desirous of performing that which would tend to the preservation of our religion, and of the duties of our sects, and guard the religious customs of each from the effects of misfortune and accidents; in every sense he treated us with attention and respect. We have represented without deceit what we have ourselves seen, and the facts that happened from him."

This, my Lords, is in page 2374 of the printed Minutes.

My Lords, we spare you the reading of a great number of these attestations; they are all written in the same style; and it must appear to your Lordships a little extraordinary, that, as they are said to be totally voluntary, as the people are represented to be crowding to make these testimonials, there should be such an unison in the heart to produce a language that is so uniform as not to vary so much as in a single tittle,—that every part of the country, every province, every district, men of every caste and of every religion, should all unite in expressing their sentiments in the very same words and in the very same phrases. I must fairly say it is a kind of miraculous concurrence, a miraculous gratitude. Mr. Hastings says that gratitude is lost in this part of the world. There it blooms and flourishes in a way not to be described. In proportion as you hear of the miseries and distresses of these very people, in the same proportion do they express their comfort and satisfaction, and that they never knew what a grievance was of any sort. Lord Cornwallis finds them aggrieved, the Court of Directors find them aggrieved, the Parliament of Great Britain find them aggrieved, and the court here find them aggrieved; but they never found themselves aggrieved. Their being turned out of house and home, and having all their land given to farmers of revenue for five years to riot in and despoil them of all they had, is what fills them with rapture. They are the only people, I believe, upon the face of the earth, that have no complaints to make of their government, in any instance whatever. Theirs must be something superior to the government of angels; for I verily believe, that, if one out of the choir of the heavenly angels were sent to govern the earth, such is the nature of man, that many would be found discontented with it. But these people have no complaint, they feel no hardships, no sorrow; Mr. Hastings has realized more than the golden age. I am ashamed for human nature, I am ashamed for our government, I am ashamed for this court of justice, that these things are brought before us; but here they are, and we must observe upon them.

My Lords, we have done, on our part; we have made out our case; and it only remains for me to make a few observations upon what Mr. Hastings has thought proper to put forward in his defence. Does he meet our case with anything but these general attestations, upon which I must first remark, that there is not one single matter of fact touched upon in them? Your Lordships will observe, and you may hunt them out through the whole body of your minutes, that you do not find a single fact mentioned in any of them. But there is an abundance of panegyric; and if we were doing nothing but making satires, as the newspapers charge us with doing, against Mr. Hastings, panegyric would be a good answer.

But Mr. Hastings sets up pleas of merit upon this occasion. Now, undoubtedly, no plea of merit can be admitted to extinguish, as your Lordships know very well, a direct charge of crime. Merit cannot extinguish crime. For instance, if Lord Howe, to whom this country owes so much as it owes this day for the great and glorious victory which makes our hearts glad, and I hope will insure the security of this country,—yet if Lord Howe, I say, was charged with embezzling the King's stores, or applying them in any manner unbecoming his situation, to any shameful or scandalous pur-

pose,—if he was accused of taking advantage of his station
to oppress any of the captains of his ships,—if he was stated
to have gone into a port of the allies of this country, and to
have plundered the inhabitants, to have robbed their women,
and broken into the recesses of their apartments,—if he had
committed atrocities like these, his glorious victory could not
change the nature and quality of such acts. My Lord Malmesbury has been lately sent to the King of Prussia; we hope and
trust that his embassy will be successful, and that this country will derive great benefit from his negotiations; but if Lord
Malmesbury, from any subsidy that was to be paid to the
King of Prussia, was to put 50,000*l.* in his own pocket, I
believe that his making a good and advantageous treaty with
the King of Prussia would never be thought a good defence
for him. We admit, that, if a man has done great and
eminent services, though they cannot be a defence against
a charge of crimes, and cannot obliterate them, yet, when
sentence comes to be passed upon such a man, you will
consider, first, whether his transgressions were common lapses
of human frailty, and whether the nature and weight of the
grievances resulting from them were light in comparison with
the services performed. I say that you cannot acquit him; but
your Lordships might think some pity due to him, that might
mitigate the severity of your sentence. In the second place,
you would consider whether the evidence of the services
alleged to be performed was as clear and undoubted as that
of the crimes charged. I confess, that, if a man has done great
services, it may be some alleviation of lighter faults; but then
they ought to be urged as such,—with modesty, with humility,
with confession of the faults, and not with a proud and
insolent defiance. They should not be stated as proofs that
he stands justified in the eye of mankind for committing unexampled and enormous crimes. Indeed, humility, suppliant
guilt, always makes impression in our bosoms, so that, when
we see it before us, we always remember that we are all frail

men; and nothing but a proud defiance of law and justice can make us forget this for one moment. I believe the Commons of Great Britain, and I hope the persons that speak to you, know very well how to allow for the faults and frailties of mankind equitably.

Let us now see what are the merits which Mr. Hastings has set up against the just vengeance of his country, and against his proved delinquencies. From the language of the prisoner, and of his counsel, you would imagine some great, known, acknowledged services had been done by him. Your Lordships recollect that most of these presumed services have been considered, and we are persuaded justly considered, as in themselves crimes. He wishes your Lordships to suppose and believe that these services were put aside either because we could not prove the facts against him or could not make out that they were criminal, and consequently that your Lordships ought to presume them to have been meritorious; and this is one of the grounds upon which he demands to be acquitted of the charges that have been brought forward and proved against him. Finding in our proceedings, and recorded upon our journals, an immense mass of criminality with which he is charged, and finding that we had selected, as we were bound to select, such parts as might be most conveniently brought before your Lordships, (for to have gone through the whole would have been nearly impossible,) he takes all the rest that we have left behind and have not brought here as charges, and converts them, by a strange metamorphosis, into merits.

My Lords, we must insist, on the part of the House of Commons, we must conjure your Lordships, for the honor of a coördinate branch of the legislature, that, whenever you are called upon to admit what we have condemned as crimes to be merits, you will at least give us an opportunity of being heard upon the matter,—that you will not suffer Mr. Hastings, when attempting to defend himself against our charges, in an indirect and oblique manner to condemn or censure the House of Commons itself, as having misrepresented to be crimes the acts of a meritorious servant of the public. Mr. Hastings has pleaded a variety of merits, and every one of these merits, without the exception of one of them, have been either directly censured by the House of Commons, and censured as a ground for legislative provision, or they remain upon the records of the House of Commons, with the vouchers for them, and proofs; and though we have not actually come to the question upon every one of them, we had come, before the year 1782, to forty-five direct resolutions upon his conduct. These resolutions were moved by a person to whom this country is under many obligations, and whom we must always mention with honor, whenever we are speaking of high situations in this country, and of great talents to support them, and of long public services in the House of Commons: I mean Mr. Dundas, then Lord Advocate of Scotland, and now one of the principal Secretaries of State, and at the head, and worthily and deservedly at the head, of the East Indian department. This distinguished statesman moved forty-five resolutions, the major part of them directly condemning these very acts which Mr. Hastings has pleaded as his merits, as being delinquencies and crimes. All that the House of Commons implore of your Lordships is, that you will not take these things, which we call crimes, to be merits, without hearing the House of Commons upon the subject-matter of them. I am sure you are too noble and too generous, as well as too just and equitable, to act in such a manner.

The first thing that Mr. Hastings brings forward in his defence is, that, whereas the Company were obliged to pay a certain tribute to the Mogul, in consideration of a grant by which the Moguls gave to us the legal title under which we hold the provinces of Bengal, Bahar, and Orissa, he did stop the payment of that tribute, or acknowledgment, small as it was,—that, though bound by a treaty recognized by the Company and recognized by the nation, though bound by the very sunnud by which he held the very office he was exercising, yet he had broken the treaty, and refused to pay the stipulated acknowledgment. Where are we, my Lords? Is this merit? Good God Almighty! the greatest blockhead, the most ignorant, miserable wretch, a person without either virtue or talents, has nothing to do but to order a clerk to strike a pen through such an account, and then to make a merit of it to you. "Oh!" says he, "I have by a mere breach of your faith, by a single dash of my pen, saved you all this money which you were bound to pay. I have exonerated you from the payment of it. I have gained you 250,000*l*. a year forever. Will you not reward a person who did you such a great and important service, by conniving a little at his delinquencies?"

But the House of Commons will not allow that this was a great and important service; on the contrary, they have declared the act itself to be censurable. There is our resolution, —Resolution the 7th:—

"That the conduct of the Company and their servants in India to the King," (meaning the Mogul king) "and Nudjif Khân, with respect to the tribute payable to the one, and the stipend to the other, and with respect to the transfer of the provinces of Corah and Allahabad to the Vizier, was contrary to policy and good faith; and that such wise and practicable measures should be adopted in future as may tend to redeem the national honor, and recover the confidence and attachment of the princes of India."

This act of injustice, against which we have fulminated the thunder of our resolutions as a heavy crime, as a crime that dishonored the nation, and which measures ought to be taken to redress, this man has the insolence to bring before your Lordships as a set-off against the crimes we charge him with. This outrageous defiance of the House of Commons, this outrageous defiance of all the laws of his country, I hope your Lordships will not countenance. You will not let it pass for nothing: on the contrary, you will consider it as aggravating heavily his crimes. And, above all, you will not suffer him to set off this, which we have declared to be injurious to our national honor and credit, and which he himself does not deny to be a breach of the public faith, against other breaches of the public faith with which we charge him,—or to justify one class of public crimes by proving that he has committed others.

Your Lordships see that he justifies this crime upon the plea of its being profitable to the Company; but he shall not march off even on this ground with flying colors. My Lords, pray observe in what manner he calculates these profits. Your Lordships will find that he makes up the account of them much in the same manner as he made up the account of Nobkissin's money. There is, indeed, no account which he has ever brought forth that does not carry upon it not only ill faith and national dishonor, but direct proofs of corruption. When Mr. Hastings values himself upon this shocking and outrageous breach of faith, which required nothing but a base and illiberal mind, without either talents, courage, or skill, except that courage which defies all consequences, which defies shame, which defies the judgment and opinion of his country and of mankind, no other talents than may be displayed by the dash of a pen, you will at least expect to see a clear and distinct account of what was gained by it.

In the year 1775, at a period when Mr. Hastings was under an eclipse, when honor and virtue, in the character of General Clavering, Colonel Monson, and Mr. Francis, sat for a short period at the Council-Board,—during that time, Mr. Hastings's conduct upon this occasion was called into question. They called for an account of the revenues of the country,—what was received, and what had been paid; and in the account returned they found the amount of the tribute due to the

Mogul, 250,000*l*., entered as paid up to October, 1774. Thus far all appeared fair upon the face of it; they took it for granted, as your Lordships would take it for granted, at the first view, that the tribute in reality had been paid up to the time stated. The books were balanced: you find a debtor; you find a creditor; every item posted in as regular a manner as possible. Whilst they were examining this account, a Mr. Croftes, of whom your Lordships have heard very often, as accountant-general, comes forward and declares that there was a little error in the account. And what was the error? That he had entered the Mogul's tribute for one year more than it had actually been paid. Here we have the small error of a payment to the Mogul of 250,000*l*. This appeared strange. "Why," says Mr. Croftes, "I never discovered it; nor was it ever intimated to me that it had been stopped from October, 1773, till the other day, when I was informed that I ought not to have made an entry of the last payments." These were his expressions. You will find the whole relation in the Bengal Appendix, printed by the orders of the Court of Directors. When Mr. Croftes was asked a very natural question, "Who first told you of your mistake? who acquainted you with Mr. Hastings's orders that the payment should be expunged from the account?" what is his answer? It is an answer worthy of Mr. Middleton, an answer worthy of Mr. Larkins, or of any of the other white banians of Mr. Hastings:—"Oh, I have forgotten." Here you have an accountant-general kept in ignorance, or who pretends to be ignorant, of so large a payment as 250,000*l*.; who enters it falsely in his account; and when asked who apprised him of his mistake, says that he has really forgotten.

Oh, my Lords, what resources there are in oblivion! what resources there are in bad memory! No genius ever has done so much for mankind as this mental defect has done for Mr. Hastings's accountants. It was said by one of the ancient philosophers, to a man who proposed to teach people memory,

—"I wish you could teach me oblivion; I wish you could teach me to forget." [2] These people have certainly not been taught the art of memory, but they appear perfect masters of the art of forgetting. My Lords, this is not all; and I must request your Lordships' attention to the whole of the account, as it appears in the account of the arrears due to the King, annexed to your minutes. Here is a kind of labyrinth, where fraud runs into fraud. On the credit side you find stated there, eight lacs paid to the Vizier, and to be taken from the Mogul's tribute, for the support of an army, of which he himself had stipulated to bear the whole expenses. These eight lacs are thus fraudulently accounted for upon the face of the thing; and with respect to eighteen lacs, the remainder of the tribute, there is no account given of it at all. This sum Mr. Hastings must, therefore, have pocketed for his own use, or that of his gang of peculators; and whilst he was pretending to save you eight lacs by one fraud, he committed another fraud of eighteen lacs for himself: and this is the method by which one act of peculation begets another in the economy of fraud.

Thus much of these affairs I think myself bound to state to your Lordships upon this occasion; for, although not one word has been produced by the counsel to support the allegations of the prisoner at your bar, yet, knowing that your Lordships, high as you are, are still but men, knowing also that bold assertions and confident declarations are apt to make some impression upon all men's minds, we oppose his allegations. But how do we oppose them? Not by things of the like nature. We oppose them by showing you that the House of Commons, after diligent investigation, has condemned them, and by stating the grounds upon which the House founded its condemnation. We send you to the records of the Company, if you want to pursue this matter further,

---

[2] Attributed to Themistocles (Cicero, *De Finibus,* II. 32. 104); a favorite quotation of Burke's friend, Johnson.

to enlighten your own minds upon the subject. Do not think, my Lords, that we are not aware how ridiculous it is for either party, the accuser or the accused, to make here any assertions without producing vouchers for them: we know it; but we are prepared and ready to take upon us the proof; and we should be ashamed to assert anything that we are not able directly to substantiate by an immediate reference to uncontradicted evidence.

With regard to the merits pleaded by the prisoner, we could efface that plea with a single stroke, by saying there is no evidence before your Lordships of any such merits. But we have done more: we have shown you that the things which he has set up as merits are atrocious crimes, and that there is not one of them which does not, in the very nature and circumstances of it, carry evidence of base corruption, as well as of flagrant injustice and notorious breach of public faith.

The next thing that he takes credit for is precisely an act of this description. The Mogul had, by solemn stipulation with the Company, a royal domain insured to him, consisting of two provinces, Corah and Allahabad. Of both these provinces Mr. Hastings deprived the Mogul, upon weak pretences, if proved in point of fact, but which were never proved in any sense, against him. I allude particularly to his alleged alliance with the Mahrattas,—a people, by the way, with whom we were not then at war, and with whom he had as good a right as Nudjif Khân to enter into alliance at that time. He takes these domains, almost the last wrecks of empire left to the descendant of Tamerlane, from the man, I say, to whose voluntary grants we owe it that we have put a foot in Bengal. Surely, we ought, at least, to have kept our faith in leaving this last retreat to that unfortunate prince. The House of Commons was of that opinion, and consequently they resolved, "That the transfer of Corah and Allahabad to the Vizier was contrary to policy and good faith." This is what the Commons think of this business which Mr. Hastings pleads as merits.

But I have not yet done with it. These provinces are estimated as worth twenty-two lacs, or thereabouts, that is, about 220,000*l*., a year. I believe they were improvable to a good deal more. But what does Mr. Hastings do? Instead of taking them into the Company's possession for the purpose of preserving them for the Mogul, upon the event of our being better satisfied with his conduct, or of appropriating them to the Company's advantage, he sells them to the Nabob of Oude, who he knew had the art, above all men, of destroying a country which he was to keep, or which he might fear he was not to keep, permanent possession of. And what do you think he sold them for? He sold them at a little more than two years' purchase. Will any man believe that Mr. Hastings, when he sold these provinces to the Vizier for two years' purchase, and when there was no man that would not have given ten years' purchase for them, did not put the difference between the real and pretended value into his own pocket, and that of his associates?

We charge, therefore, first, that this act for which he assumes merit was in itself a breach of faith; next, that the sale of these provinces was scandalously conducted; and thirdly, that this scale, at one fifth of the real value, was effected for corrupt purposes. Thus an act of threefold delinquency is one of the merits stated with great pomp by his counsel.

Another of his merits is the stoppage of the pension which the Company was under an obligation to pay to Nudjif Khân: a matter which, even if admitted to be a merit, is certainly not worth, as a set-off, much consideration.

But there is another set-off of merit upon which he plumes himself, and sets an exceedingly high value: the sale of the Rohilla nation to that worthless tyrant, the Vizier, their cruel and bitter enemy,—the cruelest tyrant, perhaps, that ever existed, and their most implacable enemy, if we except Mr. Hastings, who appears to have had a concealed degree of animosity, public, private, or political, against them. To this man he sold this whole nation, whose country, cultivated like a garden, was soon reduced, as Mr. Hastings, from the character of the Vizier, knew would be the consequence, to a mere desert, for 400,000*l*. He sent a brigade of our troops to assist the Vizier in extirpating these people, who were the bravest, the most honorable, and generous nation upon earth. Those who were not left slaughtered to rot upon the soil of their native country were cruelly expelled from it, and sent to publish the merciless and scandalous behavior of Great Britain from one end of India to the other. I believe there is not an honest, ingenuous, or feeling heart upon the face of the globe, I believe there is no man possessing the least degree of regard to honor and justice, humanity and good policy, that did not reprobate this act. The Court of Directors, when they heard of it, reprobated it in the strongest manner; the Court of Proprietors reprobated it in the strongest manner; by the House of Commons, after the most diligent investigation, it was, in a resolution moved by Mr. Dundas, reprobated in the strongest manner: and this is the act which Mr. Hastings brings forward before your Lordships as a merit.

But, again, I can prove that in this, perhaps the most atrocious of all his demerits, there is a most horrid and nefarious secret corruption lurking. I can tell your Lordships that Sir Robert Barker was offered by this Vizier, for about one half of this very country, namely, the country of the Rohillas, a sum of fifty lacs of rupees,—that is, 500,000*l*. Mr. Hastings was informed of this offer by Sir Robert Barker, in his letter of the 24th March, 1773. Still, in the face of this information, Mr. Hastings took for the Company only forty lacs of rupees. I leave your Lordships to draw your own conclusion from these facts. You will judge what became of the difference between the price offered and the price accounted for as taken. Nothing on earth can hide from mankind why Mr. Hastings made this wicked, corrupt bar-gain for the extermination of a brave and generous people,— why he took 400,000*l.* for the whole of that, for half of which he was offered and knew he might have had 500,000*l.*

Your Lordships will observe, that for all these facts there is no evidence, on the one side or on the other, directly be-fore you. Their merits have been insisted upon, in long and laborious details and discussions, both by Mr. Hastings him-self and by his counsel. We have answered them for that reason; but we answer them with a direct reference to records and papers, from which your Lordships may judge of them as set-offs and merits. I believe your Lordships will now hardly receive them as merits to set off guilt, since in every one of them there is both guilt in the act, and strong ground for presuming that he had corruptly taken money for himself.

The last act of merit that has been insisted upon by his counsel is the Mahratta peace. They have stated to you the distresses of the Company to justify the unhandsome and improper means that he took of making this peace. Mr. Hastings himself has laid hold of the same opportunity of magnifying the difficulties which, during his government, he had to contend with. Here he displays all his tactics. He spreads all his sails, and here catches every gale. He says, "I found all India confederated against you. I found not the Mahrattas alone; I found war through a hundred hostile states fulminated against you; I found the Peshwa, the Nizam, Hyder Ali, the Rajah of Berar, all combined together for your destruction. I stemmed the torrent: fortitude is my character. I faced and overcame all these difficulties, till I landed your affairs safe on shore, till I stood the saviour of India."

My Lords, we of the House of Commons have before heard all this; but we cannot forget that we examined into every part of it, and that we did not find a single fact stated by him that was not a ground of censure and reprobation. The House of Commons, in the resolutions to which I have alluded, have declared, that Mr. Hastings, the first author of these proceedings, took advantage of an ambiguous letter of the Court of Directors to break and violate the most solemn, the most advantageous, and useful treaty that the Company had ever made in India; and that this conduct of his produced the strange and unnatural junction which he says he found formed against the Company, and with which he had to combat. I should trouble your Lordships with but a brief statement of the facts; and if I do not enter more at large in observing upon them, it is because I cannot but feel shocked at the indecency and impropriety of your being obliged to hear of that as merit which the House of Commons has condemned in every part. Your Lordships received obliquely evidence from the prisoner at your bar upon this subject; yet, when we came and desired your full inquiry into it, your Lordships, for wise and just reasons, I have no doubt, refused our request. I must, however, again protest on the part of the Commons against your Lordships receiving such evidence at all as relevant to your judgment, unless the House of Commons is fully heard upon it.

But to proceed.—The government of Bombay had offended the Mahratta States by a most violent and scandalous aggression. They afterwards made a treaty of peace with them, honorable and advantageous to the Company. This treaty was made by Colonel Upton, and is called the Treaty of Poorunder. Mr. Hastings broke that treaty, upon his declared principle, that you are to look in war for the resources of your government. All India was at that time in peace. Hyder Ali did not dare to attack us, because he was afraid that his natural enemies, the Mahrattas, would fall upon him. The Nizam could not attack us, because he was also afraid of the Mahrattas. The Mahratta state itself was divided into such discordant branches as to make it impossible for them to unite in any one object; that commonwealth, which certainly at that time was the terror of India, was so broken as to render it either totally ineffective or easy to be resisted. There was not one government in India that did not look up to Great Britain as holding the balance of power, and in a position to control and do justice to every individual party in it. At that juncture Mr. Hastings deliberately broke the treaty of Poorunder; and afterwards, by breaking faith with and attacking all the powers, one after another, he produced that very union which one would hardly have expected that the incapacity or ill faith of any Governor could have effected. Your Lordships shall hear the best and most incontrovertible evidence both of his incapacity and ill faith, and of the consequences which they produced. It is the declaration of one of the latest of their allies concerning all these proceedings. It is contained in a letter from the Rajah of Berar, directly and strongly inculpating Mr. Hastings, upon facts which he has never denied and by arguments which he has never refuted, as being himself the cause of that very junction of all the powers of India against us.

Letter from Benaram Pundit.

"As the friendship of the English is, at all events, the first and most necessary consideration, I will therefore exert myself in establishing peace: for the power of making peace with all is the best object; to this all other measures are subservient, and will certainly be done by them, the English. You write, that, after having laid the foundation of peace with the Pundit Purdhaun, it is requisite that some troops should be sent with General Goddard against Hyder Naig, and take possession of his country, when all those engagements and proposals may be assented to. My reason is confounded in discussing this suggestion, at a time when Hyder Naig is in every respect in alliance with the Peshwa, and has assisted with his soul and life to repel the English. For us to unite our troops with those of the enemy and extirpate him, would not this fix the stamp of infamy upon us forever? Would any prince, for generations to come, ever after assist us, or unite with the Peshwa? Be yourself the judge, and say whether such a conduct would become a prince or not. Why, then, do you mention it? why do you write it?

"The case is as follows.—At first there was the utmost enmity between Hyder Naig and the Pundit Purdhaun, and there was the fullest intention of sending troops into Hyder Naig's country; and after the conclusion of the war with Bombay and the capture of Ragonaut Row, it was firmly resolved to send troops into that quarter; and a reliance was placed in the treaty which was entered into by the gentlemen of Bombay before the war. But when Ragonaut again went to them, and General Goddard was ready to commence hostilities,—when no regard was paid to the friendly proposals made by us and the Pundit Peshwa,—when they desisted from coming to Poonah, agreeable to their promise, and a categorical answer was given to the deputies from Poonah,—the ministers of Poonah then consulted among themselves, and, having advised with the Nabob Nizam ul Dowlah, they considered that as enemies were appearing on both sides, and it would be difficult to cope with both, what was to be done? Peace must be made with one of them, and war must be carried on with the other. They wished above all things, in their hearts, to make peace with the English gentlemen, and to unite with them to punish Hyder Naig; but these gentlemen had plainly refused to enter into any terms of reconciliation. It was therefore advisable to accommodate matters with Hyder Naig, although he had been long an enemy. What else could be done? Having nothing left for it, they were compelled to enter into an union with Hyder."

My Lords, this declaration, made to Mr. Hastings himself,

was never answered by him. Indeed, answered it could not be; because the thing was manifest, that all the desolation of the Carnatic by Hyder Ali, all these difficulties upon which he has insisted, the whole of that union by which he was pressed, and against which, as he says, he bore up with such fortitude, was his own work, the consequences of his bad faith, and his not listening to any reasonable terms of peace.

But, my Lords, see what sort of peace he afterwards made. I could prove, if I were called upon so to do, from this paper that they have had the folly and madness to produce to you for other purposes, that he might at any time have made a better treaty, and have concluded a more secure and advantageous peace, than that which at last he acceded to; that the treaty he made was both disadvantageous and dishonorable, inasmuch as we gave up every ally we had, and sacrificed them to the resentment of the enemy; that Mahdajee Sindia gained by it an empire of a magnitude dangerous to our very existence in India; that this chief was permitted to exterminate all the many little gallant nations that stood between us and the Mahrattas, and whose policy led them to guard against the ambitious designs of that government. Almost all these lesser powers, from Central India, quite up to the mountains that divide India from Tartary, almost all these, I say, were exterminated by him, or were brought under a cruel subjection. The peace he made with Mr. Hastings was for the very purpose of doing all this; and Mr. Hastings enabled him, and gave him the means of effecting it.

Advert next, my Lords, to what he did with other allies. By the treaty of Poorunder, made by Colonel Upton, and which he flagitiously broke, we had acquired, what, God knows, we little merited from the Mahrattas, twelve lacs, (112,000*l.*) for the expenses of the war,—and a country of three lacs of annual revenue, the province of Baroach and the isle of Salsette, and other small islands convenient for us upon that coast. This was a great, useful, and momentous accession of territory and of revenue: and we got it with honor; for not one of our allies were sacrificed by this treaty. We had even obtained from the Mahrattas for Ragonaut Row, our support of whom against that government was a principal cause of the war, an establishment of a thousand horse, to be maintained at their expense, and a jaghire for his other expenses of three lacs of rupees per annum, payable monthly, with leave to reside within their territories, with no other condition than that he should not remove from the place fixed for his residence for the purpose of exciting disturbances against their government. They also stipulated for the pardon of all his adherents except four; and the only condition they required from us was, that we should not assist him in case of any future disturbance. But Mr. Hastings, by his treaty, surrendered that country of three lacs of revenue; he made no stipulation for the expenses of the war, nor indemnity for any of the persons whom he had seduced into the rebellion in favor of Ragonaut Row; he gave them all up to the vengeance of their governments, without a stroke of a pen in their favor, to be banished, confiscated, and undone; and as to Ragonaut Row, instead of getting him this honorable and secure retreat, as he was bound to do, this unfortunate man was ordered to retire to his enemy's (Mahdajee Sindia's) country, or otherwise he was not to receive a shilling for his maintenance.

I will now ask your Lordships, whether any man but Mr. Hastings would claim a merit with his own country for having broken the treaty of Poorunder? Your Lordships know the opinion of the House of Commons respecting it; his colleagues in Council had remonstrated with him upon it, and had stated the mischiefs that would result from it; and Sir Eyre Coote, the commander of the Company's forces, writing at the same time from Madras, states, that he thought it would infallibly bring down upon them Hyder Ali, who, they had reason to think, was bent upon the utter destruction of the power of this country in India, and was only waiting for

some crisis in our affairs favorable to his designs. This, my
Lords, is to be one of the set-offs against all the crimes,
against the multiplied frauds, cruelties, and oppressions, all
the corrupt practices, prevarications, and swindlings, that we
have alleged against him.

My Lords, it would be an endless undertaking, and such as,
at this hour of the day, we, as well as your Lordships, are little fitted to engage in, if I were to attempt to search into and
unveil all the secret motives, or to expose as it deserves the
shameless audacity of this man's conduct. None of your Lordships can have observed without astonishment the selection of
his merits, as he audaciously calls them, which has been
brought before you. The last of this selection, in particular,
looks as if he meant to revile and spit upon the legislature of
his country, because we and you thought it fit and were resolved to publish to all India that we will not countenance offensive wars, and that you felt this so strongly as to pass the
first act of a kind that was ever made, namely, an act to limit
the discretionary power of government in making war solely,
—and because you have done this solely and upon no other
account and for no other reason under heaven than the abuse
which that man at your bar has made of it, and for which
abuse he now presumes to take merit to himself. I will read
this part of the act to your Lordships.

[*Mr. Burke here read* 24th *Geo. III. cap.* 25, *sect.* 34.]

"And whereas to pursue schemes of conquest and extension
of dominion in India are measures repugnant to the wish, the
honor, and policy of this nation, be it therefore further enacted by the authority aforesaid, that it shall not be lawful for
the Governor-General and Council of Fort William aforesaid,
without the express command and authority of the said Court
of Directors, or of the Secret Committee of the said Court of
Directors, in any case, (except where hostilities have actually

been commenced, or preparations actually made for the commencement of hostilities, against the British nation in India, or against some of the princes or states dependent thereon, or whose territories the said United Company shall be at such time engaged by any subsisting treaty to defend or guaranty,) either to declare war, or commence hostilities, or enter into any treaty for making war, against any of the country princes or states in India, or any treaty for guarantying the possessions of any country princes or states; and that in such case it shall not be lawful for the said Governor-General and Council to declare war, or commence hostilities, or enter into treaty for making war, against any other prince or state than such as shall be actually committing hostilities or making preparations as aforesaid, or to make such treaty for guarantying the possessions of any prince or state, but upon the consideration of such prince or state actually engaging to assist the Company against such hostilities commenced or preparations made as aforesaid; and in all cases where hostilities shall be commenced or treaty made, the said Governor-General and Council shall, by the most expeditious means they can devise, communicate the same unto the said Court of Directors, together with a full state of the information and intelligence upon which they shall have commenced such hostilities or made such treaties, and their motives and reasons for the same at large."

It is the first act of the kind that ever was made in this kingdom, the first statute, I believe, that ever was made by the legislature of any nation, upon the subject; and it was made solely upon the resolutions to which we had come against the violent, intemperate, unjust, and perfidious acts of this man at your Lordships' bar, and which acts are now produced before your Lordships as merits.

To show further to your Lordships how necessary this act was, here is a part of his own correspondence, the last thing I shall beg to read to your Lordships, and upon which I shall make no other comment than that you will learn from it how well British faith was kept by this man, and that it was the violation of British faith which prevented our having the most advantageous peace, and brought on all the calamities of war. It is part of a letter from the minister of the Rajah of Berar, a man called Benaram Pundit, with whom Mr. Hastings was at the time treating for a peace; and he tells him why he might have had peace at that time, and why he had it not,—and that the cause of it was his own ridiculous and even buffoonish perfidiousness, which exposed him to the ridicule of all the princes of India, and with him the whole British nation.

"But afterwards reflecting that it was not advisable for me to be in such haste before I had fully understood all the contents of the papers, I opened them in the presence of the Maha Rajah, when all the kharetas, letters, copies, and treaties were perused with the greatest attention and care. First, they convinced us of your great truth and sincerity, and that you never, from the beginning to this time, were inclined to the present disputes and hostilities; and next, that you have not included in the articles of the treaty any of your wishes or inclinations; and in short, the garden of the treaty appeared to us, in all its parts, green and flourishing: but though the fruit of it was excellent, yet they appeared different from those of Colonel Upton's treaty, (the particulars of which I have frequently written to you,) and, upon tasting them, proved to be bitter and very different, when compared to the former articles. How can any of the old and established obligations be omitted, and new matters agreed to, when it is plain that they will produce losses and damages? Some points which you have mentioned, under the plea of the faith and observance of treaties, are of such a nature that the Poonah ministers can never assent to them. In all engagements and important transactions, in which the words, *but,* and *although,* and *besides,* and *whereas,* and *why,* and other such words of doubt, are introduced, it gives an opening to disputes and misunderstandings. A treaty is meant for the entire removal of all differences, not for increase of them. My departure to Poonah has therefore been delayed."

My Lords, consider to what ironies and insults this nation was exposed, and how necessary it was for us to originate that bill which your Lordships passed into an act of Parliament, with his Majesty's assent. The words *but, although, besides, whereas,* and *why,* and such like, are introduced to give an opening, and so on. Then he desires him to send another treaty, fit for him to sign.

"I have therefore kept the treaty with the greatest care and caution in my possession, and, having taken a copy of it, I have added to each article another, which appeared to me proper and advisable, and without any loss or disadvantage to the English, or anything more in favor of the Pundit Purdhaun than what was contained in the former treaties. This I have sent to you, and hope that you will prepare and send a treaty conformable to that, without any *besides,* or *if,* or *why,* or *but,* and *whereas,* that, as soon as it arrives, I may depart for Poonah, and, having united with me Row Mahdajee Sindia, and having brought over the Nabob Nizam ul Dowlah to this business, I may settle and adjust all matters which are in this bad situation. As soon as I have received my dismission from thence, I would set off for Calcutta, and represent to you everything which for a long while I have had on my mind, and by this transaction erect to the view of all the world the standard of the greatness and goodness of the English and of my master, and extinguish the flames of war with the waters of friendship. The compassing all these advantages and happy prospects depends entirely upon your will and consent; and the power of bringing them to an issue is in your hands alone."

My Lords, you may here see the necessity there was for passing the act of Parliament which I have just read to you, in order to prevent in future the recurrence of that want of faith of which Mr. Hastings had been so notoriously guilty, and by which he had not only united all India against us, and had hindered us from making, for a long time, any peace at all, but had exposed the British character to the irony, scorn, derision, and insult of the whole people of that vast continent.

My Lords, in the progress of this impeachment, you have heard our charges; you have heard the prisoner's plea of merits; you have heard our observations on them. In the progress of this impeachment, you have seen the condition in which Mr. Hastings received Benares; you have seen the condition in which Mr. Hastings received the country of the Rohillas; you have seen the condition in which he received the country of Oude; you have seen the condition in which he received the provinces of Bengal; you have seen the condition of the country when the native government was succeeded by that of Mr. Hastings; you have seen the happiness and prosperity of all its inhabitants, from those of the highest to those of the lowest rank. My Lords, you have seen the very reverse of all this under the government of Mr. Hastings,—the country itself, all its beauty and glory, ending in a jungle for wild beasts. You have seen flourishing families reduced to implore that pity which the poorest man and the meanest situation might very well call for. You have seen whole nations in the mass reduced to a condition of the same distress. These things in his government at home. Abroad, scorn, contempt, and derision cast upon and covering the British name, war stirred up, and dishonorable treaties of peace made, by the total prostitution of British faith. Now take, my Lords, together, all the multiplied delinquencies which we have proved, from the highest degree of tyranny to the lowest degree of sharping and cheating, and then judge, my Lords, whether the House of

Commons could rest for one moment, without bringing these matters, which have baffled all legislation at various times, before you, to try at last what judgment will do. Judgment is what gives force, effect, and vigor to laws; laws without judgment are contemptible and ridiculous; we had better have no laws than laws not enforced by judgments and suitable penalties upon delinquents. Revert, my Lords, to all the sentences which have heretofore been passed by this high court; look at the sentence passed upon Lord Bacon, look at the sentence passed upon Lord Macclesfield; and then compare the sentences which your ancestors have given with the delinquencies which were then before them, and you have the measure to be taken in your sentence upon the delinquent now before you. Your sentence, I say, will be measured according to that rule which ought to direct the judgment of all courts in like cases, lessening it for a lesser offence, and aggravating it for a greater, until the measure of justice is completely full.

My Lords, I have done; the part of the Commons is concluded. With a trembling solicitude we consign this product of our long, long labors to your charge. Take it!—take it! It is a sacred trust. Never before was a cause of such magnitude submitted to any human tribunal.

My Lords, at this awful close, in the name of the Commons, and surrounded by them, I attest the retiring, I attest the advancing generations, between which, as a link in the great chain of eternal order, we stand. We call this nation, we call the world to witness, that the Commons have shrunk from no labor, that we have been guilty of no prevarication, that we have made no compromise with crime, that we have not feared any odium whatsoever, in the long warfare which we have carried on with the crimes, with the vices, with the exorbitant wealth, with the enormous and overpowering influence of Eastern corruption. This war, my Lords, we have

waged for twenty-two years, and the conflict has been fought
at your Lordships' bar for the last seven years. My Lords,
twenty-two years is a great space in the scale of the life of
man; it is no inconsiderable space in the history of a great nation. A business which has so long occupied the councils and
tribunals of Great Britain cannot possibly be huddled over in
the course of vulgar, trite, and transitory events. Nothing but
some of those great revolutions that break the traditionary
chain of human memory, and alter the very face of Nature itself, can possibly obscure it. My Lords, we are all elevated to
a degree of importance by it; the meanest of us will, by means
of it, more or less become the concern of posterity,—if we
are yet to hope for such a thing, in the present state of the
world, as a recording, retrospective, civilized posterity: but
this is in the hands of the great Disposer of events; it is not
ours to settle how it shall be.

My Lords, your House yet stands,—it stands as a great edifice; but let me say, that it stands in the midst of ruins,—in
the midst of the ruins that have been made by the greatest
moral earthquake that ever convulsed and shattered this globe
of ours. My Lords, it has pleased Providence to place us in
such a state that we appear every moment to be upon the
verge of some great mutations. There is one thing, and one
thing only, which defies all mutation,—that which existed before the world, and will survive the fabric of the world itself:
I mean justice,—that justice which, emanating from the Div-
inity, has a place in the breast of every one of us, given us for
our guide with regard to ourselves and with regard to others,
and which will stand, after this globe is burned to ashes, our
advocate or our accuser before the great Judge, when He
comes to call upon us for the tenor of a well-spent life.

My Lords, the Commons will share in every fate with your
Lordships; there is nothing sinister which can happen to you,
in which we shall not be involved: and if it should so happen
that we shall be subjected to some of those frightful changes

which we have seen,—if it should happen that your Lordships, stripped of all the decorous distinctions of human society, should, by hands at once base and cruel, be led to those scaffolds and machines of murder upon which great kings and glorious queens have shed their blood, amidst the prelates, amidst the nobles, amidst the magistrates who supported their thrones, may you in those moments feel that consolation which I am persuaded they felt in the critical moments of their dreadful agony!

My Lords, there is a consolation, and a great consolation it is, which often happens to oppressed virtue and fallen dignity. It often happens that the very oppressors and persecutors themselves are forced to bear testimony in its favor. I do not like to go for instances a great way back into antiquity. I know very well that length of time operates so as to give an air of the fabulous to remote events, which lessens the interest and weakens the application of examples. I wish to come nearer to the present time. Your Lordships know and have heard (for which of us has not known and heard?) of the Parliament of Paris. The Parliament of Paris had an origin very, very similar to that of the great court before which I stand; the Parliament of Paris continued to have a great resemblance to it in its constitution, even to its fall: the Parliament of Paris, my Lords, WAS; it is gone! It has passed away; it has vanished like a dream! It fell, pierced by the sword of the Comte de Mirabeau. And yet I will say, that that man, at the time of his inflicting the death-wound of that Parliament, produced at once the shortest and the grandest funeral oration that ever was or could be made upon the departure of a great court of magistracy. Though he had himself smarted under its lash, as every one knows who knows his history, (and he was elevated to dreadful notoriety in history,) yet, when he pronounced the death sentence upon that Parliament, and inflicted the mortal wound, he declared that his motives for doing it were merely political, and that their hands were as pure as those of justice itself, which they administered. A great and glorious exit, my Lords, of a great and glorious body! And never was a eulogy pronounced upon a body more deserved. They were persons, in nobility of rank, in amplitude of fortune, in weight of authority, in depth of learning, inferior to few of those that hear me. My Lords, it was but the other day that they submitted their necks to the axe; but their honor was unwounded. Their enemies, the persons who sentenced them to death, were lawyers full of subtlety, they were enemies full of malice; yet lawyers full of subtlety, and enemies full of malice, as they were, they did not dare to reproach them with having supported the wealthy, the great, and powerful, and of having oppressed the weak and feeble, in any of their judgments, or of having perverted justice, in any one instance whatever, through favor, through interest, or cabal.

My Lords, if you must fall, may you so fall! But if you stand,—and stand I trust you will, together with the fortune of this ancient monarchy, together with the ancient laws and liberties of this great and illustrious kingdom,—may you stand as unimpeached in honor as in power! May you stand, not as a substitute for virtue, but as an ornament of virtue, as a security for virtue! May you stand long, and long stand the terror of tyrants! May you stand the refuge of afflicted nations! May you stand a sacred temple, for the perpetual residence of an inviolable justice!

V THE FRENCH REVOLUTION

FROM *Reflections on the Revolution in France*[1]

It may not be unnecessary to inform the reader, that the following Reflections had their origin in a correspondence between the Author and a very young gentleman at Paris, who did him the honour of desiring his opinion upon the important transactions, which then, and ever since, have so much occupied the attention of all men. An answer was written some time in the month of October, 1789; but it was kept back upon prudential considerations. That letter is alluded to in the beginning of the following sheets. It has been since forwarded to the person to whom it was addressed. The reasons for the delay in sending it were assigned in a short letter to the same gentleman. This produced on his part a new and pressing application for the Author's sentiments.

The Author began a second and more full discussion on the subject. This he had some thoughts of publishing early in the last spring; but, the matter gaining upon him, he found that what he had undertaken not only far exceeded the measure of a letter, but that its importance required rather a more detailed consideration than at that time he had any leisure to bestow upon it. However, having thrown down his first thoughts in the form of a letter, and, indeed, when he sat

[1] Selections from "Reflections on the Revolution in France and on the Proceedings in Certain Societies in London Relative to that Event: in a Letter Intended to have been sent to a Gentleman in Paris" (1790).

down to write, having intended it for a private letter, he found it difficult to change the form of address, when his sentiments had grown into a greater extent, and had received another direction. A different plan, he is sensible, might be more favourable to a commodious division and distribution of his matter.

DEAR SIR,

You are pleased to call again, and with some earnestness, for my thoughts on the late proceedings in France. I will not give you reason to imagine that I think my sentiments of such value as to wish myself to be solicited about them. They are of too little consequence to be very anxiously either communicated or withheld. It was from attention to you, and to you only, that I hesitated at the time when you first desired to receive them. In the first letter I had the honour to write to you, and which at length I send, I wrote neither for, nor from, any description of men; nor shall I in this. My errors, if any, are my own. My reputation alone is to answer for them.

You see, Sir, by the long letter I have transmitted to you, that though I do most heartily wish that France may be animated by a spirit of rational liberty, and that I think you bound, in all honest policy, to provide a permanent body in which that spirit may reside, and an effectual organ by which it may act, it is my misfortune to entertain great doubts concerning several material points in your late transactions. . . .

I flatter myself that I love a manly, moral, regulated liberty as well as any gentleman of that society, be he who he will; and perhaps I have given as good proofs of my attachment to that cause, in the whole course of my public conduct. I think I envy liberty as little as they do, to any other nation. But I cannot stand forward, and give praise or blame to anything which relates to human actions, and human concerns, on a simple view of the object, as it stands stripped of every relation, in all the nakedness and solitude of metaphysical abstraction. Circumstances (which with some gentlemen pass for nothing) give in reality to every political principle its distinguishing colour and discriminating effect. The circumstances are what render every civil and political scheme beneficial or noxious to mankind. Abstractedly speaking, government, as well as liberty, is good; yet could I, in common sense, ten years ago, have felicitated France on her enjoyment of a government (for she then had a government) without inquiry what the nature of that government was, or how it was administered? Can I now congratulate the same nation upon its freedom? Is it because liberty in the abstract may be classed amongst the blessings of mankind, that I am seriously to felicitate a mad-man, who has escaped from the protecting restraint and wholesome darkness of his cell, on his restoration to the enjoyment of light and liberty? Am I to congratulate a highwayman and murderer, who has broke prison, upon the recovery of his natural rights? This would be to act over again the scene of the criminals condemned to the galleys, and their heroic deliverer, the metaphysic knight of the sorrowful countenance.

When I see the spirit of liberty in action, I see a strong principle at work; and this, for a while, is all I can possibly know of it. The wild *gas*, the fixed air, is plainly broke loose: but we ought to suspend our judgment until the first effervescence is a little subsided, till the liquor is cleared, and until we see something deeper than the agitation of a troubled and frothy surface. I must be tolerably sure, before I venture publicly to congratulate men upon a blessing, that they have really received one. Flattery corrupts both the receiver and the giver; and adulation is not of more service to the people than to kings. I should therefore suspend my congratulations on the new liberty of France, until I was informed how it had been combined with government; with public force; with the discipline and obedience of armies; with the collection of an effective and well-distributed revenue; with morality and religion; with the solidity of property; with peace and order; with civil and social manners. All these (in their way) are good things too; and, without them, liberty is not a benefit whilst it lasts, and is not likely to continue long. The effect of liberty to individuals is, that they may do what they please: we ought to see what it will please them to do, before we risk congratulations, which may be soon turned into complaints. Prudence would dictate this in the case of separate, insulated, private men; but liberty, when men act in bodies, is *power*. Considerate people, before they declare themselves, will observe the use which is made of *power;* and particularly of so trying a thing as *new* power in *new* persons, of whose principles, tempers, and dispositions they have little or no experience, and in situations, where those who appear the most stirring in the scene may possibly not be the real movers. . . .

On the forenoon of the 4th of November last, Doctor Richard Price, a non-conforming minister of eminence, preached at the dissenting meeting-house of the Old Jewry, to his club or society, a very extraordinary miscellaneous sermon, in which there are some good moral and religious sentiments, and not ill expressed, mixed up in a sort of porridge of various political opinions and reflections; but the Revolution in France is the grand ingredient in the cauldron. I consider the address transmitted by the Revolution Society to the National Assembly, through Earl Stanhope, as originating in the principles of the sermon, and as a corollary from them. It was moved by the preacher of that discourse. It was passed by those who came reeking from the effect of the sermon, without any censure or qualification, expressed or implied. If, however, any of the gentlemen concerned shall wish to separate the sermon from the resolution, they know how to acknowledge the one, and to disavow the other. They may do it: I cannot.

For my part, I looked on that sermon as the public declaration of a man much connected with literary caballers, and intriguing philosophers; with political theologians, and theological politicians, both at home and abroad. I know they set him up as a sort of oracle; because, with the best intentions in the world, he naturally *philippizes,* and chants his prophetic songs in exact unison with their designs.

That sermon is in a strain which I believe has not been heard in this kingdom, in any of the pulpits which are tolerated or encouraged in it, since the year 1648; when a predecessor of Dr. Price, the Rev. Hugh Peters, made the vault of the king's own chapel at St. James's ring with the honour and privilege of the saints, who, with the "high praises of God in their mouths, and a *two*-edged sword in their hands, were to execute judgment on the heathen, and punishments upon the *people;* to bind their *kings* with chains, and their *nobles* with fetters of iron." [2] Few harangues from the pulpit, except in the days of your league in France, or in the days of our solemn league and covenant in England, have ever breathed less of the spirit of moderation than this lecture in the Old Jewry. Supposing, however, that something like moderation were visible in this political sermon; yet politics and the pulpit are terms that have little agreement. No sound ought to be heard in the church but the healing voice of Christian charity. The cause of civil liberty and civil government gains as little as that of religion by this confusion of duties. Those who quit their proper character, to assume what does not belong to them, are, for the greater part, ignorant both of the character they leave, and of the character they assume. Wholly unacquainted with the world in which they are so fond of meddling and inexperience in all its affairs, on which they pronounce with so much confidence, they have nothing of politics but the passions they excite. Surely the church is a place where one day's truce ought to be allowed to the dissensions and animosities of mankind.

This pulpit style, revived after so long a discontinuance, had

---

[2] Psalm cxlix. [Burke]

to me the air of novelty, and of a novelty not wholly without
danger. I do not charge this danger equally to every part of
the discourse. The hint given to a noble and reverend lay-
divine, who is supposed high in office in one of our universities,[3] and other lay-divines "of *rank* and literature," may be
proper and seasonable, though somewhat new. If the noble
Seekers should find nothing to satisfy their pious fancies in
the old staple of the national church, or in all the rich variety
to be found in the well-assorted warehouses of the dissenting
congregations, Dr. Price advises them to improve upon non-
conformity; and to set up, each of them, a separate meeting-
house upon his own particular principles. It is somewhat remarkable that this reverend divine should be so earnest for
setting up new churches, and so perfectly indifferent concerning the doctrine which may be taught in them. His zeal is of
a curious character. It is not for the propagation of his own
opinions, but of any opinions. It is not for the diffusion of
truth, but for the spreading of contradiction. Let the noble
teachers but dissent, it is no matter from whom or from what.
This great point once secured, it is taken for granted their
religion will be rational and manly. I doubt whether religion
would reap all the benefits which the calculating divine com-
putes from this "great company of great preachers." It would
certainly be a valuable addition of non-descripts to the ample
collection of known classes, genera and species, which at
present beautify the *hortus siccus* of dissent. A sermon from
a noble duke, or a noble marquis, or a noble earl, or baron
bold, would certainly increase and diversify the amusements
of this town, which begins to grow satiated with the uniform
round of its vapid dissipations. I should only stipulate that
these new *Mess-Johns* in robes and coronets should keep some
sort of bounds in the democratic and levelling principles
which are expected from their titled pulpits. The new evange-
lists will, I dare say, disappoint the hopes that are conceived

---

[3] "Discourse on the Love of our Country," Nov. 4th, 1789, by Dr.
Richard Price, 3rd edition, pp. 17 and 18. [Burke]

of them. They will not become, literally as well as figuratively, polemic divines, nor be disposed so to drill their congregations, that they may, as in former blessed times, preach their doctrines to regiments of dragoons and corps of infantry and artillery. Such arrangements, however favourable to the cause of compulsory freedom, civil and religious, may not be equally conducive to the national tranquillity. These few restrictions I hope are no great stretches of intolerance, no very violent exertions of despotism.

But I may say of our preacher, *"utinam nugis tota illa dedisset tempora sævitiæ."* [4]—All things in this his fulminating bull are not of so innoxious a tendency. His doctrines affect our constitution in its vital parts. He tells the Revolution Society in this political sermon, that his Majesty "is almost the *only* lawful king in the world, because the *only* one who owes his crown to the *choice of his people.*" As to the kings of *the world,* all of whom (except one) this archpontiff of the *rights of men,* with all the plenitude, and with more than the boldness, of the papal deposing power in its meridian fervour of the twelfth century, puts into one sweeping clause of ban and anathema, and proclaims usurpers by circles of longitude and latitude, over the whole globe, it behoves them to consider how they admit into their territories these apostolic missionaries, who are to tell their subjects they are not lawful kings. That is their concern. It is ours, as a domestic interest of some moment, seriously to consider the solidity of the *only* principle upon which these gentlemen acknowledge a king of Great Britain to be entitled to their allegiance.

This doctrine, as applied to the prince now on the British throne, either is nonsense, and therefore neither true nor false, or it affirms a most unfounded, dangerous, illegal, and unconstitutional position. According to this spiritual doctor of politics, if his Majesty does not owe his crown to the choice of his people, he is no *lawful king.* Now nothing can be more un-

---

[4] Juvenal, IV. 150.

true than that the crown of this kingdom is so held by his
Majesty. Therefore if you follow their rule, the king of Great
Britain, who most certainly does not owe his high office to any
form of popular election, is in no respect better than the rest
of the gang of usurpers, who reign, or rather rob, all over the
face of this our miserable world, without any sort of right or
title to the allegiance of their people. The policy of this
general doctrine, so qualified, is evident enough. The propaga-
tors of this political gospel are in hopes that their abstract
principle (their principle that a popular choice is necessary
to the legal existence of the sovereign magistracy) would be
overlooked, whilst the king of Great Britain was not affected
by it. In the meantime the ears of their congregations would
be gradually habituated to it, as if it were a first principle
admitted without dispute. For the present it would only
operate as a theory, pickled in the preserving juices of pulpit
eloquence, and laid by for future use. *Condo et compono
quæ mox depromere possim.*[5] By this policy, whilst our government is soothed with a reservation in its favour, to which
it has no claim, the security, which it has in common with all
governments, so far as opinion is security, is taken away.

Thus these politicians proceed, whilst little notice is taken
of their doctrines; but when they come to be examined upon
the plain meaning of their words, and the direct tendency of
their doctrines, then equivocations and slippery constructions
come into play. When they say the king owes his crown to the
choice of his people, and is therefore the only lawful sovereign
in the world, they will perhaps tell us they mean to say no
more than that some of the king's predecessors have been called
to the throne by some sort of choice; and therefore he owes his
crown to the choice of his people. Thus, by a miserable sub-
terfuge, they hope to render their proposition safe, by rendering it nugatory. They are welcome to the asylum they seek

---

[5] Horace, *Epistles,* I. 1. 12.

for their offence, since they take refuge in their folly. For, if you admit this interpretation, how does their idea of election differ from our idea of inheritance? And how does the settlement of the crown in the Brunswick line derived from James the First come to legalize our monarchy, rather than that of any of the neighbouring countries? At some time or other, to be sure, all the beginners of dynasties were chosen by those who called them to govern. There is ground enough for the opinion that all the kingdoms of Europe were, at a remote period, elective, with more or fewer limitations in the objects of choice. But whatever kings might have been here, or elsewhere, a thousand years ago, or in whatever manner the ruling dynasties of England or France may have begun, the king of Great Britain is, at this day, king by a fixed rule of succession, according to the laws of his country; and whilst the legal conditions of the compact of sovereignty are performed by him, (as they are performed,) he holds his crown in contempt of the choice of the Revolution Society, who have not a single vote for a king amongst them, either individually or collectively; though I make no doubt they would soon erect themselves into an electoral college, if things were ripe to give effect to their claim. His Majesty's heirs and successors, each in his time and order, will come to the crown with the same contempt of their choice with which his Majesty has succeeded to that he wears.

Whatever may be the success of evasion in explaining away the gross error of *fact,* which supposes that his Majesty (though he holds it in concurrence with the wishes) owes his crown to the choice of his people, yet nothing can evade their full explicit declaration, concerning the principle of a right in the people to choose; which right is directly maintained, and tenaciously adhered to. All the oblique insinuations concerning election bottom in this proposition, and are referable to it. Lest the foundation of the king's exclusive legal title should pass for a mere rant of adulatory freedom, the political divine proceeds dogmatically to assert, that, by the principles of the Revolution,[6] the people of England have acquired three fundamental rights, all which, with him, compose one system, and lie together in one short sentence; namely, that we have acquired a right,

1. "To choose our own governors."
2. "To cashier them for misconduct."
3. "To frame a government for ourselves."

This new, and hitherto unheard-of, bill of rights, though made in the name of the whole people, belongs to those gentlemen and their faction only. The body of the people of England have no share in it. They utterly disclaim it. They will resist the practical assertion of it with their lives and fortunes. They are bound to do so by the laws of their country, made at the time of that very Revolution which is appealed to in favour of the fictitious rights claimed by the Society which abuses its name.

These gentlemen of the Old Jewry, in all their reasonings on the Revolution of 1688, have a Revolution which happened in England about forty years before,[7] and the late French Revolution, so much before their eyes, and in their hearts, that they are constantly confounding all the three together. It is necessary that we should separate what they confound. We must recall their erring fancies to the *acts* of the Revolution which we revere, for the discovery of its true *principles*. If the *principles* of the Revolution of 1688 are anywhere to be found, it is in the statute called the *Declaration of Right*. In that most wise, sober, and considerate declaration, drawn up by great lawyers and great statesmen, and not by warm and inexperienced enthusiasts, not one word is said, nor one suggestion made, of a general right "to choose our own *governors;* to cashier them for misconduct; and to *form* a government for *ourselves*."

This Declaration of Right (the act of the 1st of William

---

[6] The English "Glorious Revolution" of 1688.
[7] The English Civil War (1642-49).

and Mary, sess. 2, ch. 2) is the corner-stone of our constitution, as reinforced, explained, improved, and in its fundamental principles for ever settled. It is called "An Act for declaring the rights and liberties of the subject, and for *settling* the *succession* of the crown." You will observe, that these rights and this succession are declared in one body, and bound indissolubly together.

A few years after this period, a second opportunity offered for asserting a right of election to the crown. On the prospect of a total failure of issue from King William, and from the Princess, afterwards Queen Anne, the consideration of the settlement of the crown, and of a further security for the liberties of the people, again came before the legislature. Did they this second time make any provision for legalizing the crown on the spurious revolution principles of the Old Jewry? No. They followed the principles which prevailed in the Declaration of Right; indicating with more precision the persons who were to inherit in the Protestant line. This act also incorporated, by the same policy, our liberties, and an hereditary succession in the same act. Instead of a right to choose our own governors, they declared that the *succession* in that line (the Protestant line drawn from James the First) was absolutely necessary "for the peace, quiet, and security of the realm," and that it was equally urgent on them "to maintain a *certainty in the succession* thereof, to which the subjects may safely have recourse for their protection." Both these acts, in which are heard the unerring, unambiguous oracles of revolution policy, instead of countenancing the delusive, gipsy predictions of a "right to choose our governors," prove to a demonstration how totally adverse the wisdom of the nation was from turning a case of necessity into a rule of law.

Unquestionably there was at the Revolution, in the person of King William, a small and a temporary deviation from the strict order of a regular hereditary succession; but it is against all genuine principles of jurisprudence to draw a principle from a law made in a special case, and regarding an individual person. *Privilegium non transit in exemplum.* If ever there was a time favourable for establishing the principle, that a king of popular choice was the only legal king, without all doubt it was at the Revolution. Its not being done at that time is a proof that the nation was of opinion it ought not to be done at any time. There is no person so completely ignorant of our history as not to know, that the majority in parliament of both parties were so little disposed to anything resembling that principle, that at first they were determined to place the vacant crown, not on the head of the Prince of Orange, but on that of his wife Mary, daughter of King James, the eldest born of the issue of that king, which they acknowledged as undoubtedly his. It would be to repeat a very trite story, to recall to your memory all those circumstances which demonstrated that their accepting King William was not properly a *choice;* but to all those who did not wish, in effect, to recall King James, or to deluge their country in blood, and again to bring their religion, laws, and liberties into the peril they had just escaped, it was an act of *necessity,* in the strictest moral sense in which necessity can be taken. . . .

It is far from impossible to reconcile, if we do not suffer ourselves to be entangled in the mazes of metaphysic sophistry, the use both of a fixed rule and an occasional deviation; the sacredness of an hereditary principle of succession in our government, with a power of change in its application in cases of extreme emergency. Even in that extremity, (if we take the measure of our rights by our exercise of them at the Revolution,) the change is to be confined to the peccant part only; to the part which produced the necessary deviation; and even then it is to be effected without a decomposition of the whole civil and political mass, for the purpose of originating a new civil order out of the first elements of society.

A state without the means of some change is without the means of its conservation. Without such means it might even risk the loss of that part of the constitution which it wished the most religiously to preserve. The two principles of conservation and correction operated strongly at the two critical periods of the Restoration and Revolution, when England found itself without a king. At both those periods the nation had lost the bond of union in their ancient edifice; they did not, however, dissolve the whole fabric. On the contrary, in both cases they regenerated the deficient part of the old constitution through the parts which were not impaired. They kept these old parts exactly as they were, that the part recovered might be suited to them. . . .

The second claim of the Revolution Society is "a right of cashiering their governors for *misconduct*." Perhaps the apprehensions our ancestors entertained of forming such a precedent as that "of cashiering for misconduct," was the cause that the declaration of the act, which implied the abdication of King James, was, if it had any fault, rather too guarded, and too circumstantial. But all this guard, and all this accumulation of circumstances, serves to show the spirit of caution which predominated in the national councils in a situation in which men, irritated by oppression, and elevated by a triumph over it, are apt to abandon themselves to violent and extreme courses: it shows the anxiety of the great men who influenced the conduct of affairs at that great event to make the Revolution a parent of settlement, and not a nursery of future revolutions.

No government could stand a moment, if it could be blown down with anything so loose and indefinite as an opinion of "*misconduct*." They who led at the Revolution grounded the virtual abdication of King James upon no such light and uncertain principle. They charged him with nothing less than a design, confirmed by a multitude of illegal overt acts, to *subvert the Protestant church and state,* and their *fundamental,* unquestionable laws and liberties: they charged him with having broken the *original contract* between king and people. This was more than *misconduct*. A grave and overruling necessity obliged them to take the step they took, and took with infinite reluctance, as under that most rigorous of all laws. Their trust for the future preservation of the constitution was not in future revolutions. The grand policy of all their regulations was to render it almost impracticable for any future sovereign to compel the states of the kingdom to have again recourse to those violent remedies. They left the crown what, in the eye and estimation of law, it had ever been, perfectly irresponsible. In order to lighten the crown still further, they aggravated responsibility on ministers of state. By the statute of the 1st of King William, sess. 2nd, called *"the act for declaring the rights and liberties of the subject, and for settling the succession to the crown,"* they enacted, that the ministers should serve the crown on the terms of that declaration. They secured soon after the *frequent meetings of parliament,* by which the whole government would be under the constant inspection and active control of the popular representative and of the magnates of the kingdom. In the next great constitutional act, that of the 12th and 13th of King William, for the further limitation of the crown, and *better* securing the rights and liberties of the subject, they provided, "that no pardon under the great seal of England should be pleadable to an impeachment by the Commons in parliament." The rule laid down for government in the Declaration of Right, the constant inspection of parliament, the practical claim of impeachment, they thought infinitely a better security not only for their constitutional liberty, but against the vices of administration, than the reservation of a right so difficult in the practice, so uncertain in the issue, and often so mischievous in the consequences, as that of "cashiering their governors." . . .

You will observe, that from Magna Charta to the Declaration of Right, it has been the uniform policy of our constitution to claim and assert our liberties, as an *entailed inheritance* derived to us from our forefathers, and to be transmitted to our posterity; as an estate specially belonging to the people of this kingdom, without any reference whatever to any other more general or prior right. By this means our constitution preserves a unity in so great a diversity of its parts. We have an inheritable crown; an inheritable peerage; and a House of Commons and a people inheriting privileges, franchises, and liberties, from a long line of ancestors.

This policy appears to me to be the result of profound reflection; or rather the happy effect of following nature, which is wisdom without reflection, and above it. A spirit of innovation is generally the result of a selfish temper, and confined views. People will not look forward to posterity, who never look backward to their ancestors. Besides, the people of England well know, that the idea of inheritance furnishes a sure principle of conservation, and a sure principle of transmission; without at all excluding a principle of improvement. It leaves acquisition free; but it secures what it acquires. Whatever advantages are obtained by a state proceeding on these maxims, are locked fast as in a sort of family settlement; grasped as in a kind of mortmain for ever. By a constitutional policy, working after the pattern of nature, we receive, we hold, we transmit our government and our privileges, in the same manner in which we enjoy and transmit our property and our lives. The institutions of policy, the goods of fortune, the gifts of providence, are handed down to us, and from us, in the same course and order. Our political system is placed in a just correspondence and symmetry with the order of the world, and with the mode of existence decreed to a permanent body composed of transitory parts; wherein, by the disposition of a stupendous wisdom, moulding together the great mysterious incorporation of the human race, the whole, at one time, is never old, or middle-aged, or young, but, in a condition of unchangeable constancy, moves on through the varied tenor of perpetual decay, fall, renovation, and progression. Thus, by preserving the method of nature in the conduct of the state, in what we improve, we are never wholly new; in what we retain, we are never wholly obsolete. By adhering in this manner and on those principles to our forefathers, we are guided not by the superstition of antiquarians, but by the spirit of philosophic analogy. In this choice of inheritance we have given to our frame of polity the image of a relation in blood; binding up the constitution of our country with our dearest domestic ties; adopting our fundamental laws into the bosom of our family affections; keeping inseparable, and cherishing with the warmth of all their combined and mutually reflected charities, our state, our hearths, our sepulchres, and our altars.

Through the same plan of a conformity to nature in our artificial institutions, and by calling in the aid of her unerring and powerful instincts, to fortify the fallible and feeble contrivances of our reason, we have derived several other, and those no small benefits, from considering our liberties in the light of an inheritance. Always acting as if in the presence of cannonized forefathers, the spirit of freedom, leading in itself to misrule and excess, is tempered with an awful gravity. This idea of a liberal descent inspires us with a sense of habitual native dignity, which prevents that upstart insolence almost inevitably adhering to and disgracing those who are the first acquirers of any distinction. By this means our liberty becomes a noble freedom. It carries an imposing and majestic aspect. It has a pedigree and illustrating ancestors. It has its bearings and its ensigns armorial. It has its gallery of portraits; its monumental inscriptions; its records, evidences, and titles. We procure reverence to our civil institutions on the principle upon which nature teaches us to revere individual men; on account of their age, and on account of those from whom they are descended. All your sophisters cannot produce anything better adapted to preserve a rational and manly freedom than the course that we have pursued, who have chosen our nature rather than our speculations, our breasts rather than our inventions, for the great conservatories and magazines of our rights and privileges.

You might, if you pleased, have profited of our example, and have given to your recovered freedom a correspondent dignity. Your privileges, though discontinued, were not lost to memory. Your constitution, it is true, whilst you were out of possession, suffered waste and dilapidation; but you possessed in some parts the walls, and, in all, the foundations, of a noble and venerable castle. You might have repaired those walls; you might have built on those old foundations. Your constitution was suspended before it was perfected; but you had the elements of a constitution very nearly as good as could be wished. In your old states you possessed that variety of parts corresponding with the various descriptions of which your community was happily composed; you had all that combination, and all that opposition of interests, you had that action and counteraction, which, in the natural and in the political world, from the reciprocal struggle of discordant powers, draws out the harmony of the universe. These opposed and conflicting interests, which you considered as so great a blemish in your old and in our present constitution, interpose a salutary check to all precipitate resolutions. They render deliberation a matter not of choice, but of necessity; they make all change a subject of *compromise,* which naturally begets moderation; they produce *temperaments* preventing the sore evil of harsh, crude, unqualified reformations; and rendering all the headlong exertions of arbitrary power, in the few or in the many, for ever impracticable. Through that diversity of members and interests, general liberty had as many securities as there were separate views in the several orders; whilst by pressing down the whole by the weight of a real monarchy, the separate parts would have been prevented from warping, and starting from their allotted places.

You had all these advantages in your ancient states; but you chose to act as if you had never been moulded into civil society, and had everything to begin anew. You began ill, because you began by despising everything that belonged to you. You set up your trade without a capital. If the last generations of your country appeared without much lustre in your eyes, you might have passed them by, and derived your claims from a more early race of ancestors. Under a pious predilection for those ancestors, your imaginations would have realized in them a standard of virtue and wisdom, beyond the vulgar practice of the hour: and you would have risen with the example to whose imitation you aspired. Respecting your forefathers, you would have been taught to respect yourselves. You would not have chosen to consider, the French as a people of yesterday, as a nation of low-born servile wretches until the emancipating year of 1789. In order to furnish, at the expense of your honour, an excuse to your apologists here for several enormities of yours, you would not have been content to be represented as a gang of Maroon slaves, suddenly broke loose from the house of bondage, and therefore to be pardoned for your abuse of the liberty to which you were not accustomed, and ill fitted. Would it not, my worthy friend, have been wiser to have you thought, what I, for one, always thought you, a generous and gallant nation, long misled to your disadvantage by your high and romantic sentiments of fidelity, honour, and loyalty; that events had been unfavourable to you, but that you were not enslaved through any illiberal or servile disposition; that in your most devoted submission, you were actuated by a principle of public spirit, and that it was your country you worshipped, in the person of your king? Had you made it to be understood, that in the delusion of this amiable error you had gone further than your wise ancestors; that you were resolved to resume your ancient privileges, whilst you preserved the spirit of your ancient and your recent loyalty and honour; or if, diffident of yourselves, and not clearly discerning the almost obliterated constitution of your ancestors, you had looked to your neighbours in this land, who had kept alive the ancient principles and models of the old common law of Europe meliorated and adapted to its present state—by following wise examples you would have given new examples of wisdom to the world. You would have rendered the cause of liberty venerable in the eyes of every worthy mind in every nation. You would have shamed despotism from the earth, by showing that freedom was not only reconcilable, but, as when well disciplined it is, auxiliary to law. You would have had an unoppressive but a productive revenue. You would have had a flourishing commerce to feed it. You would have had a free constitution; a potent monarchy; a disciplined army; a reformed and venerated clergy; a mitigated but spirited nobility, to lead your virtue, not to overlay it; you would have had a liberal order of commons, to emulate and to recruit that nobility; you would have had a protected, satisfied, laborious, and obedient people, taught to seek and to recognise the happiness that is to be found by virtue in all conditions; in which consists the true moral equality of mankind, and not in that monstrous fiction, which, by inspiring false ideas and vain expectations into men destined to travel in the obscure walk of laborious life, serves only to aggravate and embitter that real inequality, which it never can remove; and which the order of civil life establishes as much for the benefit of those whom it must leave in an humble state, as those whom it is able to exalt to a condition more splendid, but not more happy. You had a smooth and easy career of felicity and glory laid open to you, beyond anything recorded in the history of the world; but you have shown that difficulty is good for man.

Compute your gains: see what is got by those extravagant and presumptuous speculations which have taught your leaders to despise all their predecessors, and all their contemporaries, and even to despise themselves, until the moment in which they became truly despicable. By following those false lights, France has bought undisguised calamities at a higher price than any nation has purchased the most unequivocal blessings! France has bought poverty by crime! France has not sacrificed her virtue to her interest, but she has abandoned her interest, that she might prostitute her virtue. All other nations have begun the fabric of a new government, or the reformation of an old, by establishing originally, or by enforcing with greater exactness, some rites or other of religion. All other people have laid the foundations of civil freedom in severer manners, and a system of a more austere and masculine morality. France, when she let loose the reins of regal authority, doubled the licence of a ferocious dissoluteness in manners, and of an insolent irreligion in opinions and practices; and has extended through all ranks of life, as if she were communicating some privilege, or laying open some secluded benefit, all the unhappy corruptions that usually were the disease of wealth and power. This is one of the new principles of equality in France.

France, by the perfidy of her leaders, has utterly disgraced the tone of lenient council in the cabinets of princes, and disarmed it of its most potent topics. She has sanctified the dark, suspicious maxims of tyrannous distrust; and taught kings to tremble at (what will hereafter be called) the delusive plausibilities of moral politicians. Sovereigns will consider those, who advise them to place an unlimited confidence in their people, as subverters of their thrones; as traitors who aim at their destruction, by leading their easy good-nature, under specious pretences, to admit combinations of bold and faithless men into a participation of their power. This alone (if there were nothing else) is an irreparable calamity to you and to mankind. Remember that your parliament of Paris told your king, that, in calling the states together, he had nothing to fear but the prodigal excess of their zeal in providing for the support of the throne. It is right that these men should hide their heads. It is right that they should bear their part in the ruin which their counsel has brought on their sovereign and their country. Such sanguine declarations tend to lull authority asleep; to encourage it rashly to engage in perilous adventures of untried policy; to neglect those provisions, preparations, and precautions, which distinguished benevolence from imbecility; and without which no man can answer for the salutary effect of any abstract plan of government or of freedom. For want of these, they have seen the medicine of the state corrupted into its poison. They have seen the French rebel against a mild and lawful monarch, with more fury, outrage, and insult, than ever any people has been known to rise against the most illegal usurper, or the most sanguinary tyrant. Their resistance was made to concession; their revolt was from protection; their blow was aimed at a hand holding out graces, favours, and immunities.

This was unnatural. The rest is in order. They have found their punishment in their success. Laws overturned; tribunals subverted; industry without vigour; commerce expiring; the revenue unpaid, yet the people impoverished; a church pillaged, and a state not relieved; civil and military anarchy made the constitution of the kingdom; everything human and divine sacrificed to the idol of public credit, and national bankruptcy the consequence; and, to crown all, the paper securities of new, precarious, tottering power, the discredited paper securities of impoverished fraud and beggared rapine, held out as a currency for the support of an empire, in lieu of the two great recognised species that represent the lasting, conventional credit of mankind, which disappeared and hid themselves in the earth from whence they came, when the principle of property, whose creatures and representatives they are, was systematically subverted.

Were all these dreadful things necessary? Were they the inevitable results of the desperate struggle of determined patriots, compelled to wade through blood and tumult, to the quiet shore of a tranquil and prosperous liberty? No! nothing like it. The fresh ruins of France, which shock our feelings wherever we can turn our eyes, are not the devastation of civil war; they are the sad but instructive monuments of rash and ignorant counsel in time of profound peace. They are the display of inconsiderate and presumptuous, because unresisted and irresistible, authority. The persons who have thus squandered away the precious treasure of their crimes,

the persons who have made this prodigal and wild waste of
public evils, (the last stake reserved for the ultimate ransom
of the state,) have met in their progress with little, or rather
with no opposition at all. Their whole march was more like
a triumphal procession, than the progress of a war. Their
pioneers have gone before them, and demolished and laid
everything level at their feet. Not one drop of *their* blood
have they shed in the cause of the country they have ruined.
They have made no sacrifices to their projects of greater consequence than their shoebuckles, whilst they were imprisoning
their king, murdering their fellow-citizens, and bathing in tears,
and plunging in poverty and distress, thousands of worthy men
and worthy families. Their cruelty has not ever been the base result of fear. It has been the effect of their sense of perfect safety,
in authorizing treasons, robberies, rapes, assassinations, slaugh-
ters, and burnings, throughout their harassed land. But the
cause of all was plain from the beginning.

This unforced choice, this fond election of evil, would appear perfectly unaccountable, if we did not consider the composition of the National Assembly: I do not mean its formal
constitution, which, as it now stands, is exceptionable enough,
but the materials of which, in a great measure, it is composed,
which is of ten thousand times greater consequence than all
the formalities in the world. If we were to know nothing of
this assembly but by its title and function, no colours could
paint to the imagination anything more venerable. In that light
the mind of an inquirer, subdued by such an awful image as
that of the virtue and wisdom of a whole people collected into
a focus, would pause and hesitate in condemning things even
of the very worst aspect. Instead of blameable, they would
appear only mysterious. But no name, no power, no function,
no artificial institution whatsoever, can make the men of
whom any system of authority is composed, any other than
God, and nature, and education, and their habits of life have
made them. Capacities beyond these the people have not to

give. Virtue and wisdom may be the objects of their choice; but their choice confers neither the one nor the other on those upon whom they lay their ordaining hands. They have not the engagement of nature, they have not the promise of revelation, for any such powers. . . .

I see that your example is held out to shame us. I know that we are supposed a dull, sluggish race, rendered passive by finding our situation tolerable, and prevented by a mediocrity of freedom from ever attaining to its full perfection. Your leaders in France began by affecting to admire, almost to adore, the British constitution; but as they advanced, they came to look upon it with a sovereign contempt. The friends of your National Assembly amongst us have full as mean an opinion of what was formerly thought the glory of their country. The Revolution Society has discovered that the English nation is not free. They are convinced that the inequality in our representation is a "defect in our constitution *so gross and palpable,* as to make it excellent chiefly in *form* and *theory.*" [8] That a representation in the legislature of a kingdom is not only the basis of all constitutional liberty in it, but of *"all legitimate government;* that without it a *government* is nothing but an *usurpation;"*—that "when the representation is *partial,* the kingdom possesses liberty only *partially;* and if extremely partial, it gives only a *semblance;* and if not only extremely partial, but corruptly chosen, it becomes a *nuisance."* Dr. Price considers this inadequacy of representation as our *fundamental grievance;* and though, as to the corruption of this semblance of representation, he hopes it is not yet arrived to its full perfection of depravity, he fears that "nothing will be done towards gaining for us this *essential blessing,* until some *great abuse of power* again provokes our resentment, or some *great calamity* again alarms our fears, or perhaps till the acquisition of a *pure and equal representation by other coun-*

---

[8] [Price,] "Discourse on the Love of our Country," 3rd edit., p. 39. [Burke]

tries, whilst we are *mocked* with the *shadow,* kindles our shame." To this he subjoins a note in these words: "A representation chosen chiefly by the treasury, and a *few* thousands of the *dregs* of the people, who are generally paid for their votes."

You will smile here at the consistency of those democratists, who, when they are not on their guard, treat the humbler part of the community with the greatest contempt, whilst, at the same time, they pretend to make them the depositories of all power. It would require a long discourse to point out to you the many fallacies that lurk in the generality and equivocal nature of the terms "inadequate representation." I shall only say here, in justice to that old-fashioned constitution, under which we have long prospered, that our representation has been found perfectly adequate to all the purposes for which a representation of the people can be desired or devised. I defy the enemies of our constitution to show the contrary. To detail the particulars in which it is found so well to promote its ends, would demand a treatise on our practical constitution. I state here the doctrine of the Revolutionists, only that you and others may see what an opinion these gentlemen entertain of the constitution of their country, and why they seem to think that some great abuse of power, or some great calamity, as giving a chance for the blessing of a constitution according to their ideas, would be much palliated to their feelings; you see *why they* are so much enamoured of your fair and equal representation, which being once obtained, the same effects might follow. You see they consider our House of Commons as only "a semblance," "a form," "a theory," "a shadow," "a mockery," perhaps "a nuisance."

These gentlemen value themselves on being systematic; and not without reason. They must therefore look on this gross and palpable defect of representation, this fundamental grievance, (so they call it,) as a thing not only vicious in itself, but as rendering our whole government absolutely *illegitimate,* and not at all better than a downright *usurpation.* Another revolution, to get rid of this illegitimate and usurped government, would of course be perfectly justifiable, if not absolutely necessary. Indeed their principle, if you observe it with any attention, goes much further than to an alteration in the election of the House of Commons; for, if popular representation, or choice, is necessary to the *legitimacy* of all government, the House of Lords is, at one stroke, bastardized and corrupted in blood. That House is no representative of the people at all, even in "semblance or in form." The case of the crown is altogether as bad. In vain the crown may endeavour to screen itself against these gentlemen by the authority of the establishment made on the Revolution. The Revolution which is resorted to for a title, on their system, wants a title itself. The Revolution is built, according to their theory, upon a basis not more solid than our present formalities, as it was made by a House of Lords, not representing any one but themselves; and by a House of Commons exactly such as the present, that is, as they term it, by a mere "shadow and mockery" of representation.

Something they must destroy, or they seem to themselves to exist for no purpose. One set is for destroying the civil power through the ecclesiastical; another, for demolishing the ecclesiastic through the civil. They are aware that the worst consequences might happen to the public in accomplishing this double ruin of church and state; but they are so heated with their theories, that they give more than hints, that this ruin, with all the mischiefs that must lead to it and attend it, and which to themselves appear quite certain, would not be unacceptable to them, or very remote from their wishes. A man amongst them of great authority, and certainly of great talents, speaking of a supposed alliance between church and state, says, "perhaps *we must wait for the fall of the civil powers* before this most unnatural alliance be broken.

Calamitous no doubt will that time be. But what convulsion
in the political world ought to be a subject of lamentation, if
it be attended with so desirable an effect?" You see with
what a steady eye these gentlemen are prepared to view the
greatest calamities which can befall their country.

It is no wonder therefore, that with these ideas of everything
in their constitution and government at home, either in church
or state, as illegitimate and usurped, or at best as a vain
mockery, they look abroad with an eager and passionate
enthusiasm. Whilst they are possessed by these notions, it is
vain to talk to them of the practice of their ancestors, the
fundamental laws of their country, the fixed form of a
constitution, whose merits are confirmed by the solid test of
long experience, and an increasing public strength and
national prosperity. They despise experience as the wisdom
of unlettered men; and as for the rest, they have wrought
under-ground a mine that will blow up, at one grand
explosion, all examples of antiquity, all precedents, charters,
and acts of parliament. They have "the rights of men."
Against these there can be no prescription; against these no
agreement is binding: these admit no temperament, and no
compromise: anything withheld from their full demand is so
much of fraud and injustice. Against these their rights of men
let no government look for security in the length of its continuance, or in the justice and lenity of its administration.
The objections of these speculatists, if its forms do not
quadrate with their theories, are as valid against such an old
and beneficent government, as against the most violent
tyranny, or the greenest usurpation. They are always at issue
with governments, not on a question of abuse, but a question
of competency, and a question of title. I have nothing to say
to the clumsy subtilty of their political metaphysics. Let them
be their amusement in the schools.—"Illa *se jactat in aula—
Æolus, et clauso ventorum carcere regnet.*" [9]—But let them

---

[9] Virgil, *Aeneid,* I. 140.

not break prison to burst like a *Levanter,* to sweep the earth with their hurricane, and to break up the fountains of the great deep to overwhelm us.

Far am I from denying in theory, full as far is my heart from withholding in practice, (if I were of power to give or to withhold,) the *real* rights of men. In denying their false claims of right, I do not mean to injure those which are real, and are such as their pretended rights would totally destroy. If civil society be made for the advantage of man, all the advantages for which it is made become his right. It is an institution of beneficence; and law itself is only beneficence acting by a rule. Men have a right to live by that rule; they have a right to do justice, as between their fellows, whether their fellows are in public function or in ordinary occupation. They have a right to the fruits of their industry; and to the means of making their industry fruitful. They have a right to the acquisitions of their parents; to the nourishment and im-provement of their offspring; to instruction in life, and to consolation in death. Whatever each man can separately do, without trespassing upon others, he has a right to do for himself; and he has a right to a fair portion of all which society, with all its combinations of skill and force, can do in his favour. In this partnership all men have equal rights; but not to equal things. He that has but five shillings in the partnership, has as good a right to it, as he that has five hundred pounds has to his larger proportion. But he has not a right to an equal dividend in the product of the joint stock; and as to the share of power, authority, and direction which each individual ought to have in the management of the state, that I must deny to be amongst the direct original rights of man in civil society; for I have in my contempla-tion the civil social man, and no other. It is a thing to be settled by convention.

If civil society be the offspring of convention, that con-vention must be its law. That convention must limit and modify all the descriptions of constitution which are formed under it. Every sort of legislative, judicial, or executory power are its creatures. They can have no being in any other state of things; and how can any man claim under the conventions of civil society, rights which do not so much as suppose its existence? rights which are absolutely repugnant to it? One of the first motives to civil society, and which becomes one of its fundamental rules, is, *that no man should be judge in his own cause.* By this each person has at once divested himself of the first fundamental right of un-covenanted man, that is, to judge for himself, and to assert his own cause. He abdicates all rights to be his own governor. He inclusively, in a great measure, abandons the right of self-defence, the first law of nature. Men cannot enjoy the rights of an uncivil and of a civil state together. That he may obtain justice, he gives up his right of determining what it is in points the most essential to him. That he may secure some liberty, he makes a surrender in trust of the whole of it.

Government is not made in virtue of natural rights, which may and do exist in total independence of it; and exist in much greater clearness, and in a much greater degree of abstract perfection: but their abstract perfection is their practical defect. By having a right to everything they want everything. Government is a contrivance of human wisdom to provide for human *wants.* Men have a right that these wants should be provided for by this wisdom. Among these wants is to be reckoned the want, out of civil society, of a sufficient restraint upon their passions. Society requires not only that the passions of individuals should be subjected, but that even in the mass and body, as well as in the individuals, the inclinations of men should frequently be thwarted, their will controlled, and their passions brought into subjection. This can only be done *by a power out of themselves;* and not, in the exercise of its function, subject to that will and to those passions which it is its office to bridle and subdue. In this sense the restraints on men, as well as their liberties, are to be reckoned among their rights. But as the liberties and the restrictions vary with times and circumstances, and admit of infinite modifications, they cannot be settled upon any abstract rule; and nothing is so foolish as to discuss them upon that principle.

The moment you abate anything from the full rights of men, each to govern himself, and suffer any artificial, positive limitation upon those rights, from that moment the whole organization of government becomes a consideration of convenience. This it is which makes the constitution of a state, and the due distribution of its powers, a matter of the most delicate and complicated skill. It requires a deep knowledge of human nature and human necessities, and of the things which facilitate or obstruct the various ends, which are to be pursued by the mechanism of civil institutions. The state is to have recruits to its strength, and remedies to its distempers. What is the use of discussing a man's abstract right to food or medicine? The question is upon the method of procuring and administering them. In that deliberation I shall always advise to call in the aid of the farmer and the physician, rather than the professor of metaphysics.

The science of constructing a commonwealth, or renovating it, or reforming it, is, like every other experimental science, not to be taught *à priori*. Nor is it a short experience that can instruct us in that practical science; because the real effects of moral causes are not always immediate; but that which in the first instance is prejudicial may be excellent in its remoter operation; and its excellence may arise even from the ill effects it produces in the beginning. The reverse also happens: and very plausible schemes, with very pleasing commencements, have often shameful and lamentable conclusions. In states there are often some obscure and almost latent causes, things which appear at first view of little moment, on which a very great part of its prosperity or adversity may most essentially depend. The science of government being therefore so practical in itself, and intended for such practical purposes, a matter which requires experience,

and even more experience than any person can gain in his
whole life, however sagacious and observing he may be, it is
with infinite caution that any man ought to venture upon
pulling down an edifice, which has answered in any tolerable
degree for ages the common purposes of society, or on
building it up again, without having models and patterns of
approved utility before his eyes.

These metaphysic rights entering into common life, like
rays of light which pierce into a dense medium, are, by the
laws of nature, refracted from their straight line. Indeed in
the gross and complicated mass of human passions and
concerns, the primitive rights of men undergo such a variety
of refractions and reflections, that it becomes absurd to talk
of them as if they continued in the simplicity of their original
direction. The nature of man is intricate; the objects of
society are of the greatest possible complexity: and therefore
no simple disposition or direction of power can be suitable
either to man's nature, or to the quality of his affairs. When
I hear the simplicity of contrivance aimed at and boasted
of in any new political constitutions, I am at no loss to decide
that the artificers are grossly ignorant of their trade, or totally
negligent of their duty. The simple governments are fundamentally defective, to say no worse of them. If you were to
contemplate society in but one point of view, all these simple
modes of polity are infinitely captivating. In effect each
would answer its single end much more perfectly than the
more complex is able to attain all its complex purposes. But
it is better that the whole should be imperfectly and anoma-
lously answered, than that, while some parts are provided for
with great exactness, others might be totally neglected, or
perhaps materially injured, by the over-care of a favourite
member.

The pretended rights of these theorists are all extremes:
and in proportion as they are metaphysically true, they are
morally and politically false. The rights of men are in a sort

of *middle,* incapable of definition, but not impossible to be discerned. The rights of men in governments are their advantages; and these are often in balances between differences of good; in compromises sometimes between good and evil, and sometimes between evil and evil. Political reason is a computing principle; adding, subtracting, multiplying, and dividing, morally and not metaphysically, or mathematically, true moral denominations.

By these theorists the right of the people is almost always sophistically confounded with their power. The body of the community, whenever it can come to act, can meet with no effectual resistance; but till power and right are the same, the whole body of them has no right inconsistent with virtue, and the first of all virtues, prudence. Men have no right to what is not reasonable, and to what is not for their benefit; for though a pleasant writer said, *Liceat perire poetis,* when one of them, in cold blood, is said to have leaped into the flames of a volcanic revolution, *Ardentem frigidus Ætnam insiluit,*[10] I consider such a frolic rather as an unjustifiable poetic license, than as one of the franchises of Parnassus; and whether he were poet, or divine, or politician, that chose to exercise this kind of right, I think that more wise, because more charitable, thoughts would urge me rather to save the man, than to preserve his brazen slippers as the monuments of his folly.

The kind of anniversary sermons to which a great part of what I write refers, if men are not shamed out of their present course, in commemorating the fact, will cheat many out of the principles, and deprive them of the benefits, of the revolution they commemorate. I confess to you, Sir, I never liked this continual talk of resistance, and revolution, or the practice of making the extreme medicine of the constitution its daily bread. It renders the habit of society dan-

[10] Horace, *Art of Poetry,* 11. 465-66.

gerously valetudinary: it is taking periodical doses of mercury sublimate, and swallowing down repeated provocatives of cantharides to our love of liberty.

This distemper of remedy, grown habitual, relaxes and wears out, by a vulgar and prostituted use, the spring of that spirit which is to be exerted on great occasions. It was in the most patient period of Roman servitude that themes of tyrannicide made the ordinary exercise of boys at school— *cum perimit sævos classis numerosa tyrannos.*[11] In the ordinary state of things, it produces in a country like ours the worst effects, even on the cause of that liberty which it abuses with the dissoluteness of an extravagant speculation. Almost all the high-bred republicans of my time have, after a short space, become the most decided, thorough-paced courtiers; they soon left the business of a tedious, moderate, but practical resistance, to those of us whom, in the pride and intoxication of their theories, they have slighted as not much better than Tories. Hypocrisy, of course, delights in the most sublime speculations; for, never intending to go beyond speculation, it costs nothing to have it magnificent. But even in cases where rather levity than fraud was to be suspected in these ranting speculations, the issue has been much the same. These professors, finding their extreme principles not applicable to cases which call only for a qualified, or, as I may say, civil and legal resistance, in such cases employ no resistance at all. It is with them a war or a revolution, or it is nothing. Finding their schemes of politics not adapted to the state of the world in which they live, they often come to think lightly of all public principle; and are ready, on their part, to abandon for a very trivial interest what they find of very trivial value. Some indeed are of more steady and persevering natures; but these are eager politicians out of parliament, who have little to tempt them to abandon their favourite projects. They have some change in the church or

---

[11] Juvenal, VII. 151.

state, or both, constantly in their view. When that is the case, they are always bad citizens, and perfectly unsure connexions. For, considering their speculative designs as of infinite value, and the actual arrangement of the state as of no estimation, they are at best indifferent about it. They see no merit in the good, and no fault in the vicious, management of public affairs; they rather rejoice in the latter, as more propitious to revolution. They see no merit or demerit in any man, or any action, or any political principle, any further than as they may forward or retard their design of change: they therefore take up, one day, the most violent and stretched prerogative, and another time the wildest democratic ideas of freedom, and pass from the one to the other without any sort of regard to cause, to person, or to party.

In France you are now in the crisis of a revolution, and in the transit from one form of government to another— you cannot see that character of men exactly in the same situation in which we see it in this country. With us it is militant; with you it is triumphant; and you know how it can act when its power is commensurate to its will. I would not be supposed to confine those observations to any description of men, or to comprehend all men of any description within them—No! far from it. I am as incapable of that injustice, as I am of keeping terms with those who profess principles of extremities; and who, under the name of religion, teach little else than wild and dangerous politics. The worst of these politics of revolution is this: they temper and harden the breast, in order to prepare it for the desperate strokes which are sometimes used in extreme occasions. But as these occasions may never arrive, the mind receives a gratuitous taint; and the moral sentiments suffer not a little, when no political purpose is served by the depravation. This sort of people are so taken up with their theories about the rights of man, that they have totally forgotten his nature. Without opening one new avenue to the understanding, they have succeeded in stopping up those that lead to the heart. They have perverted in themselves, and in those that attend to them, all the well-placed sympathies of the human breast.

This famous sermon of the Old Jewry breathes nothing but this spirit through all the political part. Plots, massacres, assassinations, seem to some people a trivial price for obtaining a revolution. A cheap, bloodless reformation, a guiltless liberty, appear flat and vapid to their taste. There must be a great change of scene; there must be a magnificent stage effect; there must be a grand spectacle to rouse the imagination, grown torpid with the lazy enjoyment of sixty years' security, and the still unanimating repose of public prosperity. The preacher found them all in the French Revolution. This inspires a juvenile warmth through his whole frame. His enthusiasm kindles as he advances; and when he arrives at his peroration it is in a full blaze. Then viewing, from the Pisgah of his pulpit, the free, moral, happy, flourishing, and glorious state of France, as in a bird's-eye landscape of a promised land, he breaks out into the following rapture:

"What an eventful period is this! I am *thankful* that I have lived to it; I could almost say, *Lord, now lettest thou thy servant depart in peace, for mine eyes have seen thy salvation.*—I have lived to see a *diffusion* of knowledge, which has undermined superstition and error.—I have lived to see *the rights of men* better understood than ever; and nations panting for liberty which seemed to have lost the idea of it.—I have lived to see *thirty millions of people,* indignant and resolute, spurning at slavery, and demanding liberty with an irresistible voice. *Their king led in triumph, and an arbitrary monarch surrendering himself to his subjects.*" [12]

Before I proceed further, I have to remark, that Dr. Price seems rather to overvalue the great acquisitions of light which

[12] Another of these reverend gentlemen, who was witness to some of the spectacles which Paris has lately exhibited, expresses himself thus:—*"A king dragged in submissive triumph by his conquering subjects,* is one of those appearances of grandeur which seldom rise in the prospect of human affairs, and which, during the remainder of my life, I shall think of with wonder and gratification." These gentlemen agree marvellously in their feelings. [Burke]

he has obtained and diffused in this age. The last century appears to me to have been quite as much enlightened. It had, though in a different place, a triumph as memorable as that of Dr. Price; and some of the great preachers of that period partook of it as eagerly as he has done in the triumph of France. On the trial of the Rev. Hugh Peters for high treason, it was deposed, that when King Charles was brought to London for his trial, the Apostle of Liberty in that day conducted the *triumph*. "I saw," says the witness, "his Majesty in the coach with six horses, and Peters riding before the king, *triumphing*." Dr. Price, when he talks as if he had made a discovery, only follows a precedent; for, after the commencement of the king's trial, this precursor, the same Dr. Peters, concluding a long prayer at the Royal Chapel at Whitehall, (he had very triumphantly chosen his place,) said, "I have prayed and preached these twenty years; and now I may say with old Simeon, *Lord, now lettest thou thy servant depart in peace, for mine eyes have seen thy salvation.*" Peters had not the fruits of his prayer; for he neither departed so soon as he wished, nor in peace. He became (what I heartily hope none of his followers may be in this country) himself a sacrifice to the triumph which he led as pontiff. They dealt at the Restoration, perhaps, too hardly with this poor good man. But we owe it to his memory and his sufferings that he had as much illumination, and as much zeal, and had as effectually undermined all *the superstition and error* which might impede the great business he was engaged in, as any who follow and repeat after him, in this age, which would assume to itself an exclusive title to the knowledge of the rights of men, and all the glorious consequences of that knowledge.

After this sally of the preacher of the Old Jewry, which differs only in place and time, but agrees perfectly with the spirit and letter of the rapture of 1648, the Revolution Society, the fabricators of governments, the heroic band of *cashierers* of *monarchs,* electors of sovereigns, and leaders of kings in triumph, strutting with a proud consciousness of the diffusion of the knowledge they had thus gratuitously received. To make this bountiful communication, they adjourned from the church in the Old Jewry to the London Tavern; where the same Dr. Price, in whom the fumes of his oracular tripod were not entirely evaporated, moved and carried the resolution, or address of congratulation, transmitted by Lord Stanhope to the National Assembly of France.

I find a preacher of the gospel profaning the beautiful and prophetic ejaculation, commonly called *"nunc dimittis,"* made on the first presentation of our Saviour in the temple, and applying it, with an inhuman and unnatural rapture, to the most horrid, atrocious, and afflicting spectacle that perhaps ever was exhibited to the pity and indignation of mankind. This *"leading in triumph,"* a thing in its best form unmanly and irreligious, which fills our preacher with such unhallowed transports, must shock, I believe, the moral taste of every well-born mind. Several English were the stupefied and in-dignant spectators of that triumph. It was (unless we have been strangely deceived) a spectacle more resembling a procession of American savages, entering into Onondaga, after some of their murders called victories, and leading into hovels hung round with scalps, their captives, overpowered with the scoffs and buffets of women as ferocious as themselves, much more than it resembled the triumphal pomp of a civilized, martial nation;—if a civilized nation, or any men who had a sense of generosity, were capable of a personal triumph over the fallen and afflicted.

This, my dear Sir, was not the triumph of France. I must believe that, as a nation, it overwhelmed you with shame and horror. I must believe that the National Assembly find them-selves in a state of the greatest humiliation in not being able to punish the authors of this triumph, or the actors in it; and that they are in a situation in which any inquiry they may make upon the subject must be destitute even of the ap-pearance of liberty or impartiality. The apology of that assembly is found in their situation; but when we approve what they *must* bear, it is in us the degenerate choice of a vitiated mind.

With a compelled appearance of deliberation, they vote under the dominion of a stern necessity. They sit in the heart, as it were, of a foreign republic: they have their residence in a city whose constitution has emanated neither from the charter of their king, nor from their legislative power. There they are surrounded by an army not raised either by the authority of their crown, or by their command; and which, if they should order to dissolve itself, would instantly dissolve them. There they sit, after a gang of assassins had driven away some hundreds of the members; whilst those who held the same moderate principles, with more patience or better hope, continued every day exposed to outrageous insults and murderous threats. There a majority, sometimes real, sometimes pretended, captive itself, compels a captive king to issue as royal edicts, at third hand, the polluted nonsense of their most licentious and giddy coffeehouses. It is notorious, that all their measures are decided before they are debated. It is beyond doubt, that under the terror of the bayonet, and the lamp-post, and the torch to their houses, they are obliged to adopt all the crude and desperate measures suggested by clubs composed of a monstrous medley of all conditions, tongues, and nations. Among these are found persons, in comparison of whom Catiline would be thought scrupulous, and Cethegus a man of sobriety and moderation. Nor is it in these clubs alone that the public measures are deformed into monsters. They undergo a previous distortion in academies, intended as so many seminaries for these clubs, which are set up in all the places of public resort. In these meetings of all sorts, every counsel, in proportion as it is daring, and violent, and perfidious, is taken for the mark of superior genius. Humanity and compassion are ridiculed as the fruits of superstition and ignorance. Tenderness to individuals is considered as treason to the public. Liberty is always to be estimated perfect as property is rendered insecure. Amidst assassination, massacre, and confiscation, perpetrated or meditated, they are forming plans for the good order of future society. Embracing in their arms the carcases of base criminals, and promoting their relations on the title of their offences, they drive hundreds of virtuous persons to the same end, by forcing them to subsist by beggary or by crime.

The assembly, their organ, acts before them the farce of deliberation with as little decency as liberty. They act like the comedians of a fair before a riotous audience; they act amidst the tumultuous cries of a mixed mob of ferocious men, and of women lost to shame, who, according to their insolent fancies, direct, control, applaud, explode them; and sometimes mix and take their seats amongst them; domineering over them with a strange mixture of servile petulance and proud, presumptuous authority. As they have inverted order in all things, the gallery is in the place of the house. This assembly, which overthrows kings and kingdoms, has not even the physiognomy and aspect of a grave legislative body—*nec color imperii, nec frons ulla senatûs.*[13] They have a power given to them, like that of the evil principle, to subvert and destroy; but none to construct, except such machines as may be fitted for further subversion and further destruction.

Who is it that admires, and from the heart is attached to, national representative assemblies, but must turn with horror and disgust from such a profane burlesque, and abominable perversion of that sacred institute? Lovers of monarchy, lovers of republics, must alike abhor it. The members of your assembly must themselves groan under the tyranny of which they have all the shame, none of the direction, and little of the profit. I am sure many of the members who compose even the majority of that body must feel as I do, notwithstanding the applauses of the Revolution Society. Miserable king!

[13] Lucan, IX. 207.

miserable assembly! How must that assembly be silently scandalized with those of their members, who could call a day which seemed to blot the sun out of heaven, *"un beau jour!"* [14] How must they be inwardly indignant at hearing others, who thought fit to declare to them, "that the vessel of the state would fly forward in her course towards regeneration with more speed than ever," from the stiff gale of treason and murder, which preceded our preacher's triumph! What must they have felt, whilst, with outward patience, and inward indignation, they heard of the slaughter of innocent gentlemen in their houses, that "the blood spilled was not the most pure!" What must they have felt, when they were besieged by complaints of disorders which shook their country to its foundations, at being compelled coolly to tell the complainants, that they were under the protection of the law, and that they would address the king (the captive king) to cause the laws to be enforced for their protection; when the enslaved ministers of that captive king had formally notified to them, that there were neither law, nor authority, nor power left to protect! What must they have felt at being obliged, as a felicitation on the present new year, to request their captive king to forget the stormy period of the last, on account of the great good which *he* was likely to produce to his people; to the complete attainment of which good they adjourned the practical demonstrations of their loyalty, assuring him of their obedience, when he should no longer possess any authority to command!

This address was made with much good nature and affection, to be sure. But among the revolutions in France must be reckoned a considerable revolution in their ideas of politeness. In England we are said to learn manners at second-hand from your side of the water, and that we dress our behaviour in the frippery of France. If so, we are still in the old cut; and have not so far conformed to the new

---

[14] 6th of October, 1789. [Burke]

Parisian mode of good breeding, as to think it quite in the most refined strain of delicate compliment (whether in condolence or congratulation) to say, to the most humiliated creature that crawls upon the earth, that great public benefits are derived from the murder of his servants, the attempted assassination of himself and of his wife, and the mortification, disgrace, and degradation, that he has personally suffered. It is a topic of consolation which our ordinary of Newgate would be too humane to use to a criminal at the foot of the gallows. I should have thought that the hangman of Paris, now that he is liberalized by the vote of the National Assembly, and is allowed his rank and arms in the herald's college of the rights of men, would be too generous, too gallant a man, too full of the sense of his new dignity, to employ that cutting consolation to any of the persons whom the *leze nation* might bring under the administration of his *executive power*.

A man is fallen indeed, when he is thus flattered. The anodyne draught of oblivion, thus drugged, is well calculated to preserve a galling wakefulness, and to feel the living ulcer of a corroding memory. Thus to administer the opiate portion of amnesty, powdered with all the ingredients of scorn and contempt, is to hold to his lips, instead of "the balm of hurt minds," the cup of human misery full to the brim, and to force him to drink it to the dregs.

Yielding to reasons, at least as forcible as those which were so delicately urged in the compliment on the new year, the king of France will probably endeavour to forget these events and that compliment. But history, who keeps a durable record of all our acts, and exercises her awful censure over the proceedings of all sorts of sovereigns, will not forget either those events, or the era of this liberal refinement in the intercourse of mankind. History will record, that on the morning of the 6th of October, 1789, the king and queen of France, after a day of confusion, alarm, dismay, and slaughter, lay down, under the pledged security of public faith, to indulge nature in a few hours of respite, and troubled, melancholy repose. From this sleep the queen was first startled by the voice of the sentinel at her door, who cried out to her to save herself by flight—that this was the last proof of fidelity he could give--that they were upon him, and he was dead. Instantly he was cut down. A band of cruel ruffians and assassins, reeking with his blood, rushed into the chamber of the queen, and pierced with a hundred strokes of bayonets and poniards the bed, from whence this persecuted woman had but just time to fly almost naked, and, through ways unknown to the murderers, had escaped to seek refuge at the feet of a king and husband, not secure of his own life for a moment.

This king, to say no more of him, and this queen, and their infant children, (who once would have been the pride and hope of a great and generous people,) were then forced to abandon the sanctuary of the most splendid palace in the world, which they left swimming in blood, polluted by massacre, and strewed with scattered limbs and mutilated carcases. Thence they were conducted into the capital of their kingdom. Two had been selected from the unprovoked, unresisted, promiscuous slaughter, which was made of the gentlemen of birth and family who composed the king's body guard. These two gentlemen, with all the parade of an execution of justice, were cruelly and publicly dragged to the block, and beheaded in the great court of the palace. Their heads were stuck upon spears, and led the procession; whilst the royal captives who followed in the train were slowly moved along, amidst the horrid yells, and shrilling screams, and frantic dances, and infamous contumelies, and all the unutterable abominations of the furies of hell, in the abused shape of the vilest of women. After they had been made to taste, drop by drop, more than the bitterness of death, in the slow torture of a journey of twelve miles, protracted to six hours, they were, under a guard, composed of those very soldiers who had thus conducted them through this famous triumph, lodged in one of the old palaces of Paris, now converted into a bastile for kings.

Is this a triumph to be consecrated at altars? to be commemorated with grateful thanksgiving? to be offered to the divine humanity with fervent prayer and enthusiastic ejaculation?—These Theban and Thracian orgies, acted in France, and applauded only in the Old Jewry, I assure you, kindle prophetic enthusiasm in the minds but of very few people in this kingdom: although a saint and apostle, who may have revelations of his own, and who has so completely vanquished all the mean superstitions of the heart, may incline to think it pious and decorous to compare it with the entrance into the world of the Prince of Peace, proclaimed in a holy temple by a venerable sage, and not long before not worse announced by the voice of angels to the quiet innocence of shepherds.

At first I was at a loss to account for this fit of unguarded transport. I knew, indeed, that the sufferings of monarchs make a delicious repast to some sort of palates. There were reflections which might serve to keep this appetite within some bounds of temperance. But when I took one circumstance into my consideration, I was obliged to confess, that much allowance ought to be made for the society, and that the temptation was too strong for common discretion; I mean, the circumstance of the Io Pæan of the triumph, the animating cry which called "for *all* the BISHOPS to be hanged on the lamp-posts," might well have brought forth a burst of enthusiasm on the foreseen consequences of this happy day. I allow to so much enthusiasm some little deviation from prudence. I allow this prophet to break forth into hymns of joy and thanksgiving on an event which appears like the precursor of the Millennium, and the projected fifth monarchy, in the destruction of all church establishments.

There was, however, (as in all human affairs there is,) in the midst of this joy, something to exercise the patience of these worthy gentlemen, and to try the long-suffering of their faith. The actual murder of the king and queen, and their child, was wanting to the other auspicious circumstances of this *"beautiful day."* The actual murder of the bishops, though called for by so many holy ejaculations, was also wanting. A group of regicide and sacrilegious slaughter, was indeed boldly sketched. It unhappily was left unfinished, in this great history-piece of the massacre of innocents. What hardy pencil of a great master, from the school of rights of men, will finish it, is to be seen hereafter. The age has not yet the complete benefit of that diffusion of knowledge that has undermined superstition and error; and the king of France wants another object or two to consign to oblivion, in consideration of all the good which is to arise from his own sufferings, and the patriotic crimes of an enlightened age.

Although this work of our new light and knowledge did not go to the length that in all probability it was intended it should be carried, yet I must think that such treatment of any human creatures must be shocking to any but those who are made for accomplishing revolutions. But I cannot stop here. Influenced by the inborn feelings of my nature, and not being illuminated by a single ray of this new-sprung modern light, I confess to you, Sir, that the exalted rank of the persons suffering, and particularly the sex, the beauty, and the amiable qualities of the descendant of so many kings and emperors, with the tender age of royal infants, insensible only through infancy and innocence of the cruel outrages to which their parents were exposed, instead of being a subject of exultation, adds not a little to my sensibility on that most melancholy occasion.

I hear that the august person, who was the principal object of our preacher's triumph, though he supported himself, felt much on that shameful occasion. As a man, it became him to feel for his wife and his children, and the faithful guards of his person, that were massacred in cold blood about him; as a prince, it became him to feel for the strange and frightful transformation of his civilized subjects, and to be more grieved for them than solicitous for himself. It derogates little from his fortitude, while it adds infinitely to the honour of his humanity. I am very sorry to say it, very sorry indeed, that such personages are in a situation in which it is not becoming in us to praise the virtues of the great.

I hear, and I rejoice to hear, that the great lady, the other object of the triumph, has borne that day, (one is interested that beings made for suffering should suffer well,) and that she bears all the succeeding days, that she bears the imprisonment of her husband, and her own captivity, and the exile of her friends, and the insulting adulation of addresses, and the whole weight of her accumulated wrongs, with a serene patience, in a manner suited to her rank and race, and becoming the offspring of a sovereign distinguished for her piety and her courage: that, like her, she has lofty sentiments; that she feels with the dignity of a Roman matron; that in the last extremity she will save herself from the last disgrace; and that, if she must fall, she will fall by no ignoble hand.

It is now sixteen or seventeen years since I saw the queen of France, then the dauphiness, at Versailles; and surely never lighted on this orb, which she hardly seemed to touch, a more delightful vision. I saw her just above the horizon, decorating and cheering the elevated sphere she just began to move in, —glittering like the morning-star, full of life, and splendour, and joy. Oh! what a revolution! and what a heart must I have to contemplate without emotion that elevation and that fall! Little did I dream when she added titles of veneration to those of enthusiastic, distant, respectful love, that she should ever be obliged to carry the sharp antidote against disgrace concealed in that bosom; little did I dream that I should have lived to see such disasters fallen upon her in a nation of gallant men, in a nation of men of honour, and of cavaliers. I thought ten thousand swords must have leaped from their scabbards to avenge even a look that threatened her with insult. But the age of chivalry is gone. That of sophisters, economists, and calculators, has succeeded; and the glory of Europe is extinguished for ever. Never, never more shall we behold that generous loyalty to rank and sex, that proud sub-mission, that dignified obedience, that subordination of the heart, which kept alive, even in servitude itself, the spirit of an exalted freedom. The unbought grace of life, the cheap defence of nations, the nurse of manly sentiment and heroic enterprise, is gone! It is gone, that sensibility of principle, that chastity of honour, which felt a stain like a wound, which inspired courage whilst it mitigated ferocity, which ennobled whatever it touched, and under which vice itself lost half its evil, by losing all its grossness.

This mixed system of opinion and sentiment had its origin in the ancient chivalry; and the principle, though varied in its appearance by the varying state of human affairs, subsisted and influenced through a long succession of generations, even to the time we live in. If it should ever be totally extinguished, the loss I fear will be great. It is this which has given its character to modern Europe. It is this which has distinguished it under all its forms of government, and distinguished it to its advantage, from the states of Asia, and possibly from those states which flourished in the most brilliant periods of the antique world. It was this, which, without confounding ranks, had produced a noble equality, and handed it down through all the gradations of social life. It was this opinion which mitigated kings into companions, and raised private men to be fellows with kings. Without force or opposition, it sub-dued the fierceness of pride and power; it obliged sovereigns to submit to the soft collar of social esteem, compelled stern authority to submit to elegance, and gave a dominating van-quisher of laws to be subdued by manners.

But now all is to be changed. All the pleasing illusions, which made power gentle and obedience liberal, which harmonized the different shades of life, and which, by a bland assimilation, incorporated into politics the sentiments which beautify and soften private society, are to be dissolved by this new conquering empire of light and reason. All the decent drapery of life is to be rudely torn off. All the superadded ideas, furnished from the wardrobe of a moral imagination, which the heart owns, and the understanding ratifies, as necessary to cover the defects of our naked, shivering nature, and to raise it to dignity in our own estimation, are to be exploded as a ridiculous, absurd, and antiquated fashion.

On this scheme of things, a king is but a man, a queen is but a woman; a woman is but an animal, and an animal not of the highest order. All homage paid to the sex in general as such, and without distinct views, is to be regarded as romance and folly. Regicide, and parricide, and sacrilege, are but fictions of superstition, corrupting jurisprudence by destroying its simplicity. The murder of a king, or a queen, or a bishop, or a father, are only common homicide; and if the people are by any chance, or in any way, gainers by it, a sort of homicide much the most pardonable, and into which we ought not to make too severe a scrutiny.

On the scheme of this barbarous philosophy, which is the offspring of cold hearts and muddy understandings, and which is as void of solid wisdom as it is destitute of all taste and elegance, laws are to be supported only by their own terrors, and by the concern which each individual may find in them from his own private speculations, or can spare to them from his own private interests. In the groves of *their* academy, at the end of every vista, you see nothing but the gallows. Nothing is left which engages the affections on the part of the commonwealth. On the principles of this mechanic philosophy, our institutions can never be embodied, if I may use the expression, in persons; so as to create in us love, veneration, admiration, or attachment. But that sort of reason which banishes the affections is incapable of filling their place. These public affections, combined with manners, are required sometimes as supplements, sometimes as correctives, always as aids to law. The precept given by a wise man, as well as a great critic, for the construction of poems, is equally true as to states:—*Non satis est pulchra esse poemata, dulcia sunto*.[15] There ought to be a system of manners in every nation, which a well-formed mind would be disposed to relish. To make us love our country, our country ought to be lovely.

But power, of some kind or other, will survive the shock in which manners and opinions perish; and it will find other and worse means for its support. The usurpation which, in order to subvert ancient institutions, has destroyed ancient principles, will hold power by arts similar to those by which it has acquired it. When the old feudal and chivalrous spirit of *fealty,* which, by freeing kings from fear, freed both kings and subjects from the precautions of tyranny, shall be extinct in the minds of men, plots and assassinations will be anticipated by preventive murder and preventive confiscation, and that long roll of grim and bloody maxims, which form the political code of all power, not standing on its own honour, and the honour of those who are to obey it. Kings will be tyrants from policy, when subjects are rebels from principle.

When ancient opinions and rules of life are taken away, the loss cannot possibly be estimated. From that moment we have no compass to govern us; nor can we know distinctly to what port we steer. Europe, undoubtedly, taken in a mass, was in a flourishing condition the day on which your revolution was completed. How much of that prosperous state was owing to the spirit of our old manners and opinions is not

---

[15] Horace, *Art of Poetry,* 1. 99.

easy to say; but as such causes cannot be indifferent in their operation, we must presume, that, on the whole, their operation was beneficial.

We are but too apt to consider things in the state in which we find them, without sufficiently adverting to the causes by which they have been produced, and possibly may be upheld. Nothing is more certain, than that our manners, our civilization, and all the good things which are connected with manners and with civilization, have, in this European world of ours, depended for ages upon two principles; and were indeed the result of both combined; I mean the spirit of a gentleman, and the spirit of religion. The nobility and the clergy, the one by profession, the other by patronage, kept learning in existence, even in the midst of arms and confusions, and whilst governments were rather in their causes, than formed. Learning paid back what it received to nobility and to priesthood; and paid it with usury, by enlarging their ideas, and by furnishing their minds. Happy if they had all continued to know their indissoluble union, and their proper place! Happy if learning, not debauched by ambition, had been satisfied to continue the instructor, and not aspired to be the master! Along with its natural protectors and guardians, learning will be cast into the mire, and trodden down under the hoofs of a swinish multitude.

If, as I suspect, modern letters owe more than they are always willing to own to ancient manners, so do other interests which we value full as much as they are worth. Even commerce, and trade, and manufacture, the gods of our economical politicians, are themselves perhaps but creatures; are themselves but effects, which, as first causes, we choose to worship. They certainly grew under the same shade in which learning flourished. They too may decay with their natural protecting principles. With you, for the present at least, they all threaten to disappear together. Where trade and manufactures are wanting to a people, and the spirit of nobility and religion remains, sentiment supplies, and not always ill supplies, their place; but if commerce and the arts should be lost in an experiment to try how well a state may stand without these old fundamental principles, what sort of a thing must be a nation of gross, stupid, ferocious, and, at the same time, poor and sordid, barbarians, destitute of religion, honour, or manly pride, possessing nothing at present, and hoping for nothing hereafter?

I wish you may not be going fast, and by the shortest cut, to that horrible and disgustful situation. Already there appears a poverty of conception, a coarseness and vulgarity, in all the proceedings of the Assembly and of all their instructors. Their liberty is not liberal. Their science is presumptuous ignorance. Their humanity is savage and brutal.

It is not clear, whether in England we learned those grand and decorous principles and manners, of which considerable traces yet remain, from you, or whether you took them from us. But to you, I think, we trace them best. You seem to me to be—*gentis incunabula nostræ*.[16] France has always more or less influenced manners in England; and when your fountain is choked up and polluted, the stream will not run long, or not run clear, with us, or perhaps with any nation. This gives all Europe, in my opinion, but too close and connected a concern in what is done in France. Excuse me, therefore, if I have dwelt too long on the atrocious spectacle of the 6th of October, 1789, or have given too much scope to the reflections which have arisen in my mind on occasion of the most important of all revolutions, which may be dated from that day, I mean a revolution in sentiments, manners, and moral opinions. As things now stand, with everything respectable destroyed without us, and an attempt to destroy within us every principle of respect, one is almost forced to apologize for harbouring the common feelings of men.

---

[16] Virgil, *Aeneid,* III. 105.

Why do I feel so differently from the Reverend Dr. Price, and those of his lay flock who will choose to adopt the sentiments of his discourse?—For this plain reason—because it is *natural* I should; because we are so made, as to be affected at such spectacles with melancholy sentiments upon the unstable condition of mortal prosperity, and the tremendous uncertainty of human greatness; because in those natural feelings we learn great lessons; because in events like these our passions instruct our reason; because when kings are hurled from their thrones by the Supreme Director of this great drama, and become the objects of insult to the base, and of pity to the good, we behold such disasters in the moral, as we should behold a miracle in the physical, order of things. We are alarmed into reflection; our minds (as it has long since been observed) are purified by terror and pity; our weak, unthinking pride is humbled under the dispensations of a mysterious wisdom. Some tears might be drawn from me, if such a spectacle were exhibited on the stage. I should be truly ashamed of finding in myself that superficial, theatric sense of painted distress, whilst I could exult over it in real life. With such a perverted mind, I could never venture to show my face at a tragedy. People would think the tears that Garrick formerly, or that Siddons not long since, have extorted from me, were the tears of hypocrisy; I should know them to be the tears of folly.

Indeed the theatre is a better school of moral sentiments than churches, where the feelings of humanity are thus outraged. Poets who have to deal with an audience not yet graduated in the school of the rights of men, and who must apply themselves to the moral constitution of the heart, would not dare to produce such a triumph as a matter of exultation. There, where men follow their natural impulses, they would not bear the odious maxims of a Machiavelian policy, whether applied to the attainment of monarchial or democratic tyranny. They would reject them on the modern.

as they once did on the ancient stage, where they could not bear even the hypothetical proposition of such wickedness in the mouth of a personated tyrant, though suitable to the character he sustained. No theatric audience in Athens would bear what has been borne, in the midst of the real tragedy of this triumphal day; a principal actor weighing, as it were in scales hung in a shop of horrors,—so much actual crime against so much contingent advantage,—and after putting in and out weights, declaring that the balance was on the side of the advantages. They would not bear to see the crimes of new democracy posted as in a ledger against the crimes of old despotism, and the bookkeepers of politics finding democracy still in debt, but by no means unable or unwilling to pay the balance. In the theatre, the first intuitive glance, without any elaborate process of reasoning, will show, that this method of political computation would justify every extent of crime. They would see, that on these principles, even where the very worst acts were not perpetrated, it was owing rather to the fortune of the conspirators, than to their parsimony in the expenditure of treachery and blood. They would soon see, that criminal means once tolerated are soon preferred. They present a shorter cut to the object than through the highway of the moral virtues. Justifying perfidy and murder for public benefit, public benefit would soon become the pretext, and perfidy and murder the end; until rapacity, malice, revenge, and fear more dreadful than revenge, could satiate their insatiable appetites. Such must be the consequences of losing, in the splendour of these triumphs of the rights of men, all natural sense of wrong and right.

But the reverend pastor exults in this "leading in triumph," because truly Louis the Sixteenth was "an arbitrary monarch;" that is, in other words, neither more nor less than because he was Louis the Sixteenth, and because he had the misfortune to be born king of France, with the prerogatives of

which, a long line of ancestors, and a long acquiescence of
the people, without any act of his, had put him in possession.
A misfortune it has indeed turned out to him, that he was
born king of France. But misfortune is not crime, nor is
indiscretion always the greatest guilt. I shall never think that
a prince, the acts of whose whole reign was a series of concessions to his subjects, who was willing to relax his authority,
to remit his prerogatives, to call his people to a share of
freedom, not known, perhaps not desired, by their ancestors;
such a prince, though he should be subjected to the common
frailties attached to men and to princes, though he should have
once thought it necessary to provide force against the
desperate designs manifestly carrying on against his person,
and the remnants of his authority; though all this should be
taken into consideration, I shall be led with great difficulty to
think he deserves the cruel and insulting triumph of Paris,
and of Dr. Price. I tremble for the cause of liberty, from such
an example to kings. I tremble for the cause of humanity, in
the unpunished outrages of the most wicked of mankind. But
there are some people of that low and degenerate fashion of
mind, that they look up with a sort of complacent awe and
admiration to kings, who know how to keep firm in their
seat, to hold a strict hand over their subjects, to assert their
prerogative, and, by the awakened vigilance of a severe
despotism, to guard against the very first approaches of freedom. Against such as these they never elevate their voice.
Deserters from principle, listed with fortune, they never see
any good in suffering virtue, nor any crime in prosperous
usurpation. . . .

I have often been astonished, considering that we are
divided from you but by a slender dyke of about twenty-four
miles, and that the mutual intercouse between the two
countries has lately been very great, to find how little you
seem to know of us. I suspect that this is owing to your forming a judgment of this nation from certain publications,

which do, very erroneously, if they do at all, represent the opinions and dispositions generally prevalent in England. The vanity, restlessness, petulance, and spirit of intrigue, of several petty cabals, who attempt to hide their total want of consequence in bustle and noise, and puffing, and mutual quotation of each other, makes you imagine that our contemptuous neglect of their abilities is a mark of general acquiescence in their opinions. No such thing, I assure you. Because half a dozen grasshoppers under a fern make the field ring with their importunate chink, whilst thousands of great cattle, reposed beneath the shadow of the British oak, chew the cud and are silent, pray do not imagine that those who make the noise are the only inhabitants of the field; that, of course, they are many in number; or that, after all, they are other than the little, shrivelled, meagre, hopping, though loud and troublesome, insects of the hour.

I almost venture to affirm, that not one in a hundred amongst us participates in the "triumph" of the Revolution Society. If the king and queen of France, and their children, were to fall into our hands by the chance of war, in the most acrimonious of all hostilities, (I deprecate such an event, I deprecate such hostility,) they would be treated with another sort of triumphal entry into London. We formerly have had a king of France in that situation; you have read how he was treated by the victor in the field; and in what manner he was afterwards received in England. Four hundred years have gone over us; but I believe we are not materially changed since that period. Thanks to our sullen resistance to innovation, thanks to the cold sluggishness of our national character, we still bear the stamp of our forefathers. We have not (as I conceive) lost the generosity and dignity of thinking of the fourteenth century; nor as yet have we subtilized ourselves into savages. We are not the converts of Rousseau; we are not the disciples of Voltaire; Helvetius has made no progress amongst us. Atheists are not our preachers; madmen

are not our lawgivers. We know that *we* have made no discoveries, and we think that no discoveries are to be made, in
morality; nor many in the great principles of government, nor
in the ideas of liberty, which were understood long before we
were born, altogether as well as they will be after the grave
has heaped its mould upon our presumption, and the silent
tomb shall have imposed its law on our pert loquacity. In
England we have not yet been completely embowelled of our
natural entrails; we still feel within us, and we cherish and
cultivate, those inbred sentiments which are the faithful
guardians, the active monitors of our duty, the true supporters of all liberal and manly morals. We have not been
drawn and trussed, in order that we may be filled, like
stuffed birds in a museum, with chaff and rags and paltry
blurred shreds of paper about the rights of man. We preserve the whole of our feelings still native and entire,
unsophisticated by pedantry and infidelity. We have real
hearts of flesh and blood beating in our bosoms. We fear
God; we look up with awe to kings; with affection to parliaments; with duty to magistrates; with reverence to priests; and
with respect to nobility.[17] Why? Because such ideas are
brought before our minds, it is *natural* to be so affected;
because all other feelings are false and spurious, and tend to
corrupt our minds, to vitiate our primary morals, to render
us unfit for rational liberty; and by teaching us a servile,
licentious, and abandoned insolence, to be our low sport for
a few holidays, to make us perfectly fit for, and justly deserving of, slavery, through the whole course of our lives.

---

[17] The English are, I conceive, misrepresented in a letter published in
one of the papers, by a gentleman thought to be a dissenting minister.—
When writing to Dr. Price of the spirit which prevails at Paris, he says,
"The spirit of the people in this place has abolished all the proud
distinctions which the *king* and *nobles* had usurped in their minds;
whether they talk of *the king, the noble, or the priest,* their whole
language is that of the most *enlightened and liberal amongst the English.*" If this gentleman means to confine the terms *enlightened and
liberal* to one set of men in England, it may be true. It is not generally
so. [Burke]

You see, Sir, that in this enlightened age I am bold enough to confess, that we are generally men of untaught feeling; that instead of casting away all our old prejudices, we cherish them to a very considerable degree, and, to take more shame to ourselves, we cherish them because they are prejudices; and the longer they have lasted, and the more generally they have prevailed, the more we cherish them. We are afraid to put men to live and trade each on his own private stock of reason; because we suspect that this stock in each man is small, and that the individuals would do better to avail themselves of the general bank and capital of nations and of ages. Many of our men of speculation, instead of exploding general prejudices, employ their sagacity to discover the latent wisdom which prevails in them. If they find what they seek, and they seldom fail, they think it more wise to continue the prejudice, with the reason involved, than to cast away the coat of prejudice, and to leave nothing but the naked reason; because prejudice, with its reason, has a motive to give action to that reason, and an affection which will give it permanence. Prejudice is of ready application in the emergency; it previously engages the mind in a steady course of wisdom and virtue, and does not leave the man hesitating in the moment of decision, sceptical, puzzled, and unresolved. Prejudice renders a man's virtue his habit; and not a series of unconnected acts. Through just prejudice, his duty becomes a part of his nature.

Your literary men, and your politicians, and so do the whole clan of the enlightened among us, essentially differ in these points. They have no respect for the wisdom of others; but they pay it off by a very full measure of confidence in their own. With them it is a sufficient motive to destroy an old scheme of things, because it is an old one. As to the new, they are in no sort of fear with regard to the duration of a building run up in haste; because duration is no object to those who think little or nothing has been done before their time, and who place all their hopes in discovery. They conceive, very systematically, that all things which give perpetuity are mischievous, and therefore they are at inexpiable war with all establishments. They think that government may vary like modes of dress, and with as little ill effect: that there needs no principle of attachment, except a sense of present conveniency, to any constitution of the state. They always speak as if they were of opinion that there is a singular species of compact between them and their magistrates, which binds the magistrate, but which has nothing reciprocal in it, but that the majesty of the people has a right to dissolve it without any reason, but its will. Their attachment to their country itself is only so far as it agrees with some of their fleeting projects; it begins and ends with that scheme of polity which falls in with their momentary opinion.

These doctrines, or rather sentiments, seem prevalent with your new statesmen. But they are wholly different from those on which we have always acted in this country.

I hear it is sometimes given out in France, that what is doing among you is after the example of England. I beg leave to affirm, that scarcely anything done with you has originated from the practice or the prevalent opinions of this people, either in the act or in the spirit of the proceeding. Let me add, that we are as unwilling to learn these lessons from France, as we are sure that we never taught them to that nation. The cabals here, who take a sort of share in your transactions, as yet consist of but a handful of people. If unfortunately by their intrigues, their sermons, their publications, and by a confidence derived from an expected union with the counsels and forces of the French nation, they should draw considerable numbers into their faction, and in consequence should seriously attempt anything here in imitation of what has been done with you, the event, I dare venture to prophesy, will be, that, with some trouble to their country, they will soon accomplish their own destruction. This people refused to change their law in remote ages from respect to the infallibility of popes; and they will not now alter it from a pious implicit faith in the dogmatism of philosophers; though the former was armed with the anathema and crusade, and though the latter should act with the libel and the lamp-iron.

Formerly your affairs were your own concern only. We felt for them as men; but we kept aloof from them, because we were not citizens of France. But when we see the model held up to ourselves, we must feel as Englishmen, and feeling, we must provide as Englishmen. Your affairs, in spite of us, are made a part of our interest; so far at least as to keep at a distance your panacea, or your plague. If it be a panacea, we do not want it. We know the consequences of unnecessary physic. If it be a plague, it is such a plague that the precautions of the most severe quarantine ought to be established against it.

I hear on all hands that a cabal, calling itself philosophic, receives the glory of many of the late proceedings; and that their opinions and systems are the true actuating spirit of the whole of them. I have heard of no party in England, literary or political, at any time, known by such a description. It is not with you composed of those men, is it? whom the vulgar, in their blunt, homely style, commonly call atheists and infidels? If it be, I admit that we too have had writers of that description, who made some noise in their day. At present they repose in lasting oblivion. Who, born within the last forty years, has read one word of Collins, and Toland, and Tindal, and Chubb, and Morgan, and that whole race who called themselves Freethinkers? Who now reads Bolingbroke? Who ever read him through? Ask the booksellers of London what is become of all these lights of the world. In a few years their few successors will go to the family vault of "all the Capulets." But whatever they were, or are, with us, they were and are wholly unconnected individuals. With us they kept the common nature of their kind, and were not gregarious. They never acted in corps, or were known as a faction in the state, nor presumed to influence in that name or character, or for the purposes of such a faction, on any of our public concerns. Whether they ought so to exist, and so be permitted to act, is another question. As such cabals have not existed in England, so neither has the spirit of them had any influence in establishing the original frame of our constitution, or in any one of the several reparations and improvements it has undergone. The whole has been done under the auspices, and is confirmed by the sanctions, of religion and piety. The whole has emanated from the simplicity of our national character, and from a sort of native plainness and directness of understanding, which for a long time characterized those men who have successively obtained authority amongst us. This disposition still remains; at least in the great body of the people.

We know, and what is better, we feel inwardly, that religion is the basis of civil society, and the source of all good and of all comfort. In England we are so convinced of this, that there is no rust of superstition, with which the accumulated absurdity of the human mind might have crusted it over in the course of ages, that ninety-nine in a hundred of the people of England would not prefer to impiety. We shall never be such fools as to call in an enemy to the substance of any system to remove its corruptions, to supply its defects, or to perfect its construction. If our religious tenets should ever want a further elucidation, we shall not call on atheism to explain them. We shall not light up our temple from that unhallowed fire. It will be illuminated with other lights. It will be perfumed with other incense, than the infectious stuff which is imported by the smugglers of adulterated metaphysics. If our ecclesiastical establishment should want a revision, it is not avarice or rapacity, public or private, that we shall employ for the audit, or receipt, or application of its consecrated revenue. Violently condemning neither the Greek nor the Armenian, nor, since heats are subsided, the Roman system of religion, we prefer the Protestant; not because we think it has less of the Christian religion in it, but because, in our judgment it has more. We are Protestants, not from indifference, but from zeal.

We know, and it is our pride to know, that man is by his constitution a religious animal; that atheism is against, not only our reason, but our instincts; and that it cannot prevail long. But if, in the moment of riot, and in a drunken delirium from the hot spirit drawn out of the alembic of hell, which in France is now so furiously boiling, we should uncover our nakedness, by throwing off that Christian religion which has hitherto been our boast and comfort, and one great source of civilization amongst us, and amongst many other nations, we are apprehensive (being well aware that the mind will not endure a void) that some uncouth, pernicious, and degrading superstition might take place of it.

For that reason, before we take from our establishment the natural, human means of estimation, and give it up to contempt, as you have done, and in doing it have incurred the penalties you well deserve to suffer, we desire that some other may be presented to us in the place of it. We shall then form our judgment.

On these ideas, instead of quarrelling with establishments, as some do, who have made a philosophy and a religion of their hostility to such institutions, we cleave closely to them. We are resolved to keep an established church, and established monarchy, an established aristocracy, and an established democracy, each in the degree it exists, and in no greater. I shall show you presently how much each of these we possess.

It has been the misfortune (not, as these gentlemen think it, the glory) of this age, that everything is to be discussed, as if the constitution of our country were to be always a subject rather of altercation, than enjoyment. For this reason, as well as for the satisfaction of those among you (if any such you have among you) who may wish to profit of examples, I venture to trouble you with a few thoughts upon each of these establishments. I do not think they were unwise in ancient Rome, who, when they wished to new-model their laws, set commissioners to examine the best constituted republics within their reach.

First, I beg leave to speak of our church establishment, which is the first of our prejudices, not a prejudice destitute of reason, but involving in it profound and extensive wisdom. I speak of it first. It is first, and last, and midst in our minds. For, taking ground on that religious system, of which we are now in possession, we continue to act on the early received and uniformly continued sense of mankind. That sense not only, like a wise architect, hath built up the august fabric of states, but like a provident proprietor, to preserve the structure from profanation and ruin, as a sacred temple purged from all the impurities of fraud, and violence, and injustice, and tyranny, hath solemnly and for ever consecrated the commonwealth, and all that officiate in it. This consecration is made, that all who administer in the government of men, in which they stand in the person of God himself, should have high and worthy notions of their function and destination; that their hope should be full of immortality; that they should not look to the paltry pelf of the moment, nor to the temporary and transient praise of the vulgar, but to a solid, permanent existence, in the permanent part of their nature, and to a permanent fame and glory, in the example they leave as a rich inheritance to the world.

Such sublime principles ought to be infused into persons of exalted situations; and religious establishments provided, that may continually revive and enforce them. Every sort of moral, every sort of civil, every sort of politic institution, aiding the rational and natural ties that connect the human understanding and affections to the divine, are not more than necessary, in order to build up that wonderful structure, Man; whose prerogative it is, to be in a great degree a creature of his own making; and who, when made as he ought to be made, is destined to hold no trivial place in the creation. But whenever man is put over men, as the better nature ought ever to preside, in that case more particularly, he should as nearly as possible be approximated to his perfection.

The consecration of the state, by a state religious establishment, is necessary also to operate with a wholesome awe upon free citizens; because, in order to secure their freedom, they must enjoy some determinate portion of power. To them therefore a religion connected with the state, and with their duty towards it, becomes even more necessary than in such societies, where the people, by the terms of their subjection, are confined to private sentiments, and the management of their own family concerns. All persons possessing any portion of power ought to be strongly and awfully impressed with an idea that they act in trust: and that they are to account for their conduct in that trust to the one great Master, Author, and Founder of society.

This principle ought even to be more strongly impressed upon the minds of those who compose the collective sovereignty, than upon those of single princes. Without instruments, these princes can do nothing. Whoever uses instruments, in finding helps, finds also impediments. Their power is therefore by no means complete; nor are they safe in extreme abuse. Such persons, however elevated by flattery, arrogance, and self-opinion, must be sensible, that, whether covered or not by positive law, in some way or other they are accountable even here for the abuse of their trust. If they are not cut off by a rebellion of their people, they may be strangled by the very janissaries kept for their security against all other rebellion. Thus we have seen the king of France sold by his soldiers for an increase of pay. But where popular authority is absolute and unrestrained, the people have an infinitely greater, because a far better founded, confidence in their own power. They are themselves, in a great measure, their own instruments. They are nearer to their objects. Besides, they are less under responsibility to one of the greatest controlling powers on earth, the sense of fame and estimation. The share of infamy, that is likely to fall to the lot of each individual in public acts, is small indeed; the operation of opinion being in the inverse ratio to the number of those who abuse power. Their own approbation of their own acts has to them the appearance of a public judgment in their favour. A perfect democracy is therefore the most shameless thing in the world. As it is the most shameless, it is also the most fearless. No man apprehends in his person that he can be made subject to punishment. Certainly the people at large never ought: for as all punishments are for example towards the conservation of the people at large, the people at large can never become the subject of punishment by human hand. It is therefore of infinite importance that they should not be suffered to imagine that their will, any more than that of kings, is the standard of right and wrong. They ought to be persuaded that they are full as little entitled, and far less qualified, with safety to themselves, to use any arbitrary power whatsoever; that therefore they are not, under a false show of liberty, but in truth, to exercise an unnatural, inverted domination, tyrannically to exact, from those who officiate in the state, not an entire devotion to their interest, which is their right, but an abject submission to their occasional will; extinguishing thereby, in all those who serve them, all moral principle, all sense of dignity, all use of judgment, and all consistency of character; whilst by the very same process they give themselves up a proper, a suitable, but a most contemptible prey to the servile ambition of popular sycophants, or courtly flatterers.

When the people have emptied themselves of all the lust of selfish will, which without religion it is utterly impossible they ever should, when they are conscious that they exercise, and exercise perhaps in a higher link of the order of delegation, the power, which to be legitimate must be according to that eternal, immutable law, in which will and reason are the same, they will be more careful how they place power in base and incapable hands. In their nomination to office, they will not appoint to the exercise of authority, as to a pitiful job, but as to a holy function; not according to their sordid, selfish interest, nor to their wanton caprice, nor to their arbitrary will; but they will confer that power (which any man may well tremble to give or to receive) on those only, in whom they may discern that predominant proportion of active virtue and wisdom, taken together and fitted to the charge, such, as in the great and inevitable mixed mass of human imperfections and infirmities, is to be found.

When they are habitually convinced that no evil can be acceptable, either in the act or the permission, to him whose essence is good, they will be better able to extirpate out of the minds of all magistrates, civil, ecclesiastical, or military, anything that bears the least resemblance to a proud and lawless domination.

But one of the first and most leading principles on which the commonwealth and the laws are consecrated, is lest the temporary possessors and life-renters in it, unmindful of what they have received from their ancestors, or of what is due to their posterity, should act as if they were the entire masters; that they should not think it among their rights to cut off the entail, or commit waste on the inheritance, by destroying at their pleasure the whole original fabric of their society; hazarding to leave to those who come after them a ruin instead of an habitation—and teaching these successors as little to respect their contrivances, as they had themselves respected the institutions of their forefathers. By this unprincipled facility of changing the state as often, and as much, and in as many ways, as there are floating fancies or fashions, the whole chain and continuity of the commonwealth would be broken. No one generation could link with the other. Men would become little better than the flies of a summer.

And first of all, the science of jurisprudence, the pride of the human intellect, which, with all its defects, redundancies, and errors, is the collected reason of ages, combining the principles of original justice with the infinite variety of human concerns, as a heap of old exploded errors, would be no longer studied. Personal self-sufficiency and arrogance (the certain attendants upon all those who have never experienced a wisdom greater than their own) would usurp the tribunal. Of course no certain laws, establishing invariable grounds of hope and fear, would keep the actions of men in a certain course, or direct them to a certain end. Nothing stable in the modes of holding property, or exercising function, could form a solid ground on which any parent could speculate in the education of his offspring, or in a choice for their future establishment in the world. No principles would be early worked into the habits. As soon as the most able instructor had completed his laborious course of instruction, instead of sending forth his pupil, accomplished in a virtuous discipline, fitted to procure him attention and respect, in his place in society, he would find everything altered; and that he had turned out a poor creature to the contempt and derision of the world, ignorant of the true grounds of estimation. Who would insure a tender and delicate sense of honour to beat almost with the first pulses of the heart, when no man could know what would be the test of honour in a nation, continually varying the standard of its coin? No part of life would retain its acquisitions. Barbarism with regard to science and literature, unskilfulness with regard to arts and manufactures, would infallibly succeed to the want of a steady education and settled principle; and thus the commonwealth itself would, in a few generations, crumble away, be disconnected into the dust and powder of individuality, and at length dispersed to all the winds of heaven.

To avoid therefore the evils of inconstancy and versatility, ten thousand times worse than those of obstinacy and the blindest prejudice, we have consecrated the state, that no man should approach to look into its defects or corruptions but with due caution; that he should never dream of beginning its reformation by its subversion; that he should approach to the faults of the state as to the wounds of a father, with pious awe and trembling solicitude. By this wise prejudice we are taught to look with horror on those children of their country, who are prompt rashly to hack that aged parent in pieces, and put him into the kettle of magicians, in hopes that by their poisonous weeds, and wild incantations, they may regenerate the paternal constitution, and renovate their father's life.

Society is indeed a contract. Subordinate contracts for objects of mere occasional interest may be dissolved at pleasure— but the state ought not to be considered as nothing better than a partnership agreement in a trade of pepper and coffee, calico or tobacco, or some other such low concern, to be taken up for a little temporary interest, and to be dissolved by the fancy of the parties. It is to be looked on with other reverence; because it is not a partnership in things subservient only to the gross animal existence of a temporary and perishable nature. It is a partnership in all science; a partnership in all art; a partnership in every virtue, and in all perfection. As the ends of such a partnership cannot be obtained in many generations, it becomes a partnership not only between those who are living, but between those who are living, those who are dead, and those who are to be born. Each contract of each particular state is but a clause in the great primæval contract of eternal society, linking the lower with the higher natures, connecting the visible and invisible world, according to a fixed compact sanctioned by the inviolable oath which holds all physical and all moral natures, each in their appointed place. This law is not subject to the will of those, who by an obligation above them, and infinitely superior, are bound to submit their will to that law. The municipal corporations of that universal kingdom are not morally at liberty at their pleasure, and on their speculations of a contingent improvement, wholly to separate and tear asunder the bands of their subordinate community, and to dissolve it into an unsocial, uncivil, unconnected chaos of elementary principles. It is the first and supreme necessity only, a necessity that is not chosen, but chooses, a necessity paramount to deliberation, that admits no discussion, and demands no evidence, which alone can justify a resort to anarchy. This necessity is no exception to the rule; because this necessity itself is a part too of that moral and physical disposition of things, to which man must be obedient by consent or force: but if that which is only submission to necessity should be made the object of choice, the law is broken, nature is disobeyed, and the rebellious are outlawed, cast forth, and exiled, from this world of reason, and order, and peace, and virtue, and fruitful penitence, into the antagonist world of madness, discord, vice, confusion, and unavailing sorrow. . . .

You may suppose that we do not approve your confiscation of the revenues of bishops, and deans, and chapters, and parochial clergy possessing independent estates arising from land, because we have the same sort of establishment in England. That objection, you will say, cannot hold as to the confiscation of the goods of monks and nuns, and the abolition of their order. It is true that this particular part of your general confiscation does not affect England, as a precedent in point: but the reason implies, and it goes a great way. The long parliament confiscated the lands of deans and chapters in England on the same ideas upon which your assembly set to sale the lands of the monastic orders. But it is in the principle of injustice that the danger lies, and not in the description of persons on whom it is first exercised. I see, in a country very near us, a course of policy pursued, which sets justice, the common concern of mankind, at defiance. With the National Assembly of France, possession is nothing, law and usage are nothing. I see the National Assembly openly reprobate the doctrine of prescription, which one of the greatest of their own lawyers tells us, with great truth, is a part of the law of nature. He tells us, that the positive ascertainment of its limits, and its security from invasion, were among the causes for which civil society itself has been instituted. If prescription be once shaken, no species of property is secure, when it once becomes an object large enough to tempt the cupidity of indigent power. I see a practice perfectly correspondent to their contempt of this great fundamental part of natural law. I see the confiscators begin with bishops, and chapters, and monasteries; but I do not see them end there. I see the princes of the blood, who, by the oldest usages of that kingdom, held large landed estates, (hardly with the compliment of a debate,) deprived of their possessions, and, in lieu of their stable, independent property, reduced to the hope of some precarious, charitable pension, at the pleasure of an assembly, which of course will pay little regard to the rights of pensioners at pleasure, when it despises those of legal proprietors. Flushed with the insolence of their first inglorious victories, and pressed by the distresses caused by their lust of unhallowed lucre, disappointed but not discouraged, they have at length ventured completely to subvert all property of all descriptions throughout the extent of a great kingdom. They have compelled all men, in all transactions of commerce, in the disposal of lands, in civil dealing, and through the whole communion of life, to accept as perfect payment and good and lawful tender, the symbols of their speculations on a projected sale of their plunder. What vestiges of liberty or property have they left? The tenant-right of a cabbage-garden, a year's interest in a hovel, the good-will of an ale-house or a baker's shop, the very shadow of a constructive property, are more ceremoniously treated in our parliament, than with you the oldest and most valuable landed possessions, in the hands of the most respectable personages, or than the whole body of the monied and commercial interest of your country. We entertain a high opinion of the legislative authority; but we have never dreamt that parliaments had any right whatever to violate property, to overrule prescription, or to force a currency of their own fiction in the place of that which is real, and recognised by the law of nations. But you, who began with refusing to submit to the most moderate restraints, have ended by establishing an unheard-of despotism. I find the ground upon which your confiscators go is this; that indeed their proceedings could not be supported in a court of justice; but that the rules of prescription cannot bind a legislative assembly.[18] So that this legislative assembly of a free nation sits, not for the security, but for the destruction, of property, and not of property only, but of every rule and maxim which can give it stability, and of those instruments which can alone give it circulation.

When the Anabaptists of Munster, in the sixteenth century, had filled Germany with confusion, by their system of levelling, and their wild opinions concerning property, to what country in Europe did not the progress of their fury furnish just cause of alarm? Of all things, wisdom is the most terrified with epidemical fanaticism, because of all enemies it is that against which she is the least able to furnish any kind of resource. We cannot be ignorant of the spirit of atheistical fanaticism, that is inspired by a multitude of writings, dispersed with incredible assiduity and expense, and by sermons delivered in all the streets and places of public resort in Paris. These writings and sermons have filled the populace with a black and savage atrocity of mind, which supersedes in them

---

[18] Speech of Mr. Camus, published by order of the National Assembly. [Burke]

the common feelings of nature, as well as all sentiments of morality and religion; insomuch that these wretches are induced to bear with a sullen patience the intolerable distresses brought upon them by the violent convulsions and permutations that have been made in property. The spirit of proselytism attends this spirit of fanaticism. They have societies to cabal and correspond at home and abroad for the propagation of their tenets. The republic of Berne, one of the happiest, the most prosperous, and the best governed countries upon earth, is one of the great objects, at the destruction of which they aim. I am told they have in some measure succeeded in sowing there the seeds of discontent. They are busy throughout Germany. Spain and Italy have not been untried. England is not left out of the comprehensive scheme of their malignant charity: and in England we find those who stretch out their arms to them, who recommend their example from more than one pulpit, and who choose in more than one periodical meeting, publicly to correspond with them, to applaud them, and to hold them up as objects for imitation; who receive from them tokens of confraternity, and standards consecrated amidst their rights and mysteries, who suggest to them leagues of perpetual amity, at the very time when the power, to which our constitution has exclusively delegated the federative capacity of this kingdom, may find it expedient to make war upon them.

It is not the confiscation of our church property from this example in France that I dread, though I think this would be no trifling evil. The great source of my solicitude is, lest it should ever be considered in England as the policy of a state to seek a resource in confiscations of any kind; or that any one description of citizens should be brought to regard any of the others as their proper prey. Nations are wading deeper and deeper into an ocean of boundless debt. Public debts, which at first were a security to governments, by interesting many in the public tranquillity, are likely in their excess to become

the means of their subversion. If governments provide for
these debts by heavy impositions, they perish by becoming
odious to the people. If they do not provide for them they
will be undone by the efforts of the most dangerous of all
parties; I mean an extensive, discontented monied interest, injured and not destroyed. The men who compose this interest
look for their security, in the first instance, to the fidelity of
government; in the second, to its power. If they find the old
governments effete, worn out, and with their springs relaxed,
so as not to be of sufficient vigour for their purposes, they
may seek new ones that shall be possessed of more energy;
and this energy will be derived, not from an acquisition of
resources, but from a contempt of justice. . . .

Rage and phrensy will pull down more in half an hour,
than prudence, deliberation, and foresight can build up in a
hundred years. The errors and defects of old establishments
are visible and palpable. It calls for little ability to point them
out; and where absolute power is given, it requires but a word
wholly to abolish the vice and the establishment together.
The same lazy but restless disposition, which loves sloth and
hates quiet, directs the politicians, when they come to work
for supplying the place of what they have destroyed. To make
everything the reverse of what they have seen is quite as easy
as to destroy. No difficulties occur in what has never been
tried. Criticism is almost baffled in discovering the defects
of what has not existed; and eager enthusiasm and cheating
hope have all the wide field of imagination, in which they
may expatiate with little or no opposition.

At once to preserve and to reform is quite another thing.
When the useful parts of an old establishment are kept, and
what is superadded is to be fitted to what is retained, a vigorous mind, steady, persevering attention, various powers of
comparison and combination, and the resources of an understanding fruitful in expedients, are to be exercised; they are to
be exercised in a continued conflict with the combined force

of opposite vices, with the obstinacy that rejects all improvement, and the levity that is fatigued and disgusted with everything of which it is in possession. But you may object—"A process of this kind is slow. It is not fit for an assembly, which glories in performing in a few months the work of ages. Such a mode of reforming, possibly, might take up many years." Without question it might; and it ought. It is one of the excellencies of a method in which time is amongst the assistants, that its operation is slow, and in some cases almost imperceptible. If circumspection and caution are a part of wisdom, when we work only upon inanimate matter, surely they become a part of duty too, when the subject of our demolition and construction is not brick and timber, but sentient beings, by the sudden alteration of whose state, condition, and habits, multitudes may be rendered miserable. But it seems as if it were the prevalent opinion in Paris, that an unfeeling heart, and an undoubting confidence, are the sole qualifications for a perfect legislator. Far different are my ideas of that high office. The true lawgiver ought to have a heart full of sensibility. He ought to love and respect his kind, and to fear himself. It may be allowed to his temperament to catch his ultimate object with an intuitive glance; but his movements towards it ought to be deliberate. Political arrangement, as it is a work for social ends, is to be only wrought by social means. There mind must conspire with mind. Time is required to produce that union of minds which alone can produce all the good we aim at. Our patience will achieve more than our force. If I might venture to appeal to what is so much out of fashion in Paris, I mean to experience, I should tell you, that in my course I have known, and, according to my measure, have co-operated with great men; and I have never yet seen any plan which has not been mended by the observations of those who were much inferior in understanding to the person who took the lead in the business. By a slow but well-sustained progress, the effect of each step is watched; the good or ill success of the first gives light to us in the second; and so, from light to light, we are conducted with safety through the whole series. We see that the parts of the system do not clash. The evils latent in the most promising contrivances are provided for as they arise. One advantage is as little as possible sacrificed to another. We compensate, we reconcile, we balance. We are enabled to unite into a consistent whole the various anomalies and contending principles that are found in the minds and affairs of men. From hence arises, not an excellence in simplicity, but one far superior, an excellence in composition. Where the great interests of mankind are concerned through a long succession of generations, that succession ought to be admitted into some share in the councils which are so deeply to affect them. If justice requires this, the work itself requires the aid of more minds than one age can furnish. It is from this view of things that the best legislators have been often satisfied with the establishment of some sure, solid, and ruling principle in government; a power like that which some of the philosophers have called a plastic nature; and having fixed the principle, they have left it afterwards to its own operation.

To proceed in this manner, that is, to proceed with a presiding principle, and a prolific energy, is with me the criterion of profound wisdom. What your politicians think the marks of a bold, hardy genius, are only proofs of a deplorable want of ability. By their violent haste and their defiance of the process of nature, they are delivered over blindly to every projector and adventurer, to every alchymist and empiric. They despair of turning to account anything that is common. Diet is nothing in their system of remedy. The worst of it is, that this their despair of curing common distempers by regular methods, arises not only from defect of comprehension, but, I fear, from some malignity of disposition. Your legislators seem to have taken their opinions of all professions, ranks, and offices, from the declamations and buffooneries of satirists;

who would themselves be astonished if they were held to the letter of their own descriptions. By listening only to these, your leaders regard all things only on the side of their vices and faults, and view those vices and faults under every colour of exaggeration. It is undoubtedly true, though it may seem paradoxical; but in general, those who are habitually employed in finding and displaying faults, are unqualified for the work of reformation: because their minds are not only unfurnished with patterns of the fair and good, but by habit they come to take no delight in the contemplation of those things. By hating vices too much, they come to love men too little. It is therefore not wonderful, that they should be indisposed and unable to serve them. From hence arises the complexional disposition of some of your guides to pull everything in pieces. At this malicious game they display the whole of their *quadrimanous* activity. As to the rest, the paradoxes of eloquent writers, brought forth purely as a sport of fancy, to try their talents, to rouse attention and excite surprise, are taken up by these gentlemen, not in the spirit of the original authors, as means of cultivating their taste and improving their style. These paradoxes become with them serious grounds of action, upon which they proceed in regulating the most important concerns of the state. Cicero ludicrously describes Cato as endeavouring to act, in the commonwealth, upon the school paradoxes, which exercised the wits of the junior students in the Stoic philosophy. If this was true of Cato, these gentlemen copy after him in the manner of some persons who lived about his time—*pede nudo Catonem.*[19] Mr. Hume told me that he had from Rousseau himself the secret of his principles of composition. That acute though eccentric observer had perceived, that to strike and interest the public, the marvellous must be produced; that the marvellous of the heathen mythology had long since lost its effects; that giants,

---

[19] Horace, *Epistles*, I. 19. 12-14. Horace ridicules those who, by "bare feet" and a sour face, think they imitate the austere virtue of Cato.

magicians, fairies, and heroes of romance which succeeded, had exhausted the portion of credulity which belonged to their age; that now nothing was left to the writer but that species of the marvellous which might still be produced, and with as great an effect as ever, though in another way; that is, the marvellous in life, in manners, in characters, and in extraordinary situations, giving rise to new and unlooked-for strokes in politics and morals. I believe, that were Rousseau alive, and in one of his lucid intervals, he would be shocked at the practical phrensy of his scholars, who in their paradoxes are servile imitators, and even in their incredulity discover an implicit faith. . . .

The legislators who framed the ancient republics knew that their business was too arduous to be accomplished with no better apparatus than the metaphysics of an under-graduate, and the mathematics and arithmetic of an exciseman. They had to do with men, and they were obliged to study human nature. They had to do with citizens, and they were obliged to study the effects of those habits which are communicated by the circumstances of civil life. They were sensible that the operation of this second nature on the first produced a new combination; and thence arose many diversities amongst men, according to their birth, their education, their professions, the periods of their lives, their residence in towns or in the country, their several ways of acquiring and of fixing property, and according to the quality of the property itself, all which rendered them as it were so many different species of animals. From hence they thought themselves obliged to dispose their citizens into such classes, and to place them in such situations in the state, as their peculiar habits might qualify them to fill, and to allot to them such appropriated privileges as might secure to them what their specific occasions required, and which might furnish to each description such force as might protect it in the conflict caused by the diversity of interests, that must exist, and must contend, in all complex society: for

the legislator would have been ashamed, that the coarse husbandman should well know how to assort and to use his
sheep, horses, and oxen, and should have enough of common
sense, not to abstract and equalize them all into animals, without providing for each kind an appropriate food, care, and
employment; whilst he, the economist, disposer, and shepherd
of his own kindred, subliming himself into an airy metaphysician, was resolved to know nothing of his flocks but as men
in general. It is for this reason that Montesquieu observed
very justly, that in their classification of the citizens, the great
legislators of antiquity made the greatest display of their
powers, and even soared above themselves. It is here that your
modern legislators have gone deep into the negative series,
and sunk even below their own nothing. As the first sort of
legislators attended to the different kinds of citizens, and
combined them into one commonwealth, the others, the
metaphysical and alchemistical legislators, have taken the
direct contrary course. They have attempted to confound all
sorts of citizens, as well as they could, into one homogeneous
mass; and then they divided this their amalgama into a number of incoherent republics. They reduce men to loose coun-
ters, merely for the sake of simple telling, and not to figures
whose power is to arise from their place in the table. The
elements of their own metaphysics might have taught them
better lessons. The troll of their categorical table might have
informed them that there was something else in the intellectual
world besides *substance* and *quantity*. They might learn from
the catechism of metaphysics that there were eight heads
more, in every complex deliberation, which they have never
thought of; though these, of all the ten, are the subjects on
which the skill of man can operate anything at all. . . .

It is boasted that the geometrical policy has been adopted,
that all local ideas should be sunk, and that the people should
no longer be Gascons, Picards, Bretons, Normans; but
Frenchmen, with one country, one heart, and one Assembly.

But instead of being all Frenchmen, the greater likelihood is, that the inhabitants of that region will shortly have no country. No man ever was attached by a sense of pride, partiality, or real affection, to a description of square measurement. He never will glory in belonging to the Chequer No. 71, or to any other badge-ticket. We begin our public affections in our families. No cold relation is a zealous citizen. We pass on to our neighbourhoods, and our habitual provincial connexions. These are inns and restingplaces. Such divisions of our country as have been formed by habit, and not by a sudden jerk of authority, were so many little images of the great country in which the heart found something which it could fill. The love to the whole is not extinguished by this subordinate partiality. Perhaps it is a sort of elemental training to those higher and more large regards, by which alone men come to be affected, as with their own concern, in the prosperity of a kingdom so extensive as that of France. . . .

What you may do finally does not appear; nor is it of much moment, whilst the strange and contradictory relation between your army and all the parts of your republic, as well as the puzzled relation of those parts to each other and to the whole, remain as they are. You seem to have given the provisional nomination of the officers, in the first instance, to the king, with a reserve of approbation by the National Assembly. Men who have an interest to pursue are extremely sagacious in discovering the true seat of power. They must soon perceive that those, who can negative indefinitely, in reality appoint. The officers must therefore look to their intrigues in that Assembly, as the sole, certain road to promotion. Still, however, by your new constitution they must begin their solicitation at court. This double negotiation for military rank seems to me a contrivance as well adapted, as if it were studied for no other end, to promote faction in the Assembly itself, relative to this vast military patronage; and then to poison the corps of officers with factions of a nature still more dangerous to the safety of government, upon any bottom on which it can be placed, and destructive in the end to the efficiency of the army itself. Those officers, who lose the promotions intended for them by the crown, must become of a faction opposite to that of the Assembly which has rejected their claims, and must nourish discontents in the heart of the army against the ruling powers. Those officers, on the other hand, who, by carrying their point through an interest in the Assembly, feel themselves to be at best only second in the goodwill of the crown, though first in that of the Assembly, must slight an authority which would not advance and could not retard their promotion. If to avoid these evils you will have no other rule for command or promotion than seniority, you will have an army of formality; at the same time it will become more independent, and more of a military republic. Not they, but the king is the machine. A king is not to be deposed by halves. If he is not everything in the command of an army, he is nothing. What is the effect of a power placed nominally at the head of the army, who to that army is no object of gratitude, or of fear? Such a cipher is not fit for the administration of an object, of all things the most delicate, the supreme command of military men. They must be constrained (and their inclinations lead them to what their necessities require) by a real, vigorous, effective, decided, personal authority. The authority of the Assembly itself suffers by passing through such a debilitating channel as they have chosen. The army will not long look to an assembly acting through the organ of false show, and palpable imposition. They will not seriously yield obedience to a prisoner. They will either despise a pageant, or they will pity a captive king. This relation of your army to the crown will, if I am not greatly mistaken, become a serious dilemma in your politics.

It is besides to be considered, whether an assembly like yours, even supposing that it was in possession of another sort of organ through which its orders were to pass, is fit for promoting the obedience and discipline of an army. It is known, that armies have hitherto yielded a very precarious and uncertain obedience to any senate, or popular authority; and they will least of all yield it to an assembly which is only to have a continuance of two years. The officers must totally lose the characteristic disposition of military men, if they see with perfect submission and due admiration, the dominion of pleaders; especially when they find that they have a new court to pay to an endless succession of those pleaders; whose military policy, and the genius of whose command, (if they should have any,) must be as uncertain as their duration is transient. In the weakness of one kind of authority, and in the fluctuation of all, the officers of an army will remain for some time mutinous and full of faction, until some popular general, who understands the art of conciliating the soldiery, and who possesses the true spirit of command, shall draw the eyes of all men upon himself. Armies will obey him on his personal account. There is no other way of securing military obedience in this state of things. But the moment in which that event shall happen, the person who really commands the army is your master; the master (that is little) of your king, the master of your Assembly, the master of your whole republic. . . .

To make a government requires no great prudence. Settle the seat of power; teach obedience: and the work is done. To give freedom is still more easy. It is not necessary to guide; it only requires to let go the rein. But to form a *free government;* that is, to temper together these opposite elements of liberty and restraint in one consistent work, requires much thought, deep reflection, a sagacious, powerful, and combining mind. This I do not find in those who take the lead in the National Assembly. Perhaps they are not so miserably deficient as they appear. I rather believe it. It would put them below the common level of human understanding. But when the leaders choose to make themselves bidders at an auction of popularity, their talents, in the construction of the state, will be of no service. They will become flatterers instead of legislators; the instruments, not the guides, of the people. If any of them should happen to propose a scheme of liberty, soberly limited, and defined with proper qualifications, he will be immediately outbid by his competitors, who will produce something more splendidly popular. Suspicions will be raised of his fidelity to his cause. Moderation will be stigmatized as the virtue of cowards; and compromise as the prudence of traitors: until, in hopes of preserving the credit which may enable him to temper, and moderate, on some occasions, the popular leader is obliged to become active in propagating doctrines, and establishing powers, that will afterwards defeat any sober purpose at which he ultimately might have aimed.

But am I so unreasonable as to see nothing at all that deserves commendation in the indefatigable labours of this Assembly? I do not deny that, among an infinite number of acts of violence and folly, some good may have been done. They who destroy everything certainly will remove some grievance. They who make everything new, have a chance that they may establish something beneficial. To give them credit for what they have done in virtue of the authority they have usurped, or which can excuse them in the crimes by which that authority has been acquired, it must appear, that the same things could not have been accomplished without producing such a revolution. Most assuredly they might; because almost every one of the regulations made by them, which is not very equivocal, was either in the cession of the king, voluntarily made at the meeting of the states, or in the concurrent instructions to the orders. Some usages have been abolished on just grounds; but they were such, that if they had stood as they were to all eternity, they would little detract from the happiness and prosperity of any state. The improvements of the National Assembly are superficial, their errors fundamental.

Whatever they are, I wish my countrymen rather to recommend to our neighbours the example of the British constitution, than to take models from them for the improvement of our own. In the former they have got an invaluable treasure. They are not, I think, without some causes of apprehension and complaint; but these they do not owe to their constitution, but to their own conduct. I think our happy situation owing to our constitution; but owing to the whole of it, and not any part singly; owing in a great measure to what we have left standing in our several reviews and reformations, as well as to what we have altered or superadded. Our people will find employment enough for a truly patriotic, free, and independent spirit, in guarding what they possess from violation. I would not exclude alteration neither; but even when I changed, it should be to preserve. I should be led to my remedy by a great grievance. In what I did, I should follow the example of our ancestors. I would make the reparation as nearly as possible in the style of the building. A politic caution, a guarded circumspection, a moral rather than a complexional timidity, were among the ruling principles of our forefathers in their most decided conduct. Not being illuminated with the light of which the gentlemen of France tell us they have got so abundant a share, they acted under a strong impression of the ignorance and fallibility of mankind. He that had made them thus fallible, rewarded them for having in their conduct attended to their nature. Let us imitate their caution, if we wish to deserve their fortune, or to retain their bequests. Let us add, if we please, but let us preserve what they have left; and standing on the firm ground of the British constitution, let us be satisfied to admire, rather than attempt to follow in their desperate flights, the aëronauts of France.

I have told you candidly my sentiments. I think they are not likely to alter yours. I do not know that they ought. You are young; you cannot guide, but must follow the fortune of your country. But hereafter they may be of some use to you, in some future form which your commonwealth may take. In the present it can hardly remain; but before its final settlement it may be obliged to pass, as one of our poets says, "through great varieties of untried beings," and in all its transmigrations to be purified by fire and blood.

I have little to recommend my opinions but long observation and much impartiality. They come from one who has been no tool of power, no flatterer of greatness; and who in his last acts does not wish to belie the tenour of his life. They come from one, almost the whole of whose public exertion has been a struggle for the liberty of others; from one in whose breast no anger durable or vehement has ever been kindled, but by what he considered as tyranny; and who snatches from his share in the endeavours which are used by good men to discredit opulent oppression, the hours he has employed on your affairs; and who in so doing persuades himself he has not departed from his usual office: they come from one who desires honours, distinctions, and emoluments, but little; and who expects them not at all; who has no contempt for fame, and no fear of obloquy; who shuns contention, though he will hazard an opinion: from one who wishes to preserve consistency, but who would preserve consistency by varying his means to secure the unity of his end; and, when the equipoise of the vessel in which he sails may be endangered by overloading it upon one side, is desirous of carrying the small weight of his reasons to that which may preserve its equipoise.

Thoughts on French Affairs

(DECEMBER, 1791)

In all our transactions with France, and at all periods, we have treated with that state on the footing of a monarchy. Monarchy was considered in all the external relations of that kingdom with every power in Europe as its legal and constitutional government, and that in which alone its federal capacity was vested.

It is not yet a year since Monsieur de Montmorin formally, and with as little respect as can be imagined to the king, and to all crowned heads, announced a total Revolution in that country. He has informed the British ministry that its frame of government is wholly altered,—that he is one of the ministers of the new system,—and, in effect, that the king is no longer his master, (nor does he even call him such,) but the *"first of the ministers,"* in the new system.

The second notification was that of the king's acceptance of the new Constitution, accompanied with fanfaronades in the modern style of the French bureaus: things which have much more the air and character of the saucy declamations of their clubs than the tone of regular office.

It has not been very usual to notify to foreign courts anything concerning the internal arrangements of any state. In the present case, the circumstance of these two notifications, with the observations with which they are attended, does not leave it in the choice of the sovereigns of Christendom to appear ignorant either of this French Revolution or (what is more important) of its principles.

We know, that, very soon after this manifesto of Monsieur de Montmorin, the king of France, in whose name it was made, found himself obliged to fly, with his whole family,— leaving behind him a declaration in which he disavows and annuls that Constitution, as having been the effect of force on his person and usurpation on his authority. It is equally notorious, that this unfortunate prince was, with many circumstances of insult and outrage, brought back prisoner by a deputation of the pretended National Assembly, and afterwards suspended by their authority from his government. Under equally notorious constraint, and under menaces of total deposition, he has been compelled to accept what they call a Constitution, and to agree to whatever else the usurped power which holds him in confinement thinks proper to impose.

His next brother, who had fled with him, and his third brother, who had fled before him, all the princes of his blood who remained faithful to him, and the flower of his magistracy, his clergy, and his nobility, continue in foreign countries, protesting against all acts done by him in his present situation, on the grounds upon which he had himself protested against them at the time of his flight,—with this addition, that they deny his very competence (as on good grounds they may) to abrogate the royalty, or the ancient constitutional orders of the kingdom. In this protest they are joined by three hundred of the late Assembly itself, and, in effect, by a great part of the French nation. The new government (so far as the people dare to disclose their sentiments) is disdained, I am persuaded, by the greater number,—who, as M. de La Fayette complains, and as the truth is, have declined to take any share in the new elections to the National Assembly, either as candidates or electors.

In this state of things, (that is, in the case of a *divided* kingdom,) by the law of nations,[1] Great Britain, like every other power, is free to take any part she pleases. She may decline, with more or less formality, according to her discretion, to acknowledge this new system; or she may recognize it as a government *de facto,* setting aside all discussion of its original legality, and considering the ancient monarchy as at an end. The law of nations leaves our court open to its choice. We have no direction but what is found in the well-understood policy of the king and kingdom.

This declaration of a *new species* of government, on new principles, (such it professes itself to be,) is a real crisis in the politics of Europe. The conduct which prudence ought to dictate to Great Britain will not depend (as hitherto our connection or quarrel with other states has for some time depended) upon merely *external* relations, but in a great measure also upon the system which we may think it right to adopt for the internal government of our own country.

If it be our policy to assimilate our government to that of France, we ought to prepare for this change by encouraging the schemes of authority established there. We ought to wink at the captivity and deposition of a prince with whom, if not in close alliance, we were in friendship. We ought to fall in with the ideas of Monsieur Montmorin's circular manifesto, and to do business of course with the functionaries who act under the new power by which that king to whom his Majesty's minister has been sent to reside has been deposed and imprisoned. On that idea we ought also to withhold all sorts of direct or indirect countenance from those who are treating in Germany for the reëstablishment of the French monarchy and the ancient orders of that state. This conduct is suitable to this policy.

The question is, whether this policy be suitable to the in-

---

[1] See Vattel, B. II. c. 4, sect. 56, and B. III. c. 18, sect. 296. [Burke]

terests of the crown and subjects of Great Britain. Let us, therefore, a little consider the true nature and probable effects of the Revolution which, in such a very unusual manner, has been twice diplomatically announced to his Majesty.

There have been many internal revolutions in the government of countries, both as to persons and forms, in which the neighboring states have had little or no concern. Whatever the government might be with respect to those persons and those forms, the stationary interests of the nation concerned have most commonly influenced the new governments in the same manner in which they influenced the old; and the revolution, turning on matter of local grievance or of local accommodation, did not extend beyond its territory.

The present Revolution in France seems to me to be quite of another character and description, and to bear little resemblance or analogy to any of those which have been brought about in Europe, upon principles merely political. *It is a Revolution of doctrine and theoretic dogma.* It has a much greater resemblance to those changes which have been made upon religious grounds, in which a spirit of proselytism makes an essential part.

The last revolution of doctrine and theory which has happened in Europe is the Reformation. It is not for my purpose to take any notice here of the merits of that revolution, but to state one only of its effects.

That effect was, *to introduce other interests into all countries than those which arose from their locality and natural circumstances.* The principle of the Reformation was such as, by its essence, could not be local or confined to the country in which it had its origin. For instance, the doctrine of "Justification by Faith or by Works," which was the original basis of the Reformation, could not have one of its alternatives true as to Germany and false as to every other country. Neither are questions of theoretic truth and falsehood governed by circumstances any more than by places. On that occasion, therefore, the spirit of proselytism expanded itself with great elasticity upon all sides: and great divisions were everywhere the result.

These divisions, however in appearance merely dogmatic, soon became mixed with the political; and their effects were rendered much more intense from this combination. Europe was for a long time divided into two great factions, under the name of Catholic and Protestant, which not only often alienated state from state, but also divided every state within itself. The warm parties in each state were more affectionately attached to those of their own doctrinal interest in some other country than to their fellow-citizens or to their natural government, when they or either of them happened to be of a different persuasion. These factions, wherever they prevailed, if they did not absolutely destroy, at least weakened and distracted the locality of patriotism. The public affections came to have other motives and other ties.

It would be to repeat the history of the two last centuries to exemplify the effects of this revolution.

Although the principles to which it gave rise did not operate with a perfect regularity and constancy, they never wholly ceased to operate. Few wars were made, and few treaties were entered into, in which they did not come in for some part. They gave a color, a character, and direction to all the politics of Europe.

These principles of internal as well as external division and coalition are but just now extinguished. But they who will examine into the true character and genius of some late events must be satisfied that other sources of faction, combining parties among the inhabitants of different countries into one connection, are opened, and that from these sources are likely to arise effects full as important as those which had formerly arisen from the jarring interests of the religious sects. The intention of the several actors in the change in France is not a matter of doubt. It is very openly professed.

In the modern world, before this time, there has been no

instance of this spirit of general political faction, separated from religion, pervading several countries, and forming a principle of union between the partisans in each. But the thing is not less in human nature. The ancient world has furnished a strong and striking instance of such a ground for faction, full as powerful and full as mischievous as our spirit of religious system had ever been, exciting in all the states of Greece (European and Asiatic) the most violent animosities and the most cruel and bloody persecutions and proscriptions. These ancient factions in each commonwealth of Greece connected themselves with those of the same description in some other states; and secret cabals and public alliances were carried on and made, not upon a conformity of general political interests, but for the support and aggrandizement of the two leading states which headed the aristocratic and democratic factions. For as, in later times, the king of Spain was at the head of a Catholic, and the king of Sweden of a Protestant interest, (France, though Catholic, acting subordinately to the latter,) in the like manner the Lacedemonians were everywhere at the head of the aristocratic interests, and the Athenians of the democratic. The two leading powers kept alive a constant cabal and conspiracy in every state, and the political dogmas concerning the constitution of a republic were the great instruments by which these leading states chose to aggrandize themselves. Their choice was not unwise; because the interest in opinions, (merely as opinions, and without any experimental reference to their effects,) when once they take strong hold of the mind, become the most operative of all interests, and indeed very often supersede every other.

I might further exemplify the possibility of a political sentiment running through various states, and combining factions in them, from the history of the Middle Ages in the Guelfs and Ghibellines. These were political factions originally in favor of the Emperor and the Pope, with no mixture of religious dogmas: or if anything religiously doctrinal they had in them originally, it very soon disappeared; as their first

political objects disappeared also, though the spirit remained.
They became no more than names to distinguish factions: but
they were not the less powerful in their operation, when they
had no direct point of doctrine, either religious or civil, to
assert. For a long time, however, those factions gave no small
degree of influence to the foreign chiefs in every commonwealth in which they existed. I do not mean to pursue further
the track of these parties. I allude to this part of history only
as it furnishes an instance of that species of faction which
broke the locality of public affections, and united descriptions
of citizens more with strangers than with their countrymen
of different opinions.

The political dogma, which, upon the new French system,
is to unite the factions of different nations, is this: "That the
majority, told by the head, of the taxable people in every
country, is the perpetual, natural, unceasing, indefeasible
sovereign; that this majority is perfectly master of the form as
well as the administration of the state, and that the magistrates, under whatever names they are called, are only functionaries to obey the orders (general as laws or particular as
decrees) which that majority may make; that this is the only
natural government; that all others are tyranny and usurpation."

In order to reduce this dogma into practice, the republicans
in France, and their associates in other countries, make it always their business, and often their public profession, to destroy all traces of ancient establishments, and to form a new
commonwealth in each country, upon the basis of the French
Rights of Men. On the principle of these rights, they mean to
institute in every country, and as it were the germ of the
whole, parochial governments, for the purpose of what they
call equal representation. From them is to grow, by some media, a general council and representative of all the parochial
governments. In that representative is to be vested the whole
national power,—totally abolishing hereditary name and office,
levelling all conditions of men, (except where money *must*

make a difference,) breaking all connection between territory and dignity, and abolishing every species of nobility, gentry, and Church establishments: all their priests and all their magistrates being only creatures of election and pensioners at will.

Knowing how opposite a permanent landed interest is to that scheme, they have resolved, and it is the great drift of all their regulations, to reduce that description of men to a mere peasantry for the sustenance of the towns, and to place the true effective government in cities, among the tradesmen, bankers, and voluntary clubs of bold, presuming young persons,—advocates, attorneys, notaries, managers of newspapers, and those cabals of literary men called academies. Their republic is to have a first functionary, (as they call him,) under the name of King, or not, as they think fit. This officer, when such an officer is permitted, is, however, neither in fact nor name to be considered as sovereign, nor the people as his subjects. The very use of these appellations is offensive to their ears.

This system, as it has first been realized, dogmatically as well as practically, in France, makes France the natural head of all factions formed on a similar principle, wherever they may prevail, as much as Athens was the head and settled ally of all democratic factions, wherever they existed. The other system has no head.

This system has very many partisans in every country in Europe, but particularly in England, where they are already formed into a body, comprehending most of the Dissenters of the three leading denominations. To these are readily aggregated all who are Dissenters in character, temper, and disposition, though not belonging to any of their congregations: that is, all the restless people who resemble them, of all ranks and all parties,—Whigs, and even Tories; the whole race of half-bred speculators; all the Atheists, Deists, and Socinians; all those who hate the clergy and envy the nobility; a good many among the moneyed people; the East Indians almost to a man, who cannot bear to find that their present importance does not bear a proportion to their wealth. These latter have united themselves into one great, and, in my opinion, formidable club,[2] which, though now quiet, may be brought into action with considerable unanimity and force.

Formerly, few, except the ambitious great or the desperate and indigent, were to be feared as instruments in revolutions. What has happened in France teaches us, with many other things, that there are more causes than have commonly been taken into our consideration, by which government may be subverted. The moneyed men, merchants, principal tradesmen, and men of letters (hitherto generally thought the peaceable and even timid part of society) are the chief actors in the French Revolution. But the fact is, that, as money increases and circulates, and as the circulation of news in politics and letters becomes more and more diffused, the persons who diffuse this money and this intelligence become more and more important. This was not long undiscovered. Views of ambition were in France, for the first time, presented to these classes of men: objects in the state, in the army, in the system of civil offices of every kind. Their eyes were dazzled with this new prospect. They were, as it were, electrified, and made to lose the natural spirit of their situation. A bribe, great without example in the history of the world, was held out to them,—the whole government of a very large kingdom.

There are several who are persuaded that the same thing cannot happen in England, because here (they say) the occupations of merchants, tradesmen, and manufacturers are not held as degrading situations. I once thought that the low estimation in which commerce was held in France might be reckoned among the causes of the late Revolution; and I am still of opinion that the exclusive spirit of the French

---

[2] Originally called the Bengal Club; but since opened to persons from the other Presidencies, for the purpose of consolidating the whole Indian interest. [Burke]

nobility did irritate the wealthy of other classes. But I found long since, that persons in trade and business were by no means despised in France in the manner I had been taught to believe. As to men of letters, they were so far from being despised or neglected, that there was no country, perhaps, in the universe, in which they were so highly esteemed, courted, caressed, and even feared: tradesmen naturally were not so much sought in society, (as not furnishing so largely to the fund of conversation as they do to the revenues of the state,) but the latter description got forward every day. M. Bailly, who made himself the popular mayor on the rebellion of the Bastile, and is a principal actor in the revolt, before the change possessed a pension or office under the crown of six hundred pound English a year,—for that country, no contemptible provision; and this he obtained solely as a man of letters, and on no other title. As to the moneyed men, whilst the monarchy continued, there is no doubt, that, merely as such, they did not enjoy the *privileges* of nobility; but nobility was of so easy an acquisition, that it was the fault or neglect of all of that description who did not obtain its privileges, for their lives at least, in virtue of office. It attached under the royal government to an innumerable multitude of places, real and nominal, that were vendible; and such nobility were as capable of everything as their degree of influence or interest could make them,—that is, as nobility of no considerable rank or consequence. M. Necker, so far from being a French gentleman, was not so much as a Frenchman born, and yet we all know the rank in which he stood on the day of the meeting of the States.

As to the mere matter of estimation of the mercantile or any other class, this is regulated by opinion and prejudice. In England, a security against the envy of men in these classes is not so very complete as we may imagine. We must not impose upon ourselves. What institutions and manners together had done in France manners alone do here. It is the natural operation of things, where there exists a crown, a court,

splendid orders of knighthood, and an hereditary nobility,—
where there exists a fixed, permanent, landed gentry, continued
in greatness and opulence by the law of primogeniture, and by
a protection given to family settlements,—where there exists
a standing army and navy,—where there exists a Church
establishment, which bestows on learning and parts an
interest combined with that of religion and the state;—in a
country where such things exist, wealth, new in its acquisition,
and precarious in its duration, can never rank first, or even
near the first: though wealth has its natural weight further
than as it is balanced and even preponderated amongst us, as
amongst other nations, by artificial institutions and opinions
growing out of them. At no period in the history of England
have so few peers been taken out of trade or from families
newly created by commerce. In no period has so small a
number of noble families entered into the counting-house. I
can call to mind but one in all England, and his is of near
fifty years' standing. Be that as it may, it appears plain to me,
from my best observation, that envy and ambition may, by
art, management, and disposition, be as much excited amongst
these descriptions of men in England as in any other country,
and that they are just as capable of acting a part in any
great change.

What direction the French spirit of proselytism is likely to
take, and in what order it is likely to prevail in the several
parts of Europe, it is not easy to determine. The seeds are sown
almost everywhere, chiefly by newspaper circulations, infinitely more efficacious and extensive than ever they were.
And they are a more important instrument than generally is
imagined. They are a part of the reading of all; they are the
whole of the reading of the far greater number. There are
thirty of them in Paris alone. The language diffuses them
more widely than the English,—though the English, too, are
much read. The writers of these papers, indeed, for the greater
part, are either unknown or in contempt, but they are like a
battery, in which the stroke of any one ball produces no

great effect, but the amount of continual repetition is decisive. Let us only suffer any person to tell us his story, morning and evening, but for one twelve-month, and he will become our master.

All those countries in which several states are comprehended under some general geographical description, and loosely united by some federal constitution,—countries of which the members are small, and greatly diversified in their forms of government, and in the titles by which they are held,—these countries, as it might be well expected, are the principal objects of their hopes and machinations. Of these, the chief are Germany and Switzerland; after them, Italy has its place, as in circumstances somewhat similar.

As to Germany, (in which, from their relation to the Emperor, I comprehend the Belgic Provinces,) it appears to me to be, from several circumstances, internal and external, in a very critical situation; and the laws and liberties of the Empire are by no means secure from the contagion of the French doctrines and the effect of French intrigues, or from the use which two of the greater German powers may make of a general derangement to the general detriment. I do not say that the French do not mean to bestow on these German states liberties, and laws too, after their mode; but those are not what have hitherto been understood as the laws and liberties of the Empire. These exist and have always existed under the principles of feodal tenure and succession, under imperial constitutions, grants and concessions of sovereigns, family compacts, and public treaties, made under the sanction, and some of them guarantied by the sovereign powers of other nations, and particularly the old government of France, the author and natural support of the Treaty of Westphalia.

In short, the Germanic body is a vast mass of heterogeneous states, held together by that heterogeneous body of old principles which formed the public law positive and doctrinal. The modern laws and liberties, which the new power in France proposes to introduce into Germany, and to support

with all its force of intrigue and of arms, is of a very
different nature, utterly irreconcilable with the first, and indeed fundamentally the reverse of it: I mean the *rights and
liberties of the man*, the *droit de l' homme*. That this doctrine
has made an amazing progress in Germany there cannot be
a shadow of doubt. They are infected by it along the whole
course of the Rhine, the Maese, the Moselle, and in the
greater part of Suabia and Franconia. It is particularly prevalent amongst all the lower people, churchmen and laity, in
the dominions of the Ecclesiastical Electors. It is not easy
to find or to conceive governments more mild and indulgent
than these Church sovereignties; but good government is
as nothing, when the rights of man take possession of the
mind. Indeed, the loose rein held over the people in these
provinces must be considered as one cause of the facility
with which they lend themselves to any schemes of innovation,
by inducing them to think lightly of their governments, and
to judge of grievances, not by feeling, but by imagination.

It is in these Electorates that the first impressions of
France are likely to be made; and if they succeed, it is over
with the Germanic body, as it stands at present. A great
revolution is preparing in Germany, and a revolution, in my
opinion, likely to be more decisive upon the general fate of
nations than that of France itself,—other than as in France
is to be found the first source of all the principles which are
in any way likely to distinguish the troubles and convulsions
of our age. If Europe does not conceive the independence and
the equilibrium of the Empire to be in the very essence of
the system of balanced power in Europe, and if the scheme
of public law, or mass of laws, upon which that independence
and equilibrium are founded, be of no leading consequence
as they are preserved or destroyed, all the politics of Europe
for more than two centuries have been miserably erroneous.

If the two great leading powers of Germany do not regard
this danger (as apparently they do not) in the light in which
it presents itself so naturally, it is because they are powers

too great to have a social interest. That sort of interest belongs only to those whose state of weakness or mediocrity is such as to give them greater cause of apprehension from what may destroy them than of hope from anything by which they may be aggrandized.

As long as those two princes are at variance, so long the liberties of Germany are safe. But if ever they should so far understand one another as to be persuaded that they have a more direct and more certainly defined interest in a proportioned mutual aggrandizement than in a reciprocal reduction, that is, if they come to think that they are more likely to be enriched by a division of spoil than to be rendered secure by keeping to the old policy of preventing others from being spoiled by either of them, from that moment the liberties of Germany are no more.

That a junction of two in such a scheme is neither impossible nor improbable is evident from the partition of Poland in 1773, which was effected by such a junction as made the interposition of other nations to prevent it not easy. Their circumstances at that time hindered any other three states, or indeed any two, from taking measures in common to prevent it, though France was at that time an existing power, and had not yet learned to act upon a system of politics of her own invention. The geographical position of Poland was a great obstacle to any movements of France in opposition to this, at that time, unparalleled league. To my certain knowledge, if Great Britain had at that time been willing to concur in preventing the execution of a project so dangerous in the example, even exhausted as France then was by the preceding war, and under a lazy and unenterprising prince, she would have at every risk taken an active part in this business. But a languor with regard to so remote an interest, and the principles and passions which were then strongly at work at home, were the causes why Great Britain would not give France any encouragement in such an enterprise. At that time, however, and with regard to that object, in my opinion, Great Britain and France had a common interest.

But the position of Germany is not like that of Poland, with regard to France, either for good or for evil. If a conjunction between Prussia and the Emperor should be formed for the purpose of secularizing and rendering hereditary the Ecclesiastical Electorates and the Bishopric of Münster, for settling two of them on the children of the Emperor, and uniting Cologne and Münster to the dominions of the king of Prussia on the Rhine, or if any other project of mutual aggrandizement should be in prospect, and that, to facilitate such a scheme, the modern French should be permitted and encouraged to shake the internal and external security of these Ecclesiastical Electorates, Great Britain is so situated that she could not with any effect set herself in opposition to such a design. Her principal arm, her marine, could here be of no sort of use.

France, the author of the Treaty of Westphalia, is the natural guardian of the independence and balance of Germany. Great Britain (to say nothing of the king's concern as one of that august body) has a serious interest in preserving it; but, except through the power of France, *acting upon the common old principles of state policy,* in the case we have supposed, she has no sort of means of supporting that interest. It is always the interest of Great Britain that the power of France should be kept within the bounds of moderation. It is not her interest that that power should be wholly annihilated in the system of Europe. Though at one time through France the independence of Europe was endangered, it is, and ever was, through her alone that the common liberty of Germany can be secured against the single or the combined ambition of any other power. In truth, within this century the aggrandizement of other sovereign houses has been such that there has been a great change in the whole state of Europe; and other nations as well as France may become objects of jealousy and apprehension.

In this state of things, a new principle of alliances and wars is opened. The Treaty of Westphalia is, with France, an· antiquated fable. The rights and liberties she was bound to maintain are now a system of wrong and tyranny which she is bound to destroy. Her good and ill dispositions are shown by the same means. *To communicate peaceably* the rights of men is the true mode of her showing her *friendship;* to force sovereigns to *submit* to those rights is her mode of *hostility.* So that, either as friend or foe, her whole scheme has been, and is, to throw the Empire into confusion; and those statesmen who follow the old routine of politics may see in this general confusion, and in the danger of the *lesser* princes, an occasion, as protectors or enemies, of connecting their territories to one or the other of the *two great* German powers. They do not take into consideration that the means which they encourage, as leading to the event they desire, will with certainty not only ravage and destroy the Empire, but, if they should for a moment seem to aggrandize the two great houses, will also establish principles and confirm tempers amongst the people which will preclude the two sovereigns from the possibility of holding what they acquire, or even the dominions which they have inherited. It is on the side of the Ecclesiastical Electorates that the dikes raised to support the German liberty first will give way.

The French have begun their general operations by seizing upon those territories of the Pope the situation of which was the most inviting to the enterprise. Their method of doing it was by exciting sedition and spreading massacre and desolation through these unfortunate places, and then, under an idea of kindness and protection, bringing forward an antiquated title of the crown of France, and annexing Avignon and the two cities of the Comtat, with their territory, to the French republic. They have made an attempt on Geneva, in which they very narrowly failed of success. It is known that they hold out from time to time the idea of uniting all the other provinces of which Gaul was anciently composed, including Savoy on the other side, and on this side bounding themselves by the Rhine.

As to Switzerland, it is a country whose long union, rather than its possible division, is the matter of wonder. Here I know they entertain very sanguine hopes. The aggregation to France of the democratic Swiss republics appears to them to be a work half done by their very form; and it might seem to them rather an increase of importance to these little commonwealths than a derogation from their independency or a change in the manner of their government. Upon any quarrel amongst the Cantons, nothing is more likely than such an event. As to the aristocratic republics, the general clamor and hatred which the French excite against the very name, (and with more facility and success than against monarchs,) and the utter impossibility of their government making any sort of resistance against an insurrection, where they have no troops, and the people are all armed and trained, render their hopes in that quarter far indeed from unfounded. It is certain that the republic of Bern thinks itself obliged to a vigilance next to hostile, and to imprison or expel all the French whom it finds in its territories. But, indeed, those aristocracies, which comprehend whatever is considerable, wealthy, and valuable in Switzerland, do now so wholly depend upon opinion, and the humor of their multitude, that the lightest puff of wind is sufficient to blow them down. If France, under its ancient regimen, and upon the ancient principles of policy, was the support of the Germanic Constitution, it was much more so of that of Switzerland, which almost from the very origin of that confederacy rested upon the closeness of its connection with France, on which the Swiss Cantons wholly reposed themselves for the preservation of the parts of their body in their respective rights and permanent forms, as well as for the maintenance of all in their general independency.

Switzerland and Germany are the first objects of the new French politicians. When I contemplate what they have done at home, which is, in effect, little less than an amazing conquest, wrought by a change of opinion, in a great part (to be sure far from altogether) very sudden, I cannot help letting my thoughts run along with their designs, and, without attending to geographical order, to consider the other states of Europe, so far as they may be any way affected by this astonishing Revolution. If early steps are not taken in some way or other to prevent the spreading of this influence, I scarcely think any of them perfectly secure.

Italy is divided, as Germany and Switzerland are, into many smaller states, and with some considerable diversity as to forms of government; but as these divisions and varieties in Italy are not so considerable, so neither do I think the danger altogether so imminent there as in Germany and Switzerland. Savoy I know that the French consider as in a very hopeful way, and I believe not at all without reason. They view it as an old member of the kingdom of France, which may be easily reunited in the manner and on the principles of the reunion of Avignon. This country communicates with Piedmont; and as the king of Sardinia's dominions were long the key of Italy, and as such long regarded by France, whilst France acted on her old maxims, and with views on Italy,—so, in this new French empire of sedition, if once she gets that key into her hands, she can easily lay open the barrier which hinders the entrance of her present politics into that inviting region. Milan, I am sure, nourishes great disquiets; and if Milan should stir, no part of Lombardy is secure to the present possessors,—whether the Venetian or the Austrian. Genoa is closely connected with France.

The first prince of the House of Bourbon has been obliged to give himself up entirely to the new system, and to pretend even to propagate it with all zeal: at least, that club of intriguers who assemble at the Feuillants, and whose cabinet meets at Madame de Staël's, and makes and directs all the ministers, is the real executive government of France. The

Emperor is perfectly in concert, and they will not long suffer any prince of the House of Bourbon to keep by force the French emissaries out of their dominions; nor whilst France has a commerce with them, especially through Marseilles, (the hottest focus of sedition in France,) will it be long possible to prevent the intercourse or the effects.

Naples has an old, inveterate disposition to republicanism, and (however for some time past quiet) is as liable to explosion as its own Vesuvius. Sicily, I think, has these dispositions in full as strong a degree. In neither of these countries exists anything which very well deserves the name of government or exact police.

In the States of the Church, notwithstanding their strictness in banishing the French out of that country, there are not wanting the seeds of a revolution. The spirit of nepotism prevails there nearly as strong as ever. Every Pope of course is to give origin or restoration to a great family by the means of large donations. The foreign revenues have long been gradually on the decline, and seem now in a manner dried up. To supply this defect, the resource of vexatious and impolitic jobbing at home, if anything, is rather increased than lessened. Various well-intended, but ill-understood practices, some of them existing, in their spirit at least, from the time of the old Roman Empire, still prevail; and that government is as blindly attached to old abusive customs as others are wildly disposed to all sorts of innovations and experiments. These abuses were less felt whilst the Pontificate drew riches from abroad, which in some measure counterbalanced the evils of their remiss and jobbish government at home. But now it can subsist only on the resources of domestic management; and abuses in that management of course will be more intimately and more severely felt.

In the midst of the apparently torpid languor of the Ecclesiastical State, those who have had opportunity of a near observation have seen a little rippling in that smooth water, which indicates something alive under it. There is in the Ecclesiastical State a personage who seems capable of acting (but with more force and steadiness) the part of the tribune Rienzi. The people, once inflamed, will not be destitute of a leader. They have such an one already in the Cardinal or Archbishop Boncompagni. He is, of all men, if I am not ill-informed, the most turbulent, seditious, intriguing, bold, and desperate. He is not at all made for a Roman of the present day. I think he lately held the first office of their state, that of Great Chamberlain, which is equivalent to High Treasurer. At present he is out of employment, and in disgrace. If he should be elected Pope, or even come to have any weight with a new Pope, he will infallibly conjure up a democratic spirit in that country. He may, indeed, be able to effect it without these advantages. The next interregnum will probably show more of him. There may be others of the same character, who have not come to my knowledge. This much is certain,—that the Roman people, if once the blind reverence they bear to the sanctity of the Pope, which is their only bridle, should relax, are naturally turbulent, ferocious, and headlong, whilst the police is defective, and the government feeble and resourceless beyond all imagination.

As to Spain, it is a nerveless country. It does not possess the use, it only suffers the abuse, of a nobility. For some time, and even before the settlement of the Bourbon dynasty, that body has been systematically lowered, and rendered incapable by exclusion, and for incapacity excluded from affairs. In this circle the body is in a manner annihilated; and so little means have they of any weighty exertion either to control or to support the crown, that, if they at all interfere, it is only by abetting desperate and mobbish insurrections, like that at Madrid, which drove Squillace from his place. Florida Blanca is a creature of office, and has little connection and no sympathy with that body.

As to the clergy, they are the only thing in Spain that looks like an independent order; and they are kept in some respect by the Inquisition, the sole, but unhappy resource of public tranquillity and order now remaining in Spain. As in Venice, it is become mostly an engine of state,—which, indeed, to a degree, it has always been in Spain. It wars no longer with Jews and heretics: it has no such war to carry on. Its great object is, to keep atheistic and republican doctrines from making their way in that kingdom. No French book upon any subject can enter there which does not contain such matter. In Spain, the clergy are of moment from their influence, but at the same time with the envy and jealousy that attend great riches and power. Though the crown has by management with the Pope got a very great share of the ecclesiastical revenues into its own hands, much still remains to them. There will always be about that court those who look out to a farther division of the Church property as a resource, and to be obtained by shorter methods than those of negotiations with the clergy and their chief. But at present I think it likely that they will stop, lest the business should be taken out of their hands,—and lest that body, in which remains the only life that exists in Spain, and is not a fever, may with their property lose all the influence necessary to preserve the monarchy, or, being poor and desperate, may employ whatever influence remains to them as active agents in its destruction.

The Castilians have still remaining a good deal of their old character, their *gravedad, lealtad,* and *el temor de Dios;* but that character neither is, nor ever was, exactly true, except of the Castilians only. The several kingdoms which compose Spain have, perhaps, some features which run through the whole; but they are in many particulars as different as nations who go by different names: the Catalans, for instance, and the Aragonians too, in a great measure, have the spirit of the Miquelets, and much more of republicanism than of an attachment to royalty. They are more in the way of trade and intercourse with France, and, upon the least internal movement, will disclose and probably let loose a spirit that may throw the whole Spanish monarchy into convulsions.

It is a melancholy reflection, that the spirit of melioration which has been going on in that part of Europe, more or less, during this century, and the various schemes very lately on foot for further advancement, are all put a stop to at once. Reformation certainly is nearly connected with innovation; and where that latter comes in for too large a share, those who undertake to improve their country may risk their own safety. In times where the correction, which includes the confession, of an abuse, is turned to criminate the authority which has long suffered it, rather than to honor those who would amend it, (which is the spirit of this malignant French distemper,) every step out of the common course becomes critical, and renders it a task full of peril for princes of moderate talents to engage in great undertakings. At present the only safety of Spain is the old national hatred to the French. How far that can be depended upon, if any great ferments should be excited, it is impossible to say.

As to Portugal, she is out of the high-road of these politics. I shall, therefore, not divert my thoughts that way, but return again to the North of Europe, which at present seems the part most interested, and there it appears to me that the French speculation on the Northern countries may be valued in the following or some such manner.

Denmark and Norway do not appear to furnish any of the materials of a democratic revolution, or the dispositions to it. Denmark can only be *consequentially* affected by anything done in France; but of Sweden I think quite otherwise. The present power in Sweden is too new a system, and too green and too sore from its late Revolution, to be considered as perfectly assured. The king, by his astonishing activity, his boldness, his decision, his ready versatility, and by rousing and employing the old military spirit of Sweden, keeps up the top with continual agitation and lashing. The moment it ceases to spin, the royalty is a dead bit of box. Whenever Sweden is quiet externally for some time, there is great danger that all the republican elements she contains will be animated by the new French spirit, and of this I believe the king is very sensible.

The Russian government is of all others the most liable to be subverted by military seditions, by court conspiracies, and sometimes by headlong rebellions of the people, such as the turbinating movement of Pugatchef. It is not quite so probable that in any of these changes the spirit of system may mingle, in the manner it has done in France. The Muscovites are no great speculators; but I should not much rely on their uninquisitive disposition, if any of their ordinary motives to sedition should arise. The little catechism of the Rights of Men is soon learned; and the inferences are in the passions.

Poland, from one cause or other, is always unquiet. The new Constitution only serves to supply that restless people with new means, at least new modes, of cherishing their turbulent disposition. The bottom of the character is the same. It is a great question, whether the joining that crown with the Electorate of Saxony will contribute most to strengthen the royal authority of Poland or to shake the ducal in Saxony. The Elector is a Catholic; the people of Saxony are, six sevenths at the very least, Protestants. He *must* continue a Catholic, according to the Polish law, if he accepts that crown. The pride of the Saxons, formerly flattered by having a crown in the house of their prince, though an honor which cost them dear,—the German probity, fidelity, and loyalty,—the weight of the Constitution of the Empire under the Treaty of Westphalia,—the good temper and good-nature of the princes of the House of Saxony, had formerly removed from the people all apprehension with regard to their religion, and kept them perfectly quiet, obedient, and even affectionate. The Seven Years' War made some change in the minds of the Saxons. They did not, I believe, regret the loss of what might be considered almost as the succession to the crown of Poland, the possession of which, by annexing them to a foreign interest, had often obliged them to act an arduous part, towards the support of which that foreign interest afforded no proportionable strength. In this very delicate situation of their political interests, the speculations of the French and German *Economists,* and the cabals, and the secret, as well as public doctrines of the *Illuminatenorden* and *Freemasons,* have made a considerable progress in that country; and a turbulent spirit, under color of religion, but in reality arising from the French rights of man, has already shown itself, and is ready on every occasion to blaze out.

The present Elector is a prince of a safe and quiet temper, of great prudence and goodness. He knows, that, in the actual state of things, not the power and respect belonging to sovereigns, but their very existence, depends on a reasonable frugality. It is very certain that not one sovereign in Europe can either promise for the continuance of his authority in a state of indigence and insolvency, or dares to venture on a new imposition to relieve himself. Without abandoning wholly the ancient magnificence of his court, the Elector has conducted his affairs with infinitely more economy than any of his predecessors, so as to restore his finances beyond what was thought possible from the state in which the Seven Years' War had left Saxony. Saxony, during the whole of that dreadful period, having been in the hands of an exasperated enemy, rigorous by resentment, by nature, and by necessity, was obliged to bear in a manner the whole burden of the war; in the intervals when their allies prevailed, the inhabitants of that country were not better treated.

The moderation and prudence of the present Elector, in my opinion, rather, perhaps, respites the troubles than secures the peace of the Electorate. The offer of the succession to the crown of Poland is truly critical, whether he

accepts or whether he declines it. If the States will consent
to his acceptance, it will add to the difficulties, already great,
of his situation between the king of Prussia and the Emperor.
—But these thoughts lead me too far, when I mean to speak
only of the interior condition of these princes. It has always,
however, some necessary connection with their foreign
politics.

With regard to Holland, and the ruling party there, I do
not think it at all tainted, or likely to be so, except by fear,—
or that it is likely to be misled, unless indirectly and cir-
cuitously. But the predominant party in Holland is not
Holland. The suppressed faction, though suppressed, exists.
Under the ashes, the embers of the late commotions are still
warm. The anti-Orange party has from the day of its origin
been French, though alienated in some degree for some time,
through the pride and folly of Louis the Fourteenth. It will
ever hanker after a French connection; and now that the
internal government in France has been assimilated in so
considerable a degree to that which the immoderate republicans began so very lately to introduce into Holland,
their connection, as still more natural, will be more desired.
I do not well understand the present exterior politics of the
Stadtholder, nor the treaty into which the newspapers say he
has entered for the States with the Emperor. But the
Emperor's own politics with regard to the Netherlands seem
to me to be exactly calculated to answer the purpose of the
French Revolutionists. He endeavors to crush the aristocratic
party, and to nourish one in avowed connection with the
most furious democratists in France.

These Provinces in which the French game is so well
played they consider as part of the old French Empire: certainly they were amongst the oldest parts of it. These they
think very well situated, as their party is well disposed to a
reunion. As to the greater nations, they do not aim at making
a direct conquest of them, but, by disturbing them through a
propagation of their principles, they hope to weaken, as they

will weaken them, and to keep them in perpetual alarm and agitation, and thus render all their efforts against them utterly impracticable, whilst they extend the dominion of their sovereign anarchy on all sides.

As to England, there may be some apprehension from vicinity, from constant communication, and from the very name of liberty, which, as it ought to be very dear to us, in its worst abuses carries something seductive. It is the abuse of the first and best of the objects which we cherish. I know that many, who sufficiently dislike the system of France, have yet no apprehensions of its prevalence here. I say nothing to the ground of this security in the attachment of the people to their Constitution, and their satisfaction in the discreet portion of liberty which it measures out to them. Upon this I have said all I have to say, in the Appeal I have published. That security is something, and not inconsiderable; but if a storm arises, I should not much rely upon it.

There are other views of things which may be used to give us a perfect (though in my opinion a delusive) assurance of our own security. The first of these is from the weakness and rickety nature of the new system in the place of its first formation. It is thought that the monster of a commonwealth cannot possibly live,—that at any rate the ill contrivance of their fabric will make it fall in pieces of itself,—that the Assembly must be bankrupt,—and that this bankruptcy will totally destroy that system from the contagion of which apprehensions are entertained.

For my part I have long thought that one great cause of the stability of this wretched scheme of things in France was an opinion that it could not stand, and therefore that all external measures to destroy it were wholly useless.

As to the bankruptcy, that event has happened long ago, as much as it is ever likely to happen. As soon as a nation compels a creditor to take paper currency in discharge of his debt, there is a bankruptcy. The compulsory paper has in some degree answered,—not because there was a surplus from

Church lands, but because faith has not been kept with the clergy. As to the holders of the old funds, to them the payments will be dilatory, but they will be made; and whatever may be the discount on paper, whilst paper is taken, paper will be issued.

As to the rest, they have shot out three branches of revenue to supply all those which they have destroyed: that is, *the Universal Register of all Transactions*, the heavy and universal *Stamp Duty*, and the new *Territorial Impost*, levied chiefly on the reduced estates of the gentlemen. These branches of the revenue, especially as they take assignats in payment, answer their purpose in a considerable degree, and keep up the credit of their paper: for, as they receive it in their treasury, it is in reality funded upon all their taxes and future resources of all kinds, as well as upon the Church estates. As this paper is become in a manner the only visible maintenance of the whole people, the dread of a bankruptcy is more apparently connected with the delay of a counter-revolution than with the duration of this republic; because the interest of the new republic manifestly leans upon it, and, in my opinion, the counter-revolution cannot exist along with it. The above three projects ruined some ministers under the old government, merely for having conceived them. They are the salvation of the present rulers.

As the Assembly has laid a most unsparing and cruel hand on all men who have lived by the bounty, the justice, or the abuses of the old government, they have lessened many expenses. The royal establishment, though excessively and ridiculously great for *their* scheme of things, is reduced at least one half; the estates of the king's brothers, which under the ancient government had been in truth royal revenues, go to the general stock of the confiscation; and as to the crown lands, though under the monarchy they never yielded two hundred and fifty thousand a year, by many they are thought at least worth three times as much.

As to the ecclesiastical charge, whether as a compensation for losses, or a provision for religion, of which they made at first a great parade, and entered into a solemn engagement in favor of it, it was estimated at a much larger sum than they could expect from the Church property, movable or im-movable: they are completely bankrupt as to that article. It is just what they wish; and it is not productive of any serious inconvenience. The non-payment produces discontent and occasional sedition; but is only by fits and spasms, and amongst the country people, who are of no consequence. These seditions furnish new pretexts for non-payment to the Church establishment, and help the Assembly wholly to get rid of the clergy, and indeed of any form of religion, which is not only their real, but avowed object.

They are embarrassed, indeed, in the highest degree, but not wholly resourceless. They are without the species of money. Circulation of money is a great convenience, but a substitute for it may be found. Whilst the great objects of production and consumption, corn, cattle, wine, and the like, exist in a country, the means of giving them circulation, with more or less convenience, cannot be *wholly* wanting. The great confiscation of the Church and of the crown lands, and of the appanages of the princes, for the purchase of all which their paper is always received at par, gives means of con-tinually destroying and continually creating; and this per-petual destruction and renovation feeds the speculative market, and prevents, and will prevent, till that fund of confiscation begins to fail, a *total* depreciation.

But all consideration of public credit in France is of little avail at present. The action, indeed, of the moneyed interest was of absolute necessity at the beginning of this Revolution; but the French republic can stand without any assistance from that description of men, which, as things are now cir-cumstanced, rather stands in need of assistance itself from the power which alone substantially exists in France: I mean the several districts and municipal republics, and the several clubs which direct all their affairs and appoint all their magistrates. This is the power now paramount to everything, even to the Assembly itself called National and that to which tribunals, priesthood, laws, finances, and both descriptions of military power are wholly subservient, so far as the military power of either description yields obedience to any name of authority.

The world of contingency and political combination is much larger than we are apt to imagine. We never can say what may or may not happen, without a view to all the actual circumstances. Experience, upon other data than those, is of all things the most delusive. Prudence in new cases can do nothing on grounds of retrospect. A constant vigilance and attention to the train of things as they successively emerge, and to act on what they direct, are the only sure courses. The physician that let blood, and by blood-letting cured one kind of plague, in the next added to its ravages. That power goes with property is not universally true, and the idea that the operation of it is certain and invariable may mislead us very fatally.

Whoever will take an accurate view of the state of those republics, and of the composition of the present Assembly deputed by them, (in which Assembly there are not quite fifty persons possessed of an income amounting to 100*l.* sterling yearly,) must discern clearly, *that the political and civil power of France is wholly separated from its property of every description,* and of course that neither the landed nor the moneyed interest possesses the smallest weight or consideration in the direction of any public concern. The whole kingdom is directed by *the refuse of its chicane,* with the aid of the bustling, presumptuous young clerks of counting-houses and shops, and some intermixture of young gentlemen of the same character in the several towns. The rich peasants are bribed with Church lands; and the poorer of that description are, and can be, counted for nothing. They may rise in ferocious, ill-directed tumults,—but they can only disgrace themselves and signalize the triumph of their adversaries.

The *truly* active citizens, that is, the above descriptions, are all concerned in intrigue respecting the various objects in their local or their general government. The rota, which the French have established for their National Assembly, holds out the highest objects of ambition to such vast multitudes as in an unexampled measure to widen the bottom of a new species of interest merely political, and wholly unconnected with birth or property. This scheme of a rota, though it enfeebles the state, considered as one solid body, and indeed wholly disables it from acting as such, gives a great, an equal, and a diffusive strength to the democratic scheme. Seven hundred and fifty people, every two years raised to the supreme power, has already produced at least fifteen hundred bold, acting politicians: a great number for even so great a country as France. These men never will quietly settle in ordinary occupations, nor submit to any scheme which must reduce them to an entirely private condition, or to the exercise of a steady, peaceful, but obscure and unimportant industry. Whilst they sit in the Assembly, they are denied offices of trust and profit,—but their short duration makes this no restraint: during their probation and apprenticeship they are all salaried with an income to the greatest part of them immense; and after they have passed the novitiate, those who take any sort of lead are placed in very lucrative offices, according to their influence and credit, or appoint those who divide their profits with them.

This supply of recruits to the corps of the highest civil ambition goes on with a regular progression. In very few years it must amount to many thousands. These, however, will be as nothing in comparison to the multitude of municipal officers, and officers of district and department, of all sorts, who have tasted of power and profit, and who hunger for the periodical return of the meal. To these needy agitators, the glory of the state, the general wealth and prosperity of the nation, and the rise or fall of public credit are as dreams; nor have arguments deduced from these topics any sort of weight with them. The indifference with which the Assembly regards the state of their colonies, the only valuable part of the French commerce, is a full proof how little they are likely to be affected by anything but the selfish game of their own ambition, now universally diffused.

It is true, amidst all these turbulent means of security to their system, very great discontents everywhere prevail. But they only produce misery to those who nurse them at home, or exile, beggary, and in the end confiscation, to those who are so impatient as to remove from them. Each municipal republic has a *Committee,* or something in the nature of a *Committee of Research.* In these petty republics the tyranny is so near its object that it becomes instantly acquainted with every act of every man. It stifles conspiracy in its very first movements. Their power is absolute and uncontrollable. No stand can be made against it. These republics are besides so disconnected, that very little intelligence of what happens in them is to be obtained beyond their own bounds, except by the means of their clubs, who keep up a constant correspondence, and who give what color they please to such facts as they choose to communicate out of the track of their correspondence. They all have some sort of communication, just as much or as little as they please, with the centre. By this confinement of all communication to the ruling faction, any combination, grounded on the abuses and discontents in one, scarcely can reach the other. There is not one man, in any one place, to head them. The old government had so much abstracted the nobility from the cultivation of provincial interest, that no man in France exists, whose power, credit, or consequence extends to two districts, or who is capable of uniting them in any design, even if any man could assemble ten men together without being sure of a speedy lodging in a prison. One must not judge of the state of France by what has been observed elsewhere. It does not in the least resemble any other country. Analogical reasoning from history or from recent experience in other places is wholly delusive.

In my opinion, there never was seen so strong a government internally as that of the French municipalities. If ever any rebellion can arise against the present system, it must begin, where the Revolution which gave birth to it did, at the capital. Paris is the only place in which there is the least freedom of intercourse. But even there, so many servants as any man has, so many spies and irreconcilable domestic enemies.

But that place being the chief seat of the power and intelligence of the ruling faction, and the place of occasional resort for their fiercest spirits, even there a revolution is not likely to have anything to feed it. The leaders of the aristocratic party have been drawn out of the kingdom by order of the princes, on the hopes held out by the Emperor and the king of Prussia at Pilnitz; and as to the democratic factions in Paris, amongst them there are no leaders possessed of an influence for any other purpose but that of maintaining the present state of things. The moment they are seen to warp, they are reduced to nothing. They have no attached army,—no party that is at all personal.

It is not to be imagined, because a political system is, under certain aspects, very unwise in its contrivance, and very mischievous in its effects, that it therefore can have no long duration. Its very defects may tend to its stability, because they are agreeable to its nature. The very faults in the Constitution of Poland made it last; the *veto* which destroyed all its energy preserved its life. What can be conceived so monstrous as the republic of Algiers, and that no less strange republic of the Mamelukes in Egypt? They are of the worst form imaginable, and exercised in the worst manner, yet they have existed as a nuisance on the earth for several hundred years.

From all these considerations, and many more that crowd upon me, three conclusions have long since arisen in my mind.

First, that no counter revolution is to be expected in France from internal causes solely.

Secondly, that, the longer the present system exists, the greater will be its strength, the greater its power to destroy discontents at home, and to resist all foreign attempts in favor of these discontents.

Thirdly, that, as long as it exists in France, it will be the interest of the managers there, and it is in the very essence of their plan, to disturb and distract all other governments, and their endless succession of restless politicians will continually stimulate them to new attempts.

Princes are generally sensible that this is their common cause; and two of them have made a public declaration of their opinion to this effect. Against this common danger, some of them, such as the king of Spain, the king of Sardinia, and the republic of Bern, are very diligent in using defensive measures.

If they were to guard against an invasion from France, the merits of this plan of a merely defensive resistance might be supported by plausible topics; but as the attack does not operate against these countries externally, but by an internal corruption, (a sort of dry rot,) they who pursue this merely defensive plan against a danger which the plan itself supposes to be serious cannot possibly escape it. For it is in the nature of all defensive measures to be sharp and vigorous under the impressions of the first alarm, and to relax by degrees, until at length the danger, by not operating instantly, comes to appear as a false alarm,—so much so, that the next menacing appearance will look less formidable, and will be less provided against. But to those who are on the offensive it is not necessary to be always alert. Possibly it is more their interest not to be so. For their unforeseen attacks contribute to their success.

In the mean time a system of French conspiracy is gaining ground in every country. This system, happening to be founded on principles the most delusive indeed, but the most flattering to the natural propensities of the unthinking multitude, and to the speculations of all those who think, without thinking very profoundly, must daily extend its influence. A predominant inclination towards it appears in all those who have no religion, when otherwise their disposition leads them to be advocates even for despotism. Hence Hume, though I cannot say that he does not throw out some expressions of disapprobation on the proceedings of the levellers in the reign of Richard the Second, yet affirms that the doctrines of John Ball were "conformable to the ideas of primitive equality *which are engraven in the hearts of all men.*"

Boldness formerly was not the character of atheists as such. They were even of a character nearly the reverse; they were formerly like the old Epicureans, rather an unenterprising race. But of late they are grown active, designing, turbulent, and seditious. They are sworn enemies to kings, nobility, and priesthood. We have seen all the Academicians at Paris, with Condorcet, the friend and correspondent of Priestley, at their head, the most furious of the extravagant republicans.

The late Assembly, after the last captivity of the king, had actually chosen this Condorcet, by a majority on the ballot, for preceptor to the Dauphin, who was to be taken out of the hands and direction of his parents, and to be delivered over to this fanatic atheist and furious democratic republican. His untractability to these leaders, and his figure in the club of Jacobins, which at that time they wished to bring under, alone prevented that part of the arrangement, and others in the same style, from being carried into execution. Whilst he was candidate for this office, he produced his title to it by promulgating the following ideas of the title of his royal

pupil to the crown. In a paper written by him, and published
with his name, against the reëstablishment even of the appearance of monarchy under any qualifications, he says:—

"Jusqu'à ce moment, ils [l'Assemblée Nationale] n'ont rien
préjugé encore. En se réservant de nommer un gouverneur au
Dauphin, ils n'ont pas prononcé *que cet enfant dût régner,*
mais seulement qu'il *était possible* que la Constitution l'y
destinât; ils ont voulu que l'éducation effaçât tout ce que *les
prestiges du trône* ont pu lui inspirer de préjugés sur les droits
prétendus de sa naissance: qu'elle lui fît connaître de bonne
heure et *l'égalité naturelle des hommes et la souveraineté du
peuple;* qu'elle lui apprît à ne pas oublier que c'est *du peuple*
qu'il tiendra le titre de Roi, et que *le peuple n'a pas même le
droit de renoncer à celui de l'en dépouiller.*

"Ils ont voulu que cette éducation le rendît également
digne, par ses lumières et ses vertus, de recevoir *avec
résignation* le fardeau dangereux d'une couronne, ou de la
déposer avec joie entre les mains de ses frères; qu'il sentît
que le devoir et la gloire du roi d'un peuple libre sont de
hâter le moment de n'être plus qu'un citoyen ordinaire.

"Ils ont voulu que *l'inutilité d'un roi,* la nécessité de cher-
cher les moyens de remplacer *un pouvoir fondé sur des
illusions,* fût une des premières vérités offertes à sa raison;
*l'obligation d'y concourir lui-même, un des premiers devoirs
de sa morale; et le désir de n'être plus affranchi du joug de la
loi par une injurieuse inviolabilité, le premier sentiment de
son cœur.* Ils n'ignorent pas que dans ce moment il s'agit bien
moins de former un roi que de lui apprende *à savoir à vouloir
ne plus l'être.*" [3]

---

[3] "Until now, they [the National Assembly] have prejudged nothing.
Reserving to themselves a right to appoint a preceptor to the Dauphin,
they did not declare *that this child was to reign,* but only that *possibly*
the Constitution *might* destine him to it: they willed. that. while education should efface from his mind all the prejudices arising from *the delusions of the throne* respecting his pretended birthright, it should also
teach him not to forget that it is *from the people* he is to receive the
title of King, and that *the people do not even possess the right of
giving up their power to take it from him.*

Such are the sentiments of the man who has occasionally filled the chair of the National Assembly, who is their perpetual secretary, their only standing officer, and the most important by far. He leads them to peace or war. He is the great theme of the republican faction in England. These ideas of M. Condorcet are the principles of those to whom kings are to intrust their successors and the interests of their succession. This man would be ready to plunge the poniard in the heart of his pupil, or to whet the axe for his neck. Of all men, the most dangerous is a warm, hot-headed, zealous atheist. This sort of man aims at dominion, and his means are the words he always has in his mouth,—*"L'égalité naturelle des hommes, et la souveraineté du peuple."*

All former attempts, grounded on these rights of men, had proved unfortunate. The success of this last makes a mighty difference in the effect of the doctrine. Here is a principle of a nature to the multitude the most seductive, always existing before their eyes *as a thing feasible in practice.* After so many failures, such an enterprise, previous to the French experiment, carried ruin to the contrivers, on the face of it; and if any enthusiast was so wild as to wish to engage in a scheme of that nature, it was not easy for him to find followers: now there is a party almost in all countries, ready-made, animated with success, with a sure ally in the very centre of Europe. There is no cabal so obscure in any

---

"They willed that this education should render him worthy, by his knowledge and by his virtues, both to receive *with submission* the dangerous burden of a crown, and *to resign it with pleasure* into the hands of his brethren; that he should be conscious that the hastening of that moment when he is to be only a common citizen constitutes the duty and the glory of a king of a free people.

"They willed that *the uselessness of a king,* the necessity of seeking means to establish something in lieu of a *power founded on illusions,* should be one of the first truths offered to his reason; *the obligation of conforming himself to this, the first of his moral duties; and the desire of no longer being freed from the yoke of the law by an injurious inviolability, the first and chief sentiment of his heart.* They are not ignorant that in the present moment the object is less to form a king than to teach him *that he should know how to wish no longer to be such."* [Burke]

place, that they do not protect, cherish, foster, and endeavor to raise it into importance at home and abroad. From the lowest, this intrigue will creep up to the highest. Ambition, as well as enthusiasm, may find its account in the party and in the principle.

The ministers of other kings, like those of the king of France, (not one of whom was perfectly free from this guilt, and some of whom were very deep in it,) may themselves be the persons to foment such a disposition and such a faction. Hertzberg, the king of Prussia's late minister, is so much of what is called a philosopher, that he was of a faction with that sort of politicians in everything, and in every place. Even when he defends himself from the imputation of giving extravagantly into these principles, he still considers the Revolution of France as a great public good, by giving credit to their fraudulent declaration of their universal benevolence and love of peace. Nor are his Prussian Majesty's present ministers at all disinclined to the same system. Their ostentatious preamble to certain late edicts demonstrates (if their actions had not been sufficiently explanatory of their cast of mind) that they are deeply infected with the same distemper of dangerous, because plausible, though trivial and shallow, speculation.

Ministers, turning their backs on the reputation which properly belongs to them, aspire at the glory of being speculative writers. The duties of these two situations are in general directly opposite to each other. Speculators ought to be neutral. A minister cannot be so. He is to support the interest of the public as connected with that of his master. He is his master's trustee, advocate, attorney, and steward,—and he is not to indulge in any speculation which contradicts that character, or even detracts from its efficacy. Necker had an extreme thirst for this sort of glory; so had others; and this pursuit of a misplaced and misunderstood reputation was one of the causes of the ruin of these ministers, and of their unhappy master. The Prussian ministers in foreign courts have (at least not long since) talked the most democratic language with regard to France, and in the most unmanaged terms.

The whole *corps diplomatique,* with very few exceptions, leans that way. What cause produces in them a turn of mind which at first one would think unnatural to their situation it is not impossible to explain. The discussion would, however, be somewhat long and somewhat invidious. The fact itself is indisputable, however they may disguise it to their several courts. This disposition is gone to so very great a length in that corps, in itself so important, and so important as *furnishing* the intelligence which sways all cabinets, that, if princes and states do not very speedily attend with a vigorous control to that source of direction and information, very serious evils are likely to befall them.

But, indeed, kings are to guard against the same sort of dispositions in themselves. They are very easily alienated from all the higher orders of their subjects, whether civil or military, laic or ecclesiastical. It is with persons of condition that sovereigns chiefly come into contact. It is from them that they generally experience opposition to their will. It is with *their* pride and impracticability that princes are most hurt. It is with *their* servility and baseness that they are most commonly disgusted. It is from their humors and cabals that they find their affairs most frequently troubled and distracted. But of the common people, in pure monarchical governments, kings know little or nothing; and therefore being unacquainted with their faults, (which are as many as those of the great, and much more decisive in their effects, when accompanied with power,) kings generally regard them with tenderness and favor, and turn their eyes towards that description of their subjects, particularly when hurt by opposition from the higher orders. It was thus that the king of France (a perpetual example to all sovereigns) was ruined. I have it from very

Louis XVI

sure information, (and it was, indeed, obvious enough, from the measures which were taken previous to the assembly of the States and afterwards,) that the king's counsellors had filled him with a strong dislike to his nobility, his clergy, and the corps of his magistracy. They represented to him, that he had tried them all severally, in several ways, and found them all untractable: that he had twice called an assembly (the Notables) composed of the first men of the clergy, the nobility, and the magistrates; that he had himself named every one member in those assemblies, and that, though so picked out, he had not, in this their collective state, found them more disposed to a compliance with his will than they had been separately; that there remained for him, with the least prospect of advantage to his authority in the States-General, which were to be composed of the same sorts of men, but not chosen by him, only the *Tiers État:* in this alone he could repose any hope of extricating himself from his difficulties, and of settling him in a clear and permanent authority. They represented, (these are the words of one of my informants,) "that the royal authority, compressed with the weight of these aristocratic bodies, full of ambition and of faction, when once unloaded, would rise of itself, and occupy its natural place without disturbance or control"; that the common people would protect, cherish, and support, instead of crushing it. "The people" (it was said) "could entertain no objects of ambition"; they were out of the road of intrigue and cabal, and could possibly have no other view than the support of the mild and parental authority by which they were invested, for the first time collectively, with real importance in the state, and protected in their peaceable and useful employments.

This unfortunate king (not without a large share of blame to himself) was deluded to his ruin by a desire to humble and reduce his nobility, clergy, and his corporate magistracy: not that I suppose he meant wholly to eradicate these bodies, in the manner since effected by the democratic power; I rather believe that even Necker's designs did not go to that extent. With his own hand, however, Louis the Sixteenth pulled down the pillars which upheld his throne; and this he did, because he could not bear the inconveniences which are attached to everything human,—because he found himself cooped up, and in durance, by those limits which Nature prescribes to desire and imagination, and was taught to consider as low and degrading that mutual dependence which Providence has ordained that all men should have on one another. He is not at this minute, perhaps, cured of the dread of the power and credit like to be acquired by those who would save and rescue him. He leaves those who suffer in his cause to their fate,— and hopes, by various mean, delusive intrigues, in which I am afraid he is encouraged from abroad, to regain, among traitors and regicides, the power he has joined to take from his own family, whom he quietly sees proscribed before his eyes, and called to answer to the lowest of his rebels, as the vilest of all criminals.

It is to be hoped that the Emperor may be taught better things by this fatal example. But it is sure that he has advisers who endeavor to fill him with the ideas which have brought his brother-in-law to his present situation. Joseph the Second was far gone in this philosophy, and some, if not most, who serve the Emperor, would kindly initiate him into all the mysteries of this freemasonry. They would persuade him to look on the National Assembly, not with the hatred of an enemy, but the jealousy of a rival. They would make him desirous of doing, in his own dominions, by a royal despotism, what has been done in France by a democratic. Rather than abandon such enterprises, they would persuade him to a strange alliance between those extremes. Their grand object being now, as in his brother's time, at any rate to destroy the higher orders, they think he cannot compass this end, as certainly he cannot, without elevating the lower. By depressing the one and by raising the other they hope in the first place to increase his treasures and his army; and with

these common instruments of royal power they flatter him
that the democracy, which they help in his name to create,
will give him but little trouble. In defiance of the freshest
experience, which might show him that old impossibilities
are become modern probabilities, and that the extent to
which evil principles may go, when left to their own operation, is beyond the power of calculation, they will endeavor
to persuade him that such a democracy is a thing which cannot subsist by itself; that in whose ever hands the military
command is placed, he must be, in the necessary course of
affairs, sooner or later the master; and that, being the master
of various unconnected countries, he may keep them all in
order by employing a military force which to each of them
is foreign. This maxim, too, however formerly plausible, will
not now hold water. This scheme is full of intricacy, and may
cause him everywhere to lose the hearts of his people. These
counsellors forget that a corrupted army was the very cause
of the ruin of his brother-in-law, and that he is himself far
from secure from a similar corruption.

Instead of reconciling himself heartily and *bonâ fide*,
according to the most obvious rules of policy, to the States
of Brabant, *as they are constituted*, and who in *the present
state of things* stand on the same foundation with the
monarchy itself, and who might have been gained with the
greatest facility, they have advised him to the most unkingly
proceeding which, either in a good or in a bad light, has ever
been attempted. Under a pretext taken from the spirit of the
lowest chicane, they have counselled him wholly to break the
public faith, to annul the amnesty, as well as the other
conditions through which he obtained an entrance into the
Provinces of the Netherlands under the guaranty of Great
Britain and Prussia. He is made to declare his adherence to
the indemnity in a criminal sense, but he is to keep alive in
his own name, and to encourage in others, a *civil* process in
the nature of an action of damages for what has been

suffered during the troubles. Whilst he keeps up this hopeful lawsuit in view of the damages he may recover against individuals, he loses the hearts of a whole people, and the vast subsidies which his ancestors had been used to receive from them.

This design once admitted unriddles the mystery of the whole conduct of the Emperor's ministers with regard to France. As soon as they saw the life of the king and queen of France no longer, as they thought, in danger, they entirely changed their plan with regard to the French nation. I believe that the chiefs of the Revolution (those who led the constituting Assembly) have contrived, as far as they can do it, to give the Emperor satisfaction on this head. He keeps a continual tone and posture of menace to secure this his only point. But it must be observed, that he all along grounds his departure from the engagement at Pilnitz to the princes on the will and actions of *the king* and the majority of the people, without any regard to the natural and constitutional orders of the state, or to the opinions of the whole House of Bourbon. Though it is manifestly under the constraint of imprisonment and the fear of death that this unhappy man has been guilty of all those humilities which have astonished mankind, the advisers of the Emperor will consider nothing but the *physical* person of Louis, which, even in his present degraded and infamous state, they regard as of sufficient authority to give a complete sanction to the persecution and utter ruin of all his family, and of every person who has shown any degree of attachment or fidelity to him or to his cause, as well as competent to destroy the whole ancient constitution and frame of the French monarchy.

The present policy, therefore, of the Austrian politicians is, to recover despotism through democracy,—or, at least, at any expense, everywhere to ruin the description of men who are everywhere the objects of their settled and systematic aversion, but more especially in the Netherlands. Compare

this with the Emperor's refusing at first all intercourse with
the present powers in France, with his endeavoring to excite
all Europe against them, and then, his not only withdrawing
all assistance and all countenance from the fugitives who
had been drawn by his declarations from their houses, situations, and military commissions, many even from the means of
their very existence, but treating them with every species of
insult and outrage.

Combining this unexampled conduct in the Emperor's
advisers with the timidity (operating as perfidy) of the king
of France, a fatal example is held out to all subjects, tending
to show what little support, or even countenance, they are to
expect from those for whom their principle of fidelity may
induce them to risk life and fortune. The Emperor's advisers
would not for the world rescind one of the acts of this or of
the late French Assembly; nor do they wish anything better
at present for their master's brother of France than that he
should really be, as he is nominally, at the head of the system
of persecution of religion and good order, and of all descriptions of dignity, natural and instituted: they only wish all this
done with a little more respect to the king's person, and with
more appearance of consideration for his new subordinate
office,—in hopes, that, yielding himself for the present to the
persons who have effected these changes, he may be able to
game for the rest hereafter. On no other principles than these
can the conduct of the court of Vienna be accounted for.
The subordinate court of Brussels talks the language of a
club of Feuillants and Jacobins.

In this state of general rottenness among subjects, and of
delusion and false politics in princes, comes a new experiment. The king of France is in the hands of the chiefs of the
regicide faction,—the Barnaves, Lameths, Fayettes, Périgords,
Duports, Robespierres, Camuses, &c., &c., &c. They who
had imprisoned, suspended, and conditionally deposed him
are his confidential counsellors. The next desperate of the

desperate rebels call themselves the *moderate* party. They
are the chiefs of the first Assembly, who are confederated to
support their power during their suspension from the present,
and to govern the existent body with as sovereign a sway
as they had done the last. They have, for the greater part,
succeeded; and they have many advantages towards procuring their success in future. Just before the close of their
regular power, they bestowed some appearance of prerogatives on the king, which in their first plans they had refused
to him,—particularly the mischievous, and, in his situation,
dreadful prerogative of a *veto*. This prerogative, (which they
hold as their bit in the mouth of the National Assembly for
the time being,) without the direct assistance of their club,
it was impossible for the king to show even the desire of
exerting with the smallest effect, or even with safety to his
person. However, by playing, through this *veto,* the Assembly
against the king, and the king against the Assembly, they
have made themselves masters of both. In this situation,
having destroyed the old government by their sedition, they
would preserve as much of order as is necessary for the
support of their own usurpation.

It is believed that this, by far the worst party of the miscreants of France, has received direct encouragement from
the counsellors who betray the Emperor. Thus strengthened
by the possession of the captive king, (now captive in his
mind as well as in body,) and by a good hope of the Emperor,
they intend to send their ministers to every court in Europe,
—having sent before them such a denunciation of terror and
superiority to every nation without exception as has no example in the diplomatic world. Hitherto the ministers to
foreign courts had been of the appointment of the sovereign
of France *previous to the Revolution;* and, either from inclination, duty, or decorum, most of them were contented
with a merely passive obedience to the new power. At present,
the king, being entirely in the hands of his jailors, and his

mind broken to his situation, can send none but the enthusiasts of the system,—men framed by the secret committee of the Feuillants, who meet in the house of Madame de Staël, M. Necker's daughter. Such is every man whom they have talked of sending hither. These ministers will be so many spies and incendiaries, so many active emissaries of democracy. Their houses will become places of rendezvous here, as everywhere else, and centres of cabal for whatever is mischievous and malignant in this country, particularly among those of rank and fashion. As the minister of the National Assembly will be admitted at this court, at least with his usual rank, and as entertainments will be naturally given and received by the king's own ministers, any attempt to discountenance the resort of other people to that minister would be ineffectual, and indeed absurd, and full of contradiction. The women who come with these ambassadors will assist in fomenting factions amongst ours, which cannot fail of extending the evil. Some of them I hear are already arrived. There is no doubt they will do as much mischief as they can.

Whilst the public ministers are received under the general law of the communication between nations, the correspondences between the factious clubs in France and ours will be, as they now are, kept up; but this pretended embassy will be a closer, more steady, and more effectual link between the partisans of the new system on both sides of the water. I do not mean that these Anglo-Gallic clubs in London, Manchester, &c., are not dangerous in a high degree. The appointment of festive anniversaries has ever in the sense of mankind been held the best method of keeping alive the spirit of any institution. We have one settled in London; and at the last of them, that of the 14th of July, the strong discountenance of government, the unfavorable time of the year, and the then uncertainty of the disposition of foreign powers, did not hinder the meeting of at least nine hundred people, with good coats on their backs, who could afford to pay half a guinea a head to show their zeal for the new principles. They were with great difficulty, and all possible address, hindered from inviting the French ambassador. His real indisposition, besides the fear of offending any party, sent him out of town. But when our court shall have recognized a government in France founded on the principles announced in Montmorin's letter, how can the French ambassador be frowned upon for an attendance on those meetings wherein the establishment of the government he represents is celebrated? An event happened a few days ago, which in many particulars was very ridiculous; yet, even from the ridicule and absurdity of the proceedings, it marks the more strongly the spirit of the French Assembly: I mean the reception they have given to the Frith Street Alliance. This, though the delirium of a low, drunken alehouse club, they have publicly announced as a formal alliance with the people of England, as such ordered it to be presented to their king, and to be published in every province in France. This leads, more directly and with much greater force than any proceeding with a regular and rational appearance, to two very material considerations. First, it shows that they are of opinion that the current opinions of the English have the greatest influence on the minds of the people in France, and indeed of all the people in Europe, since they catch with such astonishing eagerness at every the most trifling show of such opinions in their favor. Next, and what appears to me to be full as important, it shows that they are willing publicly to countenance, and even to adopt, every factious conspiracy that can be formed in this nation, however low and base in itself, in order to excite in the most miserable wretches here an idea of their own sovereign importance, and to encourage them to look up to France, whenever they may be matured into something of more force, for assistance in the subversion of their domestic government. This address of the alehouse club was actually proposed and accepted by the Assembly as an

Infl. on England

alliance. The procedure was in my opinion a high misdemeanor in those who acted thus in England, if they were not so very low and so very base that no acts of theirs can be called high, even as a description of criminality; and the Assembly, in accepting, proclaiming, and publishing this forged alliance, has been guilty of a plain aggression, which would justify our court in demanding a direct disavowal, if our policy should not lead us to wink at it.

Whilst I look over this paper to have it copied, I see a manifesto of the Assembly, as a preliminary to a declaration of war against the German princes on the Rhine. This manifesto contains the whole substance of the French politics with regard to foreign states. They have ordered it to be circulated amongst the people in every country of Europe,—even previously to its acceptance by the king, and his new privy council, the club of the Feuillants. Therefore, as a summary of their policy avowed by themselves, let us consider some of the circumstances attending that piece, as well as the spirit and temper of the piece itself.

It was preceded by a speech from Brissot, full of unexampled insolence towards all the sovereign states of Germany, if not of Europe. The Assembly, to express their satisfaction in the sentiments which it contained, ordered it to be printed. This Brissot had been in the lowest and basest employ under the deposed monarchy,—a sort of thief-taker, or spy of police,— in which character he acted after the manner of persons in that description. He had been employed by his master, the *Lieutenant de Police,* for a considerable time in London, in the same or some such honorable occupation. The Revolution, which has brought forward all merit of that kind, raised him, with others of a similar class and disposition, to fame and eminence. On the Revolution he became a publisher of an infamous newspaper, which he still continues. He is charged, and I believe justly, as the first mover of the troubles in Hispaniola. There is no wickedness, if I am rightly informed, in which he is not versed, and of which he is not perfectly capable. His quality of news-writer, now an employment of the first dignity in France, and his practices and principles, procured his election into the Assembly, where he is one of the leading members. M. Condorcet produced on the same day a draught of a declaration to the king, which the Assembly published before it was presented.

Condorcet (though no marquis, as he styled himself before the Revolution) is a man of another sort of birth, fashion, and occupation from Brissot,—but in every principle, and every disposition to the lowest as well as the highest and most determined villanies, fully his equal. He seconds Brissot in the Assembly, and is at once his coadjutor and his rival in a newspaper, which, in his own name, and as successor to M. Garat, a member also of the Assembly, he has just set up in that empire of gazettes. Condorcet was chosen to draw the first declaration presented by the Assembly to the king, as a threat to the Elector of Treves, and the other princes on the Rhine. In that piece, in which both Feuillants and Jacobins concurred, they declared publicly, and most proudly and insolently, the principle on which they mean to proceed in their future disputes with any of the sovereigns of Europe; for they say, "that it is not with fire and sword they mean to attack their territories, but by what will be *more dreadful* to them, the introduction of liberty."—I have not the paper by me, to give the exact words, but I believe they are nearly as I state them.—*Dreadful,* indeed, will be their hostility, if they should be able to carry it on according to the example of *their* modes of introducing liberty. They have shown a perfect model of their whole design, very complete, though in little. This gang of murderers and savages have wholly laid waste and utterly ruined the beautiful and happy country of the Comtat Venaissin and the city of Avignon. This cruel and treacherous outrage the sovereigns of Europe, in my opinion, with a great mistake of their honor and interest, have permitted, even without a remonstrance, to be carried to the desired point, on the principles on which they are now themselves threatened in their own states; and this, because, according to the poor and narrow spirit now in fashion, their brother sovereign, whose subjects have been thus traitorously and inhumanly treated in violation of the law of Nature and of nations, has a name somewhat different from theirs, and, instead of being styled King, or Duke, or Landgrave, is usually called Pope.

The Electors of Treves and Mentz were frightened with the menace of a similar mode of war. The Assembly, however, not thinking that the Electors of Treves and Mentz had done enough under their first terror, have again brought forward Condorcet, preceded by Brissot, as I have just stated. The declaration, which they have ordered now to be circulated in all countries, is in substance the same as the first, but still more insolent, because more full of detail. There they have the impudence to state that they aim at no conquest: insinuating that all the old, lawful powers of the world had each made a constant, open profession of a design of subduing his neighbors. They add, that, if they are provoked, their war will be directed only against those who assume to be *masters;* but to the *people* they will bring peace, law, liberty, &c., &c. There is not the least hint that they consider those whom they call persons *"assuming to be masters"* to be the lawful government of their country, or persons to be treated with the least management or respect. They regard them as usurpers and enslavers of the people. If I do not mistake, they are described by the name of tyrants in Condorcet's first draught. I am sure they are so in Brissot's speech, ordered by the Assembly to be printed at the same time and for the same purposes. The whole is in the same strain, full of false philosophy and false rhetoric,—both, however, calculated to captivate and influence the vulgar mind, and to excite sedition in the countries in which it is ordered to be circulated. Indeed, it is such, that, if any of the lawful, acknowledged sovereigns of Europe had publicly ordered such a manifesto to be circulated in the dominions of another, the ambassador of that power would instantly be ordered to quit every court without an audience.

The powers of Europe have a pretext for concealing their fears, by saying that this language is not used by the king; though they well know that there is in effect no such person,—that the Assembly is in reality, and by that king is acknowledged to be, *the master,*—that what he does is but matter of formality,—and that he can neither cause nor hinder, accelerate nor retard, any measure whatsoever, nor add to nor soften the manifesto which the Assembly has directed to be published, with the declared purpose of exciting mutiny and rebellion in the several countries governed by these powers. By the generality also of the menaces contained in this paper, (though infinitely aggravating the outrage,) they hope to remove from each power separately the idea of a distinct affront. The persons first pointed at by the menace are certainly the princes of Germany, who harbor the persecuted House of Bourbon and the nobility of France; the declaration, however, is general, and goes to every state with which they may have a cause of quarrel. But the terror of France has fallen upon all nations. A few months since all sovereigns seemed disposed to unite against her; at present they all seem to combine in her favor. At no period has the power of France ever appeared with so formidable an aspect, In particular the liberties of the Empire can have nothing more than an existence the most tottering and precarious, whilst France exists with a great power of fomenting rebellion, and the greatest in the weakest, —but with neither power nor disposition to support the smaller states in their independence against the attempts of the more powerful.

I wind up all in a full conviction within my own breast, and the substance of which I must repeat over and over again, that the state of France is the first consideration in the politics of Europe, and of each state, externally as well as internally considered.

Most of the topics I have used are drawn from fear and apprehension. Topics derived from fear or addressed to it are, I well know, of doubtful appearance. To be sure, hope is in general the incitement to action. Alarm some men,—you do not drive them to provide for their security; you put them to a stand; you induce them, not to take measures to prevent the approach of danger, but to remove so unpleasant an idea from their minds; you persuade them to remain as they are, from a new fear that their activity may bring on the apprehended mischief before its time. I confess freely that this evil sometimes happens from an overdone precaution; but it is when the measures are rash, ill-chosen, or ill-combined, and the effects rather of blind terror than of enlightened foresight. But the few to whom I wish to submit my thoughts are of a character which will enable them to see danger without astonishment, and to provide against it without perplexity.

To what lengths this method of circulating mutinous manifestoes, and of keeping emissaries of sedition in every court under the name of ambassadors, to propagate the same principles and to follow the practices, will go, and how soon they will operate, it is hard to say; but go on it will, more or less rapidly, according to events, and to the humor of the time. The princes menaced with the revolt of their subjects, at the same time that they have obsequiously obeyed the sovereign mandate of the new Roman senate, have received with distinction, in a public character, ambassadors from those who in the same act had circulated the manifesto of sedition in their dominions. This was the only thing wanting to the degradation and disgrace of the Germanic body.

The ambassadors from the rights of man, and their admission into the diplomatic system, I hold to be a new era in this business. It will be the most important step yet taken to affect the existence of sovereigns, and the higher classes of life: I do not mean to exclude its effects upon all classes; but the first blow is aimed at the more prominent parts in the ancient order of things.

What is to be done?

It would be presumption in me to do more than to make a case. Many things occur. But as they, like all political measures, depend on dispositions, tempers, means, and external circumstances, for all their effect, not being well assured of these, I do not know how to let loose any speculations of mine on the subject. The evil is stated, in my opinion, as it exists. The remedy must be where power, wisdom, and information, I hope, are more united with good intentions than they can be with me. I have done with this subject I believe, forever. It has given me many anxious moments for the two last years. If a great change is to be made in human affairs, the minds of men will be fitted to it, the general opinions and feelings will draw that way. Every fear, every hope, will forward it; and then they who persist in opposing this mighty current in human affairs will appear rather to resist the decrees of Providence itself than the mere designs of men. They will not be resolute and firm, but perverse and obstinate.

FROM *Letters on a Regicide Peace*[1]

. . . The operation of dangerous and delusive first principles obliges us to have recourse to the true ones. In the intercourse between nations, we are apt to rely too much on the instrumental part. We lay too much weight upon the formality of treaties and compacts. We do not act much more wisely, when we trust to the interests of men as guaranties of their engagements. The interests frequently tear to pieces the engagements, and the passions trample upon both. Entirely to trust to either is to disregard our own safety, or not to know mankind. Men are not tied to one another by papers and seals. They are led to associate by resemblances, by conformities, by sympathies. It is with nations as with individuals. Nothing is so strong a tie of amity between nation and nation as correspondence in laws, customs, manners, and habits of life. They have more than the force of treaties in themselves. They are obligations written in the heart. They approximate men to men without their knowledge, and sometimes against their intentions. The secret, unseen, but irrefragable bond of habitual intercourse holds them together, even when their per-

[1] From "Four Letters on the Proposals for Peace with the Regicide Directory of France." The following selections are from the close of Letter I and the beginning of Letter II (written in late 1795 and early 1796).

verse and litigious nature sets them to equivocate, scuffle, and fight about the terms of their written obligations.

As to war, if it be the means of wrong and violence, it is the sole means of justice amongst nations. Nothing can banish it from the world. They who say otherwise, intending to impose upon us, do not impose upon themselves. But it is one of the greatest objects of human wisdom to mitigate those evils which we are unable to remove. The conformity and analogy of which I speak, incapable, like everything else, of preserving perfect trust and tranquillity among men, has a strong tendency to facilitate accommodation, and to produce a generous oblivion of the rancor of their quarrels. With this similitude, peace is more of peace, and war is less of war. I will go further. There have been periods of time in which communities apparently in peace with each other have been more perfectly separated than in later times many nations in Europe have been in the course of long and bloody wars. The cause must be sought in the similitude throughout Europe of religion, laws, and manners. At bottom, these are all the same. The writers on public law have often called this *aggregate* of nations a commonwealth. They had reason. It is virtually one great state, having the same basis of general law, with some diversity of provincial customs and local establishments. The nations of Europe have had the very same Christian religion, agreeing in the fundamental parts, varying a little in the ceremonies and in the subordinate doctrines. The whole of the polity and economy of every country in Europe has been derived from the same sources. It was drawn from the old Germanic or Gothic Custumary,—from the feudal institutions, which must be considered as an emanation from that Custumary; and the whole has been improved and digested into system and discipline by the Roman law. From hence arose the several orders, with or without a monarch, (which are called States,) in every European country; the strong traces of which, where monarchy predominated, were never wholly extinguished or merged in despotism. In the few places where monarchy was cast off, the spirit of European monarchy was still left. Those countries still continued countries of States,— that is, of classes, orders, and distinctions, such as had before subsisted, or nearly so. Indeed, the force and form of the institution called States continued in greater perfection in those republican communities than under monarchies. From all those sources arose a system of manners and of education which was nearly similar in all this quarter of the globe,— and which softened, blended, and harmonized the colors of the whole. There was little difference in the form of the universities for the education of their youth, whether with regard to faculties, to sciences, or to the more liberal and elegant kinds of erudition. From this resemblance in the modes of intercourse, and in the whole form and fashion of life, no citizen of Europe could be altogether an exile in any part of it. There was nothing more than a pleasing variety to recreate and instruct the mind, to enrich the imagination, and to meliorate the heart. When a man travelled or resided, for health, pleasure, business, or necessity, from his own country, he never felt himself quite abroad.

The whole body of this new scheme of manners, in support of the new scheme of politics, I consider as a strong and decisive proof of determined ambition and systematic hostility. I defy the most refining ingenuity to invent any other cause for the total departure of the Jacobin Republic from every one of the ideas and usages, religious, legal, moral, or social, of this civilized world, and for her tearing herself from its communion with such studied violence, but from a formed resolution of keeping no terms with that world. It has not been, as has been falsely and insidiously represented, that these miscreants had only broke with their old government. They made a schism with the whole universe, and that schism extended to almost everything, great and small. For one, I wish, since it is gone thus far, that the breach had been so complete as to make all intercourse impracticable: but, partly by accident, partly by design, partly from the resistance of the matter, enough is left to preserve intercourse, whilst amity is destroyed or corrupted in its principle.

This violent breach of the community of Europe we must conclude to have been made (even if they had not expressly declared it over and over again) either to force mankind into an adoption of their system or to live in perpetual enmity with a community the most potent we have ever known. Can any person imagine, that, in offering to mankind this desperate alternative, there is no indication of a hostile mind, because men in possession of the ruling authority are supposed to have a right to act without coercion in their own territories? As to the right of men to act anywhere according to their pleasure, without any moral tie, no such right exists. Men are never in a state of *total* independence of each other. It is not the condition of our nature: nor is it conceivable how any man can pursue a considerable course of action without its having some effect upon others, or, of course, without producing some degree of responsibility for his conduct. The *situations* in which men relatively stand produce the rules and principles of that responsibility, and afford directions to prudence in exacting it. . . .

My ideas and my principles led me, in this contest, to encounter France, not as a state, but as a faction. The vast territorial extent of that country, its immense population, its riches of production, its riches of commerce and convention, the whole aggregate mass of what in ordinary cases constitutes the force of a state, to me were but objects of secondary consideration. They might be balanced; and they have been often more than balanced. Great as these things are, they are not what make the faction formidable. It is the faction that makes them truly dreadful. That faction is the evil spirit that possesses the body of France,—that informs it as a soul,—that stamps upon its ambition, and upon all its pursuits, a characteristic mark, which strongly distinguishes them from the same general passions and the same general views in other men and in other communities. It is that spirit which inspires into them a new, pernicious, a desolating activity. Constituted as France was ten years ago, it was not in that France to shake, to shatter, and to overwhelm Europe in the manner that we behold. A sure destruction impends over those infatuated princes who, in the conflict with this new and unheard-of power, proceed as if they were engaged in a war that bore a resemblance to their former contests, or that they can make peace in the spirit of their former arrangements of pacification. Here the beaten path is the very reverse of the safe road.

As to me, I was always steadily of opinion that this disorder was not in its nature intermittent. I conceived that the contest, once begun, could not be laid down again, to be resumed at our discretion, but that our first struggle with this evil would also be our last. I never thought we could make peace with the system; because it was not for the sake of an object we pursued in rivalry with each other, but with the system itself that we were at war. As I understood the matter, we were at war, not with its conduct, but with its existence,—convinced that its existence and its hostility were the same.

The faction is not local or territorial. It is a general evil. Where it least appears in action, it is still full of life. In its sleep it recruits its strength and prepares its exertion. Its spirit lies deep in the corruptions of our common nature. The social order which restrains it feeds it. It exists in every country in Europe, and among all orders of men in every country, who look up to France as to a common head. The centre is there. The circumference is the world of Europe, wherever the race of Europe may be settled. Everywhere else the faction is militant; in France it is triumphant. In France is the bank of deposit and the bank of circulation of all the pernicious principles that are forming in every state. It will be a folly scarcely deserving of pity, and too mischievous for contempt, to think of restraining it in any other country whilst it is predominant there. War, instead of being the cause of its force, has suspended its operation. It has given a reprieve, at least, to the Christian world.

The true nature of a Jacobin war, in the beginning, was by most of the Christian powers felt, acknowledged, and even in the most precise manner declared. In the joint manifesto published by the Emperor and the King of Prussia, on the 4th of August, 1792, it is expressed in the clearest terms, and on principles which could not fail, if they had adhered to them, of classing those monarchs with the first benefactors of mankind. This manifesto was published, as they themselves express it, "to lay open to the present generation, as well as to posterity, their motives, their intentions, and the *disinterestedness* of their personal views: taking up arms for the purpose of preserving social and political order amongst all civilized nations, and to secure to *each* state its religion, happiness, independence, territories, and real constitution."—"On this ground they hoped that all empires and all states would be unanimous, and, becoming the firm guardians of the happiness of mankind, that they could not fail to unite their efforts to rescue a numerous nation from its own fury, to preserve Europe from the return of barbarism, and the universe from the subversion and anarchy with which it was threatened." The whole of that noble performance ought to be read at the first meeting of any congress which may assemble for the purpose of pacification. In that piece "these powers expressly renounce all views of personal aggrandizement," and confine themselves to objects worthy of so generous, so heroic, and so perfectly wise and politic an enterprise. It was to the principles of this confederation, and to no other, that we wished our sovereign and our country to accede, as a part of the commonwealth of Europe. To these principles, with some trifling exceptions and limitations, they did fully accede.[2] And all our friends who took office acceded to the ministry, (whether wisely or not,) as I always understood the matter, on the faith and on the principles of that declaration.

As long as these powers flattered themselves that the menace of force would produce the effect of force, they acted on those declarations; but when their menaces failed of success, their efforts took a new direction. It did not appear to them that virtue and heroism ought to be purchased by millions of rix-dollars. It is a dreadful truth, but it is a truth that cannot be concealed: in ability, in dexterity, in the distinctness of their views, the Jacobins are our superiors. They saw the thing right from the very beginning. Whatever were the first motives to the war among politicians, they saw that in its spirit, and for its objects, it was a *civil war;* and as such they pursued it. It is a war between the partisans of the ancient civil, moral, and political order of Europe against a sect of fanatical and ambitious atheists which means to change them all. It is not France extending a foreign empire over other nations: it is a sect aiming at universal empire, and beginning with the conquest of France. The leaders of that sect secured *the centre of Europe;* and that secured, they knew, that, whatever might be the event of battles and sieges, their *cause* was victorious. Whether its territory had a little more or a little less peeled from its surface, or whether an island or two was detached from its commerce, to them was of little moment. The conquest of France was a glorious acquisition. That once well laid as a basis of empire, opportunities never could be wanting to regain or to replace what had been lost, and dreadfully to avenge themselves on the faction of their adversaries. . . .

---

[2] See Declaration, Whitehall, Oct. 29, 1793. [Burke]

VI
LETTER TO
A NOBLE LORD

Letter to a Noble Lord [1]

My Lord: I could hardly flatter myself with the hope, that so very early in the season I should have to acknowledge obligations to the Duke of BEDFORD, and to the Earl of LAUDERDALE. [2] These noble persons have lost no time in conferring upon me that sort of honour, which it is alone within their competence, and which it is certainly most congenial to their nature, and to their manners, to bestow.

To be ill spoken of, in whatever language they speak, by the zealots of the new sect in philosophy and politics, of which these noble persons think so charitably, and of which others think so justly, to me, is no matter of uneasiness or surprise. To have incurred the displeasure of the Duke of Orleans or the Duke of Bedford, to fall under the censure of citizen Brissot or of his friend the Earl of Lauderdale, I ought to consider as proofs, not the least satisfactory, that I have produced some part of the effect I proposed by my endeavours. I have laboured hard to earn, what the noble lords are generous enough to pay. Personal offence I have given them none. The part they take against me is from zeal

---

[1] "A letter from the Right Hon. Edmund Burke to a Noble Lord on the Attacks Made upon Him and his Pension, in the House of Lords, by the Duke of Bedford and the Earl of Lauderdale, Early in the Present Session of Parliament" (1795). Bedford and Lauderdale, attempting to embarrass the Government, had attacked Burke's pension (which was conferred directly by the Crown) as having been made without the consent of Parliament, as excessive in amount, and as inconsistent with the principles of economic reform Burke himself had advocated.

[2] James Maitland (1759-1839), Eighth Earl.

to the cause. It is well! It is perfectly well! I have to do homage to their justice. I have to thank the Bedfords and the Lauderdales for having so faithfully and so fully acquitted towards me whatever arrear of debt was left undischarged by the Priestleys and the Paines.[3]

Some, perhaps, may think them executors in their own wrong; I at least have nothing to complain of. They have gone beyond the demands of justice. They have been (a little perhaps beyond their intention) favourable to me. They have been the means of bringing out, by their invectives, the handsome things which Lord Grenville has had the goodness and condescension to say in my behalf. Retired as I am from the world, and from all its affairs and all its pleasures, I confess it does kindle, in my nearly extinguished feelings, a very vivid satisfaction to be so attacked and so commended. It is soothing to my wounded mind, to be commended by an able, vigorous, and well-informed statesman, and at the very moment when he stands forth with a manliness and resolution, worthy of himself and of his cause, for the preservation of the person and government of our sovereign, and therein for the security of the laws, the liberties, the morals, and the lives of his people. To be in any fair way connected with such things, is indeed a distinction. No philosophy can make me above it; no melancholy can depress me so low, as to make me wholly insensible to such an honour.

Why will they not let me remain in obscurity and inaction? Are they apprehensive, that if an atom of me remains, the sect has something to fear? Must I be annihilated, lest, like old *John Zisca's*,[4] my skin might be made into a drum, to animate Europe to eternal battle, against a tyranny that threatens to overwhelm all Europe, and all the human race?

---

[3] Joseph Priestley and Thomas Paine, both strong sympathizers with the Revolution.
[4] John Zisca (1360-1424), the Hussite leader, who supposedly asked that his skin, at his death, be made into drumheads.

My Lord, it is the subject of awful meditation. Before this of France, the annals of all time have not furnished an instance of a *complete* revolution. That Revolution seems to have extended even to the constitution of the mind of man. It has this of wonderful in it, that it resembles what Lord Verulam[5] says of the operations of nature. It was perfect, not only in its elements and principles, but in all its members and its organs from the very beginning. The moral scheme of France furnishes the only pattern ever known, which they who admire will *instantly* resemble. It is indeed an inexhaustible repertory of one kind of examples. In my wretched condition, though hardly to be classed with the living, I am not safe from them. They have tigers to fall upon animated strength. They have hyenas to prey upon carcasses. The national menagerie is collected by the first physiologists of the time; and it is defective in no description of savage nature. They pursue even such as me, into the obscurest retreats, and haul them before their revolutionary tribunals. Neither sex, nor age, nor the sanctuary of the tomb, is sacred to them. They have so determined a hatred to all privileged orders, that they deny even to the departed the sad immunities of the grave. They are not wholly without an object. Their turpitude purveys to their malice; and they unplumb the dead for bullets to assassinate the living. If all revolutionists were not proof against all caution, I should recommend it to their consideration, that no persons were ever known in history, either sacred or profane, to vex the sepulchre, and, by their sorceries, to call up the prophetic dead, with any other event, than the prediction of their own disastrous fate.—"Leave me, oh leave me to repose!"

In one thing I can excuse the Duke of Bedford for his attack upon me and my mortuary pension. He cannot readily comprehend the transaction he condemns. What I have ob-

---

[5] Francis Bacon.

tained was the fruit of no bargain; the production of no intrigue; the result of no compromise; the effect of no solicitation. The first suggestion of it never came from me mediately or immediately, to his Majesty or any of his ministers. It was long known that the instant my engagements would permit it, and before the heaviest of all calamities had for ever condemned me to obscurity and sorrow, I had resolved on a total retreat. I had executed that design. I was entirely out of the way of serving or of hurting any statesman, or any party, when the ministers so generously and so nobly carried into effect the spontaneous bounty of the Crown. Both descriptions have acted as became them. When I could no longer serve them, the ministers have considered my situation. When I could no longer hurt them, the revolutionists have trampled on my infirmity. My gratitude, I trust, is equal to the manner in which the benefit was conferred. It came to me indeed, at a time of life, and in a state of mind and body, in which no circumstances of fortune could afford me any real pleasure. But this was no fault in the royal donor, or in his ministers, who were pleased, in acknowledging the merits of an invalid servant of the public, to assuage the sorrows of a desolate old man.

It would ill become me to boast of anything. It would as ill become me, thus called upon, to depreciate the value of a long life, spent with unexampled toil in the service of my country. Since the total body of my services, on account of the industry which was shown in them, and the fairness of my intentions, have obtained the acceptance of my sovereign, it would be absurd in me to range myself on the side of the Duke of Bedford and the corresponding society, or, as far as in me lies, to permit a dispute on the rate at which the authority appointed by *our* constitution to estimate such things has been pleased to set them.

Loose libels ought to be passed by in silence and contempt. By me they have been so always. I knew that as long as I remained in public, I should live down the calumnies of malice, and the judgments of ignorance. If I happened to be now and then in the wrong, (as who is not?) like all other men, I must bear the consequence of my faults and my mistakes. The libels of the present day are just of the same stuff as the libels of the past. But they derive an importance from the rank of the persons they came from, and the gravity of the place where they were uttered. In some way or other I ought to take some notice of them. To assert myself thus traduced is not vanity or arrogance. It is a demand of justice; it is a demonstration of gratitude. If I am unworthy, the ministers are worse than prodigal. On that hypothesis, I perfectly agree with the Duke of Bedford.

For whatever I have been (I am now no more) I put myself on my country. I ought to be allowed a reasonable freedom, because I stand upon my deliverance; and no culprit ought to plead in irons. Even in the utmost latitude of defensive liberty, I wish to preserve all possible decorum. Whatever it may be in the eyes of these noble persons themselves, to me their situation calls for the most profound respect. If I should happen to trespass a little, which I trust I shall not, let it always be supposed, that a confusion of characters may produce mistakes; that, in the masquerades of the grand carnival of our age, whimsical adventures happen; odd things are said and pass off. If I should fail a single point in the high respect I owe to those illustrious persons, I cannot be supposed to mean the Duke of Bedford and the Earl of Lauderdale of the House of Peers, but the Duke of Bedford and the Earl of Lauderdale of Palace-Yard!—The Dukes and Earls of Brentford. There they are on the pavement; there they seem to come nearer to my humble level; and, virtually at least, to have waived their high privilege.

Making this protestation, I refuse all revolutionary tribunals, where men have been put to death for no other reason, than that they had obtained favours from the Crown. I claim, not the letter, but the spirit, of the English law, that is, to be tried by my peers. I decline his Grace's jurisdiction as a judge. I challenge the Duke of Bedford as a juror to pass upon the value of my services. Whatever his natural parts may be, I cannot recognize, in his few and idle years, the comp.- tence to judge of my long and laborious life. If I can help it, he shall not be on the inquest of my *quantum meruit*.[6] Poor rich man! He can hardly know anything of public industry in its exertions, or can estimate its compensations when its work is done. I have no doubt of his Grace's readiness in all the calculations of vulgar arithmetic; but I shrewdly suspect that he is little studied in the theory of moral proportions; and has never learned the rule of three in the arithmetic of policy and state.

His Grace thinks I have obtained too much. I answer, that my exertions, whatever they have been, were such as no hopes of pecuniary reward could possibly excite; and no pecuniary compensation can possibly reward them. Between money and such services, if done by abler men than I am, there is no common principle of comparison: they are quantities incom- mensurable. Money is made for the comfort and convenience of animal life. It cannot be a reward for what mere animal life must indeed sustain, but never can inspire. With sub- mission to his Grace, I have not had more than sufficient. As to any noble use, I trust I know how to employ, as well as he, a much greater fortune than he possesses. In a more confined application, I certainly stand in need of every kind of relief and easement much more than he does. When I say I have not received more than I deserve, is this the language I hold to Majesty? No! Far, very far, from it! Before that presence, I claim no merit at all. Everything towards me is favour and bounty. One style to a gracious benefactor; another to a proud and insulting foe.

---

[6] Used legally ("what is the value?").

His Grace is pleased to aggravate my guilt, by charging my acceptance of his Majesty's grant as a departure from my ideas, and the spirit of my conduct with regard to economy. If it be, my ideas of economy were false and ill-founded. But they are the Duke of Bedford's ideas of economy I have contradicted, and not my own. If he means to allude to certain bills brought in by me on a message from the throne in 1782, I tell him that there is nothing in my conduct that can contradict either the letter or the spirit of those acts. Does he mean the pay-office act? I take it for granted he does not. The act to which he alludes, is, I suppose, the establishment act. I greatly doubt whether his Grace has ever read the one or the other. The first of these systems cost me, with every assistance which my then situation gave me, pains incredible. I found an opinion common through all the offices, and general in the public at large, that it would prove impossible to reform and methodize the office of paymaster-general. I undertook it, however; and I succeeded in my undertaking. Whether the military service, or whether the general economy of our finances, have profited by that act, I leave to those who are acquainted with the army, and with the treasury, to judge.

An opinion full as general prevailed also at the same time, that nothing could be done for the regulation of the civil-list establishment. The very attempt to introduce method into it, and any limitations to its services, was held absurd. I had not seen the man, who so much as suggested one economical principle, or an economical expedient, upon that subject. Nothing but coarse amputation, or coarser taxation, were then talked of, both of them without design, combination, or the least shadow of principle. Blind and headlong zeal, or factious fury, were the whole contribution brought by the most noisy on that occasion, towards the satisfaction of the public, or the relief of the Crown.

Let me tell my youthful censor, that the necessities of that time required something very different from what others then suggested, or what his Grace now conceives. Let me inform him, that it was one of the most critical periods in our annals.

Astronomers have supposed, that if a certain comet, whose path intercepted the ecliptic, had met the earth in some (I forget what) sign, it would have whirled us along with it, in its eccentric course, into God knows what regions of heat and cold. Had the portentous comet of the rights of man, (which "from its horrid hair shakes pestilence and war," and "with fear of change perplexes monarchs,")[7] had that comet crossed upon us in that internal state of England, nothing human could have prevented our being irresistibly hurried, out of the highway of heaven, into all the vices, crimes, horrors, and miseries of the French Revolution.

Happily, France was not then Jacobinized. Her hostility was at a good distance. We had a limb cut off; but we preserved the body. We lost our colonies; but we kept our constitution. There was, indeed, much intestine heat; there was a dreadful fermentation. Wild and savage insurrection quitted the woods, and prowled about our streets in the name of reform. Such was the distemper of the public mind, that there was no madman, in his maddest ideas, and maddest project, who might not count upon numbers to support his principles and execute his designs.

Many of the changes, by a great misnomer called parliamentary reforms, went, not in the intention of all the professors and supporters of them, undoubtedly, but went in their certain, and, in my opinion, not very remote effect, home to the utter destruction of the constitution of this kingdom. Had they taken place, not France, but England, would have had the honour of leading up the death-dance of democratic revolution. Other projects, exactly coincident in time with those, struck at the very existence of the kingdom under any constitution. There are who remember the blind fury of some, and

---

[7] *Paradise Lost,* II. 710 and I. 598.

the lamentable helplessness of others; here, a torpid confusion, from a panic fear of the danger; there, the same inaction from a stupid insensibility to it; here, well-wishers to the mischief; there, indifferent lookers-on. At the same time, a sort of national convention, dubious in its nature, and perilous in its example, nosed parliament in the very seat of its authority; sat with a sort of superintendence over it; and little less than dictated to it, not only laws, but the very form and essence of legislature itself. In Ireland things ran in a still more eccentric course. Government was unnerved, confounded, and in a manner suspended. Its equipoise was totally gone. I do not mean to speak disrespectfully of Lord North. He was a man of admirable parts; of general knowledge; of a versatile understanding fitted for every sort of business; of infinite wit and pleasantry; of a delightful temper; and with a mind most perfectly disinterested. But it would be only to degrade myself by a weak adulation, and not to honour the memory of a great man, to deny that he wanted something of the vigilance and spirit of command, that the time required. Indeed, a darkness, next to the fog of this awful day, loured over the whole region. For a little time the helm appeared abandoned—

> *Ipse diem noctemque negat discernere cœlo,*
> *Nec meminisse viæ mediâ Palinurus in undâ.*[8]

At that time I was connected with men of high place in the community. They loved liberty as much as the Duke of Bedford can do; and they understood it at least as well. Perhaps their politics, as usual, took a tincture from their character, and they cultivated what they loved. The liberty they pursued was a liberty inseparable from order, from virtue, from morals, and from religion; and was neither hypocritically nor fanatically followed. They did not wish, that liberty, in itself one of the first of blessings, should in its perversion became

[8] *Virgil,* Aeneid, III. 201-2.

the greatest curse which could fall upon mankind. To preserve the constitution entire, and practically equal to all the great ends of its formation, not in one single part, but in all its parts, was to them the first object. Popularity and power they regarded alike. These were with them only different means of obtaining that object; and had no preference over each other in their minds, but as one or the other might afford a surer or a less certain prospect of arriving at that end. It is some consolation to me in the cheerless gloom, which darkens the evening of my life, that with them I commenced my political career, and never for a moment, in reality, nor in appearance, for any length of time, was separated from their good wishes and good opinion.

By what accident it matters not, nor upon what desert, but just then, and in the midst of that hunt of obloquy, which ever has pursued me with a full cry through life, I had obtained a very considerable degree of public confidence. I know well enough how equivocal a test this kind of popular opinion forms of the merit that obtained it. I am no stranger to the insecurity of its tenure. I do not boast of it. It is mentioned to show, not how highly I prize the thing, but my right to value the use I made of it. I endeavoured to turn that short-lived advantage to myself into a permanent benefit to my country. Far am I from detracting from the merit of some gentlemen, out of office or in it, on that occasion. No!—It is not my way to refuse a full and heaped measure of justice to the aids that I receive. I have, through life, been willing to give everything to others; and to reserve nothing for myself, but the inward conscience, that I had omitted no pains to discover, to animate, to discipline, to direct the abilities of the country for its service, and to place them in the best light to improve their age, or to adorn it. This conscience I have. I have never suppressed any man; never checked him for a moment in his course, by any jealousy, or by any policy. I was always ready to the height of my means, (and they were always infinitely below my desires,) to forward those abilities which overpowered my own. He is an ill-furnished undertaker, who has no machinery but his own hands to work with. Poor in my own faculties, I ever thought myself rich in theirs. In that period of difficulty and danger more especially, I consulted, and sincerely coöperated with, men of all parties, who seem disposed to the same ends, or to any main part of them. Nothing to prevent disorder was omitted: when it appeared, nothing to subdue it was left uncounselled, nor unexecuted, as far as I could prevail. At the time I speak of, and having a momentary lead, so aided and so encouraged, and as a feeble instrument in a mighty hand—I do not say I saved my country; I am sure I did my country important service. There were few, indeed, that did not at that time acknowledge it, and that time was thirteen years ago. It was but one voice, that no man in the kingdom better deserved an honourable provision should be made for him.

So much for my general conduct through the whole of the portentous crisis from 1780 to 1782, and the general sense then entertained of that conduct by my country. But my character, as a reformer, in the particular instances which the Duke of Bedford refers to, is so connected in principle with my opinions on the hideous changes, which have since barbarized France, and, spreading thence, threatened the political and moral order of the whole world, that it seems to demand something of a more detailed discussion.

My economical reforms were not, as his Grace may think, the suppression of a paltry pension or employment, more or less. Economy in my plans was, as it ought to be, secondary, subordinate, instrumental. I acted on state principles. I found a great distemper in the commonwealth: and, according to the nature of the evil and of the object, I treated it. The malady was deep; it was complicated, in the causes and in the symptoms. Throughout it was full of contraindicants. On one hand government, daily growing more invidious from an apparent increase of the means of strength, was every day growing more contemptible by real weakness. Nor was this dissolution confined to government commonly so called. It extended to parliament; which was losing not a little in its dignity and estimation, by an opinion of its not acting on worthy motives. On the other hand, the desires of the people (partly natural and partly infused into them by art) appeared in so wild and inconsiderate a manner, with regard to the economical object, (for I set aside for a moment the dreadful tampering with the body of the constitution itself,) that, if their petitions had literally been complied with, the state would have been convulsed; and a gate would have been opened, through which all property might be sacked and ravaged. Nothing could have saved the public from the mischiefs of the false reform but its absurdity; which would soon have brought itself, and with it all real reform, into discredit. This would have left a rankling wound in the hearts of the people, who would know they had failed in the accomplishment of their wishes, but who, like the rest of mankind in all ages, would impute the blame to anything rather than to their own proceedings. But there were then persons in the world, who nourished complaint; and would have been thoroughly disappointed if the people were ever satisfied. I was not of that humor. I wished that they *should* be satisfied. It was my aim to give to the people the substance of what I knew they desired, and what I thought was right, whether they desired it or not, before it had been modified for them into senseless petitions. I knew that there is a manifest, marked distinction, which ill men with ill designs, or weak men incapable of any design, will constantly be confounding, that is, a marked distinction between change and reformation. The former alters the substance of the objects themselves; and gets rid of all their essential good, as well as of all the accidental evil, annexed to them. Change is novelty; and whether it is to operate any one of the effects of reformation at all, or whether it may not contradict the very principle upon which reformation is desired, cannot be certainly known beforehand. Reform is, not a change in the substance, or in the primary modification, of the object, but, a direct application of a remedy to the grievance complained of. So far as that is removed, all is sure. It stops there; and, if it fails, the substance which underwent the operation, at the very worst, is but where it was.

All this, in effect, I think, but am not sure, I have said elsewhere. It cannot at this time be too often repeated; line upon line; precept upon precept; until it comes into the currency of a proverb, *to innovate is not to reform*. The French revolutionists complained of everything; they refused to reform anything; and they left nothing, no, nothing at all *unchanged*. The consequences are *before us,*—not in remote history; not in future prognostication: they are about us; they are upon us. They shake the public security; they menace private enjoyment. They dwarf the growth of the young; they break the quiet of the old. If we travel, they stop our way. They infest us in town; they pursue us to the country. Our business is interrupted; our repose is troubled; our pleasures are saddened; our very studies are poisoned and perverted, and knowledge is rendered worse than ignorance, by the enormous evils of this dreadful innovation. The revolution harpies of France, sprung from night and hell, or from that chaotic anarchy, which generates equivocally "all monstrous, all prodigious things," cuckoo-like, adulterously lay their eggs, and brood over, and hatch them in the nest of every neighbouring state. These obscene harpies, who deck themselves in I know not what divine attributes, but who in reality are foul and ravenous birds of prey, (both mothers and daughters,) flutter over our heads, and souse down upon our tables, and leave nothing unrent, unrifled, unravaged, or unpolluted with the slime of their filthy offal.[9]

---

[9] Tristius haud illis monstrum, nec sævior ulla
   Pestis, et ira Deûm Stygiis sese extulit undis.
   Virginei volucrum voltus; fædissima ventris
   Proluvies; uncæque manus; et pallida semper
   Ora fame——[*Aeneid*, III. 214-18]
Here the poet breaks the line, because he (and that he is Virgil) had not verse or language to describe that monster even as he had conceived her. Had he lived in our time, he would have been more

If his Grace can contemplate the result of this complete innovation, or, as some friends of his will call it, *reform,* in the whole body of its solidity and compounded mass, at which, as Hamlet says, the face of heaven glows with horror and indignation, and which, in truth, makes every reflecting mind, and every feeling heart, perfectly thought-sick, without a thorough abhorrence of everything they say, and everything they do, I am amazed at the morbid strength or the natural infirmity of his mind.

It was then not my love, but my hatred, to innovation, that produced my plan of reform. Without troubling myself with the exactness of the logical diagram, I considered them as things substantially opposite. It was to prevent that evil, that I proposed the measures, which his Grace is pleased, and I am not sorry he is pleased, to recall to my recollection. I had (what I hope that noble duke will remember in all its operations) a state to preserve, as well as a state to reform. I had a people to gratify, but not to inflame, or to mislead. I do not claim half the credit for what I did, as for what I prevented from being done. In that situation of the public mind, I did not undertake, as was then proposed, to new-model the House of Commons or the House of Lords; or to change the authority under which any officer of the Crown acted, who was suffered at all to exist. Crown, Lords, Commons, judicial system, system of administration, existed as they had existed before; and in the mode and manner in which they had always existed. My measures were, what I then truly stated them to the House to be, in their intent, healing and mediatorial. A complaint was made of too much influence in the House of Commons; I reduced it in both Houses; and I gave my reasons article by article for every reduction, and showed why I

overpowered with the reality than he was with the imagination. Virgil only knew the horror of the times before him. Had he lived to see the revolutionists and constitutionalists of France, he would have had more horrid and disgusting features of his harpies to describe, and more frequent failures in the attempt to describe them. [Burke] thought it safe for the service of the state. I heaved the lead every inch of way I made. A disposition to expense was complained of; to that I opposed, not mere retrenchment, but a system of economy, which would make a random expense, without plan or foresight, in future not easily practicable. I proceeded upon principles of research to put me in possession of my matter; on principles of method to regulate it; and on principles in the human mind and in civil affairs to secure and perpetuate the operation. I conceived nothing arbitrarily; nor proposed anything to be done by the will and pleasure of others, or my own; but by reason, and by reason only. I have ever abhorred, since the first dawn of my understanding to this its obscure twilight, all the operations of opinion, fancy, inclination, and will, in the affairs of government, where only a sovereign reason, paramount to all forms of legislation and administration, should dictate. Government is made for the very purpose of opposing that reason to will and caprice, in the reformers or in the reformed, in the governors or in the governed, in kings, in senates, or in people.

On a careful review, therefore, and analysis, of all the component parts of the civil list, and on weighing them against each other, in order to make, as much as possible, all of them a subject of estimate, (the foundation and corner-stone of all regular provident economy,) it appeared to me evident, that this was impracticable, whilst that part, called the pension list, was totally discretionary in its amount. For this reason, and for this only, I proposed to reduce it, both in its gross quantity, and in its larger individual proportions, to a certainty; lest, if it were left without a *general* limit, it might eat up the civil-list service; if suffered to be granted in portions too great for the fund, it might defeat its own end; and, by unlimited allowances to some, it might disable the Crown in means of providing for others. The pension list was to be kept as a sacred fund; but it could not be kept as a constant, open fund, sufficient for growing demands, if some demands would wholly devour it. The tenour of the act will show that it regarded the civil list *only*, the reduction of which to some sort of estimate was my great object.

No other of the Crown funds did I meddle with, because they had not the same relations. This of the four and a half per cents does his Grace imagine had escaped me, or had escaped all the men of business, who acted with me in those regulations? I know that such a fund existed, and that pensions had been always granted on it, before his Grace was born. This fund was full in my eye. It was full in the eyes of those who worked with me. It was left on principle. On principle I did what was then done; and on principle what was left undone was omitted. I did not dare to rob the nation of all funds to reward merit. If I pressed this point too close, I acted contrary to the avowed principles on which I went. Gentlemen are very fond of quoting me; but if any one thinks it worth his while to know the rules that guided me in my plan of reform, he will read my printed speech on that subject; at least what is contained from page 230 to page 241 in the second volume of the collection which a friend has given himself the trouble to make of my publications. Be this as it may, these two bills, (though achieved with the greatest labour, and management of every sort, both within and without the House,) were only a part, and but a small part, of a very large system, comprehending all the objects I stated in opening my proposition, and, indeed, many more, which I just hinted at in my speech to the electors of Bristol, when I was put out of that representation. All these, in some state or other of forwardness, I have long had by me.

But do I justify his Majesty's grace on these grounds? I think them the least of my services! The time gave them an occasional value. What I have done in the way of political economy was far from confined to this body of measures. I did not come into parliament to con my lesson. I had earned my pension before I set my foot in St. Stephen's chapel.[10] I was prepared and disciplined to this political warfare. The first session I sat in parliament, I found it necessary to analyze the whole commercial, financial, constitutional, and foreign interests of Great Britain and its empire. A great deal was then done; and more, far more, would have been done, if more had been permitted by events. Then in the vigour of my manhood, my constitution sunk under my labour. Had I then died, (and I seemed to myself very near death,) I had then earned for those who belonged to me, more than the Duke of Bedford's ideas of service are of power to estimate. But, in truth, these services I am called to account for are not those on which I value myself the most. If I were to call for a reward, (which I have never done,) it should be for those in which for fourteen years, without intermission, I showed the most industry, and had the least success: I mean in the affairs of India. They are those on which I value myself the most; most for the importance; most for the labour; most for the judgment; most for constancy and perseverance in the pursuit. Others may value them most for the *intention*. In that, surely, they are not mistaken.

Does his Grace think, that they, who advised the Crown to make my retreat easy, consider me only as an economist? That, well understood, however, is a good deal. If I had not deemed it of some value, I should not have made political economy an object of my humble studies, from my very early youth to near the end of my services in parliament, even before (at least to any knowledge of mine) it had employed the thoughts of speculative men in other parts of Europe. At that time it was still in its infancy in England, where, in the last century, it had its origin. Great and learned men thought my studies were not wholly thrown away, and deigned to com-

---

[10] Where the House of Commons convened.

municate with me now and then on some particulars of their immortal works. Something of these studies may appear incidentally in some of the earliest things I published. The House has been witness to their effect, and has profited of them more or less for above eight and twenty years.

To their estimate I leave the matter. I was not, like his Grace of Bedford, swaddled, and rocked, and dandled into a legislator; "*Nitor in adversum*" [11] is the motto of a man like me. I possessed not one of the qualities, nor cultivated one of the arts, that recommend men to the favour and protection of the great. I was not made for a minion or a tool. As little did I follow the trade of winning the hearts, by imposing on the understandings, of the people. At every step of my progress in life, (for in every step was I traversed and opposed,) and at every turnpike I met, I was obliged to show my passport, and again and again to prove my sole title to the honour of being useful to my country, by a proof that I was not wholly unacquainted with its laws, and the whole system of its interests both abroad and at home. Otherwise no rank, no toleration, even for me. I had no arts but manly arts. On them I have stood, and, please God, in spite of the Duke of Bedford and the Earl of Lauderdale, to the last gasp will I stand.

Had his Grace condescended to inquire concerning the person, whom he has not thought it below him to reproach, he might have found, that, in the whole course of my life, I have never, on any pretence of economy, or on any other pretence, so much as in a single instance, stood between any man and his reward of service, or his encouragement in useful talent and pursuit, from the highest of those services and pursuits to the lowest. On the contrary I have, on an hundred occasions, exerted myself with singular zeal to forward every man's even tolerable pretensions. I have more than once had good-natured reprehensions from my friends for carrying the

---

[11] Ovid, *Metamorphoses*, II. 72.

matter to something bordering on abuse. This line of conduct, whatever its merits might be, was partly owing to natural disposition; but I think full as much to reason and principle. I looked on the consideration of public service, or public ornament, to be real and very justice: and I ever held a scanty and penurious justice to partake of the nature of a wrong. I held it to be, in its consequences, the worst economy in the world. In saving money, I soon can count up all the good I do: but when, by a cold penury, I blast the abilities of a nation, and stunt the growth of its active energies, the ill I may do is beyond all calculation. Whether it be too much or too little, whatever I have done has been general and systematic. I have never entered into those trifling vexations, and oppressive details, that have been falsely, and most ridiculously, laid to my charge.

Did I blame the pensions given to Mr. Barré and Mr. Dunning between the proposition and execution of my plan? No! surely no! Those pensions were within my principles. I assert it, those gentlemen deserved their pensions, their titles —all they had; and more had they had, I should have been but pleased the more. They were men of talents; they were men of service. I put the profession of the law out of the question in one of them. It is a service that rewards itself. But their *public service,* though, from their abilities un-questionably of more value than mine, in its quantity and its duration was not to be mentioned with it. But I never could drive a hard bargain in my life, concerning any matter what-ever; and least of all do I know how to haggle and huckster with merit. Pension for myself I obtained none; nor did I solicit any. Yet I was loaded with hatred for everything that was withheld, and with obloquy for everything that was given. I was thus left to support the grants of a name ever dear to me, and ever venerable to the world, in favour of those, who were no friends of mine or of his, against the rude attacks of those who were at that time friends to the grantees, and their own zealous partisans. I have never heard

the Earl of Lauderdale complain of these pensions. He finds
nothing wrong till he comes to me. This is impartiality, in the
true, modern, revolutionary style.

Whatever I did at that time, so far as it regarded order
and economy, is stable and eternal; as all principles must be.
A particular order of things may be altered; order itself cannot lose its value. As to other particulars, they are variable by
time and by circumstances. Laws of regulation are not fundamental laws. The public exigencies are the masters of all such
laws. They rule the laws, and are not to be ruled by them.
They who exercise the legislative power at the time must
judge.

It may be new to his Grace, but I beg leave to tell him, that
mere parsimony is not economy. It is separable in theory
from it; and in fact it may, or it may not, be a *part* of
economy, according to circumstances. Expense, and great
expense, may be an essential part in true economy. If parsimony were to be considered as one of the kinds of that
virtue, there is however another and a higher economy.
Economy is a distributive virtue, and consists not in saving,
but in selection. Parsimony requires no providence, no
sagacity, no powers of combination, no comparison, no
judgment. Mere instinct, and that not an instinct of the
noblest kind, may produce this false economy in perfection.
The other economy has larger views. It demands a discriminating judgment, and a firm, sagacious mind. It shuts
one door to impudent importunity, only to open another, and
a wider, to unpresuming merit. If none but meritorious service
or real talent were to be rewarded, this nation has not wanted,
and this nation will not want, the means of rewarding all the
service it ever will receive, and encouraging all the merit it
ever will produce. No state, since the foundation of society,
has been impoverished by that species of profusion. Had the
economy of selection and proportion been at all times observed, we should not now have had an overgrown Duke of
Bedford, to oppress the industry of humble men, and to

limit, by the standard of his own conceptions, the justice, the bounty, or, if he pleases, the charity of the Crown.

His Grace may think as meanly as he will of my deserts in the far greater part of my conduct in life. It is free for him to do so. There will always be some difference of opinion in the value of political services. But there is one merit of mine, which he, of all men living, ought to be the last to call in question. I have supported with very great zeal, and I am told with some degree of success, those opinions, or if his Grace likes another expression better, those old prejudices, which buoy up the ponderous mass of his nobility, wealth, and titles. I have omitted no exertion to prevent him and them from sinking to that level, to which the meretricious French factions, his Grace at least coquets with, omit no exertion to reduce both. I have done all I could to discountenance their inquiries into the fortunes of those, who hold large portions of wealth without any apparent merit of their own. I have strained every nerve to keep the Duke of Bedford in that situation, which alone makes him my superior. Your Lordship has been a witness of the use he makes of that pre-eminence.

But be it, that this is virtue! Be it, that there is virtue in this well-selected rigour; yet all virtues are not equally becoming to all men and at all times. There are crimes, undoubtedly there are crimes, which in all seasons of our existence, ought to put a generous antipathy in action; crimes that provoke an indignant justice, and call forth a warm and animated pursuit. But all things that concern, what I may call, the preventive police of morality, all things merely rigid, harsh, and censorial, the antiquated moralists, at whose feet I was brought up, would not have thought these the fittest matter to form the favourite virtues of young men of rank. What might have been well enough, and have been received with a veneration mixed with awe and terror, from an old, severe, crabbed Cato, would have wanted something of propriety in the young Scipios, the ornament of the Roman nobility, in the flower of their life. But the times, the morals, the masters, the scholars, have all undergone a thorough revolution. It is a vile illiberal school, this new French academy of the *sans culottes*. There is nothing in it that is fit for a gentleman to learn.

Whatever its vogue may be, I still flatter myself, that the parents of the growing generation will be satisfied with what is to be taught to their children in Westminister, in Eton, or in Winchester; I still indulge the hope that no *grown* gentleman or nobleman of our time will think of finishing at Mr. Thelwall's lecture whatever may have been left incomplete at the old universities of his country. I would give to Lord Grenville and Mr. Pitt for a motto, what was said of a Roman censor or prætor (or what was he?) who, in virtue of a Senatus consultum, shut up certain academies,

"Claudere ludum impudentiæ jussit." [12]

Every honest father of a family in the kingdom will rejoice at the breaking up for the holidays, and will pray that there may be a very long vacation in all such schools.

The awful state of the time, and not myself, or my own justification, is my true object in what I now write; or in what I shall ever write or say. It little signifies to the world what becomes of such things as me, or even as the Duke of Bedford. What I say about either of us is nothing more than a vehicle, as you, my Lord, will easily perceive, to convey my sentiments on matters far more worthy of your attention. It is when I stick to my apparent first subject that I ought to apologize, not when I depart from it. I therefore must beg your Lordship's pardon for again resuming it after this very short digression; assuring you that I shall never altogether lose sight of such matter as persons abler than I am may turn to some profit.

The Duke of Bedford conceives, that he is obliged to call the attention of the House of Peers to his Majesty's grant to

---

[12] Tacitus, *De Oratoribus*, 35.

me, which he considers as excessive, and out of all bounds.

I know not how it has happened, but it really seems, that, whilst his Grace was meditating his well-considered censure upon me, he fell into a sort of sleep. Homer nods; and the Duke of Bedford may dream; and as dreams (even his golden dreams) are apt to be ill-pieced and incongruously put together, <u>his Grace preserved his idea of reproach to *me*, but took the subject-matter from the Crown grants *to his own family.*</u> This is "the stuff of which his dreams are made." In that way of putting things together his Grace is perfectly in the right. The grants to the house of Russell were so enormous, as not only to outrage economy, but even to stagger credibility. <u>The Duke of Bedford is the leviathan among all the creatures of the Crown.</u> He tumbles about his unwieldly bulk; he plays and frolics in the ocean of the royal bounty. Huge as he is, and whilst "he lies floating many a rood," [13] he is still a creature. His ribs, his fins, his whale-bone, his blubber, the very spiracles through which he spouts a torrent of brine against his origin, and covers me all over with the spray,—everything of him and about him is from the throne. Is it for *him* to question the dispensation of the royal favour?

I really am at a loss to draw any sort of parallel between the public merits of his Grace, by which he justifies the grants he holds, and these services of mine, on the favourable construction of which I have obtained what his Grace so much disapproves. In private life, I have not at all the honour of acquaintance with the noble Duke. But I ought to presume, and it costs me nothing to do so, that he abundantly deserves the esteem and love of all who live with him. But as to public service, why truly it would not be more ridiculous for me to compare myself in rank, in fortune, in splendid descent, in youth, strength, or figure, with the Duke of Bedford, than to make a parallel between his services and my

---

[13] *Paradise Lost*, I. 196.

attempts to be useful to my country. It would not be gross
adulation, but uncivil irony, to say, that he has any public
merit of his own to keep alive the idea of the services, by
which his vast landed pensions were obtained. My merits,
whatever they are, are original and personal; his are derivative. It is his ancestor, the original pensioner, that has laid
up this inexhaustible fund of merit, which makes his Grace
so very delicate and exceptious about the merit of all other
grantees of the Crown. Had he permitted me to remain in
quiet, I should have said, 'tis his estate; that's enough. It
is his by law; what have I to do with it or its history? He
would naturally have said on his side, 'tis this man's fortune.
—He is as good now as my ancestor was two hundred and
fifty years ago. I am a young man with very old pensions; he
is an old man with very young pensions,—that's all.

Why will his Grace, by attacking me, force me reluctantly
to compare my little merit with that which obtained from the
Crown those prodigies of profuse donation, by which he
tramples on the mediocrity of humble and laborious individuals? I would willingly leave him to the herald's college,
which the philosophy of the *sans culottes* (prouder by far
than all the Garters, and Norroys, and Clarencieux, and Rouge
Dragons, that ever pranced in a procession of what his friends
call aristocrats and despots) will abolish with contumely and
scorn. These historians, recorders, and blazoners of virtues
and arms, differ wholly from that other description of
historians, who never assign any act of politicians to a good
motive. These gentle historians, on the contrary, dip their
pens in nothing but the milk of human kindness. They seek
no further for merit than the preamble of a patent, or the
inscription on a tomb. With them every man created a peer
is first a hero ready made. They judge of every man's
capacity for office by the offices he has filled; and the more
offices the more ability. Every general officer with them is a
Marlborough; every statesman a Burleigh; every judge a
Murray or a Yorke. They who, alive, were laughed at or

pitied by all their acquaintance, make as good a figure as the best of them in the pages of Guillim, Edmondson, and Collins.

To these recorders, so full of good nature to the great and prosperous, I would willingly leave the first Baron Russell, and Earl of Bedford, and the merits of his grants. But the aulnager, the weigher, the meter of grants, will not suffer us to acquiesce in the judgment of the prince reigning at the time when they were made. They are never good to those who earn them. Well then; since the new grantees have war made on them by the old, and that the word of the sovereign is not to be taken, let us turn our eyes to history, in which great men have always a pleasure in contemplating the heroic origin of their house.

The first peer of the name, the first purchaser of the grants, was a Mr. Russell, a person of an ancient gentleman's family raised by being a minion of Henry the Eighth. As there generally is some resemblance of character to create these relations, the favourite was in all likelihood much such another as his master. The first of those immoderate grants was not taken from the ancient demesne of the Crown, but from the recent confiscation of the ancient nobility of the land. The lion having sucked the blood of his prey, threw the offal carcass to the jackal in waiting. Having tasted once the food of confiscation, the favourites became fierce and ravenous. This worthy favourite's first grant was from the lay nobility. The second, infinitely improving on the enormity of the first, was from the plunder of the church. In truth his Grace is somewhat excusable for his dislike to a grant like mine, not only in its quantity, but in its kind so different from his own.

Mine was from a mild and benevolent sovereign; his from Henry the Eighth.

Mine had not its fund in the murder of any innocent person of illustrious rank, or in the pillage of any body of unoffending men. His grants were from the aggregate and consolidated funds of judgments iniquitously legal, and from possessions voluntarily surrendered by the lawful proprietors, with the gibbet at their door.

The merit of the grantee whom he derives from was that of being a prompt and greedy instrument of a *levelling* tyrant, who oppressed all descriptions of his people, but who fell with particular fury on everything that was *great and noble*. Mine has been, in endeavouring to screen every man, in every class, from oppression, and particularly in defending the high and eminent, who in the bad times of confiscating princes, confiscating chief governors, or confiscating demagogues, are the most exposed to jealousy, avarice, and envy.

The merit of the original grantee of his Grace's pensions was in giving his hand to the work and partaking the spoil with a prince, who plundered a part of the national church of his time and country. Mine was in defending the whole of the national church of my own time and my own country, and the whole of the national churches of all countries, from the principles and the examples which lead to ecclesiastical pillage, thence to a contempt of *all* prescriptive titles, thence to the pillage of *all* property, and thence to universal desolation.

The merit of the origin of his Grace's fortune was in being a favourite and chief adviser to a prince, who left no liberty to their native country. My endeavour was to obtain liberty for the municipal country in which I was born, and for all descriptions and denominations in it. Mine was to support with unrelaxing vigilance every right, every privilege, every franchise, in this my adopted, my dearer, and more comprehensive country; and not only to preserve those rights in this chief seat of empire, but in every nation, in every land, in every climate, language, and religion, in the vast domain that is still under the protection, and the larger that was once under the protection, of the British Crown.

His founder's merits were, by arts in which he served his master and made his fortune, to bring poverty, wretchedness, and depopulation on his country. Mine were, under a benevolent prince, in promoting the commerce, manufactures, and agriculture of his kingdom; in which his Majesty shows an eminent example, who even in his amusements is a patriot, and in hours of leisure an improver of his native soil.

His founder's merit was the merit of a gentleman raised by the arts of a court, and the protection of a Wolsey, to the eminence of a great and potent lord. His merit in that eminence was, by instigating a tyrant to injustice, to provoke a people to rebellion. My merit was, to awaken the sober part of the country, that they might put themselves on their guard against any one potent lord, or any greater number of potent lords, or any combination of great leading men of any sort, if ever they should attempt to proceed in the same courses, but in the reverse order; that is, by instigating a corrupted populace to rebellion, and, through that rebellion, introducing a tyranny yet worse than the tyranny which his Grace's ancestor supported, and of which he profited in the manner we behold in the despotism of Henry the Eighth.

The political merit of the first pensioner of his Grace's house was that of being concerned as a counsellor of state in advising, and in his person executing, the conditions of a dishonourable peace with France; the surrendering the fortress of Boulogne, then our out-guard on the Continent. By that surrender, Calais, the key of France, and the bridle in the mouth of that power, was, not many years afterwards, finally lost. My merit has been in resisting the power and pride of France, under any form of its rule; but in opposing it with the greatest zeal and earnestness, when that rule appeared in the worst form it could assume; the worst indeed which the prime cause and principle of all evil could possibly give it. It was my endeavour by every means to excite a spirit in the House where I had the honour of a

seat, for carrying on, with early vigour and decision, the
most clearly just and necessary war, that this or any nation
ever carried on; in order to save my country from the iron
yoke of its power, and from the more dreadful contagion of
its principles; to preserve, while they can be preserved, pure
and untainted, the ancient, inbred integrity, piety, good
nature, and good humour of the people of England, from
the dreadful pestilence, which, beginning in France, threatens
to lay waste the whole moral, and in a great degree the
whole physical world, having done both in the focus of its
most intense malignity.

The labours of his Grace's founder merited the curses, not
loud but deep, of the Commons of England, on whom *he*
and his master had effected a *complete parliamentary reform*,
by making them, in their slavery and humiliation, the true
and adequate representatives of a debased, degraded, and
undone people. My merits were, in having had an active,
though not always an ostentatious, share, in every one act,
without exception, of undisputed constitutional utility in
my time, and in having supported, on all occasions, the
authority, the efficiency, and the privileges of the Commons
of Great Britain. I ended my services by a recorded and fully
reasoned assertion on their own journals of their constitutional rights, and a vindication of their constitutional conduct.
I laboured in all things to merit their inward approbation, and
(along with the assistance of the largest, the greatest, and
best of my endeavours) I received their free, unbiassed,
public, and solemn thanks.

Thus stands the account of the comparative merits of the
Crown grants which compose the Duke of Bedford's fortune
as balanced against mine. In the name of common sense,
why should the Duke of Bedford think, that none but of the
House of Russell are entitled to the favour of the Crown?
Why should he imagine that no king of England has been
capable of judging of merit but King Henry the Eighth?
Indeed, he will pardon me; he is a little mistaken; all virtue

did not end in the first Earl of Bedford. All discernment did not lose its vision when his Creator closed his eyes. Let him remit his rigour on the disproportion between merit and reward in others, and they will make no inquiry into the origin of his fortune. They will regard with much more satisfaction, as he will contemplate with infinitely more advantage, whatever in his pedigree has been dulcified by an exposure to the influence of heaven in a long flow of generations, from the hard, acidulous, metallic tincture of the spring. It is little to be doubted, that several of his forefathers in that long series have degenerated into honour and virtue. Let the Duke of Bedford (I am sure he will) reject with scorn and horror the counsels of the lecturers, those wicked panders to avarice and ambition, who would tempt him, in the troubles of his country, to seek another enormous fortune from the forfeitures of another nobility, and the plunder of another church. Let him (and I trust that yet he will) employ all the energy of his youth, and all the resources of his wealth, to crush rebellious principles which have no foundation in morals, and rebellious movements that have no provocation in tyranny.

Then will be forgot the rebellions, which, by a doubtful priority in crime, his ancestor had provoked and extinguished. On such a conduct in the noble Duke, many of his countrymen might, and with some excuse might, give way to the enthusiasm of their gratitude, and, in the dashing style of some of the old declaimers, cry out, that if the fates had found no other way in which they could give a Duke of Bedford and his opulence as props to a tottering world, then the butchery of the Duke of Buckingham might be tolerated; it might be regarded even with complacency, whilst in the heir of confiscation they saw the sympathizing comforter of the martyrs, who suffer under the cruel confiscation of this day; whilst they behold with admiration his zealous protection of the virtuous and loyal nobility of France, and his manly support of his brethren, the yet standing nobility and gentry of his native land. Then his Grace's merit would be pure, and new, and sharp, as fresh from the mint of honour. As he pleased he might reflect honour on his predecessors, or throw it forward on those who were to succeed him. He might be the propagator of the stock of honour, or the root of it, as he thought proper.

Had it pleased God to continue to me the hopes of succession, I should have been, according to my mediocrity, and the mediocrity of the age I live in, a sort of founder of a family; I should have left a son, who, in all the points in which personal merit can be viewed, in science, in erudition, in genius, in taste, in honour, in generosity, in humanity, in every liberal sentiment, and every liberal accomplishment, would not have shown himself inferior to the Duke of Bedford, or to any of those whom he traces in his line. His Grace very soon would have wanted all plausibility in his attack upon that provision which belonged more to mine than to me. HE would soon have supplied every deficiency, and symmetrized every disproportion. It would not have been for that successor to resort to any stagnant wasting reservoir of merit in me, or in any ancestry. He had in himself a salient, living spring of generous and manly action. Every day he lived he would have re-purchased the bounty of the Crown, and ten times more, if ten times more he had received. He was made a public creature; and had no enjoyment whatever, but in the performance of some duty. At this exigent moment, the loss of a finished man is not easily supplied.

But a Disposer whose power we are little able to resist, and whose wisdom it behoves us not at all to dispute, has ordained it in another manner, and (whatever my querulous weakness might suggest) a far better. The storm has gone over me; and I lie like one of those old oaks which the late hurricane has scattered about me. I am stripped of all my honours, I am torn up by the roots, and lie prostrate on the earth! There, and prostrate there, I most unfeignedly recognize the Divine justice, and in some degree submit to it. But whilst I humble myself before God, I do not know that it is forbidden to repel the attacks of unjust and inconsiderate men. The patience of Job is proverbial. After some of the convulsive struggles of our irritable nature, he submitted himself, and repented in dust and ashes. But even so, I do not find him blamed for reprehending, and with a considerable degree of verbal asperity, those ill-natured neighbours of his, who visited his dunghill to read moral, political, and economical lectures on his misery. I am alone. I have none to meet my enemies in the gate. Indeed, my Lord, I greatly deceive myself, if in this hard season I would give a peck of refuse wheat for all that is called fame and honour in the world. This is the appetite but of a few. It is a luxury, it is a privilege, it is an indulgence for those who are at their ease. But we are all of us made to shun disgrace, as we are made to shrink from pain, and poverty, and disease. It is an instinct; and under the direction of reason, instinct is always in the right. I live in an inverted order. They who ought to have succeeded me are gone before me. They who should have been to me as posterity are in the place of ancestors. I owe to the dearest relation (which ever must subsist in memory) that act of piety, which he would have performed to me; I owe it to him to show that he was not descended, as the Duke of Bedford would have it, from an unworthy parent.

The Crown has considered me after long service; the Crown has paid the Duke of Bedford by advance. He has had a long credit for any services which he may perform hereafter. He is secure, and long may he be secure, in his advance, whether he performs any services or not. But let him take care how he endangers the safety of that constitution which secures his own utility or his own insignificance; or how he discourages those, who take up, even puny arms, to defend an order of things, which, like the sun of heaven, shines alike on the useful and the worthless. His grants are ingrafted on the public law of Europe, covered with the awful hoar of innumerable ages. They are guarded by the sacred rules of prescription, found in that full treasury of jurisprudence from which the jejuneness and penury of our municipal law has, by degrees, been enriched and strengthened. This prescription I had my share (a very full share) in bringing to its perfection. The Duke of Bedford will stand as long as prescriptive law endures; as long as the great stable laws of property, common to us with all civilized nations, are kept in their integrity, and without the smallest intermixture of laws, maxims, principles, or precedents of the grand Revolution. They are secure against all changes but one. The whole revolutionary system, institutes, digest, code, novels, text, gloss, comment, are, not only not the same, but they are the very reverse, and the reverse fundamentally, of all the laws, on which civil life has hitherto been upheld in all the governments of the world. The learned professors of the rights of man regard prescription, not as a title to bar all claim, set up against all possession—but they look on prescription as itself a bar against the possessor and proprietor. They hold an immemorial possession to be no more than a long-continued, and therefore an aggravated injustice.

Such are *their* ideas; such *their* religion, and such *their* law. But as to *our* country and *our* race, as long as the well-compacted structure of our church and state, the sanctuary, the holy of holies of that ancient law, defended by reverence, defended by power, a fortress at once and a temple, shall stand inviolate on the brow of the British Sion—as long as the British monarchy, not more limited than fenced by the orders of the state, shall, like the proud Keep of Windsor, rising in the majesty of proportion, and girt with the double belt of its kindred and coeval towers, as long as this awful structure shall oversee and guard the subjected land—so long the mounds and dykes of the low, fat Bedford level will have nothing to fear from all the pickaxes of all the levellers of France. As long as our sovereign lord the king, and his faithful subjects, the Lords and Commons of this realm,—the triple cord which no man can break; the solemn, sworn, constitutional frank-pledge of this nation; the firm guarantees of each other's being, and each other's rights; the joint and several securities, each in its place and order, for every kind and every quality, of property and of dignity; as long as these endure, so long the Duke of Bedford is safe: and we are all safe together—the high from the blights of envy and the spoliations of rapacity; the low from the iron hand of oppression and the insolent spurn of contempt. Amen! and so be it: and so it will be,

> *Dum domus Æneæ Capitoli immobile saxum*
> *Accolet; imperiumque pater Romanus habebit.*—[14]

But if the rude inroad of Gallic tumult, with its sophistical rights of man, to falsify the account, and its sword as a make-weight to throw into the scale, shall be introduced into our city by a misguided populace, set on by proud great men, themselves blinded and intoxicated by a frantic ambition, we shall, all of us, perish and be overwhelmed in a common ruin. If a great storm blow on our coast, it will cast the whales on the strand as well as the periwinkles. His Grace will not survive the poor grantee he despises, no, not for a twelvemonth. If the great look for safety in the services they render to this Gallic cause, it is to be foolish, even above the weight of privilege allowed to wealth. If his Grace be one of these whom they endeavour to proselytize, he ought to be aware of the character of the sect, whose doctrines he is invited to embrace. With them insurrection is the most sacred of revolutionary duties to the state. Ingratitude to benefactors is the first of revolutionary virtues. Ingratitude is indeed their four cardinal virtues compacted and amalgamated into one; and he will find it in everything that has happened since the commencement of the philosophic Revolution to this hour.

---

[14] Virgil, *Aeneid,* IX. 448-49.

If he pleads the merit of having performed the duty of insurrection against the order he lives in, (God forbid he ever should,) the merit of others will be to perform the duty of insurrection against him. If he pleads (again God forbid he should, and I do not suspect he will) his ingratitude to the Crown for its creation of his family, others will plead their right and duty to pay him in kind. They will laugh, indeed they will laugh, at his parchment and his wax. His deeds will be drawn out with the rest of the lumber of his evidence room, and burnt to the tune of ça ira in the courts of Bedford (then Equality) house.

Am I to blame, if I attempt to pay his Grace's hostile reproaches to me with a friendly admonition to himself? Can I be blamed, for pointing out to him in what manner he is likely to be affected, if the sect of the cannibal philosophers of France should proselytize any considerable part of this people, and, by their joint proselytizing arms, should conquer that government, to which his Grace does not seem to me to give all the support his own security demands? Surely it is proper, that he, and that others like him, should know the true genius of this sect; what their opinions are, what they have done; and to whom; and what (if a prognostic is to be formed from the dispositions and actions of men) it is certain they will do hereafter. He ought to know, that they have sworn assistance, the only engagement they ever will keep, to all in this country, who bear a resemblance to themselves, and who think as such, that *The whole duty of man* consists in destruction. They are a misallied and disparaged branch of the house of Nimrod. They are the Duke of Bedford's natural hunters; and he is their natural game. Because he is not very profoundly reflecting, he sleeps in profound security: they, on the contrary, are always vigilant, active, enterprising, and, though far removed from any knowledge which makes men estimable or useful, in all the instruments and resources of evil, their leaders are not meanly instructed, or insufficiently furnished. In the French

Revolution everything is new; and, from want of preparation to meet so unlooked-for an evil, everything is dangerous. Never, before this time, was a set of literary men converted into a gang of robbers and assassins. Never before did a den of bravoes and banditti assume the garb and tone of an academy of philosophers.

Let me tell his Grace, that an union of such characters, monstrous as it seems, is not made for producing despicable enemies. But if they are formidable as foes, as friends they are dreadful indeed. The men of property in France confiding in a force, which seemed to be irresistible, because it had never been tried, neglected to prepare for a conflict with their enemies at their own weapons. They were found in such a situation as the Mexicans were, when they were attacked by the dogs, the cavalry, the iron, and the gunpowder, of a handful of bearded men, whom they did not know to exist in nature. This is a comparison that some, I think, have made; and it is just. In France they had their enemies within their houses. They were even in the bosoms of many of them. But they had not sagacity to discern their savage character. They seemed tame, and even caressing. They had nothing but *douce humanité* in their mouth. They could not bear the punishment of the mildest laws on the greatest criminals. The slightest severity of justice made their flesh creep. The very idea that war existed in the world disturbed their repose. Military glory was no more, with them, than a splendid infamy. Hardly would they hear of self-defence, which they reduced within such bounds, as to leave it no defence at all. All this while they meditated the confiscations and massacres we have seen. Had any one told these unfortunate noblemen and gentlemen, how, and by whom, the grand fabric of the French monarchy under which they flourished would be subverted, they would not have pitied him as a visionary, but would have turned from him as what they call a *mauvais plaisant*. Yet we have seen what has happened. The persons who have suffered from the cannibal philosophy of France, are so like the Duke of Bedford, that nothing but his Grace's probably not speaking quite so good French could enable us to find out any difference. A great many of them had as pompous titles as he, and were of full as illustrious a race: some few of them had fortunes as ample: several of them, without meaning the least disparagement to the Duke of Bedford, were as wise, and as virtuous, and as valiant, and as well educated, and as complete in all the lineaments of men of honour, as he is; and to all this they had added the powerful out-guard of a military profession, which, in its nature, renders men somewhat more cautious than those, who have nothing to attend to but the lazy enjoyment of undisturbed possessions. But security was their ruin. They are dashed to pieces in the storm, and our shores are covered with the wrecks. If they had been aware that such a thing might happen, such a thing never could have happened.

I assure his Grace, that if I state to him the designs of his enemies, in a manner which may appear to him ludicrous and impossible, I tell him nothing that has not exactly happened, point by point, but twenty-four miles from our own shore. I assure him that the Frenchified faction, more encouraged, than others are warned, by what has happened in France, look at him and his landed possessions as an object at once of curiosity and rapacity. He is made for them in every part of their double character. As robbers, to them he is a noble booty; as speculatists, he is a glorious subject for their experimental philosophy. He affords matter for an extensive analysis, in all the branches of their science, geometrical, physical, civil, and political. These philosophers are fanatics; independent of any interest, which if it operated alone would make them much more tractable, they are carried with such a headlong rage towards every desperate trial, that they would sacrifice the whole human race to the slightest of their experiments. I am better able to enter into the character of this description of men than the noble Duke

Burke's habits

can be. I have lived long and variously in the world. Without any considerable pretensions to literature in myself, I have aspired to the love of letters. I have lived for a great many years in habitudes with those who professed them. I can form a tolerable estimate of what is likely to happen from a character, chiefly dependent for fame and fortune on knowledge and talent, as well in its morbid and perverted state, as in that which is sound and natural. Naturally men so formed and finished are the first gifts of Providence to the world. But when they have once thrown off the fear of God, which was in all ages too often the case, and the fear of man, which is now the case, and when in that state they come to understand one another, and to act in corps, a more dreadful calamity cannot arise out of hell to scourge mankind. Nothing can be conceived more hard than the heart of a thoroughbred metaphysician. It comes nearer to the cold malignity of a wicked spirit than to the frailty and passion of a man. It is like that of the principle of evil himself, incorporeal, pure, unmixed, dephlegmated, defecated evil. It is no easy operation to eradicate humanity from the human breast. What Shakspeare calls "the compunctious visitings of nature" [15] will sometimes knock at their hearts, and protest against their murderous speculations. But they have a means of compounding with their nature. Their humanity is not dissolved. They only give it a long prorogation. They are ready to declare, that they do not think two thousand years too long a period for the good that they pursue. It is remarkable, that they never see any way to their projected good but by the road of some evil. Their imagination is not fatigued with the contemplation of human suffering through the wild waste of centuries added to centuries of misery and desolation. Their humanity is at their horizon—and, like the horizon, it always flies before them. The geometricians, and the chemists, bring, the one from the dry bones of their

[15] *Macbeth*, I. 5. 42.

diagrams, and the other from the soot of their furnaces, dispositions that make them worse than indifferent about those feelings and habitudes, which are the support of the moral world. Ambition is come upon them suddenly; they are intoxicated with it, and it has rendered them fearless of the danger, which may from thence arise to others or to themselves. These philosophers consider men in their experiments, no more than they do mice in an air pump, or in a recipient of mephitic gas. Whatever his Grace may think of himself, they look upon him, and everything that belongs to him, with no more regard than they do upon the whiskers of that little long-tailed animal, that has been long the game of the grave, demure, insidious, spring-nailed, velvet-pawed, green-eyed philosophers, whether going upon two legs, or upon four.

His Grace's landed possessions are irresistibly inviting to an *agrarian* experiment. They are a downright insult upon the rights of man. They are more extensive than the territory of many of the Grecian republics; and they are without comparison more fertile than most of them. There are now republics in Italy, in Germany, and in Switzerland, which do not possess anything like so fair and ample a domain. There is scope for seven philosophers to proceed in their analytical experiments, upon Harrington's seven different forms of republics, in the acres of this one duke. Hitherto they have been wholly unproductive to speculation; fitted for nothing but to fatten bullocks, and to produce grain for beer, still more to stupify the dull English understanding. Abbé Sieyes has whole nests of pigeon-holes full of constitutions ready made, ticketed, sorted, and numbered; suited to every season and every fancy; some with the top of the pattern at the bottom, and some with the bottom at the top; some plain, some flowered; some distinguished for their simplicity, others for their complexity; some of blood colour; some of *boue de Paris;* some with directories, others without a direction; some with councils of elders, and councils of youngsters; some without any council at all. Some where the electors choose the representatives; others, where the representatives choose the electors. Some in long coats, and some in short cloaks; some with pantaloons; some without breeches. Some with five-shilling qualifications; some totally unqualified. So that no constitution-fancier may go unsuited from his shop, provided he loves a pattern of pillage, oppression, arbitrary imprisonment, confiscation, exile, revolutionary judgment, and legalized premeditated murder, in any shapes into which they can be put. What a pity it is, that the progress of experimental philosophy should be checked by his Grace's monopoly! Such are their sentiments, I assure him; such is their language, when they dare to speak; and such are their proceedings, when they have the means to act.

Their geographers and geometricians have been some time out of practice. It is some time since they have divided their own country into squares. That figure has lost the charms of its novelty. They want new lands for new trials. It is not only the geometricians of the republic that find him a good subject, the chemists have bespoken him after the geometricians have done with him. As the first set have an eye on his Grace's lands, the chemists are not less taken with his buildings. They consider mortar as a very anti-revolutionary invention in its present state; but properly employed, an admirable material for overturning all establishments. They have found that the gunpowder of *ruins* is far the fittest for making other *ruins,* and so *ad infinitum.* They have calculated what quantity of matter convertible into nitre is to be found in Bedford House, in Woburn Abbey, and in what his Grace and his trustees have still suffered to stand of that foolish royalist Inigo Jones, in Covent Garden. Churches, play-houses, coffee-houses, all alike are destined to be mingled, and equalized, and blended into one common rubbish; and, well sifted and lixiviated, to crystallize into true, democratic, explosive, insurrectionary nitre. Their academy del *Cimento* (per antiphrasin) with Morveau and Hassenfrats at its head, have computed that the brave *sans culottes* may make war on all the aristocracy of Europe for a twelve-month, out of the rubbish of the Duke of Bedford's buildings.[16]

While the Morveaux and Priestleys are proceeding with these experiments upon the Duke of Bedford's houses, the Sieyes, and the rest of the analytical legislators, and constitution-venders, are quite as busy in their trade of decomposing organization, in forming his Grace's vassals into primary assemblies, national guards, first, second, and third requisitioners, committees of research, conductors of the travelling guillotine, judges of revolutionary tribunals, legislative hangmen, supervisors of domiciliary visitation, exactors of forced loans, and assessors of the maximum.

The din of all this smithery may some time or other possibly wake this noble Duke, and push him to an endeavour to save some little matter from their experimental philosophy. If he pleads his grants from the Crown, he is ruined at the outset. If he pleads he has received them from the pillage of superstitious corporations, this indeed will stagger them a

---

[16] There is nothing, on which the leaders of the republic, one and indivisible, value themselves, more than on the chemical operations, by which, through science, they convert the pride of aristocracy to an instrument of its own destruction—on the operations by which they reduce the magnificent, ancient country seats of the nobility, decorated with the *feudal* titles of Duke, Marquis, or Earl, into magazines of what they call *revolutionary* gunpowder. They tell us, that hitherto things "had not yet been properly and in a *revolutionary* manner explored."—"The strong *chateaus,* those *feudal* fortresses that *were ordered to be demolished,* attracted next the attention of your committee. *Nature* there had *secretly* regained her *rights,* and had produced saltpetre for the *purpose,* as it should seem, *of facilitating the execution of your decree by preparing the means of destruction.* From these *ruins,* which *still frown* on the liberties of the republic, we have extracted the means of producing good; and those piles, which have hitherto glutted the *pride of despots* and covered the plots of La Vendée, will soon furnish wherewithal to tame the traitors, and to overwhelm the disaffected."—"The *rebellious cities,* also, have afforded a large quantity of saltpetre, *Commune Affranchie,* (that is, the noble city of Lyons reduced in many parts to a heap of ruins,) and Toulon, will pay a *second* tribute to our artillery." Report, 1st February, 1794. [Burke]

little, because they are enemies to all corporations, and to all religion. However, they will soon recover themselves, and will tell his Grace, or his learned council, that all such property belongs to the *nation;* and that it would be more wise for him, if he wishes to live the natural term of a *citizen,* (that is, according to Condorcet's calculation, six months on an average,) not to pass for an usurper upon the national property. This is what the *serjeants* at law of the rights of man will say to the puny *apprentices* of the common law of England.

Is the genius of philosophy not yet known? You may as well think the garden of the Tuilleries was well protected with the cords of ribbon insultingly stretched by the National Assembly to keep the sovereign canaille from intruding on the retirement of the poor king of the French, as that such flimsy cobwebs will stand between the savages of the Revolution and their natural prey. Deep philosophers are no triflers; brave *sans culottes* are no formalists. They will no more regard a Marquis of Tavistock than an Abbot of Tavistock; the Lord of Woburn will not be more respectable in their eyes than the Prior of Woburn; they will make no difference between the superior of a Covent Garden of nuns, and of a Covent Garden of another description. They will not care a rush whether his coat is long or short; whether the colour be purple or blue and buff. They will not trouble *their* heads, with what part of *his* head his hair is cut from; and they will look with equal respect on a tonsure and a crop. Their only question will be that of their *Legendre,* or some other of their legislative butchers, how he cuts up? how he tallows in the cawl, or on the kidneys?

Is it not a singular phenomenon, that whilst the *sans-culotte* carcass-butchers, and the philosophers of the shambles, are pricking their dotted lines upon his hide, and, like the print of the poor ox that we see in the shop-windows at Charing Cross, alive as he is, and thinking no harm in the world, he is divided into rumps, and sirloins, and briskets, and into all sorts of pieces for roasting, boiling, and stewing, that all the while they are measuring *him,* his Grace is measuring *me;* is invidiously comparing the bounty of the Crown with the deserts of the defender of his order, and in the same moment fawning on those who have the knife half out of the sheath—poor innocent!

> "Pleas'd to the last, he crops the flow'ry food,
>   And licks the hand just raised to shed his blood." [17]

No man lives too long, who lives to do with spirit, and suffer with resignation, what Providence pleases to command, or inflict; but indeed they are sharp incommodities which beset old age. It was but the other day, that, on putting in order some things which had been brought here on my taking leave of London for ever, I looked over a number of fine portraits, most of them of persons now dead, but whose society, in my better days, made this a proud and happy place. Amongst these was the picture of Lord Keppel. It was painted by an artist worthy of the subject, the excellent friend of that excellent man from their earliest youth, and a common friend of us both, with whom we lived for many years without a moment of coldness, of peevishness, of jealousy, or of jar, to the day of our final separation.

I ever looked on Lord Keppel as one of the greatest and best men of his age; and I loved and cultivated him accordingly. He was much in my heart, and I believe I was in his to the very last beat. It was after his trial at Portsmouth that he gave me this picture. With what zeal and anxious affection I attended him through that his agony of glory, what part my son took in the early flush and enthusiasm of his virtue, and the pious passion with which he attached himself to all my connexions, with what prodigality we both squandered ourselves in courting almost every sort of enmity for his sake,

[17] Pope, *Essay on Man,* 11. 83-84.

I believe he felt, just as I should have felt such friendship on such an occasion. I partook indeed of this <u>honour,</u> with several of the first, and best, and ablest in the kingdom, but I was behindhand with none of them; and I am sure, that if to the eternal disgrace of this nation, and to the total annihilation of every trace of honour and virtue in it, things had taken a different turn from what they did, I should have attended him to the quarter-deck with no less good will and more pride, though with far other feelings, than I partook of the general flow of national joy that attended the justice that was done to his virtue.

Pardon, my Lord, the feeble garrulity of age, which loves to diffuse itself in discourse of the departed great. At my years we live in retrospect alone: and, wholly unfitted for the society of vigorous life, we enjoy the best balm to all wounds, the consolation of friendship, in those only whom we have lost for ever. Feeling the loss of Lord Keppel at all times, at no time did I feel it so much as on the first day when I was attacked in the House of Lords.

Had he lived, that reverend form would have risen in its place, and, with a mild, parental reprehension to his <u>nephew the Duke of Bedford</u>, he would have told him that the favour of that gracious Prince, who had honoured his virtues with the government of the navy of Great Britain, and with a seat in the hereditary great council of his kingdom, was not undeservedly shown to the friend of the best portion of his *Burke* life, and his faithful companion and counsellor under his rudest trials. He would have told him, that to whomever else these reproaches might be becoming, they were not decorous in his near kindred. He would have told him, that when men in that rank lose <u>decorum</u> they lose everything. *

On that day I had a loss in Lord Keppel; but the public loss of him in this awful crisis—! I speak from much knowledge of the person, he never would have listened to any compromise with the rabble rout of this sans-culotterie of

France. His goodness of heart, his reason, his taste, his public duty, his principles, his prejudices, would have repelled him for ever from all connexion with that horrid medley of madness, vice, impiety, and crime.

Lord Keppel had two countries; one of descent, and one of birth. Their interest and their glory are the same; and his mind was capacious of both. His family was noble, and it was Dutch: that is, he was of the oldest and purest nobility that Europe can boast, among a people renowned above all others for love of their native land. Though it was never shown in insult to any human being, Lord Keppel was something high. It was a wild stock of pride, on which the tenderest of all hearts had grafted the milder virtues. He valued ancient nobility; and he was not disinclined to augment it with new honours. He valued the old nobility and the new, not as an excuse for inglorious sloth, but as an incitement to virtuous activity. He considered it as a sort of cure for selfishness and a narrow mind; conceiving that a man born in an elevated place in himself was nothing, but everything in what went before and what was to come after him. Without much speculation, but by the sure instinct of ingenuous feelings, and by the dictates of plain, unsophisticated, natural understanding, he felt, that no great commonwealth could by any possibility long subsist, without a body of some kind or other of nobility, decorated with honour, and fortified by privilege. This nobility forms the chain that connects the ages of a nation, which otherwise (with Mr. Paine) would soon be taught that no one generation can bind another. He felt that no political fabric could be well made without some such order of things as might, through a series of time, afford a rational hope of securing unity, coherence, consistency, and stability to the state. He felt that nothing else can protect it against the levity of courts, and the greater levity of the multitude. That to talk of hereditary monarchy, without anything else of hereditary reverence in the commonwealth, was a low-minded absurdity, fit only for those detestable "fools aspiring to be knaves," who began to forge in 1789 the false money of the French constitution.—That it is one fatal objection to all *new* fancied and *new fabricated* republics, (among a people, who, once possessing such an advantage, have wickedly and insolently rejected it,) that the *prejudice* of an old nobility is a thing that *cannot* be made. It may be improved, it may be corrected, it may be replenished; men may be taken from it or aggregated to it, but the *thing itself* is matter of *inveterate* opinion, and therefore *cannot* be matter of mere positive institution. He felt that this nobility in fact does not exist in wrong of other orders of the state, but by them, and for them.

I knew the man I speak of: and, if we can divine the future, out of what we collect from the past, no person living would look with more scorn and horror on the impious parricide committed on all their ancestry, and on the desperate attainder passed on all their posterity, by the Orleans, and the Rochefoucaults, and the Fayettes, and the Viscomtes de Noailles, and the false Perigords, and the long *et cætera* of the perfidious *sans culotttes* of the court, who act like demoniacs, possessed with a spirit of fallen pride, and inverted ambition, abdicated their dignities, disowned their families, betrayed the most sacred of all trusts, and, by breaking to pieces a great link of society and all the cramps and holdings of the state, brought eternal confusion and desolation in their country. For the fate of the miscreant parricides themselves he would have had no pity. Compassion for the myriads of men, of whom the world was not worthy, who by their means have perished in prisons, or on scaffolds, or are pining in beggary and exile, would leave no room in his, or in any well-formed mind, for any such sensation. We are not made at once to pity the oppressor and the oppressed.

Looking to his Batavian descent, how could he bear to

behold his kindred, the descendants of the brave nobility of Holland, whose blood, prodigally poured out, had, more than all the canals, meres, and inundations of their country, protected their independence, to behold them bowed in the basest servitude to the basest and vilest of the human race; in servitude to those who in no respect were superior in dignity, or could aspire to a better place than that of hangmen to the tyrants, to whose sceptered pride they had opposed an elevation of soul, that surmounted, and overpowered, the loftiness of Castile, the haughtiness of Austria, and the overbearing arrogance of France?

Could he with patience bear, that the children of that nobility, who would have deluged their country and given it to the sea, rather than submit to Louis XIV., who was then in his meridian glory, when his arms were conducted by the Turennes, by the Luxembourgs, by the Boufflers; when his councils were directed by the Colberts, and the Louvois; when his tribunals were filled by the Lamoignons and the Daguessaus—that these should be given up to the cruel sport of the Pichegrus, the Jourdans, the Santerres, under the Rolands, the Brissots, and Gorfas, and Robespierres, the Reubels, the Carnots, and Talliens, and Dantons, and the whole tribe of regicides, robbers, and revolutionary judges, that, from the rotten carcass of their own murdered country, have poured out innumerable swarms of the lowest, and at once the most destructive, of the classes of animated nature, which, like columns of locusts, have laid waste the fairest part of the world?

Would Keppel have borne to see the ruin of the virtuous patricians, that happy union of the noble and the burgher, who, with signal prudence and integrity, had long governed the cities of the confederate republic, the cherishing fathers of their country, who, denying commerce to themselves, made it flourish in a manner unexampled under their protection?

Could Keppel have borne that a vile faction should totally destroy this harmonious construction, in favour of a robbing democracy, founded on the spurious rights of man?

He was no great clerk, but he was perfectly well versed in the interests of Europe, and he could not have heard with patience, that the country of Grotius, the cradle of the law of nations, and one of the richest repositories of all law, should be taught a new code by the ignorant flippancy of Thomas Paine, the presumptuous foppery of La Fayette, with his stolen rights of man in his hand, the wild, profligate intrigue, and turbulency, of Marat, and the impious sophistry of Condorcet, in his insolent addresses to the Batavian republic.

Could Keppel, who idolized the house of Nassau, who was himself given to England along with the blessings of the British and Dutch revolutions; with revolutions of stability; with revolutions which consolidated and married the liberties and the interests of the two nations for ever, could he see the fountain of British liberty itself in servitude to France? Could he see with patience a Prince of Orange expelled as a sort of diminutive despot, with every kind of contumely, from the country, which that family of deliverers had so often rescued from slavery, and obliged to live in exile in another country, which owes its liberty to his house?

Would Keppel have heard with patience, that the conduct to be held on such an occasion was to become short by the knees to the faction of the homicides, to entreat them quietly to retire? or, if the fortunes of war should drive them from their first wicked and unprovoked invasion, that no security should be taken, no arrangement made, no barrier formed, no alliance entered into for the security of that, which under a foreign name is the most precious part of England? What would he have said, if it was even proposed that the Austrian Netherlands (which ought to be a barrier to Holland, and the tie of an alliance, to protect her against any species of rule that might be erected, or even be restored in France) should be formed into a republic under her influence, and dependent upon her power?

But above all, what would he have said, if he had heard it made a matter of accusation against me, by his nephew the Duke of Bedford, that I was the author of the war? Had I a mind to keep that high distinction to myself, as from pride I might, but from justice I dare not, he would have snatched his share of it from my hand, and held it with the grasp of a dying convulsion to his end.

It would be a most arrogant presumption in me to assume to myself the glory of what belongs to his Majesty, and to his ministers, and to his parliament, and to the far greater majority of his faithful people; but had I stood alone to counsel, and that all were determined to be guided by my advice, and to follow it implicitly—then I should have been the sole author of a war. But it should have been a war on my ideas and my principles. However, let his Grace think as he may of my demerits with regard to the war with regicide, he will find my guilt confined to that alone. He never shall, with the smallest colour of reason, accuse me of being the author of a peace with regicide. But that is high matter; and ought not to be mixed with anything of so little moment, as what may belong to me, or even to the Duke of Bedford.

I have the honour to be, &c.

EDMUND BURKE

Index

533